ESSENTIAL RESEARCH METHODS IN
PSYCHOLOGY

Sara Miller McCune founded SAGE Publishing in 1965 to support the dissemination of usable knowledge and educate a global community. SAGE publishes more than 1000 journals and over 800 new books each year, spanning a wide range of subject areas. Our growing selection of library products includes archives, data, case studies and video. SAGE remains majority owned by our founder and after her lifetime will become owned by a charitable trust that secures the company's continued independence.

Los Angeles | London | New Delhi | Singapore | Washington DC | Melbourne

ESSENTIAL RESEARCH METHODS IN PSYCHOLOGY

EDITED BY
PHILIP BANYARD,
BELINDA WINDER,
CHRISTINE NORMAN
& GAYLE DILLON

START

SAGE

Los Angeles | London | New Delhi
Singapore | Washington DC | Melbourne

SAGE

Los Angeles | London | New Delhi
Singapore | Washington DC | Melbourne

SAGE Publications Ltd
1 Oliver's Yard
55 City Road
London EC1Y 1SP

SAGE Publications Inc.
2455 Teller Road
Thousand Oaks, California 91320

SAGE Publications India Pvt Ltd
B 1/I 1 Mohan Cooperative Industrial Area
Mathura Road
New Delhi 110 044

SAGE Publications Asia-Pacific Pte Ltd
3 Church Street
#10-04 Samsung Hub
Singapore 049483

Editor: Amy Maher
Assistant editor: Esmé Carter
Production editor: Rachel Burrows
Cover design: Wendy Scott
Typeset by: C&M Digitals (P) Ltd, Chennai, India
Printed in the UK

Library of Congress Control Number: 2021947639

British Library Cataloguing in Publication data

A catalogue record for this book is available from the British Library

ISBN 978-1-4739-9907-7
ISBN 978-1-4739-9908-4 (pbk)

CONTENTS

ABOUT THE EDITORS AND CONTRIBUTORS

Phil Banyard Dr Philip Banyard is Emeritus Professor in Psychology at NTU. This position does not require him to do anything, but it does not pay him anything either. He is available for christenings, weddings and light gardening.

Gayle Dillon Dr Gayle Dillon is Deputy Head of Department for Psychology at NTU. Her teaching and research interests cover developmental and forensic psychology, with a focus on people with additional support needs. Colleagues still talk about her daring burlesque dance routines.

Christine Norman Dr Christine Norman is a senior lecturer at NTU with teaching and research interests in biological and forensic psychology as well as dabbling in the psychology of religion and spirituality.

Belinda Winder Professor Belinda Winder is Research Director of the Centre for Crime, Offending, Prevention & Engagement (COPE) at NTU. Her research expertise includes sexual crime, prison and life post-release for those serving long prison sentences. She utilises mixed methods to understand the challenges that people with convictions face as they strive to build lives post-conviction.

Lucy Betts Professor Lucy Betts explores children's experiences and perceptions of bullying and cyberbullying, including trying to find out why people feel that cyberbullying is something that happens to other people.

Nicholas Blagden Dr Nicholas Blagden is Associated Professor of Forensic Psychology at NTU and Associate Head of the Sexual Offences Crime and Misconduct Research Unit. Nick is a legend as an academic though he is the only person in the UK who has bought a second-hand Alpha Romeo and then been surprised to find himself spending days of his life at the roadside waiting for the RAC.

Andrew Clouter Dr Andrew Clouter is a senior lecturer at Nottingham Trent University, with research interests in cognitive electrophysiology and transcranial electrical stimulation.

Anna Cunningham Anna Cunningham is a senior lecturer at NTU with teaching and research interests in language and literacy development. In her spare time, she is a keen kayaker and piano player.

Amanda Edmondson Amanda Edmondson is a senior lecturer in psychology with a huge interest in the connectedness of physical and mental health. She is very passionate about designing research that enables people to express their experiences in ways that they find useful.

Caroline Flowers Dr Caroline Flowers is a forensic psychologist who had extensive experience of working in prisons before joining NTU as a senior lecturer. Her specialist areas are stalking and intimate partner violence.

Moon Halder Dr Moon Halder's research primarily focuses on understanding how group memberships and social interactions with others has an impact on an individual's health and wellbeing in different cultures. Moon is also interested in exploring the impact of online interaction in various cultures.

Lydia Harkin Dr Lydia Harkin is a senior lecturer at Nottingham Trent University. Her work centres on ways that technology can aid wellbeing and alleviate negative repercussions of chronic conditions. She is a passionate qualitative researcher and is keen to pursue research which centres the population, their interactions, and their experiences at the heart of research questions.

Andrew Harris Dr Andrew Harris is a senior lecturer in psychology at NTU. His research focuses on applying experimental methodology to investigate gambling psychology, impulse control, and gambling harm-minimisation strategies.

Rowena Hill Dr Rowena Hill is an associate professor with expertise in mixed method research within major disasters and emergencies.

Beth Jones Dr Beth Jones is a senior lecturer in social and health psychology with expertise in the health and wellbeing of trans and gender diverse people.

Rosie Kitson-Boyce Dr Rosie Kitson-Boyce is senior lecturer and psychologist with expertise in forensic psychology and criminology. Rosie is interested in why people commit crime and also why they desist from crime.

Rusi Jaspal Rusi Jaspal is Pro Vice-Chancellor and a professor of psychology at the University of Brighton. Professor Jaspal's research cuts across the fields of psychology and public health, focusing particularly on social psychological approaches to promoting good psychological and physical health outcomes.

Jennifer Mackay Dr Jenny Mackay is a senior lecturer in forensic psychology and chartered psychologist, and has many years working in practitioner-facing roles with vulnerable clients in both forensic and non-forensic settings.

Kristina Newman Dr Kristina Newman is a senior lecturer at NTU Psychology and specialises in both teaching and research in qualitative and health psychology.

Ben Oldfield Dr Ben Oldfield is a senior lecturer at NTU with a research interest in gaming and online learning

Treshi-Marie Perera Treshi-Marie Perera is a senior lecturer at NTU with research interests in multisensory integration. She explores the sensory processes underlying the perception of body ownership in healthy individuals as well as those with propensities towards clinical conditions.

Eva Prikrylova Dr Eva Prikrylova is a senior lecturer at NTU Psychology. Eva is a qualitative discursive psychologist and is interested in gender, identities and health.

Darren Rhodes Dr Darren Rhodes is a senior lecturer at NTU with teaching and research interests in Open Research, time perception, and consciousness science.

Anastasia Rousaki Anastasia Rousaki is a PhD candidate and a part-time lecturer of qualitative research methods in psychology at NTU. She is a critical discursive psychologist, researching adolescent sexting, consent and coercion.

Francesca Chloe Ryding Francesca Chloe Ryding is a lecturer at Nottingham Trent University, interested in researching and understanding the role of social networking sites on body image and well-being.

Lisa Sanderson Lisa Sanderson completed her PhD at Nottingham Trent University in 2017 on Posttraumatic Growth in Fire and Rescue Personnel.

Mark Sergeant Dr Mark Sergeant's research focuses on the topic of academic integrity, particularly student perceptions of plagiarism and other forms of academic cheating. Mark is specifically focused on the decision-making process students go through when deciding whether or not to engage in academic cheating.

Sarah Seymour-Smith Dr Sarah Seymour-Smith is an associate professor at NTU Psychology where she is Lead for Qualitative Teaching and Research. Sarah is a discursive psychologist whose main research focus is the study of masculinities and health.

James Stiller Dr James Stiller is a senior lecturer in psychology at University of Chichester, with a background in zoology, evolutionary, cognitive and applied social/developmental psychology. He previously taught at NTU for over 14 years and is currently interested in the psychology behind human–animal interactions and wellbeing.

Melina Throuvala Dr Melina Throuvala is a senior lecturer at NTU with research interests in internet addiction and online behaviour. She is also a qualified counsellor.

Russell Turk Dr Russell Turk is a senior lecturer at NTU. He teaches on a range of undergraduate modules with a focus on statistics and research methods. His research interests include psycholinguistics, cognition, and effective pedagogy.

Emma J. Vardy Dr Emma Vardy is a senior lecturer at NTU with a research interest in children's literacy, specifically attitudes to reading, reading motivation and reading for pleasure in primary and secondary school students. She also an extraordinary baker of vegan cakes.

Mike Vernon Dr Mike Vernon is a senior lecturer in the Department of Psychology at Nottingham Trent University. He teaches on a range of undergraduate and postgraduate psychology modules, and his research interests typically focus on cognitive mechanisms in applied contexts.

Janet Vousden Janet Vousden is a senior lecturer in developmental psychology at NTU with teaching and research interests in language and literacy.

Juliet Ruth Helen Wakefield Dr Juliet Wakefield is a senior lecturer at NTU. She is a social psychologist whose research and teaching involve exploring the implications of people's group memberships for their thinking, behaviour, and wellbeing.

David Wilde David Wilde is a senior lecturer in psychology with many years expertise in qualitative research and has interests in individual differences, health psychology, and the psychology of anomalous experiences.

FOREWORD

PROFESSOR DARAGH MCDERMOTT, ASSOCIATE DEAN OF PSYCHOLOGY, NOTTINGHAM TRENT UNIVERSITY

In an age where we are constantly bombarded by facts, figures, experts and 'cutting edge research' and our daily lives are a constant stream of information being shared on social media, by journalists, politicians and even our friends and family the ability to think critically and examine the credibility of a research study is now more important than ever. For readers who are starting your journey as a budding psychologist or social scientist, this reference guide – *Essential Research Methods in Psychology* – will provide you with the foundations that you need to make sense of social scientific and psychological research. Not only that, but once you are able to separate the wood from the trees and differentiate between credible and robust data – taken from studies that have been conducted appropriately, ethically and treated their data with care – from those that are not, you will be well on your way to being able to design your own robust research studies that will help us answer the questions of tomorrow.

This text brings together a range of qualitative and quantitative methodological expertise and provides a snapshot of the incredible talent currently producing ground breaking, cutting edge, world leading research at Nottingham Trent University's Department of Psychology. I am immensely proud to introduce you to their work and am confident that once you start your own journey with *Essential Research Methods in Psychology*, you will have a researcher companion that you will turn to again and again.

PREFACE

ABOUT THE BOOK

Psychology is an amazing subject to study. It stretches from the hardest of hard science through to philosophy. It deals with everything you want to know about life and the universe. To be fair it doesn't have many answers to the big questions but it retains a keen interest in all issues. One of the key aspects of psychology is its focus on evidence. If we want to have informed discussions about things then we need evidence and psychology has devised many methods for collecting and analysing that evidence. And that is what this book is about.

In this book you will find a broad selection of the methods used by psychologists. Our choice reflects the major research methods, but it is inevitably selective because of the space that is available. In each chapter, we present a method and look at how it is used. We illustrate this with an example study that will highlight some of the problems with the method as well as the many strengths.

There are a number of text additions to help the reader including examples of schoolkid errors, cultural contexts and further reading. We have also put in a number of examples from the Ig Nobels. These are prizes awarded every year to scientific studies that first make you laugh and then make you think. Good science doesn't always have to be serious.

THE AUTHORS

The book has contributions from over 30 academic staff at NTU Psychology at Nottingham Trent University. It has been edited by four of these staff and we hope that we have created a text that reads as if it has one author rather than many. We were going to include a picture of all the authors but modesty and, frankly, good taste prevailed.

One of the most striking aspects of being an editor is to watch your colleagues adopt the behaviour of students. Much of this is very positive but some of the negative aspects also crept in. At the university, we have strict deadlines and word limits for student work and it is part of the corridor culture for staff to throw their eyebrows to the ceiling when these basic rules are not met by their students. Lecturers commonly think that it is easy to keep to deadlines and word limits.

Imagine our surprise to find that these same staff used the worst excuses to explain their own lateness. Bargaining for an extension accompanied by the lamest of excuses became a daily event for the editors. Avoidance, denial and emotional blackmail became part of the daily discourse on the corridor. And as for word limits ... you don't want to know.

Students, take heart from this. If these authors had been students at this university most of them would have had their work failed for lateness, marked down for being over-length and derided for the poor quality of their excuses. It must be harder being a student than we remember, and that is a key lesson we'll take from this process.

Having said that, it has been an absolute to joy to work with colleagues on this project and I hope you find our efforts interesting and useful.

ACKNOWLEDGEMENTS

The editors would like to acknowledge their students at Nottingham Trent University who have put up with our weak attempts at humour over the years and have engaged with us in a positive and productive way. Learning is not something that stops when you get your degree, and our students help us to keep looking at material afresh and keep learning ourselves. In recognition of this, the royalties from this text go into a fund at Nottingham Trent University that is used to enhance the experience of our psychology undergraduates.

The editors would also like to acknowledge the positive and supportive working environment that they enjoy with their colleagues in NTU Psychology. This text is a companion to *Essential Psychology* that was also written by NTU staff and is now in its third edition. The fact that we have now written four texts with SAGE shows that we have a great relationship with them and value the support and confidence shown to us by their editors.

Finally, the editors would like to acknowledge ... Ken Bruce (for *PopMaster*), Covid-19 for encouraging us to have quality time with our friends and families, and also for going away so we can stop doing that now. We would also like to thank Master Jumble Griffon (as ever), Simon, Beau and Sunny (who wants a same-old same-old life anyway??) and witches everywhere (not just in fairy tales). And friends. Magnificent and wonderful friends. On top of that, a big shout out to the amazing Christian and Amelia, Kitty Fisher, Famille Wardle and The Northerners, and everyone who knows us. And, can I have a signed photo please Ken?

1

PSYCHOLOGICAL RESEARCH: DOING THE RIGHT THING?

PHILIP BANYARD

The chapter sets the context for our exploration of research methods in psychology.

We look at what we need to think about when developing a research question, especially the context for the questions. We also look at what we accept as evidence in psychology and how we judge the quality of it. We finish by looking at the way we do research, and how we try to do the right thing. This all sounds very straightforward, but it is actually anything but that.

1. QUESTIONS

> The scientist is not a person who gives the right answers, *[they are the]* one who asks the right questions.
>
> Claude Levi-Strauss

Where do research questions come from and how are they formed? Some questions derive from real life problems, and some are derived from theory. The motivation for the questions can vary from the need for a solution to a social problem to the need to satisfy the demands of a funder. The fundamental questions are predictably, why, what, how, who and what on earth does our Sharon see in him? Asking the right question is easier said than done.

We want questions that enhance our understanding of the world. They need to be big enough to develop our knowledge in a meaningful way but small enough to allow us to explore them and sometimes to test the proposition behind them. So, a question like '*is there a god?*' doesn't work for us because it is too big and also untestable. It is a matter of belief and it is not clear what evidence we could find to either challenge or support the belief. A better question for us, though, might be '*why do some people believe in gods?*'

or '*what effect does belief in a god have on their behaviour?*' These are questions that we can investigate and collect evidence on that will help us better understand this behaviour.

1.1 Curiosity

Questions start from our curiosity about our lives and experiences: what is that? Why did that happen? How can we change that? As children, we start off being very curious and ask adults about all sorts of things that help us understand the world we live in and how to behave in it. Some of these questions are about natural phenomena such as '*Why is the sky blue, mummy?*' which will tax the explanatory powers of most adults, but for which there is an established scientific answer.[1] Other questions such as '*Why is that man over there so ugly?*' are taxing for other reasons such as social embarrassment. This second question is about the categorisation and judgement of people and their qualities, and provokes further questions about the criteria for these judgements and how they come to develop. With the first question, we are asking for an explanation of the physical world and in the second question we are asking about a social world that has been created by people.

In psychology, we are more interested in the socially constructed world of human experience and human behaviour than we are with the physical world though sometimes we pretend that we are discovering physical phenomena.

Interesting fact

Where do statistics come from?

The statistics we use today commonly came from a need to answer a particular question. For example, the idea of sampling was invented by John Graunt who lived in the 17th century and is commonly seen as the first European statistician. His job was to determine the number of people who were dying at any time from the Black Death.[2] If the number of people dying was particularly high he was to inform the king, who would leave London until the disease had calmed down. Graunt could not count the total number of people dying from the disease at any time because this would have been an impossible job. Instead, he took a sample of mortuaries and visited these. At each mortuary, he estimated the number of people who had died of different diseases. From this sample he extrapolated to the number of people dying in London, and informed the king.

[1] And the even bigger question of why we experience electromagnetic radiation with a wavelength between 380–500 nm as being blue is even harder.

[2] You probably learned at school that the black death was bubonic plague, however, there are some strong suggestions that the characteristics of the black death do not match those of bubonic plague. Of course, if it wasn't bubonic plague we don't know what it was, and so we don't know how to cure it if it comes back – see Duncan and Scott (2005).

We'll look at the issues with research questions by exploring one of the most famous studies in social psychology conducted by Stanley Milgram in the 1960s. If you have studied psychology before then you will be familiar with this study. If you haven't, then check out the film Milgram made of his study which you can find on YouTube. He was curious to explain the atrocities of the Second World War when death camps were set up in central Europe to kill people deemed to be inferior, including Jews, Roma, people with disabilities, and Slavs. Milgram was Jewish and had lost family to these atrocities, so he had a personal interest in the question.

One of the narratives that developed after the war was that the people who worked in the death camps and carried out the industrial scale slaughter were just ordinary people. Hannah Arendt (1963) briefly attended the trial Adolf Eichman, who was one of the architects of the slaughter, and was taken with how mundane and normal he seemed. She introduced the idea of the **banality of evil** to describe the motivation of the man – not a sociopath but someone who was following orders and trying to be the model citizen.

This is obviously something we want to explore as behavioural scientists if we are going to make our world a better and safer place. Milgram's question mirrored Arendt's understanding of the events and asked 'in what circumstances will ordinary people do extraordinary things that will threaten the health and even existence of another human being?'

Milgram's question and his answer has been a feature of nearly every introductory psychology course in the Western world from its publication until today. It is a great question and has stimulated much student debate and reflection for every class that has come across it. In fulfils our idea of a great psychology question in that it is about a big issue that affects the lives of millions and the study is direct, accessible to the lay reader and has results that you do not expect.

We are going to argue, however, that the context in which Milgram framed his question led him to answers that we challenge today, and we will come back to that later in the chapter.

1.2 Context is everything

Context is so important in developing the right question. In his book *Schooling the Smash Street Kids*, Paul Corrigan (1979) explores the question, '*why do children truant?*' At first glance this appears a great question and something we want to know about so that we can help schools retain their children and also support children who are rejecting schooling. Corrigan points out that there is a missing corollary to this question without which you cannot make much progress with the original question. If you want to take the time to reflect on this, then stop reading and see if you can work out what is the missing component (spoiler alert – the answer is in the next paragraph).

The original question takes a social behaviour (not going to school), badges it as a social problem (truancy) and then looks at it from one quite narrow perspective (how do we get children back to school). If we want to know why children don't want to go to school Corrigan suggests we also need to ask '*why do we make all children go to school?*', and this is by no means an easy question to answer. A clue to the answer lies in the choice of words to describe this education process. The other use of the word schooling is for the training of horses which involves breaking their will and making them docile. Our industrial society needs a docile workforce with a set of limited ambitions who will accept the authority of the people in power even though they are a set of self-serving, privileged, two-faced, free-loading, incompetent, spineless bastards, yes you, Alexander Boris de Pfeffel Johnson (please see Whoa there! box). Understanding why some children reject schooling requires us to explore what is happening in our schools and why. This context allows us to see these children as the shock troops of our resistance to authority.

Whoa there!

Stating your position

At this point you might be thinking that the author has taken a political position and that this goes against the conduct of science. Indeed yes, the author is expressing a political position but no, this does not necessarily challenge a scientific approach. Science does not exist in a moral vacuum and all science questions have a political context. The important thing is that this context is clear and not disguised or denied.

1.3 Inventing criminals and patients

If we are to develop good questions then we have to understand the context in which they are framed and social context in which behaviour takes place. Nottingham (where we work) has a Category B prison which takes in a lot of offenders for short sentences. Many people return to prison on several occasions and the average number of times a new arrival has been in prison before is nine (Lievesley et al., 2018). Given that some of them must be turning up for the first time there are many prisoners who have been locked up dozens of times. The research question here might be '*why do these people continue to reoffend?*' and it is a good question to ask. However, it also needs the corollary question about what is going on in the prison. A prison sentence is either meant to act as a deterrent to future offending behaviour, or as a vehicle for **rehabilitation**. In either case, repeat incarceration is a failure of the process.

One thing to consider is that prisons need offenders, because without them they are out of business. In the same way, police need crime and fire officers need fires. They have a vested interest in maintaining the behaviour that keeps them in work. With regard to our repeat offenders, the prison is admitting someone who has already been schooled in the rules of the prison and is likely to be relatively docile. Why wouldn't the prison be pleased to receive people like this? There is no incentive for the prison to work on reducing their offending and every incentive to ease their return.

Psychologists also have a vested interest in mental distress. Over the past 150 years psychologists and psychiatrists have put a lot of effort into cataloguing different types of mental distress. During this period hundreds of new **diagnostic categories** have appeared with the big question being whether these are issues that are being uncovered or whether they are being invented. Kutchins and Kirk (2001) in their text, *Making us Crazy*, take the latter view and show how the DSM (Diagnostic and Statistical Manual of the American Psychiatric Association) is a political document that evolves to suit the interests of financial and business organisations. This is a much bigger argument than we have space for here but by changing our research question from '*what is wrong with you?*' to '*what has happened to you?*' we will come to some very different conclusions about the causes and treatments of mental and emotional distress (see Lucy Johnson, *A Straight Talking Introduction to Psychiatric Diagnosis*, 2015).

1.4 Is psychology racist?

Our questions are not formed in a social vacuum. Our society in the UK developed its wealth and power through the subjugation and exploitation of peoples in other parts of the world. The consequences of these social and political upheavals are still playing out, and the world we live in favours some groups over others. One very striking aspect of this can be seen in the **racist** attitudes and structures that are part of our lives, and are so embedded that they are often unseen by the majority of people (mainly because they are not disadvantaged by them). As a quick example, think back to when you were in school and count up how many of the staff who taught you were people of colour, and how many people of colour were there in the school management? And in our universities, there is clear evidence that Black academics experience systematic discrimination (BBC, 2021).

Is psychology immune from this? Is psychology research racist? The simple answers to these questions are, a) no, and b) yes. It is also important to add that psychology has issues to deal with around **sexism** and other discriminatory behaviours, but we will focus on racism for now. It is perhaps a good idea to explore this to see in what ways psychological research is racist and what we can do to start to address this. This section is about research questions and the context we use to frame them. Psychology has a history of asking questions that have promoted racist attitudes and behaviours, and it continues to frame its question within a white, European context.

One of the issues to address when considering this is how we understand racism. Many people are offended and upset to have their behaviour challenged as being racist and see racism as being a feature of other people and not themselves. The arbitrary division of the world into racists and non-racists is not helpful as it prevents us reflecting on our own behaviour and masks the behaviours that occur in liberal institutions like universities who position themselves as anti-racist. These institutions have clear evidence of racism in their student achievement data and also their staff recruitment. And in psychology, the demographic is skewed in predictable ways with very few people from marginalised and disadvantaged groups in positions as lecturer or professor even though the proportion of students from these groups is much higher.

The field of psychology is in an excellent position to promote and lead discussion of issues around racism and help in the emancipation of all disadvantaged people. If you are interested in reading more about these issues then we suggest *White Fragility* by Robin DiAngelo and *Discourse on Colonialism* by Aimé Césaire.

When we review our research questions for context we need to also consider the context of the power structures within our society. Later in this chapter we will look at some examples of how psychology has been used to promote and support racist ideas and consider how we can challenge this.

1.5 Who wants to know?

One source of research questions is our general curiosity in the world. We are all scientists in our daily lives as identified by George Kelly who explored this in his writings on **personal construct theory** (see Bannister and Fransella, 1986, and also Chapter 11 in this text). He argued that we devise our own set of constructs to explain the world that we are constantly testing these constructs in the way that scientists test their hypotheses. Scientific questioning is something that we all do.

Beyond this world of personal curiosity and hypothesis testing is the world of professional science. This world is still curious, but that curiosity has a purpose and that purpose is defined by the funders of the research. It is common practice now for authors of scientific papers to identify who is sponsoring the research so that we are aware of any influences that might be brought to bear on the final reports. Many of us have worked on projects where the data is owned by the funder and embargoes have been placed on us disseminating the knowledge. We highlight an example conflict of interest in the section on ethics later in this chapter.

When you look at research questions it is important to ask, who is asking this question, why do they want to know this and what will they do with the data? Who stands to gain and who stands to lose?

1.6 Summary

Doing the studies and analysing the results is the easy bit, but if you ask a stupid question the best you can hope for is a stupid answer. The hardest part of any research activity is to get the best question that you can. And that question needs to have a theoretical context, and a scope that allows for meaningful exploration, and be framed so that any answer will expand our knowledge of the topic it is addressing.

2. EVIDENCE

> Enlightenment is man's release from his self-incurred tutelage. Tutelage is man's inability to make use of his understanding without direction from another. Self-incurred is this tutelage when its cause lies not in lack of reason but in lack of resolution and courage to use it without direction from another. Sapere aude! 'Have courage to use your own reason!' – that is the motto of enlightenment.
>
> Immanuel Kant, *An Answer to the Question: What Is Enlightenment?*

Since the Enlightenment the focus of Western science has been to create evidence that is objective and can challenge the irrational beliefs and superstitions to which we are all prone. Psychology is largely still influenced by this **empiricist** tradition, which holds that knowledge comes from the senses (what we observe), it is tentative and probabilistic, and that evidence should be gathered using the scientific method.[3] Psychology aims to provide statements and theories based on evidence rather than opinions and revelations.

Ig Nobel Prize

Overestimating our competence

Two psychologists, David Dunning and Justin Kruger, were amused by a news report of a would-be bank robber (McArthur Wheeler) who rubbed his face with lemon juice to avoid being caught on camera – his logic was that, as lemon juice can be used as invisible ink, then he would become invisible. The Dunning–Kruger effect, as they called it, is the observation that in some situations people assess their ability as higher than it actually is and mistakenly trust their judgment in a situation where they really should do some further checking.

Dunning and Kruger conducted various research studies to test their idea.

In one study, they asked undergraduates to assess their abilities on a range of skills such as logical reasoning, grammar and humour. They then showed the students their test scores and ask them to estimate their position in the class. They found that those students who had poor scores (the incompetent group) actually overestimated their position in class whereas those who did well on the tests (the competent group) underestimated their position.

What is particular amusing about this effect is that most people interpret it as a comment on other people's stupidity – whereas really the observation was meant as something we should be applying to ourselves.

[3]We are not going to discuss the scientific method here, but if you are interested then pick up Fancher & Rutherford, 2012 – see the further reading at the end of this chapter.

For this work Dunning and Kruger were given the 2000 Ig Nobel Prize for Psychology.

Dunning, D., & Kruger, J. (1999). Unskilled and unaware of it: How difficulties in recognizing one's own incompetence lead to inflated self-assessments. *Journal of Personality and Social Psychology*, *77*(6), 1121–34.

Evidence comes in many forms but largely in psychology it focuses on what people do, and we can collect that evidence through a range of techniques that we match to the question we are posing. The other chapters in this text give details and examples of many of the techniques and methods used by psychologists. In this section, we will look at some of the key themes and debates in these methods.

2.1 Qualitative and quantitative data

Psychologists often make a distinction between **qualitative** and **quantitative** data. Qualitative data are about 'qualities' of things. They are descriptions, words, meanings, pictures, texts, and so forth. They are about what something is like or how something is experienced. Quantitative data are about 'quantities' of things. They are numbers, raw scores, percentages, means, standard deviations, and so forth. They are measurements of things, telling us how much of something there is.

Sometimes people refer to research as being either qualitative or quantitative. This is a shorthand way of referring to different traditions of enquiry within the discipline. However, it can be misleading, for it implies that certain methods inherently produce certain kinds of data. For example, experiments are usually referred to as quantitative and textual analysis is usually described as qualitative. However, experimental designs can be used to collect qualitative data and interviews can be used to collect qualitative data.

Of course, the decision of whether to collect qualitative or quantitative data (or both) in the course of a piece of psychological enquiry is a research design decision, which depends entirely on what it is that you are trying to find out. In other words, the type of data that are collected depend upon the nature of the research question. The following chapters consider this issue and explain the choice of qualitative or quantitative data for each study.

2.2 Operational definitions

Psychologists are interested in all sorts of phenomena such as aggression, happiness, depth perception, memory, pain, prejudice, intelligence, and so on. The problem is that most of the things we are interested in are unobservable, and therefore cannot be measured directly. We can, however, measure how people behave. So, if we want to know about some unseen psychological process, we have to select observable behaviours which represent that process, and measure them instead. It is then up to the researcher to argue that the measurements of those observable behaviours are a valid representation of the invisible thing which is the real topic of the investigation.

The behaviour we choose to observe and record is called the **operational definition** of the invisible thing that we are really trying to study, and selecting the best operational definition is trickier than it sounds.

One of the best known, and most controversial, operational definitions of a hidden psychological construct is the IQ test, a measure of intelligence. There are a number of reasons why some people argue that the IQ test is not a valid operational definition of intelligence. One reason is that the test measures our performance, whereas the construct of intelligence is really to do with competence (ability). We might be very clever but perform poorly on the test because we were in a bad mood, or because the test was in a foreign language, or because it had a cultural bias in it (see Gould, 1997). And in any case, is the collection of mental puzzles that makes up an IQ test a good measure of intelligence in the first place? It might just measure 'puzzle-solving ability'. For all these reasons it is possible to argue that a person's behaviour on an IQ test might not validly represent their intelligence.

Skoolkid error

Just because you can measure something it doesn't mean that it is important and, conversely, just because it is hard to measure something it does not mean that it is unimportant.

The key thing for the discerning reader of psychological research is to consider the quality of the chosen operational definitions used in a study, and to ask whether or not the measurements taken really do allow us to draw conclusions about the psychological phenomena they are supposed to represent.

2.3 Judging the quality of evidence

Once we've got our data we need to have some idea about how confident we can be of our findings. All measurement has some error, but psychologists will try and reduce the error by considering how reliable or valid the findings are.

One of the most important quality control checks in psychological research is to check the **reliability** of our measurements. Another word for reliability is consistency. If we are using a measurement technique we need to know whether it will give us consistent results. If we measure someone on a scale on a Wednesday afternoon, we hope to get the same results as if we had done the measurement on a Friday morning. It would remarkable if we got exactly the same result because all forms of measurement have an element of error in them, but we hope this error is relatively small. Psychologists have devised a range of techniques to estimate reliability and you will come across these in the studies described in other chapters in this text.

Associated with the notion of reliability is the concept of replication. It is a tenet of science that findings of empirical work should not be trusted unless they can be replicated. This means that an independent researcher should be able to copy the procedure of a given research study, and obtain the same pattern of results. This is why it is so important to be explicit about the details of how a research study was conducted. Sometimes replications are exact: in other words, they are conducted in exactly the same way, with the same type of participant sample. More usually they are designed slightly differently to tackle some vulnerable part of the original procedure.

Reliability is only half the story. The second major aspect to quality control in relation to measurement is **validity**. A measurement technique is said to be valid if it measures what it claims to measure. Note that this is related to, but not the same as, the notion of reliability. For a measure to be valid it must, first of all, be reliable (it cannot be valid if it gives inconsistent measurements of the same thing), but it must also have other properties.

For a start, it is possible to have a perfectly consistent (reliable) measure, which is perfectly consistently rubbish. For example, we might develop a measure of intelligence which involves measuring the circumference of a person's head, and then converting the resulting measurement into an IQ score. This would give high levels of reliability but it would not, validly, measure intelligence. So, the critical reader of psychological research must consider whether a happiness scale measures happiness, and whether an IQ test measures intelligence, and whether 'five factor' personality scales measure personality.

2.4 Sources of error

There are many things that can contaminate our data. For example, **demand characteristics** (Orne, 1962) can distort our results. The basic idea is that participants of psychological research studies will behave in accordance with their own efforts to understand the situation in which they find themselves, and their own interpretation of the 'demands' of that situation. Since the participants' understandings of the demands of the setting are likely to be at odds with the researcher's understanding this may lead to misinterpretations of the participants' behaviour. In other words, the researcher may interpret the participants' behaviour as meaning one thing, when in fact it means something completely different.

And then there are **experimenter effects**, where the results of the study are affected by the expectations of the experimenters (see Rosenthal and Fode, 1963). There is in psychological research, as in everyday life, a powerful tendency to find what you are looking for: the self-fulfilling prophecy. Incidentally, this is something that can affect all types of psychological research, not just experiments, so the label 'experimenter' effect is somewhat misleading.

2.5 Summary

Modern psychology is based on evidence. That evidence commonly comes from empirical studies and by understanding how the data was collected and analysed, we can come to a judgement about the quality of that evidence.

3. CONDUCT OF RESEARCH: DOING THE RIGHT THING

> A person may cause evil to others not only by his actions but by his inaction, and in either case he is justly accountable to them for the injury.
>
> John Stuart Mill, On Liberty (1859)

We have looked at the way we frame our research questions and we have looked at the quality of the evidence we collect. In this section, we look at how we act on those questions and collect that evidence. Psychologists devise strict guidelines for good ethical practice and this helps to keep the work at a high quality. **Ethics** though, tend to be procedural and so we also need to explore the social and political context of our work. For example, the methods and questions of psychology are largely derived from a long history of Western science and so preference that view over others. There is also the issue of bias that inevitably frames even the most objective studies.

3.1 Ethics

How do we know right from wrong, good from bad, humour from cruelty? How can we judge the behaviour of other people and set a code of conduct for our own behaviour? In professional life we develop **ethics** which are a moral framework that is applied to a narrow group of people such as doctors or psychologists. These ethics are socially agreed and under constant review.

The ethics of a behaviour can be judged using four categories: consequences, actions, character and motive (Daeg de Mott, 2001). When we look at consequences, we judge whether a behaviour is right or wrong by looking at the result of the behaviour. If it leads to a result that brings about an improvement for someone's life, we might think it is a good thing. When we look at the actions, however, we look at the act itself, and consider what is the person doing. The category of character is concerned with whether the person is a good (or virtuous) person who is generally ethical. When we look at motives, we are concerned with the intentions of the person carrying out the behaviour, and we consider whether they were trying to do something good. Nothing is clear cut in the study of ethics and these categories sometimes give us different assessments. The puzzle is to decide whether you think the behaviour is ethical or not.

The modern ethical codes and guidelines for psychology can be traced back to two key moral statements in the middle of the 20th century. The first was the Nuremberg Code (see the box on p. 13). During the Second World War (1939–45), Nazi doctors conducted many harmful experiments on prisoners. For example, the doctors tested the prisoners' reactions to fatal diseases such as typhoid, and to extreme temperatures by immersing them in freezing water to see how long it would take for them to die. After the war, a ten-point code (The Nuremburg Code) was produced which has formed the basis for many contemporary ethical codes in both medical and behavioural research. If you read through it and compare it to the standard psychology ethics codes, you'll see the similarities.

The Nuremberg Code (1946)

1. The voluntary consent of the human subject is absolutely essential.
2. The experiment should yield fruitful results for the good of society that cannot be obtained by other means.
3. The experiment should be based on previous research so that the anticipated results can justify the research.
4. All unnecessary physical and mental suffering should be avoided.
5. No experiment should be conducted where there is reason to believe that death or disabling injury may be the result.
6. The degree of risk should also be less than the potential humanitarian importance of the research.
7. Adequate precautions should be in place to protect the subjects against any possible injury.
8. Experiments should only be conducted by qualified persons.
9. The human subject should always be at liberty to end the experiment.
10. The scientist in charge should be prepared to terminate any experiment if there is probable cause to believe that continuation is likely to result in injury or death.

(Adapted from Katz, 1972)

The other statement was a declaration of human rights. Human rights are more controversial than you might think. It depends, in part, on where you think rights come from. According to Fukuyama (2001), there are three lines of argument about the source of rights: divine rights, natural rights or rights from custom and practice. In other words, rights can come from *God*, or from *nature* or from *human beings*.

Let's just consider the third option. The executive director of Amnesty International, William F. Schulz (2000) argued that human rights should be concerned with the things 'human beings possess or can claim', or in other words, human rights are anything we agree them to be. An example of this approach is the United Nations' Universal Declaration of Human Rights (UN Assembly, 1948). This was a political document written to keep both the United States and the Soviet Union engaged with the process at a time when their Cold War conflict was just beginning. If you read through it, you will find some absurdities such as article 24 which states we have a right to 'periodic holidays with pay'. In a world where less than half the population have paid employment, this is nonsense. And what about article 19, the right to freedom of expression? This sounds fine and dandy but in all societies there are limits on expression, for example, in this country, we are (rightly, we believe) forbidden from freely expressing racist views.

These key statements of ethics and rights are both written by Western academics and politicians and, not surprisingly, focus heavily on the behaviour and cultural expectations of people from Europe and the USA. This focus on the individual rather than the community puts a cultural bias into our moral and ethical judgements and is another example of how racism is embedded into our everyday lives.

3.2 Ethical guidelines and Stanley Milgram

Ethical guidelines are live documents, and institutions and professional organisations maintain ethics committees to police the conduct of their members and also to develop and maintain the guidelines. If you want to study the guidelines of the British Psychological Society, they are freely available on their website. Many textbooks use the Milgram study as an example of ethical wrong-doing, so it is time to revisit this work.

If we cut to the chase of this discussion then, contrary to many texts, we argue that the study was ethical. It was ethical in the sense that ethics are socially agreed rules of a professional association and the Milgram study was reviewed by the American Psychological Association and found to be ethical. The judgment of his peers endorsed the study. In fact, Milgram introduced some ethical controls that were previously not used such as de-briefing and follow-up interviews for the participants. Of course, no ethical committee today would agree to the procedures that Milgram used but they do still agree to worse (see the section on psychologists at Guantanamo Bay).

Ethel ethics

Psychologists at Guantanamo Bay

Sometimes ethical codes clash and resolving them can be a messy business. In 2002, the USA set up a prison camp in Guantanamo Bay on the coast of Cuba to house the people it was capturing around the world who they believed were terrorists. This camp was outside of its home territory, and therefore outside US law.

The president at the time, George W. Bush, said these people were not soldiers and hence not subject to the protection offered by the Geneva Convention. In some cases, the people were taken from conflict zones in Afghanistan and Pakistan and in some cases they were snatched from countries where there was no conflict.

To describe the full horror of Guantanamo would take a book in itself and if you want to know more about it then just search the internet. The issue we want to look at in this chapter is the role of psychologists at Guantanamo. The role of Guantanamo was not just to contain these people but to get information from them about possible attacks on Western countries and so interrogation techniques were very important. This is where psychologists come in and one of the many techniques that they were able to bring along was sensory deprivation which is regarded by most observers as torture. If you look at the image in Figure 1.1 you will see prisoners at Guantanamo in orange jump suits. If you look closer you will see that they have ear-muffs (so they can't hear anything), opaque glasses (so they can't see anything) and thick gloves (so they can't feel anything). This is sensory deprivation. And they have shackles on their ankles and wrists, that's why they appear to be praying.

Figure 1.1 Prisoners experiencing sensory deprivation torture in Guantanamo Bay

(Continued)

The involvement of psychologists in military interrogation has created a storm through the profession. In most people's eyes, the interrogation of people who are being held outside international law (in other words illegally) is unethical in itself but to then subject them to inhuman treatment that can be classed as torture and to continue with this over a period of years is beyond description. There does not appear to be an ethical dilemma here because it is clearly wrong, or is it?

In 2002, just as Guantanamo was coming on line, the American Psychological Association (APA) made a change in its ethical code. This change concerned situations where a psychologist comes into conflict between the orders they are being given and their ethical code. So, for example, if they were a member of the military and were asked to carry out an inhumane interrogation which is against the ethical code of psychologists, what should they do? Should they go with their ethical code or should they follow their orders? This is an easy decision when sat in a comfy chair reading a book but a much harder one in a real-life situation.

The response of the APA could have been to put pressure on the military and the US government not to carry out torture and not to require psychologists to be part of it. What they did, however, was to change their ethical code to give psychologists a get out clause and take part in the torture. The new code said 'If the conflict is unresolvable [between orders and ethics] psychologists may adhere to the requirements of the law, regulations, or other governing legal authority' (APA, 2002).

This addition to the APA ethics code hit a nerve in the USA and the UK because it is an echo of the Nuremberg Defence. This is the moral defence for war crimes that says 'it wasn't my fault, I was obeying orders'. It is called the Nuremberg Defence because it was used by the people who were put on trial for war crimes after the Second World War (1939–45). The defence was rejected at those trials so it made it all the more controversial to add this defence to the APA ethical code.

Finally, in 2009 there was a change in government of the USA and President Obama brought in a new attitude to Guantanamo and clearly stated that he did not want Americans involved in torture. The APA also changed its line and amended its ethical code as follows,

> The APA Ethics Committee will not accept any defence to torture in its adjudication of ethics complaints. Torture in any form, at any time, in any place, and for any reason, is unethical for psychologists and wholly inconsistent with membership in the American Psychological Association. (APA, 2009)

This all sounds like a very negative story about psychology and psychologists and it is obviously not the profession's finest hour. However, during the time that Guantanamo was operational many psychologists kept up a barrage of articles that challenged the APA's position and some decided to leave the APA (e.g. Pope and Gutheil, 2009). The debate about ethics was kept going throughout this time and eventually the APA arrived at a result that was in agreement with other similar professions such as doctors and psychiatrists.

Debates on ethics commonly focus on procedures and hence on what Milgram did during the data collection. We argue that ethics goes beyond procedures and encompasses the context of that research and the uses to which it is put. Milgram's focus on the individual and his view that ordinary people will enter into an agentic state and behave as automatons to carry out the requests of authority has framed public perceptions of these behaviours. More recently, reviews of the original evidence have questioned the integrity of Milgram's research reports, the validity of his explanations, and the broader relevance of his research (for example, see Reicher, Haslam and Smith, 2012). Instead of seeing the work as being about obedience, it can be better understood in the context of social identity theory as providing insight into processes of engaged followership, in which people are prepared to harm others because they identify with their leaders' cause and believe their actions to be virtuous.

Ethical statements give us necessary guidance on how to conduct our studies but they rarely require psychologists to consider the impact of their studies on the community. Psychology's approach to ethics commonly focuses on procedure and ignores bigger issues such as whether the research is discriminatory or racist.

3.3 Bias in research: The story of race science in psychology

Earlier in this chapter we stated our position that mainstream Western psychology is racist. It has a history of either supporting or not challenging (we argue this is effectively the same thing) discriminatory ideas and practices. To explore this will take more that a couple of paragraphs in this text but to give you a flavour of some of the arguments, we offer two examples, one from history and one that is current.

The study of **individual differences** can be traced back to the work of Francis Galton (1822–1911). Galton is credited with developing a staggering range of techniques and concepts (see Fancher, 1996) including, self-report questionnaires, twin studies, scatterplots and statistics. Galton's work was driven by one major concern – how we can best manipulate the forces of evolution to the advantage of the human race. The idea is expressed in his book *Hereditary Genius*,

> As it is easy ... to obtain by careful selection a permanent breed of dogs or horses gifted with peculiar powers of running, or of doing anything else, so would it be quite practicable to produce a highly-gifted race of men by judicious marriages during several consecutive generations. (Galton, 1869, reproduced in Fancher, 1996 p. 228)

He later coined the term eugenics to describe his project of improving the race through selective breeding. And here is the problem at the heart of mental testing from the beginning until today, the focus on perceived differences between groups of people and, in particular, between white people and peoples from historically marginalised communities. Galton wasn't interested in the human race but the white race. For example, Galton wrote,

> There exists a sentiment for the most part quite unreasonable against the gradual extinction of an inferior race. (Francis Galton, 1883, cited in Rose et al., 1984, p. 30)

Galton's work, and that of many other supporters of race science is commonly presented without mention of this aspect to the work. The history of mental testing is littered with discriminatory practices and racist ideas and if you are interested to explore this then start with *The Science and Politics of IQ* (Kamin, 1977).

Our second example concerns the way that psychology categorises people. Psychologists use the processes of diagnosis to put people into categories for personality type, or type of psychiatric distress. The issue here is that the categories are developed around the behaviour and experience of the dominant group, that is the white majority of the West. The experiences of other people are then judged against these criteria and categories. This is ongoing and is one of the ways that psychology is not including the disadvantaged and the disenfranchised within its theories and practices. If you are interested in exploring this then start with *Aliens and Alienists* by Littlewood and Lipsedge (1998).

3.4 Decolonising psychology

The impact of colonialism is rarely discussed and poorly understood. In the UK, we are largely blind to our own history and commonly portray ourselves as a force for good in the world. The rest of the world does not see us in the same light. Our colonial wars and occupations led to countless deaths and immense suffering, the effects of which can still be seen today. One of the key ideas of decolonial thinking is that the violence of colonialism was not confined to a period of history but persists today in coloniality (ways of knowing, power and being, formed during colonial occupation, that persist after the end of colonial rule – see Gómez-Ordóñez et al. 2021).

Of particular concern to this text is how we start to decolonise our methods. Much of our understanding of people comes from an examination of a narrow section of the population by that same narrow section. To understand and explore all people we can be more inclusive of who we study and ensure that their voice is heard within their own terms and not ours. The solution is clearly more taxing than these simple starting points and there is a growing body of literature to draw on when you consider these issues with your research.

3.5 Open science

There is growing pressure for our studies to be transparent and open to scrutiny. This is fueled by a replication crisis and practices to manipulate data such as p-hacking (see Andrews & Justice, 2019). To try and address some of these issues psychologists have started to carry out some major replication trials. In a report published in 2015 the Open Science Collaboration describe an attempt by 270 psychologists to replicate findings from 100 studies published in 2008 in prestigious journals (Open Science Collaboration, 2015). The Reproducibility Project is designed to estimate the 'reproducibility' of psychological findings.

The headline result from the Reproducibility Project report is that only 36% of the replication attempts showed a statistically significant effect. Or to put it another way, two-thirds of all studies could not be replicated to get the same result as the original. Some replications found the opposite effect to the one they were trying to recreate. This is despite the fact that the Project went to incredible lengths to make the replication attempts true to the original studies, including consulting with the original authors.

This doesn't mean that the original studies were faked but it does question how quickly we should accept a result before subjecting the study to replication trials and further scrutiny. The positive spin on this is that although these results are disappointing it does show Psychology as a trail blazer for examining its practices and trying to introduce more rigor, or am I clutching at straws?

3.6 Giving psychology away

In 1969 George Miller addressed the American Psychological Association (APA) as President and laid out a challenge that still resonates today. He started by saying,

> The most urgent problems of our world today are the problems we have made for ourselves. (1969: 1063).

This is even more clear today where the climate emergency and endless wars are created by human behaviour. Miller continued by stating that if psychology can help with our problems then it should try to do so. He suggested that our obligations as citizens (rather than as scientists) mean that if we have something of practical value to contribute, we should make every effort to ensure that it is implemented.

Miller recognised the revolutionary potential of psychology and went on to say,

> … if we were ever to achieve substantial progress toward our stated aim – toward the understanding, prediction and control of mental and behavioural phenomena – the implications for every aspect of society would make brave men tremble. (1969: 1065).

Miller suggested that despite this potential, nothing very revolutionary had emerged from psychology so far. Psychometric tests and factor analysis, for example, he points out as being admirable but not comparable to the impact of gunpowder, the steam engine or genetic surgery. And in the 45 years since this address, it is difficult to identify any great additions to the list. A recent discussion in *The Psychologist* (Banyard, 2015) challenged psychologists to come up with an achievement that matched the non-stick frying pan in its impact and usefulness. The responses were not encouraging.

This absence of major findings appears to create a narrative of despair about the impact of psychology but Miller offered a more positive message;

> I believe that the real impact of psychology will be felt, not through the technological products it places in the hands of powerful men, but through its effects on the public at large, through a new and different public conception of what is humanly possible and humanly desirable. (1969: 1066).

3.7 Summary

Psychology research affects lives, and if it doesn't, we have to ask what is the point of it. It attempts to regulate the conduct of research through ethical codes, and also to reflect on the social impact of its findings. Psychology has a history of not challenging racist ideas and continues to struggle with its largely Eurocentric focus.

LEARNING OBJECTIVES

After reading this chapter you should be able to:

- Consider the importance of sound questions in research and how to develop them.
- Reflect on the bias and racism that are present in Western psychological thought and practice.
- Evaluate the quality of evidence in psychological research.
- Reflect on the purpose of psychological research.

FURTHER READING

The following texts are all mentioned in the chapter and will provide some context to understanding the context in which psychological research takes place.

Césaire, A. (1972). *Discourse on colonialism*. Monthly Review Press.
Fancher, R. E., & Rutherford, A. (2012). *Pioneers of psychology* (4th ed.). W.W. Norton.
Kamin, L. (1977). *The science and politics of IQ*. Penguin.
Kutchins, H., & Kirk, S. (2001). *Making us crazy: DSM – the psychiatric bible and the creation of mental disorders*. Constable.
Littlewood, R., & Lipsedge, M. (1998). *Aliens and alienists* (2nd ed.). Unwin Hyman.

LINKS TO USEFUL RESOURCES

British Psychology Society ethical codes, www.bps.org.uk/news-and-policy/bps-code-ethics-and-conduct

UN General Assembly, *Universal Declaration of Human Rights*, www.refworld.org/docid/3ae6b3712c.html

2

EXPERIMENTAL METHOD

ANDREW HARRIS, RUSSELL TURK, MIKE VERNON AND JULIET RUTH HELEN WAKEFIELD

Psychology's relationship with the **experimental method** dates back to 1879 when Wilhelm Wundt, who is widely considered to be the father of modern psychology, opened the first laboratory of experimental psychology at the University of Leipzig. Until this point, psychology was considered a sub-discipline of philosophy, and explanations of human behaviour were focused on a person's soul. Wundt challenged those beliefs by demonstrating that psychological investigation could be conducted in a rigorous and controlled manner, thereby laying the groundwork for future experimental psychologists.

Figure 2.1 Psychology lab for motor control testing

1. EXPERIMENTS

1.1 The basics

The experimental method is one way in which psychology defines itself as a science, and some of the most well-known psychological studies were conducted using this methodology. For example, Harlow's work on attachment theory (1959), Asch's conformity study (1951), and the Bobo Doll experiments by Bandura, Ross, and Ross (1961; 1963) all used various forms of the experimental method. There are several explanations for why the experimental method is so popular, but the key reasons are the high level of control it provides to the experimenter, and that it allows the experimenter to make **causal inferences**. Over the course of this chapter we will be looking at the features of experimental research, as well as the strengths and weaknesses of this type of design. We will then explore these issues in the context of a case-study, which will be a famous piece of real-world experimental research. Throughout this chapter we encourage you to think critically about the experimental method and form your own conclusions about whether it was an appropriate choice of method for our research case study, as well as how effectively it was implemented by the experimenters.

Like any research method, the choice to use an experiment should be determined by the **research question**. Experiments can be used to compare groups of participants, gain pre- and post-variable manipulation scores for a single group of participants, and many more things besides. However, experiments cannot tell us about the lived experiences of individuals or help us identify relationships between attitudes and behaviours. For example, you could use an experimental design to see which of two stop-smoking adverts was more effective, but not how people's attitude towards cigarettes affects their likelihood to start smoking. The first step in designing a good experiment is therefore to make sure that the design is appropriate for the question you want to answer.

One of the main strengths of the experimental method is that it allows researchers to make predictions about how changes in one thing will cause a change in something else, a process known as **hypothesis** testing. In its simplest form, the experimenter hypothesises that changes in one **variable** will cause a change in a second variable. In any experiment, the variable that is being manipulated by the experimenter is known as the **independent variable** and the second variable, which is expected to change as a result of the manipulation, is called the **dependent variable**. The independent variable is split into different **levels**. These levels can be linear – e.g., giving participants five, ten, or fifteen milligrams of caffeine – but are often categorical and involve the presence or absence of the manipulation. Where only one independent variable is present, each level makes up one experimental **condition**, but more complex designs may include two or more independent variables. In these designs, the number of conditions is a product of the levels in each independent variable. For example, if you have two independent variables with two levels each, then you would have four different experimental conditions.

1.2 Controls

In the perfect experiment, all other variables should be controlled, so that the only thing changing across the different conditions is the independent variable. In this case, it is possible to conclude that any change in the dependent variable must be caused by the manipulation of the independent variable. Since researchers will often want to make causal inferences from their data, it is important to control as many aspects of the experiment as possible, starting with how the instructions are delivered to the participants.

Standardisation of the experimental procedures is an important step towards removing **extraneous variables** from an experimental design. There are numerous ways in which researchers can unintentionally introduce bias into the experiment, including inconsistent delivery of instructions, experimenter **affect**, the physical environment, as well as some that are perhaps a little more surprising. For example, the gender of the experimenter has been shown to have an effect on children's IQ scores (Back & Dana, 1977), recall of autobiographical memory (Grysman & Denney, 2017), risk-taking behaviour (Ronay & von Hippel, 2010), and pain response (Gijsbers & Nicholson, 2005). Whilst it may not always be possible to completely avoid the introduction of bias, researchers need to make every effort to recognise and reduce the impact of extraneous variables. Standardising procedures and instructions are an effective way of doing this.

Another key feature of experiments is randomisation. In most cases, participants should be randomly allocated to a condition to avoid systematic biases that may introduce extraneous variables – such as all participants being from Nottingham in one condition and Edinburgh in the other. Randomisation also allows for generalisation since, theoretically, the participants in each condition have an equal chance of being drawn from any area of the general population.

Whoa there!

The (non) perfect experiment

Although this section refers to the perfect experiment, there is in fact no such thing. The idea of experimental design is to control every aspect of the procedure and environment, so that a causal effect can be inferred between the independent and dependent variable(s). However, when designing any experiment, it is often necessary to make compromises between maintaining absolute control and being able to conduct the experiment. Therefore, the most important thing is to control for any **confounding variables,** whilst also minimising the extraneous variables most likely to affect the findings.

Since there is no such thing as perfect control, this means that all experiments are inherently flawed in some way, and that researchers need to recognise the limitations of their design in order to draw meaningful conclusions from their data. It should also be noted that whilst randomisation is an important element of experimental design, it is only effective in the long term. It is highly unlikely that a single experiment contains a truly random sample of the population, but over time, multiple experiments studying the same thing should capture a representative sample and allow for generalisable conclusions.

1.3 Experimental designs

Standardisation is especially important in experiments where each participant only takes part in one of the conditions. This type of design is known as a **between-groups design** and is characterised by having different participants in each experimental condition. A well-known example of a between-groups design is the Bobo Doll experiment (Bandura et al., 1961), which we will explore in more detail later. The alternative to this type of design is a **within-groups** design, where each participant takes part in all experimental conditions. The Stroop task (see Stroop, 1935) is an example of an experiment conducted using a within-groups design. In this experiment participants are asked to identify the ink-colour of a stimulus in different conditions whilst disregarding the stimulus itself. The stimuli were presented as words that either matched the colour of the ink (Condition 1), did not match the colour (Condition 2), or as coloured patches (Condition 3). Response time was measured to see how quickly each condition was completed.

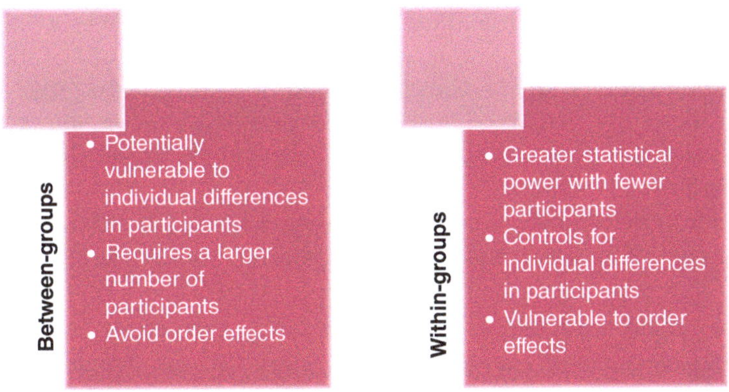

Figure 2.2 Pros and cons of between- and within-groups experimental designs

More complex experimental designs may involve multiple independent variables, each with two or more levels, as well as both between-group and within-group elements – this is often referred to as a **mixed-factorial** design. These designs allow researchers to investigate how multiple factors influence the dependent variable, but require careful thought about the effect that the independent variables might have on one another. This is known as an **interaction effect** and is an important consideration in more complex designs. Having multiple independent variables, each with several conditions, increases the complexity of the design, and requires researchers to consider more advanced methods to ensure parity across conditions and participants, including **counterbalancing** and **random allocation**. It is also possible to have more than one dependent variable, but this is less common than having multiple independent variables.

1.4 Types of experiments

So far, we have focused on what are sometimes known as **true experiments**. These are studies that meet three distinct criteria:

- The researcher(s) have manipulated a variable in order to determine a causal effect;
- All non-experimental variables are held constant across conditions and participants; and
- Participants are randomly allocated to a condition.

These types of experiments are popular in areas of psychology where it is possible to isolate and manipulate individual variables, such as memory, perception, and some types of language research. However, in many cases it is not possible to directly manipulate the variable of interest. Consider an experiment that tests the reaction time of participants based on their age, or a study that compares the performance of participants from different socio-economic backgrounds on a set of cognitive tasks. In these cases, the experimenter cannot directly manipulate the variables of interest – you cannot change where participants grew up – nor can they randomly allocate participants to different conditions. These studies are often referred to as **quasi-experimental** since they utilise the experimental **paradigm**, but are not as highly controlled as a true experiment. Quasi-experimental designs must balance the benefit of studying a given phenomenon with a lack of experimental control, and more than any other type of experiment, researchers must be careful not to overstate their findings.

When talking about experiments, a key strength of the methodology is that, when conducted in a controlled manner, it is easy for other researchers to replicate the findings. **Replicability** is an important part of the scientific process since it allows findings to be tested and either challenged, verified, or extended. However, the level of control required to make this possible can also lead to highly artificial scenarios. As such, researchers need to be careful when inferring **causality** from this type of study, since participants may not be displaying typical everyday behaviour.

Furthermore, the ability to tightly control the experimental environment may also be a weakness of this methodology. Human behaviour can rarely be attributed to a single cause, but there can be the temptation to conclude that this is the case based on experimental data, and researchers might overstate this relationship in order to highlight the importance of their findings. For example, an experiment might want participants to make a judgement on whether a string of letters is a real word (or not) when presented with the string for less than a second. This type of study is quite common in language research and has been used to make claims about how the brain processes written stimuli. A relatively obvious issue with this is that people often have much longer to respond to words in real life and rarely need to make this type of judgement, at least explicitly.

Ig Nobel Prize

Is implicit social behaviour censored?

In order to see whether people automatically imitate social gestures, researchers in Belgium and Germany used a series of experiments in which they showed participants a picture of a hand performing either a thumbs-up or a middle-finger gesture (Cracco, Genschow, Radkova, & Brass, 2018). They concluded that although there is some automatic imitation of these gestures, this is heavily influenced by the appropriateness of the gesture in a social situation. They showed that people are more likely to imitate a middle-finger gesture in an anti-social setting than they would in a prosocial one. They also found that this effect was stronger in a prosocial setting, suggesting that people automatically inhibit inappropriate behaviour rather than blindly copying it. This is a good example of a relatively simple experiment and the authors make some interesting points about the role of social norms in influencing behaviour. You can find the paper here:

Cracco, E., Genschow, O., Radkova, I., & Brass, M. (2018). Automatic imitation of pro-and antisocial gestures: Is implicit social behaviour censored? *Cognition*, *170*, 179–89.

When running an experiment, the aim is often to draw conclusions about the relationship between one (or more) independent variable(s) and a dependent variable, such as the effect of music or colour on emotional state (Anwar, Waqas, Zain, & Kee, 2020). In order to do this, we want to compare the impact of each level of the independent variable on the dependent variable. As you will learn from your statistics module, researchers use **descriptive statistics** and **inferential statistics** to help them make these comparisons.

1.5 Summary

In conclusion, experiments are a powerful tool that allow researchers to make causal inferences about specific aspects of behaviour or psychological processes. They are characterised by high levels of control and replicability but can suffer from a lack of **ecological validity** due to the (often) artificial nature of the study. Now, let us look at a famous, real-world example of a piece of research utilising the experimental method.

2. EXAMPLE STUDY: TRANSMISSION OF AGGRESSION THROUGH IMITATION OF AGGRESSIVE MODELS

2.1 The study

Transmission of aggression through imitation of aggressive models

Bandura, A., Ross, D., & Ross, S. A. (1961). Transmission of aggression through imitation of aggressive models. *The Journal of Abnormal and Social Psychology*, *63*(3), 575–82.

2.2 Background and aims

During the 1960s, Albert Bandura and colleagues conducted a series of experiments on observational learning, famously known as the Bobo doll experiments. Bandura et al. (1961) designed and conducted a **controlled experiment** to investigate if social behaviours, such as aggression, could be learned by the observation and imitation of others. This experimental study by Bandura et al. (1961) focused on the transmission of aggression through imitation of aggressive models. In the context of psychology, a model is a person or persons which performs behaviours in psychological studies. Such behaviours may or may not be imitated by the participants in the study.

Figure 2.3 Bobo doll

Interesting fact

'Psychology Pop Idol'

Psychologists of the 20th century were put to a popularity contest to determine who were the most influential psychologists of that period. The rankings were based on three criteria: number of journal citations; number of introductory textbook citations; and the survey responses of 1725 members of the American Psychological Society, who were asked to list who they felt were the most influential psychologists of the 20th century. Albert Bandura placed fourth on that list, very impressive! Can you think of other prominent psychologists who may have appeared high on this list? The full list can be found in Haggbloom et al. (2002) in the *Review of General Psychology*, *6*, 2.

The theory which the study was designed to test is the **Social Learning Theory**. Social Learning Theory argues behaviour can be learned through **vicarious learning**, which is learning via the observation of others' behaviours. Social Learning Theory emphasises the importance of observing and modelling behaviours, attitudes, and the emotional reactions of others. This may appear more obvious today, but up until the point of Bandura and colleagues' Bobo doll studies, **behaviourism** was the dominant psychological paradigm in the 20th century.

Behaviourism emphasised the role of environmental factors in shaping behaviour, to the near exclusion of innate or cognitive factors. Behaviourists argued that we learn new behaviour through classical and operant conditioning, as demonstrated in the seminal works of Pavlov (1927) and Skinner (1953) respectively. Essentially, the behaviourist approach argued that people learned through performing their own actions and that the subsequent positive or negative feedback they received would shape future behaviour. Bandura spotted a problem with this way of learning, arguing that learning would be extremely laborious and dangerous if individuals had to learn all behaviour via their own actions (Bandura & Walters, 1977). Imagine if you were a child having to learn the correct way to cross a busy road safely through trial and error learning! Instead, he argued we are able to first observe how this is done successfully and then imitate that behaviour. Therefore, Bandura argued that learning is not purely behavioural but that it is a cognitive process that takes place in a social context.

Previous research on observational learning had started to demonstrate that when we see another individual receiving reward or punishment for behaving in a specific manner, we can determine whether that behaviour should be conducted or not (Lewis & Duncan, 1958). For example, imagine we see someone cheating in a school test and they get caught and punished for doing so. As a result, we would be less likely to attempt the same behaviour. Although modern society is more critical of sex-based behavioural stereotypes, Fauls and Smith (1956) had shown that children perceive their parents as having a preference for sex-appropriate behaviour. Their findings also showed that parents did indeed reward imitation of sex-appropriate behaviour and discouraged or punished imitation of sex-inappropriate behaviour.

2.3 The hypotheses

The past research led Bandura to predict that children would be more likely to model the behaviour of a same-sex model compared to a model of the opposite sex. In addition, as aggression was viewed as a highly masculine-type behaviour, Bandura argued that boys should be more predisposed than girls toward imitating aggression, with this being even more likely if aggressive behaviour was first observed in a male model. Research had also shown that children will readily imitate the behaviour of an adult model if the model remains present (Bandura & Huston, 1961). However, it was yet to be determined how the behaviour displayed by a model could influence children's behaviour in a new setting when the model was absent. This was the **research gap** identified by Bandura et al. (1961), and their research aim was to investigate if imitations of learned behaviour could occur in the absence of a model. They made the following **hypotheses**:

1. Children shown aggressive models will show significantly more imitative aggression than those shown non-aggressive or no models.
2. Children shown non-aggressive, subdued models will show significantly less aggressive behaviour than those shown aggressive or no models.
3. Boys will show significantly more imitative aggression than girls.
4. Children will imitate same-sex model behaviour to a greater degree than opposite-sex behaviour.

The experimental method was chosen by Bandura and colleagues as they wanted to be able to identify a causal relationship between witnessing aggression and behaving aggressively. Experiments are seen as the gold standard way of establishing **causation**, where a change in an independent variable (witnessing aggression) leads to a change in a dependent variable (behaving aggressively). For this to be established, experiments need to be designed very carefully, minimising the potential impact that variables other than the independent variable of interest can have on the dependent variable. Let's take a closer look at the design and controls put in place by Bandura et al. (1961).

Cultural context

Bandura's box

When evaluating research, it is important to understand the **cultural context** in which it sits. Many things changed in people's lives in the UK and USA. in the 1950s and 1960s, but if one thing stands out as defining the age more than any other, it is arguably the evolution of television. Television was one of the most popular consumer products in the 1950s. At the start of this decade, there were approximately three million TV owners in the USA. alone, but by the end of it, this number exploded to around 55 million people who were able to watch shows on more than 500 stations (Ganzel, 2007). The public and researchers alike had growing concerns regarding how what we see on TV, particularly displays of antisocial behaviour and violence, might shape behaviour.

Considering the general shift from a more behaviourist view of learning to a more social-cognitive view, as seen with Social Learning Theory, you can see how many people became concerned that behaviour would be shaped by what people saw on TV. In fact, so much was this concern, that Bandura, Ross, and Ross (1963) later conducted an experiment specifically testing whether witnessing TV-mediated violence would have the same impact on behaviour as witnessing the violent actions of a live model. Their findings were striking, demonstrating that children exposed to a real or cartoon model acting violently on TV exhibited nearly twice as much aggression towards the Bobo doll (an inflatable clown-like doll which bounces back up after it is punched or hit) than a **control group**. The issue over the extent to which media violence *causes* aggression is still being debated today.

Some groups have implicated media violence as a causal factor in infamous school shootings, such as the Columbine incident. Families of the victims of the shooting (unsuccessfully) sued videogame companies as it was suggested that the perpetrators had copied the violent actions seen within specific videogames. There was not enough evidence to suggest this had played a causal role in the shootings. Researchers such as Chris Ferguson (2010) have argued the focus on media violence as a causal role in aggression facilitates conservative censorship and that it distracts people from looking into the real causes for aggression in our society. Unfortunately, and like many historical (and also current) studies in psychology, the issue of culture is ignored. Imagine this study if the aggressive adult model was white and the Bobo doll was black, or what if the opposite was the case? Children were brought up in the 1950s on a diet of TV shows and films that showed white people being disrespectful and violent to people of colour (and you may well feel that there are still many examples of this today). These behaviours are modelled and contribute to racism that is present in our society today.

2.4 Experimental design

To investigate if imitations of learned behaviour could occur in the absence of a model, Bandura et al. (1961) conducted a three-stage experiment examining how the dependent variable of children's imitated aggression was affected by three independent variables: (i) the observed model's behaviour (aggressive, non-aggressive, or no observation of model); (ii) the sex of the child participant (boy or girl); and (iii) the sex of the model (male or female). Before we examine the three-stage procedure, let's examine the independent and dependent variables in more depth.

One of the main considerations of an experimental design is how the variables can be **operationalised**. It must be clear how the variables are going to be measured and/or manipulated. Aggression, for instance, has many different forms, leading Bandura et al. (1961) to specify imitative physical aggression (e.g. striking the Bobo doll,) and imitative verbal aggression (e.g. repeating phrases such as '*pow*' or '*kick him*') as their measures of interest for imitated aggression. In order to measure the imitated aggression of each child, aggression was rated on five-point scales by observers via a one-way mirror in an adjoining room. This allowed the reliability of the scoring to be examined by comparing the scoring across two observers (a process known as **inter-rater reliability**) in order to ensure judgement on the observed aggression remains consistent.

The manipulation of the levels of the independent variables also involves careful consideration. When manipulating the independent variables, potential extraneous variables must be addressed. Personal characteristics of participants can affect results, meaning that the age, sex, socio-economic status, height, weight, physical impairments, and other personal attributes of the participants should ideally be controlled to ensure that the sample represents the population from which it is drawn (nursery-aged children in this case). However, it is worth noting that the influence of participants' personal characteristics will vary depending on the type of experiment. For example, an experiment where the dependent variable is balance or posture control will be far more influenced by the height and weight of the participants than an experiment where the dependent variable is imitated aggression (as in Bandura et al.'s (1961) experiment).

This means that controlling for participants' height and weight was unlikely to be a priority for Bandura. Whilst the height and weight of the participants are unlikely to influence imitated aggression in this experiment, one of the limitations of this experiment is that the findings cannot be fully generalised to the broad population as the children were all of a similar socio-economic status (upper-middle class). That being said, one of the main strengths of this experiment is that the variables in this study were well controlled, as will become clearer as we continue through this chapter. With the variables operationalised and extraneous variables considered, let's examine how participants were assigned to conditions of the independent variables. As illustrated in Figure 2.2, the seventy-two participants, aged between 37 and 69 months, were assigned to separate conditions in order to isolate cause and effect between the independent variables and the dependent

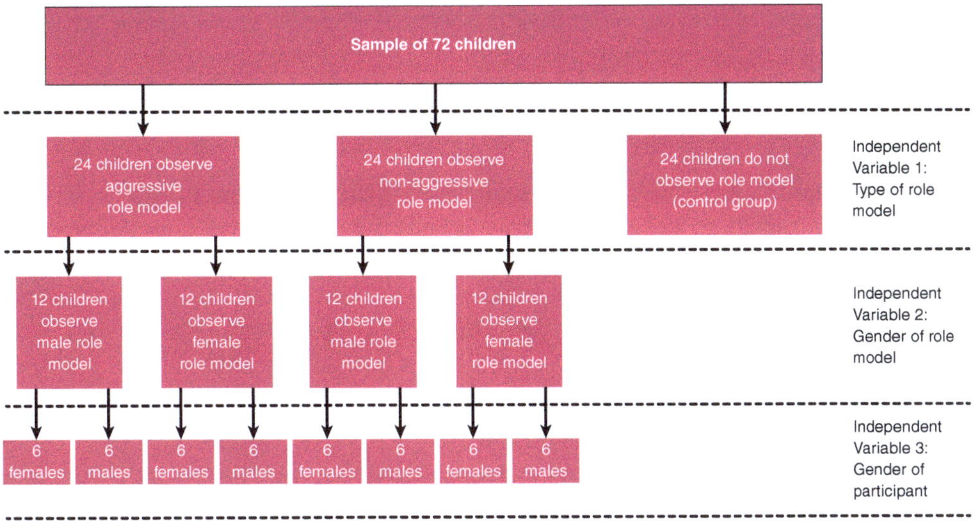

Figure 2.4 Condition structure in Bandura et al.

Source: Adapted from Bandura et al. (1961)

variable. Note that the eight experimental conditions shown at the bottom of the figure are each independent from one another, incorporating different levels of each of the three independent variables.

2.5 Experimental procedure

The type of experimental design used to assign participants to conditions in this experiment was a **matched-pairs design**. Before assigning participants to conditions, the experimenter and a nursery school teacher rated each of the participants on the aggressiveness of their behaviour from their previous observations of the children. The children were then categorised into groups of three, where each child in the group possessed similar aggression levels. One child from each group was then placed into each of the three experimental conditions. This matched-pairs design allowed for the aggressiveness of the children to be controlled across the aggressive model, non-aggressive model, and no model (control) conditions. The sex of the children and the sex of the model were also manipulated in the aggressive and non-aggressive model conditions, which would not have been possible using a within-groups design. Participants could not have participated in all conditions, as it is not possible to manipulate the sex of the children – boys can only participate as boys, and girls can only participate as girls. It would also not have been possible to employ a standard between-groups design because participants could not be randomly assigned to conditions (boys had to be assigned to the boys' conditions; girls had to be assigned to the girls' conditions).

The three stages of the experiment varied somewhat depending on the experimental condition to which the participant was assigned. The first stage allowed for the participants to observe either the aggressive or non-aggressive behaviour from the model. Only those in the experimental conditions, not those in the control condition, participated in this stage, which lasted approximately ten minutes. With a **standardised procedure** enforced, participants were individually seated in a play room where they were able to play with potato prints and picture stickers, whilst at the same time the model was seated in the opposite corner of the room with a tinker toy set (children's plastic building materials), a mallet, and a five-foot inflated Bobo doll. For the children in the non-aggressive condition, the model ignored the Bobo doll and quietly assembled the tinker toys. For the children in the aggressive condition, the model was both physically and verbally aggressive to the Bobo doll for approximately nine of the ten minutes they were in the room with the child. The model exhibited distinct aggressive acts, such as sitting on the Bobo doll and repeatedly punching it on the nose: behaviours that would not typically be performed by a child unless the behaviour was being imitated.

In the second stage, termed the aggression arousal stage, the intention was to put the children in an aggravated state to ensure that aggressive behaviour is provoked in the final stage across all conditions. Participants in both the experimental and control conditions were taken into a separate room containing reasonably attractive toys. After approximately two minutes of the child playing with the toys, the experimenter told the child that the toys were their best toys and that they were saved for the other children to play with. The child was then told that they can play with the toys in the next room (the experimental room) before being led into the experimental room for the final stage.

Ethel ethics

A child of its time

Using children under the age of 16 years old as participants requires informed consent from the child, along with additional consent from the parent or those with legal responsibility for the child. For very young children, regular monitoring is required to ensure that they are not eliciting any signs of distress or cues that they do not wish to participate (British Psychological Society, 2014). It is important to note that Bandura et al.'s (1961) study took place before such rules were in place, and many of the children were in tears during the aggressive model condition or experienced distress by being shown toys and then not being allowed to play with them. Such negative outcomes mean that the study would likely be deemed unethical in modern times.

In the third and final stage, the test for delayed imitation, the children were taken into the experimental room containing a variety of non-aggressive and aggressive toys, including a three-foot Bobo doll. To reduce any influence of the placement of toys affecting the experiment, the toys were arranged in a fixed order for all participants – another great example of how potential confounds/extraneous variables can be controlled. During this twenty-minute stage, the experimenter remained in the room with the participant to ensure the child did not feel uncomfortable being alone in an unfamiliar room. To make the presence of the experimenter as inconspicuous as possible, the experimenter worked quietly in the corner of the room and avoided interaction with the child. Throughout this time, observers were rating the behaviour of the children via the one-way mirror, allowing for the recorded data to be used to make comparisons across conditions.

In any experiment, once the data have been collected for each of the participants, descriptive statistics such as means and standard deviations can be calculated for all experimental and control conditions. This gives an indication of the trends in the data and allows us to describe how the dependent variable is affected by the manipulation of the independent variables. However, to make inferences about the data, and to test for **statistical significance**, inferential statistics must be calculated via statistical tests.

2.6 Analysis and findings

To examine the extent to which imitated aggression differed across the three role-model experimental conditions, a variation of the analysis of variance **(ANOVA)**, called the Friedman two-way analysis of variance, was conducted. A significant main effect of experimental condition was found, indicating that the type of model observed had an effect on levels of imitated aggression. To explore which experimental condition/s differed from which in terms of aggression levels, additional **post-hoc tests** were conducted. These showed that the children who observed an aggressive model were significantly more aggressive (both physically and verbally) than those who observed a non-aggressive model, and significantly more aggressive than those who did not observe a model (control condition). However, there was no statistical difference in aggression levels between participants in the non-aggressive and control conditions.

The next issue to explore was the extent to which the children's sex affected aggression levels. Interestingly, whilst the boys were significantly more physically aggressive than the girls, there was no difference between the two sexes on the imitation of verbal aggression. The statistical analysis of the data also revealed a significant interaction between the independent variable of the sex of the child and the independent variable of the sex of the model. When observing a male model, boys displayed significantly more physical and verbal aggression compared to the girls. The findings from this experiment indicated that social behaviours such as aggression can be learned via the imitation of others. The extent of this imitation appears to be different across the two sexes, with boys imitating more physical aggression than girls, boys imitating significantly more physical and verbal aggression after observing a male model, but there was no statistical difference between the two sexes in terms of imitating verbal aggression.

Skoolkid errors

Interpreting the strength of the evidence

A common school child error is assuming that the findings of a study provide concrete evidence or 'proof' for the overall interpretation(s). Even with a well-controlled experiment, the findings cannot be considered as concrete evidence. Any interpretation is made considering the information available at the time, but the findings may still have been influenced by confounding/extraneous variables that may have been overlooked or not fully controlled.

3. REFLECTION ON BANDURA AND THE EXPERIMENTAL METHOD

3.1 Findings

The main conclusion that Bandura and colleagues drew from their research is that the results provided **empirical evidence** in support of Social Learning Theory. More specifically, by showing that the children replicated the adults' behaviour, the researchers provided support for the idea that we acquire and engage in new behaviours through the observation and imitation of others. Bandura then went on to conduct additional studies in order to further test his Social Learning Theory. For instance, Bandura (1965) explored how the children reacted when they saw the adult model being praised, punished, or receiving no feedback for their aggressive behaviour towards the Bobo doll. He found that children who observed punishment were less likely to behave aggressively themselves, compared to children in the other two conditions. Bandura argued that these findings provided further support for Social Learning Theory, as they showed that we pay attention to how other people are treated after they behave in a certain way, and we use this observation to determine whether we should (or should not) imitate the behaviour ourselves.

Bandura and colleagues' studies have often been argued to have important real-world implications, particularly regarding the topic of children's exposure to violent media. This argument was further strengthened when Bandura, Ross, and Ross (1963) extended their original study by showing that children will also imitate aggressive models they see on film. Bandura and colleagues' studies have often been cited by those who argue that children should not be exposed to violent images in television programmes, films, and videogames, as it may lead to them imitating the characters they observe. Indeed, such arguments are frequently put forward in a bid to explain young people's violent behaviour, such as the often-cited Columbine High massacre perpetrators' extensive playing of the videogame *Doom* (Ferguson, 2007).

3.2 Strengths and limitations

When reflecting on the appropriateness of applying Bandura et al.'s. (1961) findings to real-life situations in this manner, it is useful to take a step back and consider the strengths and limitations of the study. There are certainly a number of important strengths in terms of how the study was designed, particularly with regards to how the researchers controlled for extraneous variables. For instance, the fact that the researchers observed the children's behaviour in the natural environment of the nursey before the study took place meant that they could create a matched-pairs design, allowing them to control for variations in the children's levels of aggression. They also controlled for other important variables, such as the time of day at which the experiment was conducted, and the sexes of the children. Additionally, in terms of categorising the children's behaviours during the study, the researchers measured inter-rater reliability by getting two observers to independently rate the aggressiveness of the children's behaviour, and then compare their ratings. The fact that a high level of agreement was observed between the raters suggests that we can be confident that the behaviours were categorised appropriately.

However, the study also has a number of limitations, and various critiques have been levelled at the work. Perhaps most notably, it has been argued that the study has low **ecological validity**, because it involves an artificial situation where a child observes a stranger (with whom they cannot interact) behaving oddly towards a toy that many of them had never encountered before (and which is designed to be hit: Ferguson, 2010). This is clearly very different to the 'real-world' modelling to which Bandura and colleagues attempted to apply the findings, which tends to happen within well-established social groups, such as families and circles of friends, and where there is a real human cost to aggression, such as people being hurt. There is also the possibility that the novelty of the Bobo doll affected the children's behaviour: Cumberbatch (1991) notes that children were found to be five times more likely to behave aggressively towards the Bobo doll if they were unfamiliar with it (compared to children who had seen a Bobo doll before), suggesting that the children's imitative behaviour in the original study may have been partially due to them never having encountered the Bobo doll before. It would thus have been beneficial for Bandura, Ross, and Ross to have added 'familiarity with Bobo dolls' to their list of matched-pairs criteria when designing the experiment.

Another issue that the researchers failed to address was the nursey the children went to: all attended the Stanford University nursery, which meant their parents were university staff or students. Stanford is a highly prestigious university, and in the 1960s, this meant that the vast majority of nursery attendees were white upper-middle class children (Hart & Kritsonis, 2006). This lack of diversity limits the researchers' ability to generalise the findings to the general population, and is also an example of the **WEIRD problem** in Psychology: the over-recruitment of participants from White, Educated, Industrialized, Rich, and Democratic backgrounds (Henrich, Heine, & Norenzayan, 2010).

Finally, some people have criticised the study on ethical grounds. For instance, the researchers never explored whether the children experienced any long-term emotional or social damage from engaging in the research, or even whether they were upset or confused during participation. Not considering such issues is a significant ethical oversight (British Psychological Society, 2018).

3.3 Reflection on the experimental method

An experiment is a powerful tool for psychologists. This is primarily because it is the only way to establish evidence of causality (or cause and effect) by showing that manipulating the independent variable causes the dependent variable to change. Experiments also give psychologists the ability to control extraneous variables that might otherwise impact upon the dependent variable, thereby increasing the psychologist's confidence in asserting that it is indeed the manipulations of the independent variable that are causing changes in the dependent variable. While this ability to control variables is a clear strength of the experimental method, it is also an important weakness within the context of psychology. This is because psychologists are interested in exploring people's **cognition** and behaviour in the real world, and there is the possibility that these cognitions and behaviours will be unduly affected by the artificial and highly-controlled laboratory environment. For instance, the experimental environment may give rise to problems such as **demand characteristics**, where the participant's behaviour is affected by their expectations regarding the study's aim, or **experimenter effects**, where the experimenter's expectations regarding the study affects the participant's behaviour. In such circumstances, the experimental environment becomes an extraneous variable itself, with the potential to affect how participants respond to stimuli.

Field experiments may be a way to escape the artificial control of the laboratory, but they open up the possibility of numerous additional extraneous variables affecting participants' behaviour. They are also often more logistically complex, time-consuming, and expensive than laboratory experiments, and the unpredictability of the real world means that they can present dangers for experimenters and/or participants. There might also be novel ethical concerns, particularly if participants are exposed to the experimental manipulation without them being aware of what is going on. For instance, is it appropriate for an experimenter to observe and record the behaviour of a train passenger who has just seen an apparently drunk person collapse on the carriage floor during rush-hour? Moreover, what if witnessing the incident upsets the passenger? Should the experimenter take time to debrief and comfort them, or should the experiment be perceived as a fabrication of an event which could have easily happened in reality, implying that the experimenter has no responsibility to provide the passenger with post-experiment support?

It is quandaries such as these that can make field experiments particularly challenging to design and conduct. Nonetheless, when approached with care, they enable studies to be conducted with ecological validity, and can produce data that would be all but impossible to gather in the laboratory. In particular, Social Psychology is replete with interesting and influential field experiments, such as Latané and Darley's (1970) seminal research into bystander intervention, which led to the conceptualisation of the famous bystander effect (the idea that people are more likely to help a person in distress when they are alone, compared to when other people are present).

3.4 Summary

In sum, experiments (like all research methods) have important strengths and weaknesses, and psychologists need to be aware of these when selecting a method for their research project. For this reason, some psychologists choose to address the same research question using multiple research methods: a process known as **triangulation**. If the results from these different research methods converge, then the psychologist can have more confidence in stating that their predictions have been supported. However, using triangulation can be expensive and time-consuming and also requires the psychologist to be experienced in the use of multiple research methods. Ultimately, as with all aspects of research, the psychologist must weigh up the pros and cons of each potential option before deciding what is best for their research project.

LEARNING OBJECTIVES

You should now know:

- What is meant by 'the experimental method'
- What led Bandura, Ross, and Ross to conduct their Bobo doll study
- The methods they used
- The results they found
- The conclusions they drew from the results
- Strengths and limitations of the study
- Strengths and limitations of the experimental method

FURTHER READING

Bandura, A., Ross, D., Ross, S., & Webb, D. (2013). *Psychology classics all psychology students should read: The Bobo doll experiment*. CreateSpace Independent Publishing Platform.

If you want to learn more about Bandura's Bobo doll experiments, this is a useful book. It provides a helpful summary of the key ideas and the theoretical rationale behind the research

Banyard, P., & Grayson, A. (2007). *Introducing psychological research*. Red Globe Press.

This highly accessible book explores some of the most famous research studies within psychology, including Bandura's Bobo doll experiments.

Field, A. (2018). *Discovering statistics using IBM SPSS statistics*. Sage.

This is a useful book if you want to learn more about how to analyse data you collect from experiments. It is also very user-friendly and humorous.

Hart-Davis, A. (2018). *Pavlov's dog and 49 other experiments that revolutionised psychology*. Modern Books.

If you would like to learn more about important historical psychology experiments, this is a useful book. It is an informative and light-hearted exploration of seminal experimental psychology.

Thomas, G. (2017). *How to do your research project: A guide for students*. Sage.

If you want to apply what you have learnt in this chapter in order to create your own experimental research project, you will find this book to be useful. It is a helpful and accessible guide to students who are beginning a research project.

LINKS TO USEFUL RESOURCES

SAGE Experimental Research Methods video series: https://methods.sagepub.com/video/experimental-design

SAGE Core Concepts in Research video series: https://methods.sagepub.com/video/sampling-tuto-s

3

SURVEY METHODS

LUCY BETTS, MOON HALDER, MARK SERGEANT AND BEN OLDFIELD

1. INTRODUCTION

Survey methods are very popular within psychology and, as Hulland and colleagues (2018) note, '*surveys are ubiquitous and inform decision making in every walk of life*' (p. 92). The survey method approach involves participants being asked a series of questions about particular topics which can be administered either face-to-face by the research, over the telephone, in paper form as a self-administered survey, or online.

1.1 Basics

One of the reasons for the popularity of surveys is the range of research questions that you can ask using surveys. For example, Neuman (2007) suggests surveys can be used to explore a range of non-mutually exclusive areas including: (1) behaviour; (2) attitudes, beliefs, and opinions; (3) characteristics; (4) expectations; (5) self-classifications; and (6) knowledge. Although surveys can be used to answer a range of research questions, Neuman cautions against using surveys to try and answer why questions as surveys are less effective than other research methods when addressing these topics. In this chapter, we will introduce you to the survey method and consider the practicalities of using this approach to collect data within psychology.

The are several advantages to the survey method including being able to collect data from many participants relatively quickly. Also, when **self-report** surveys are administered to a large randomly collected sample, it is possible to generalise the findings (Demetriou,

Ozer, & Eassau, 2014). Further, Demetriou et al. argue that when using self-report surveys, the data collected tends to be more accurate because the person who is filling out the survey is closer to the topic than other potential data sources. For example, a child may be accurate in giving their own personal experiences of bullying compared to similar reports about the child's experiences from a parent or teacher. However, surveys are not without their limitations. One of the biggest limitations of surveys is the potential for **social desirability bias** and participants not responding truthfully to the questions (Demetriou et al., 2014). As discussed later in the chapter, how the questions in a survey are worded is particularly important to avoid **response bias** and that the response options to questions avoid forcing participants to give an ambiguous answer.

Once you have decided that surveys are an appropriate method for you to collect your data, the first thing that you will need to decide is whether you will develop your own survey or whether you will use existing surveys that other researchers have developed. In the first part of the chapter we will outline some of the practical considerations that you must be mindful of when developing your own survey. Of course, a lot of these considerations also apply to all surveys, irrespective of who designed them, therefore, you should also ensure that any pre-existing survey that you use follows these guidelines as well.

2. DESIGNING SURVEYS

2.1 Considerations for designing surveys

In some circumstances, it may be preferable for you to develop you own survey. For example, to assess a new concept or when existing measures do not follow best practices that may lead to **measurement error** (Gehlbach, 2015). DeVellis (2017) outlines eight steps to developing surveys:

1. Determining what it is you want to measure
2. Generating an item pool
3. Determining the format of measurement
4. Having the item pool reviewed by 'experts'
5. Considering the inclusion of validation items
6. Administering items to a development sample
7. Evaluating the items
8. Optimising the scale length

Once you have decided what it is you want to measure, you should begin to generate an item pool (the questions that are likely to be included in your survey). There are a number of practical considerations that you should be mindful of when writing your questions which will be explored in the next section.

2.2 The questions

At the heart of designing questions and surveys is ensuring that each question has the same meaning for everyone including the researchers and all of the potential participants. Therefore, it is really important to ensure that the language that you use in your questions is clear and that you are mindful to ensure that all participants would have enough knowledge to be able to answer the questions. To help with survey design and the wording of questions, De Vaus (2002) made 17 recommendations that you should follow when you are generating your questions (these also equally apply to questions that are contained within existing surveys):

1. Keep language simple
2. Keep questions as short as possible
3. Avoid **double-barrelled** questions
4. Avoid **leading** questions
5. Be cautious of **negatively**-worded questions
6. Consider whether participants will have appropriate knowledge to answer the question
7. Ensure that language used has the same meaning for everyone
8. Avoid **prestige bias**
9. Avoid **ambiguous** questions
10. Avoid questions that are precise
11. Ensure the frame of reference clear
12. Avoid questions that artificially create opinions
13. Think about whether personal or impersonal wording is needed
14. Avoid questions that go in too much detail
15. Avoid **dangling alternatives**
16. Avoid **gratuitous qualifiers**
17. Avoid questions with all-inclusive or exclusive words.

Thinking about some the key issues that De Vaus (2002) raised, when developing questions, you should think about the language that you are using and ensure that the language is as simple as possible. For example, you should avoid the use of jargon and technical terms (unless you either give a definition or are confident that your participants will know what the terms mean). You should also think about whether you could make the question shorter. Short questions are recommended for surveys as they tend to be less confusing and less ambiguous for participants completing the survey.

You should also ensure when writing your questions that you have avoided double-barrelled questions. The challenge with double-barrelled questions is that by their very nature, because they ask about more than one thing in the question, it is hard to interpret which part of the question a participant's response relates to. For example, do you like chocolate and ice-cream? is a double-barrelled question and if someone says yes, you don't know if it's the chocolate, the ice-cream or both that they like. To overcome this problem in this example, you should ask separately about chocolate and ice-cream. Similar to double-barrelled questions, you should also avoid leading questions.

Interesting facts

The first surveys

Collecting information about people through a census has been with us for thousands of years but the first questionnaire-based survey is attributed to the Statistical Society of London. In his history of the questionnaire method, Robert Gault writes 'Among the earliest acts of the Statistical Society of London ... was the appointment of committees to enquire into industrial and social conditions. One of these committees, in 1838, used the first written questionnaire of which I have any record. The committee-men prepared and printed a list of questions "designed to elicit the complete and impartial history of strikes".' (Gault, 1907)

Leading questions are problematic because they give the participants a sense that there is a 'right answer' and this could result in some participants giving you the answer that they think you want to hear rather than the answer that they would actually give. For example, starting questions with 'do you agree that' or 'does this seem like a good idea' can lead participants. You should also be careful of ambiguous questions which also have the potential to confuse participants. Ambiguous questions tend to occur if the sentence structure of the question is not clear, if you have used words that have different meanings, there is both positive and negative phrases within the questions, or if the question is double-barrelled.

Although negatively-worded questions have the potential to be confusing to some participants, including a few negatively-worded questions in your scale can be a good thing to keep participants on their toes and ensure that they are reading the items. With negatively-worded questions, it is important that you re-code them before you begin your analysis so that they are scored in the same way as the rest of the scale. You should also think about how precise you are with the wording of the questions. Although you want to avoid questions that may give really vague or imprecise responses, if a question is too precise it may also give unreliable responses as participants may not be able to give an accurate response. For example, it may be hard to give an accurate answer to the question 'how many times have you been to university in the last 12 months?', because the time frame is so long. Similarly, you should also avoid developing questions that contain all-inclusive words (e.g., all, everyone) or exclusive words (e.g., none, no-one) as few participants are likely to disagree with them so there is likely to be little variability in these responses.

Once you have come up with the questions for your survey, it may be wise to get a peer to double check that you have followed De Vaus' (2002) recommendations. Having decided the wording for your questions, you next need to think about how the participants will answer them.

Ig Nobel Prize

Rhinotillexomania (habitual nose-picking)

The 2001 Ig Nobel Prize for Public Heath went to Andrade and Srihari for their study which was awarded for their 'probing medical discovery that nose-picking is a common activity among adolescents'. Almost the entire sample admitted to nose picking, with a median frequency of four times per day and the frequency was greater than 20 times per day in 7.6% of the sample. Nearly 17% of subjects considered that they had a serious nose-picking problem.

Andrade, C., & Srihari, B.S. (2001) A preliminary survey of rhinotillexomania in an adolescent sample. *Journal of Clinical Psychiatry*, *62*(6), 426–31.

2.3 Response format

When designing surveys as well as thinking about the questions that you ask, it is also important to think about how participants will answer them. In other words, you need to decide which **response format** you will use to collect the data. The first decision that you need to make is whether you will use closed or open questions. Closed questions are designed to limit the responses offered by the participant and typically the participant is asked to select from a range of pre-existing answers such as yes/no or strongly agree, agree, disagree, strongly disagree. The advantage of closed questions is that you can easily convert the participants' responses into numbers which you can then use in your analysis. Open questions on the other hand allow participants to write a free-text response that is not constrained by the researcher. However, the disadvantages of using open questions is that the responses may be limited by the participants' literacy skills and there are also implications for how you analyse the data (e.g., you may need to think about how you will convert the participants' text responses into numbers if you wanted to do a statistical analysis).

If you decide to use closed questions, you next need to consider the format of the responses that you will include. De Vaus (2002) suggests that there are three guiding principles for developing response formats:

1. exhaustiveness,
2. exclusiveness, and
3. balancing categories.

Exhaustiveness relates to whether the responses to the question will cover all of the possible responses that participants may have. For example, you would need a wide range of response options to capture a participant's nationality if you made your survey available online for anyone to complete. Therefore, in some cases where there are a range of possible options and you may not have listed them all, it may be useful to include an 'other' category where you ask participants to specify their response.

Exclusiveness relates to the questions and responses being written in such a way that participants may legitimately want to select more than one response to answer the question. For example, if a participant was asked about their occupation and they were a student but also worked part-time in a shop, they may want to select both shop worker and student from a list of responses. Therefore, if you end up with a question where participants are legitimately able to answer with more than one response, then you should include options such as all of the above or both 'a' and 'b'.

Balancing categories relates to the number of responses and how these are distributed around a neutral response point. A balanced approach is one where there are the same number of positive responses as negative responses; for example, strongly agree, agree, neither agree nor disagree, disagree, strongly disagree. An example of an unbalanced approach would be strongly agree, moderately agree, slightly agree, agree, neither agree nor disagree, disagree, strongly disagree. This example is unbalanced because there are more agree responses than disagree responses.

2.4 Scales

Accompanying the recommendations for response format, when thinking about responses, you also need to think which type of response formats you will use. The most common response format for scales is a **Likert** scale. Likert scales involve participants being presented with a statement and then this is followed by a series of responses from which they have to select one that reflects their agreement with the statement. For example,

I love survey design:

Strongly agree	Agree	Neither agree nor disagree	Disagree	Strongly disagree

In the original version of the Likert scales (Likert, 1932), items were coded such that the value or number 5 was always attached to the positive end of the scale and the value or number 1 to the negative end of the scale but more recently a range of response formats have been used for such scales (Hartley & Betts, 2013). The response formats for Likert scales are often worded so that they have approximately equal distance between responses. However, there are issues about what middle values mean and, also whether participants can distinguish between the number of responses. For example, whether everyone draws the same meaning between slightly agree and somewhat agree. When developing Likert scales, it is also important that you think about how many responses you need to have. This is an important consideration because having fewer response points reduces the likely variability in the participants' answers which may have implications for your data analysis. Although the consideration of the format of Likert scales may seem trivial, there is evidence that changing the position of verbal and numeric labels can change response patterns. For example, having scales that started on the left with positive verbal labels and the highest numeric value has consistently resulted in respondents having higher scores than other response patterns (Hartley & Betts, 2013). Likert scales have also been criticised because the same score can be achieved in a number of different ways, leading to questions about the reproducibility of the results (Oppenheim, 1992).

Semantic differential scales are another type of scales frequently used in Psychology surveys. These scales present opposite adjective words to describe something, someone, or an attitude. The words are presented with a corresponding numeric scale and participants are asked to report their response. For example:

Survey design is:

Important .... Unimportant

In addition to Likert scales and semantic differential scales there are of course many different response formats that you can use such as providing a rating out of 10, a feeling thermometer, and rankings of which responses are the most important. You need to decide which response format provides the most appropriate type of data and which best accompanies the questions that you are asking.

2.5 Reliability

Although thinking about the question wording and response format is important for selecting existing scales to include in your survey, two of the most important things to consider when selecting existing scales to use in research is the scale's **reliability** and **validity**.

Reliability relates to whether the survey is measuring consistently the thing that you are interested in. A scale has to measure the construct of interest consistently so that you can be confident that a high proportion of a participant's score is due to the variable that you are trying to measure rather than error. So, in other words, whether if someone completes a happiness survey on two occasions, any difference in the score they get is because of a change in their happiness rather than something associated with inconsistencies in survey itself (Oppenheim, 1992). There are several types of reliability. **Test-retest reliability** involves administering the same survey to the same group on more than one occasion over a relatively short period.

A reliable survey would mean that very similar results were obtained on both occasions. However, one issue with the short time frame that you must be mindful of is that **practice effects** could occur. **Parallel-form reliability** involves two versions of a particular survey being administered, and for reliability to be demonstrated, participants' scores on both versions of the survey must be highly correlated. Rust and Golombok (1999) argue that parallel-form reliability is one of the best forms of establishing reliability. However, because of the complexity associated with establishing at least two versions of the same survey, this method tends not to be used very often.

To overcome some of the challenges associated with identifying parallel forms of the same survey **split-half reliability** can be used. Split-half reliability involves splitting a participant's performance on a survey (e.g., their scores on even numbered questions versus their scores on odd numbered questions) and then exploring the correlation between the two scores. A high correlation between the two halves would be indicative of the reliability of the survey. Finally, you can also consider the **internal consistency** of a scale assessed using Cronbach's alpha. According to Oppenheim (1992), internal consistency is based on classical scaling theory and the premiss that if the items are designed to assess a single construct then they should have a strong association with each other and the construct. According to this logic, if there is internal consistency then it is likely the items within the scale are assessing the same variable. Kline (2000) recommends when selecting scales to use in research that high reliability assessed as both internal consistency (with 0.7 as a minimum) and test-retest reliability are a crucial consideration for reliability.

2.6 Validity

Validity relates to the extent to which the survey is assessing what it purports to. For example, taking a scale from the case study does the scale measure fear of missing out or is it measuring something different? There are several types of validity. **Face validity** considers the extent to which the items measure what they are intended to and involves considering the individual questions within a survey. However, Oppenheim (1992) cautions that this approach '*holds many dangers*' (p. 161). For example, Oppenheim raises questions about how do the items represent the broader construct?, how were the items selected?, and what do the items represent? Oppenheim suggests that one way to try and mitigate against some of these dangers of face validity is through how the survey had been constructed.

Concurrent validity is when the results of a new survey is correlated with an existing survey or external measure of the same construct. If the survey is valid, there should be an association between the new survey and the existing measure of the same construct.

Construct validity is when you look at whether the relationship between the survey score is associated with things that you would expect to be associated. Specifically, in the case of construct validity you would make use of existing theory to make predictions about how the score on the newly developed survey would be associated with other measures and if these were evidenced, then you would have established construct validity for the survey.

Predictive validity involves the extent to which survey scores can predict some future outcome. When selecting scales, Kline (2000) recommends focusing on construct validity, especially when research aims to extend psychological knowledge. However, Kline also acknowledges that validity is hard to establish.

Whether you are using pre-existing scales or whether you have developed your own scale, it is important that you check the reliability and validity of the scales that you have used for your data.

2.7 Administering your survey

Having designed or selected your pre-existing survey measures, you should also consider how the questions will be presented to the participants. For example, it is good practice to include an appropriate introduction that outlines the topic of your research to the potential participants. You should think about how you frame this introduction and the instructions for the survey(s) to ensure that the language is accessible to participants and that participants have a clear understanding of what is required of them. For example, you probably want to avoid using psychological terms (unless you are recruiting psychologists) so that participants are clear about what is being asked of them. In some cases, you may want to consider whether you need to give participants definitions of particular terms so that the participants and the researchers have a shared understanding of the constructs that are being measured. However, you should think about whether providing a definition will prime the participants to respond in a particular way and ultimately influence the data that you collect. Depending on the age of the sample you are working with and also the complexity of your survey, you may want to consider giving participants examples of how they should complete the questions.

Skoolkid errors

Not checking your data before analysis

When you have entered your data, it is important that you go through a process of data cleaning. Data cleaning involves going through the data you have collected and potentially removing data from any participants who may not have completed the survey correctly. It is important that you keep a record of decisions you make when cleaning your data so that you can report it in your method section. There are four things to look for:

1. Someone submitting your online survey more than once – check the unique identifiers to make sure that participants haven't accidently submitted their results more than once.
2. Data for **satisficing/lazy submitting** – check your data for responses where participants have given the same response throughout. Although this may be legitimate for some of the scales contained within your survey it may not be for the entire survey.
3. Participants who have missed entire scales/sections/stopped answering part way through.
4. Participants who have missed out a couple of questions – in this case you may want to think about how you will handle missing data in your analysis.

Before you collect data using a particular survey, it is really important that you know how you will score it when you have the data. In other words, you need to be sure which items (if any) need **reverse coding** and what the survey specific scoring instructions are. You should also recode any items before you explore the internal consistency of your surveys.

2.8 Cultural context

There are several challenges associated with undertaking cross-cultural research using surveys (Halder et al., 2016) including:

- Survey design
- Translation
- Selection of methodology
- Data collection
- Cultural obligation and peer pressure
- Ethical considerations and awareness
- Working as a cross-cultural research team
- Other possible challenges

Focusing on survey design, it is important to recognise that many surveys have been developed with Western samples and are based on Western theories. Therefore, researchers need to be mindful of item equivalence between samples including idioms, phrases, and grammatical details (Halder et al., 2016; Sekaran, 1983). Researchers can adopt several techniques to translate surveys including **one-way translation**, **translation by committee**, and **back translation**. When selecting a translation method, it is important to recognise that it can change the length of items and the survey (McGorry, 2000), that working with bilinguals who can read and write fluently in both languages is crucial (Marin & Marin, 1991), and consideration needs to be given to cultural phraseology paying particular attention to any regional or class differences. Cultural context can have an influence on participant responses as cultural orientation has been seen to influence how one thinks, perceives the world around us and the reaction to various situations (Cunningham et al., 1995; Dake, 1991; Kühnen & Oyserman, 2002; Oyserman & Lee, 2008) which calls for a culturally fit survey instrument.

While conducting cross-cultural research, it is recommended that survey instruments be administered in the native language using a translation method. However, care should be taken to make sure that the literal meaning of the survey items remains the same (Brislin, 1970; McGorry, 2000). An example of a back translation process is illustrated in Figure 3.1 below (adapted from Halder et al., 2016):

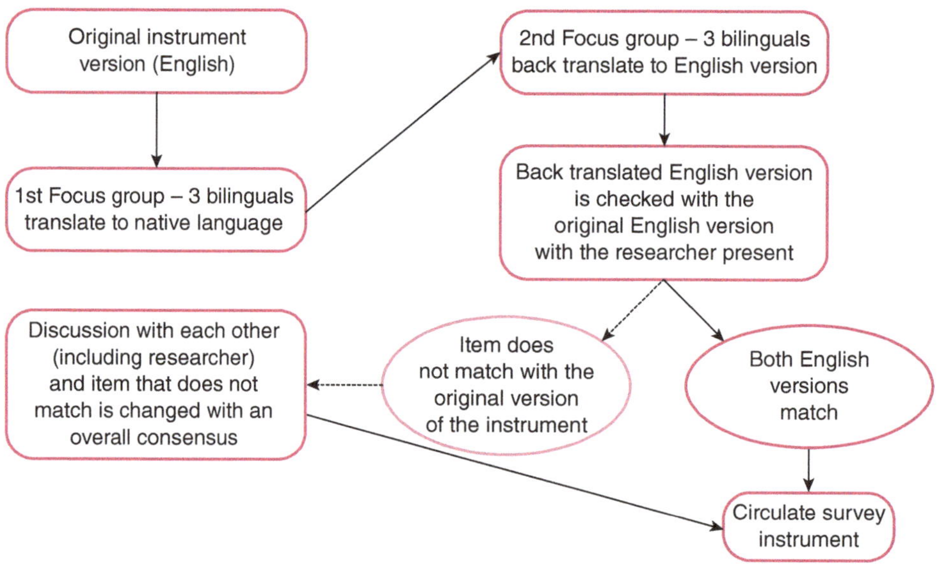

Figure 3.1 An illustration of the back translation process (adapted from Halder et al., 2016)

Selection of methodology in cross-cultural research is crucial as implications of incorrect methodological procedures can sometimes lead to adverse psychological and social issues for the participants in certain countries. For example, while a survey response from a participant on adult images might be acceptable in certain cultures, such topics might not be easily accepted in some collectivist cultures. Therefore, it is important for the researcher to anticipate the culture-specific impact of the method itself. As a researcher, measures should be taken to eliminate any possible adverse psychological impact on participants.

General familiarity with research process of participants should be taken into consideration while administering any survey cross-culturally. Any challenges in the comprehension of the research process and the survey items would be best handled by being able to address any queries first-hand (e.g., the researcher could be present in person to help address any participant query or having online communication if online).

Cultural obligation and peer pressure could force participant responses that could have an adverse impact on the results as participants might simply respond to survey items without actually being interested in the topic or could respond without understanding the meaning. This fails ethical adherence. Hence, it is important that participant recruitment and administration is closely monitored when conducting survey cross-culturally. The presence of having a researcher could help address any queries adequately either face2face or online.

Adherence to ethical standards is crucial when conducting cross-cultural study using survey instruments. An understanding of the cultural variance is important to help meet all ethical guidelines. Ethical codes and practices might not always be easy to follow in all cultures and might not address all ethical issues that a researcher might come across while conducting a cross-cultural research. Being aware of cultural values, norms, perception and behaviours in the sample could help address some of the challenges (Ponterotto & Casas, 1993). It is important to note that ethical guidelines developed in Western countries cannot be fully followed in Eastern countries (Pedersen, 1991) due to fundamental differences in cultural norms, values and behavioural patterns that exist in different cultures (Hofstede, 1980). Therefore, an understanding of how the ethical guidelines and procedures is received and is interpreted in another culture should be taken into consideration. Researchers should think about how best ethical standards in the target sample could be maintained. It is recommended that cross-cultural research should be approached with an early understanding of cultural history, values and traditions that could be incorporated while submitting ethics application.

Cross-cultural research team could benefit by maintaining support and being flexible in their research strategies. One should establish a cross-cultural research team before piloting any study as research strategies could then be adapted to cultural needs and demands.

Whoa there!

Online surveys

Although online surveys have the advantage of allowing you to potentially reach a much wider audience to recruit participants, including specialist populations, in a relatively quick and cost effective way, there are some considerations when using such an approach. First, it is worth considering whether there is a potential for a bias sample to be recruited through online methods because of who has digital connectivity. For example, the world internet usage and population statistics for 2020 (www.internetworldstats.com/stats.htm) suggests variation in the internet access according to world regions with Africa having the lowest proportion (42.2%) and North America the highest proportion (90.3%). Further, the proportion of the world region using the internet compared to the proportion of the world population is over-represented for Europe (15.1% versus 10.7%) and North America (6.9% versus 4.7%) and under-represented for Africa (11.7% versus 17.2%). Therefore, a lack of digital connectivity could limit your potential sample.

Second, it is also worth considering whether there is a lack of research control associated with online surveys. For example, ensuring that participants have followed the established protocol or instructions (note this can be overcome in some cases through **manipulation checks**) and the environment participants completed the survey in. Aligned to this is the increase in use of online paid participation services such as Amazon's MTurk, Qualitrics, and Prolific Academic. These services can be used to reach a wider participant pool in return for monetary compensation for participants. However, although some have questioned the representativeness of these methods and the quality of the data (Barends & de Veries, 2019) there is some evidence that the samples of MTurk participants are more diverse, that realistic monetary compensation for time, and that the data is at least as reliable as more traditional approaches (Buhrmester, Kwang & Gosling, 2011).

A further consideration when developing online surveys is that some of your participants will likely be completing the surveys on their smartphones. Therefore, you should seek to optimise your survey for completion on smartphones. To optimise your online survey for smartphone use it is recommended that you: (1) ensure that text is large enough to be easily read; (2) touch targets should be large to allow easy selection; (3) all content should visible on the screen without participants scrolling; (4) the design should be simple and easy for participants to use; and (5) the survey should appear in the same format on all devices (Antoun, Katz, Argueta & Wang, 2018).

When designing a study that involves multiple scales, it is important that you think about the order in which the scales are given to participants. Specifically, you need to make sure that you are not **priming** participants or introducing biases into responses such that responses are not influenced by the previous scale (e.g., a scale on honesty presented just before a scale on lying). It is also wise to think about the order of the scales from an ethical point of view to ensure that participants are not left reflecting on their answers about a potentially sensitive topic because you asked about it last.

It's really important that you pilot your survey before you collect your actual data. Piloting involves asking a couple of people, who will not take part in the actual survey, to check for: readability (e.g., are the questions and instructions clear) and any formatting issues. For online surveys you also want to consider any technical issues, problems with how the survey appears on different devices, and how the data is recorded.

When using surveys, you need to think about the participants' linguistic abilities. For example, O'Reilly, Ronzoni and Dogra (2013) suggest that when designing questions for children it is important that they are short, written in child accessible language, clear, contain a single point per question, and allow for a precise answer.

3. EXAMPLE STUDY: RELATIONAL AGGRESSION ON FACEBOOK

3.1 Paper and researchers

Abell, L., Buglass, S. L., & Betts L. R. (2019). Relational aggression on Facebook: The role of FOMO and avoiding inferiority. *Cyberpsychology, Behavior, and Social Networking, 22*, 799–803.

Loren Abell is a Senior Lecturer at NTU. Her research explores the use of indirect aggression and emotional manipulation in social contexts including banter in online and offline contexts.

Sarah Buglass is a Principal Lecturer at NTU. Her research interests primarily involve the use of digital technology and problematic/risky online behaviour.

Lucy Betts is a Professor in Social Developmental Psychology. Her research currently focuses on experiences of cyberbullying and online risks.

3.2 Introduction to the piece of research

We are spending more and more time online and engaging with social media. Engaging with social media can have many benefits including educational and enhancing our connections to others. Our engagement with social media is underpinned by numerous motives and individual differences. However, not all motives for engaging with social media are necessarily positive, for example, fear of missing out (FOMO). FOMO is a psychological state where we think that those we are connected to are having more interesting and fulfilling lives than we are (Przybylski, Murayama, DeHaan, & Gladwell, 2013). Feelings of FOMO are likely to increase when we make more frequent comparisons and, as such, we may engage in compensatory behaviours such as disclosing more about ourselves (Buglass, Binder, Betts, & Underwood, 2017; Gilbert, McEwan, Bellew, Mills, & Gale, 2009). One compensatory behaviour that had not previously been explored is relational aggression. Relational aggression involves behaviours that damage the social networks of others (Archer & Coyne, 2005; Asher, Stark, & Fireman, 2017). On Facebook, these relational aggression acts may translate to tagging individuals in embarrassing photographs, deliberately ignoring someone on chat or excluding them from seeing profile content (Abell & Brewer, 2014).

Ethel ethics

Survey ethics

Managing consent: For online surveys it is not possible to get written consent for participants as you would do if they were completing the research face-to-face. Therefore, it is necessary to give potential participants information about the study and then ask them to indicate their consent to participate through asking them to tick a series of checkboxes that relate to them giving consent.

Debriefing and providing support: For online surveys, it is possible that people may not reach the debrief because they may navigate away from the survey before they get to the end of it. Therefore, you should include all information that you want participants to receive (such as appropriate support agencies) in the information sheet that you give to participants, so you know that they have received that information should they decide to navigate away from the survey.

Anonymity: You should be mindful that whilst an IP address can be used to determine whether someone had completed your questionnaire more than once, it is also possible to identify individuals from their IP address. Therefore, you should consider whether you need to collect this information as part of your online survey. Depending on your mechanism of withdrawal, a participant's anonymity may also be compromised if you ask them to email you to withdraw their data and their email address includes their name. Therefore, you should make participants aware of this in the information sheet and also consider whether you need to provide other mechanisms to withdraw your data.

3.3 Aims of the study

The aim of the study was to explore the relationship between FOMO and Facebook relational aggression. The study also examined whether a desire to strive to avoid inferiority and engagement in interpersonal manipulation acted as serial mediators in the relationship between FOMO and Facebook relational aggression.

3.4 Design

Existing scales and subscales were selected to measure their key variables of FOMO, stiving to avoid inferiority, interpersonal manipulation, and relational aggression on Facebook. The scales were selected because their psychometrics properties had been established in previous research such that they demonstrated acceptable levels of reliability and validity. The study used four existing scales,

- The FOMO scale (Przybylski et al., 2013) which is a 10-tem measure of FOMO (e.g., 'I fear others have more rewarding experiences than me') that participants responded to a 5-point scale ranging from 1 = Not true of me to 5 = extremely true of me.
- The striving to avoid inferiority scale (Gilbert et al., 2009) which includes 31 questions designed to assess insecure striving to avoid inferiority (e.g., 'I need to match what other people achieve') and participants responded on a 5-point scale ranging from 0 = Never to 4 = Always.
- The four-item interpersonal manipulation subscale from the need for drama scale (Fankowski et al., 2016) which assessed the general tendency to manipulate others (e.g., 'sometimes it's fun to get people riled up') with participants responding on a 7-point scale ranging from 1 = strongly disagree to 7 = strongly agree.
- The relational aggression on Facebook scale (Abell & Brewer, 2014) was used to assess relational aggressive behaviour towards a friend on Facebook (e.g., 'I often ignore my friend when they try to speak to me on Facebook chat') with participants responding on a 5-point scale ranging from 1 = strongly disagree to 5 = strongly agree.

For all of the measures, items were scored and some items were reverse scored so that high scores indicated greater agreement with the questions. For each participant, the average score was calculated for the items in each scale leading to scores for FOMO, striving to avoid inferiority, interpersonal manipulation, and relational aggression on

Facebook. All of the scales had demonstrated acceptable internal consistency with scores ranging from ≥.78 and ≤ .94

The scales were administered as an online survey which included an information page, a series of statements that the participants were required to tick to indicate their consent, the various scales with accompanying instructions relating to how to complete the scales, and a debrief. The sample was UK-based university students who reported that they were active Facebook users. The final sample comprised 190 participants as data was excluded from 30 participants because of a large number of incomplete responses.

3.5 The findings

Before data analysis was undertaken, the normality of the data was examined, and the data was found to be normally distributed. Where there were missing values, these were replaced with the scale mean. Bivariate correlations were used to examine the relationship between FOMO and the other variables. These correlations revealed that FOMO was positively associated with striving to avoid inferiority, manipulation, and relational aggression. A boot-strapped serial mediation (Preacher & Hayes, 2008) undertaken using the PROCESS (Hayes, 2015) SPSS macro was used to examine the sequential relationships between FOMO, desire to strive to avoid inferiority, engagement in interpersonal manipulation, and Facebook relational aggression with age and gender entered as covariates.

The serial mediation analysis revealed that FOMO did not predict relational aggression or engagement in interpersonal manipulation. However, there was indirect effect between FOMO and relational aggression. Specifically, FOMO predicted striving to avoid manipulation which in turn predicted interpersonal manipulation and interpersonal aggression. This means that higher levels of FOMO were associated with individuals having a greater desire to avoid inferiority. A greater desire to avoid inferiority predicted higher levels of interpersonal manipulation and higher reported rates of Facebook relational aggression.

3.6 Reflections

Although there was no direct relationship between FOMO and relational aggression, the findings suggest that those Facebook users who experience FOMO engage in social manipulation to avoid the feelings of inferiority associated with FOMO and may also exclude and embarrass their Facebook friends as a way to compensate and mitigate against inferiority so that negative evaluations towards others. However, it is important to acknowledge that, as with all survey designs, approximately 14% of participants did not fully complete all of the measures. The study also did not directly assess participants' engagement with Facebook but rather relied on potential participants self-selecting to take part in the research because they identified as active Facebook users. Although due to the cross-sectional nature of the design of the study meant that it was not possible to explore potential causality in the results, the scales demonstrated acceptable internal consistency within the current sample.

LEARNING OBJECTIVES

You should now know how to:

- Create a new survey following the appropriate considerations for survey design
- Develop questions that are appropriately worded to ensure that you generate reliable data
- Select appropriate response formats for your survey questions
- Use information on a scale's reliability and validity to make informed choices about which (if any) existing scale to select for your survey
- Avoid some of the common pitfalls of survey design and survey methods
- Conduct a survey study that is ethical and will generate meaningful data
- Understand the key considerations when undertaking cross-cultural research using a survey.

FURTHER READING

De Vaus, D. (2014). *Surveys in social research*. Routledge.

This text links theory and research to the design of surveys for research in the social sciences. As well as providing background information on scale design and administration, the book also discusses how to analyse and interpret survey data.

Devellis, R. F. (2017). *Scale development: Theory and applications* (4th ed). Sage.

This text provides a comprehensive account of how to design surveys including chapters on factor analysis and item response theory.

Matsumoto, D., & van de Vijver, F. (Eds.). (2010). *Cross-cultural research methods in psychology* (Culture and Psychology). Cambridge University Press.

This book will help shed light on cross-cultural research, including methodological issues, item translation and adaptation.

Vannett, D. L., & Krosnick, J. A. (2018). *The Palgrave handbook of survey research*. Springer.

Split over five different sections, this text gives a comprehensive account of all things survey-related including conventional survey research, opportunities to expand data collection, information on improving linking surveys with external data sources, and research transparency and data dissemination.

LINKS TO USEFUL RESOURCES

Here is a video explaining the merits and practicalities of longitudinal survey methods
https://sk.sagepub.com/video/niall-bolger-defines-longitudinal-survey

This is a really useful video explaining how to make sure the items (questions) you create for your survey are both valid and reliable
http://sk.sagepub.com/video/creating-valid-and-reliable-survey-items

4

NEUROSCIENTIFIC METHODS

ANDREW CLOUTER AND DARREN RHODES

1. INTRODUCTION TO NEUROSCIENTIFIC METHODS

Neuroscience and the clinical field of neurology have provided many fascinating insights to psychologists. The work of the neurosurgeon Wilder Penfield makes a great example. At McGill University and the Royal Victoria Hospital in Montréal, Canada, he developed an innovative technique to treat **epilepsy**. As part of the procedure, he would electrically stimulate areas of the patient's brain (while keeping careful records of what sensations were elicited by the stimulation at each point in the brain). His patients often reported vivid experiences and observable behaviour, such as the movement of fingers, hearing a particular song on a radio, or smelling toast burning. Of course, no radio was playing, and there was no nearby toaster burning a slice of bread to a crisp – the electrical stimulation of the brain was generating the real, lived, experience of events that were not present in the environment … but from the perspective of the patient, the experiences were indistinguishable from real events. All of our mental processes, and all of our sensations, and all of our behaviour, are a result of activity in our brain. The link between the study of the nervous system (neuroscience) and the study of the human mind and human behaviour (psychology) is clear.

In the field of neuroscience, the scientific methods vary wildly from taking tissue samples from the nervous system, performing surgeries and implantations in rodents and non-human primates, genetic manipulations, and many more … there are hundreds of techniques to choose from. In the field of psychology, the methods borrowed from neuroscience and neurology are often related to non-invasive neuroimaging and stimulation. The use of such techniques allows psychological scientists to broaden the study of the human mind and human behaviour to include the human brain.

1.1 Computational models

As the field of **neuroscience** developed, computational models also became a complimentary technique. In fact, Alan Hodgkin and Andrew Huxley received a Nobel Prize in 1963 for their work in examining and describing how neurons in the nervous system activate. Their mathematical description of neuron activation has formed the basis of computational models that describe brain activity ever since. In the 1950s, one emerging idea was to treat the brain as an information processing unit – sort of like a computer – with processing happening in parallel or sequence (visual information is processed in the occipital cortex of the brain and passed on to other brain areas that specialise in different functions, such as integrating visual information with that from other senses, before being passed on to other processing centres (for memory storage and motor action). This allows models to be generated to predict brain activity.

But computational models need not be restricted to predicting or describing brain activity – computational models are also used to predict and describe observed human behaviour, such as response times, error rates, and memory performance. The behavioural data generated by participants in experiments, alongside predictions from computational models and techniques from neuroscience can be used as complimentary approaches to answer important questions in psychological science. If multiple methods show similar results that converge to provide evidence for a particular hypothesis, then you can be sure that the evidence is strong.

1.2 The nervous system

We should start by describing the scale of the system that we are studying with neuroscientific methods: the human **nervous system**. At the level of the smallest functional unit (but still not nearly at the smallest scale that is possible), we have the neuron. There are approximately 100 billion of them in the human brain. Neurons are connected to each other, and 'communicate' with each other, via synapses. Since each neuron connects with many others, there are approximately 100 trillion connections. Neurons often form circuits, like electrical circuits, connecting to other neurons, that themselves connect with other neurons, with some connections back to the source to create feedback loops. Many of these circuits are organised within the many anatomical structures in the brain – you will hear of many of them, such as the hippocampus, the subthalamic nucleus, the substantia nigra, the cerebellum, etc. Networks between these anatomic regions integrate and pass information around the brain.

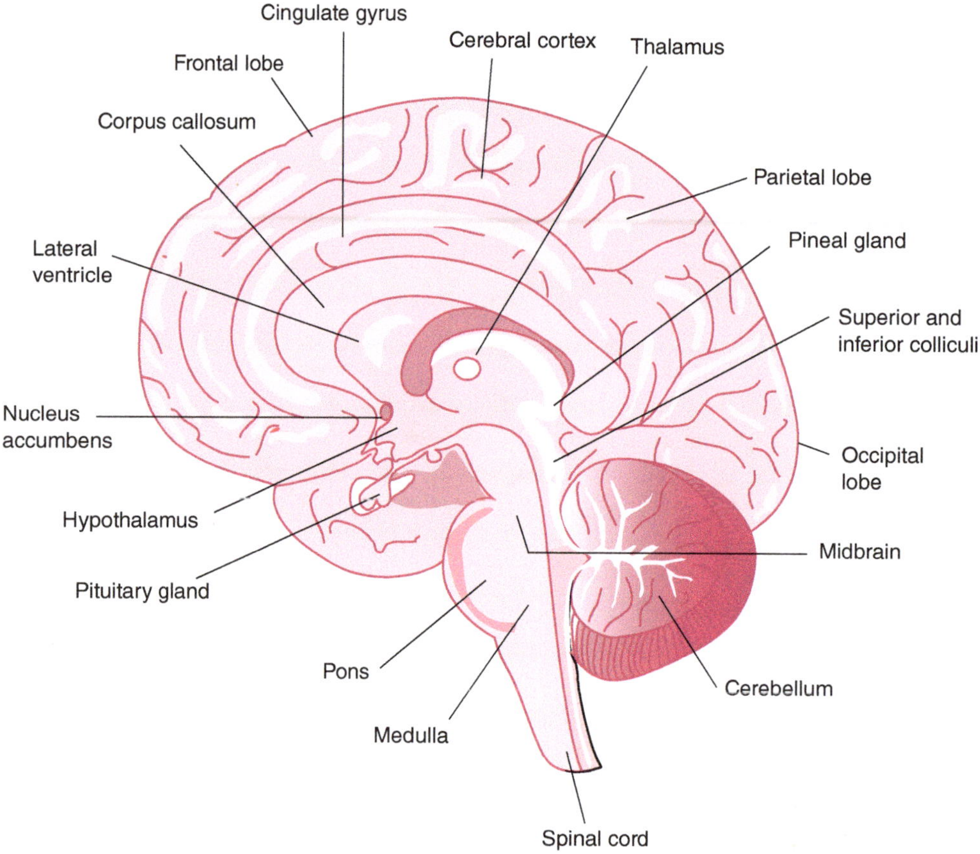

Figure 4.1 The nervous system

These networks do the brain's work such as processing sensory information from vision and audition, allowing for conscious experience, the formation of memories, and feelings of happiness and grief. The final output of all of this is what is observed as human behaviour – the basis of much of psychological science. This gives psychological scientists a 'read-out' of what might have happened in the brain, but the basis for the observed behaviour goes to the level of individual cells, molecules, and even genes. Complementing experimental psychology with methods from neuroscience, in particular those relating to neuroimaging and stimulation, allows us to go farther than simply observing behaviour – it allows us to collect data relating to activity in the brain itself. This gives us a great view of how different parts of the brain work together to subserve the observed behaviour that psychological scientists are so interested in.

1.3 Basics of methods

As you have learned in the Experimental Methods chapter, very well-designed experiments can generate reliable behavioural data from participants, which can be used to test hypotheses and make causal inferences. Within neuroscientific approaches to psychological science, the same approach of experimental manipulation is widely used. Experiments are designed and carefully controlled to manipulate the **independent variable** and observe the effects on the **dependent variable** (the measured behaviour). In a neuroscience study, we can use the same approach, for example, we can manipulate an independent variable (say, whether an image presented to a participant is of a location or an object), and the dependent (measured) variable can be related to brain activity (showing that objects and locations are processed in different anatomical regions of the brain). Or alternately, brain activity need not be the dependent variable, but it can be the variable that we manipulate.

Using **non-invasive stimulation techniques**, such as transcranial electrical or magnetic stimulation, we can manipulate activity in certain regions of the brain to see how it affects behaviour. If we do both (showing that brain region X is active when processing objects, and brain region Y is active when processing locations, and showing that interfering with the activity of the brain at regions X and Y using magnetic stimulation interferes with successful processing of objects and locations, as evidenced through behavioural measurements), we create very strong evidence that suggests that regions X and Y are important for object and location processing, respectively. Unlike the work of Wilder Penfield long ago, stimulation of the brain is these days usually done in a non-invasive way, transcranially – across the skull – rather than directly stimulating the brain itself (although direct stimulation of the brain is still widely done with patients and animals).

2. NEURO IMAGING AND STIMULATION TECHNIQUES

Neuroimaging and stimulation techniques are often described in terms of several criteria: the invasiveness of the technique, and the resolution; which can be either the temporal resolution (how good it is in detecting differences over time) and the spatial resolution (how good it is in detecting differences in spatial location). When used in psychological science, they are used functionally – that is, they are used to measure, promote, or disrupt ongoing brain activity and are most likely used differently between experimental conditions. Below are some of the common neuroimaging and stimulation techniques.

2.1 Invasive techniques

Neurosurgeons insert electrodes into the brains of patients for a variety of conditions – clearly an invasive technique. For example, advanced Parkinson's disease can be treated using the 'deep brain stimulation' technique, where electrodes are surgically implanted into the **subthalamic nuclei** of the patient. In addition to being able to electrically stimulate the brain, scientists can also record electrical activity from that part of the brain. Such electrical recordings have very high spatial resolution – pairs of contacts at the tip of the electrode ensure that electrical activity from elsewhere in the brain is 'cancelled out', leaving a recording of electrical activity specific to the very small area around the contacts. The temporal resolution is also extremely high – activity can be measured at the sub-millisecond scale.

2.2 Non-invasive techniques

Magnetoencephalography (MEG) and electroencephalography (EEG) are **non-invasive techniques** that measure the electrical activity of the brain in different ways. MEG uses specialised sensors to detect the tiny magnetic fields that are generated by the electrical activity in the brain. With EEG, electrodes are in contact with the scalp, and electrical activity generated is captured by these electrodes. There are advantages and disadvantages to these two complementary techniques, and the data generated can be analysed in a variety of ways. It can be analysed in a way that answers the questions of when and where in the brain something occurs. For this purpose, the temporal resolution of these techniques is excellent, being on the sub-millisecond scale. If the data is analysed in a way to answer questions relating to how, or which regions of the brain are mutually involved, the temporal resolution can be decreased somewhat, but still in the millisecond range. The spatial resolution of these techniques is not as good being largely confined to brain 'regions' at best – for example, 'the occipital visual area', and largely restricted to the surface of the brain (the cortex).

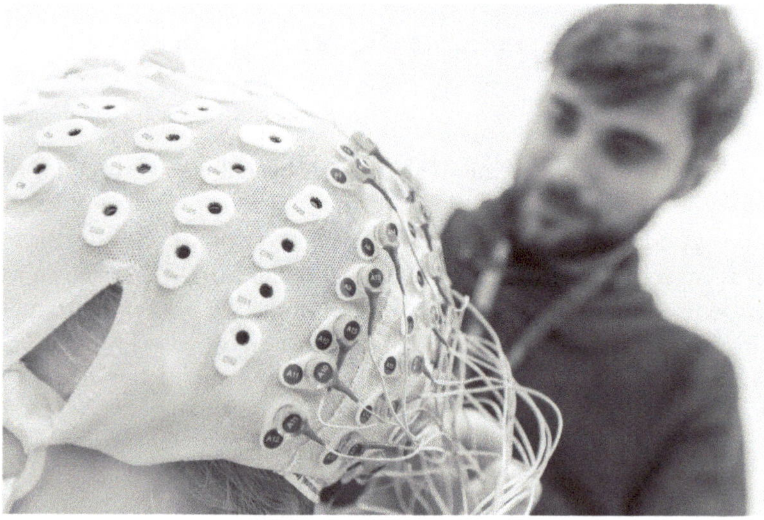

Figure 4.2 An EEG cap with electrodes attached

Source: Image from Psychology@NTU

2.3 fMRI and PET

Functional magnetic resonance imaging (fMRI) makes use of clinical MRI machines that can be used to scan any area of the body. Depending on how the machine is programmed, different tissues and substances in the body can be highlighted. In psychological science, MRI is often used to first scan the brain of the participant to get an image, and then to detect where in the brain oxygenated blood becomes deoxygenated. That is, if we know where the oxygen stored in the blood is being used in a particular experimental condition compared to another (that is, we look at the difference between at least two experimental conditions), we can be sure that that area in the brain is involved in whatever the mental process is that is being manipulated between the conditions. fMRI has high spatial resolution and is not restricted to only the surface areas of the brain (as it would be in EEG), but the temporal resolution is poor being measured only in seconds, so you can't answer questions about 'when' some brain activity happens, but fMRI can do a great job of determining 'where'.

Interesting fact

Did you know that there is currently a worldwide helium shortage? Sad news for those party balloons but what has that got to do with neuroscience I hear you ask. Well, liquid helium is necessary for MRI machines to work. In its liquid form helium is very cold and so is used to cool the wires that form the magnetic field that the MRI relies on for its function. This magnetic field is really powerful and relies on the wires being able to superconduct electricity. This produces a lot of heat so needs the helium coolant to keep the temperature down. So, next time you go to buy your party balloons remember you may be impeding scientific research in the future.

Proton emission tomography (PET) is similar to MRI in terms of the spatial and temporal resolution, but it is an invasive technique. A radioactive tracer with a short half-life is injected into the participant's bloodstream. One of the advantages of PET over fMRI is that PET is not limited to oxygenated and deoxygenated blood – the tracer can be used to find sites of glucose metabolism, dopamine storage, or the binding of different neurotransmitters. That is, the scientist can also get an answer to a question of 'how' or what neurotransmitters are involved in particular brain areas and functions.

Skoolkid errors

Research studies using brain imaging techniques such as fMRI often report their finding with a nice colourful example image of the brain 'lighting up' (see Figure 4.3). This kind of pictorial image adds a sense of trustworthiness to the findings, it makes them feel solid and factual. This together with the idea that imaging research is very biological and 'scientific' when compared to the rest of psychological research can lead to a feeling of certainty about the findings. We are more easily convinced by such images and need to be aware of this bias so we can remain critical of the findings. There are issues to consider in interpreting findings that should not be clouded by the persuasiveness of a nice brain image. If you check out the Ig Nobels example in this chapter (p. 110) you will see what we mean. We should say that techniques for statistical analysis have improved more recently to strengthen the interpretation of fMRI findings so we are not suggesting you discount them. Just be careful not to be swayed by shiny pictures.

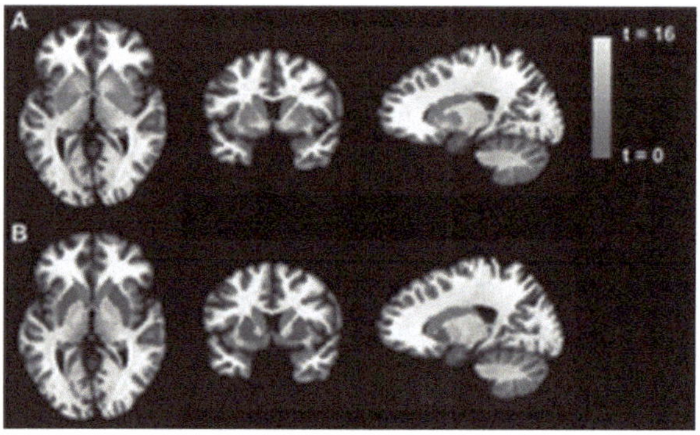

Figure 4.3 Brain image from an fMRI study on brain changes in chronic fatigue syndrome

From Miller et al. (2014)

2.4 Brain zapping

Transcranial electrical current stimulation (tECS) is a method of applying an electrical current to the brain, to influence the activity in particular regions of the brain. Like EEG and MEG, the current is largely limited to the surface areas of the brain – you will not be able to electrically stimulate deeper structures. tECS uses electrodes (often soaked in saline) that are in contact with the scalp. One method of use – transcranial direct current stimulation (tDCS) – passes an electrical current from one electrode, through the surface of the brain, to another. One area of the brain will be under the anodal electrode (where the current is 'injected' so to speak), the other area under the cathodal electrode (where the current is 'returned'). Typically, the area under the anodal electrode is the area of the brain that gets 'excited' (more likely to activate), while the area under the cathode becomes 'depressed' (less likely to activate).

A different technique using the same equipment is called transcranial alternating current stimulation (tACS), where the anodal and cathodal electrodes are constantly swapped at an experimenter-controlled frequency. This technique can be used to manipulate the communication between different areas of the brain. For example, if we know from an EEG experiment that we conducted that the left dorsolateral prefrontal cortex and the left temporoparietal cortex are involved in, say, maintaining items in working memory, and that they communicate with each other at a particular frequency, we can uses tACS to enhance or disrupt that frequency. These electrical stimulation techniques are non-invasive, and have similar temporal and spatial resolutions as EEG and MEG.

Finally, transcranial magnetic stimulation (TMS) uses an electrical discharge to create a magnetic field above the surface of a participant's head, which in turn creates a much smaller electrical event in the brain. Unlike the electrical stimulation techniques described above, which can influence brain activity but not actually elicit activity (in most cases), TMS can be strong enough to elicit activity of the brain. For example, you can hold the TMS coil above the motor cortex of your participant, discharge the device, and cause your participant's left hand fingers to twitch. The temporal resolution is similar to the electrical stimulation techniques, with slightly better spatial resolution. For example, you can cause the leftshand fingers to twitch, while not making the whole arm jump!

Whoa there!

There is a lot to consider when you decide to undertake research that uses neuroscience approaches. It's not enough to think, 'This behavioural experiment would be much cooler if I could use brain stimulation!' Some of the neuroscience techniques have risks. Of course, the safety of these methods have been carefully considered over the years, and guidelines are in place to ensure that the safety considerations are taken into account by trained researchers (never do neuroscience research without proper training!). But, despite every attempt at following safety guidelines and procedures, magnetic and electrical stimulation carries with it the risk of inducing seizure activity in a very small proportion of people, and your participants with implants for medical reasons should be excluded from your research entirely in order to ensure that the stimulation doesn't affect their medical device. And you also need to carefully consider which neuroimaging and stimulation approaches can work together. For example, you won't be able to use transcranial magnetic stimulation and magnetic resonance imaging at the same time! But you could, if you planned it very carefully, use electrical stimulation and magnetic resonance imaging. Proper training is always necessary before you begin scientific experiments that involve imaging or stimulation!

3. COMPUTATIONAL NEUROSCIENCE MODELS

One way that we can understand how the brain works is by applying **computational techniques** to neuroscience data (i.e., making statistical predictions about brain activity). Computational neuroscience is one of the fastest-growing sectors of neuroscience, with applications in areas such as machine learning, artificial intelligence, cognitive science, and supercomputing. The following section gives an overview of some very basic principles of computing and neural networks. You may also be interested in more detailed information about some specific techniques.

Computation means 'calculation', and it is done by applying mathematical rules to take data (e.g., EEG recordings) and turn them into useful information (e.g., predictions about brain activity). The brain is an immensely complex system, and the computations that it performs are also … complex. As a result, it is generally very difficult to simply apply any existing computational technique to the brain, because what works well for other systems may not always work so well in the brain. Instead, computational neuroscientists try to develop their own techniques that are specific to the brain. Several such techniques exist.

3.1 Predictive neural networks

The easiest computational technique to explain is the **predictive neural network** (PN). The basic idea of PNs is to obtain a set of data (e.g., EEG recordings) and ask: what would be the pattern of brain activity that this data would create if it were part of a much larger system? By asking 'What if?' we obtain a predictive model, which generates predictions about activity in the brain. PNs take data from multiple sources, such as EEG recordings and visual information, and then take these two inputs and calculate an output (e.g., predicting what type of image you would see when presented with photos of faces). The output layer of PNs can be used to generate predictions, which are then compared to the real data that the model is based upon in order to evaluate how accurate it was. You can then train additional layers of neurons or synapses in your neural network, based on this evaluation. The name comes from the fact that these networks are intended to simulate biologically-based neural networks, although they are much simpler in design. PNs are an example of pattern recognition systems, which are designed to recognise particular patterns in time-based data (in this case EEG recordings).

Predictive neural networks were an important early computational technique for neuroscience because they were one of the first techniques people tried on brain data. They were used at a time when more complicated techniques such as Bayesian models and hidden Markov models did not exist, and the few neural networks available at the time tended to be overly complex. They remain an important technique, although they tend to be less commonly used than the other techniques described here. Predictive neural networks can also be trained with reinforcement learning, where, instead of providing independent data for training, we train the network by rewarding it for producing accurate results. Using this approach, we can train a PN to play Space Invaders or Pacman, but it requires very careful training to avoid overfitting (i.e., learning how to play specific games rather than learning general rules about how the brain works). Don't use PNs to simulate everything! PNs are a very, very simple form of artificial neural network and can be more of a hindrance than a help. They lack the flexibility of more complex models and, although they do provide robust predictions of data, they often do not tell you why their predictions were made.

Predictive neural networks are only appropriate when trying to recognise patterns in time-based data such as EEG recordings. When predicting brain activity from other types of input such as visual information or tactile input, more complex models such as hidden Markov models, may be better suited to the task at hand.

3.2 Brain-state dependent neural networks

These neural networks are based on the concept that brain activity depends on certain conditions – for example, when you are looking at photos of faces, then certain visual areas in the brain will be more active than others. What makes these networks unique is that they can change their connections (i.e., synapses) in response to changing conditions. This makes them much more flexible models than PNs, but also makes it much harder to figure out how they work (because the network has to 'figure out' which connections to make). These models can be used very effectively when you have multiple types of data (e.g. EEG recordings and visual information), because instead of trying to predict the whole brain activity, you can individually predict each type of data (e.g., for photos, predict the activity in the V1 area; for faces, predict the activity in V4). These differences are then fed back into the network to influence how it changes connections.

Brain-state dependent networks are particularly useful for studying brain activity. When a subject performs a task, many different areas of their brain light up with different intensities. When we ask questions about what is going on in these areas, sometimes a few ones will be active at a time and obscure other parts of the network. We don't know what to expect when we look at certain brain regions, but we do know how to answer questions about other ones (e.g., 'When the subject is presented with photos of faces, then what area of the brain becomes active?'). As a result, these networks allow us to predict things like patterns of activity in the brain, but they may not be very good for simulating how it works (because they can't simulate certain brain activity). Brain-state dependent neural networks are an important tool for studying brain activity because they can offer insight into how various parts of the brain interact. Being able to predict which areas will be active in response to particular stimuli can help us draw connections between different areas of the brain.

3.3 Recurrent neural networks

A further type of neural network is **recurrent neural nets**. These are networks that allow information to flow through the net multiple times. This property, known as recurrent or time series input, can be used to model data that has temporal patterns. For example, one type of data that could be modelled with an RNN is time-series data. Time series data can include physiological measurements such as heart-rate, blood-pressure , and brain activity recorded by an EEG or fMRI scanner.

Recurrent neural networks are very versatile models because they generalise easily to new situations, making them very useful for modelling complex systems. New types of connections can be included in the network to represent new aspects of the system (e.g., two subjects may also have high blood pressure). They are also useful in making predictions about short timescales – for example, heart rate data may be analyzed to predict a patient's blood-pressure 90 seconds later (after their blood pressure has had time to respond to the change in heart-rate). Recurrent neural networks can also be used to make predictions about both behavioural data, and neuroimaging data in psychology. They can be very powerful in making predictions about how we behave or what we think under many different circumstances, and it is easy to imagine that these types of networks would also be very useful in understanding human brain activity. However, like any type of network, recurrent neural networks require a lot of computational power and may not be the best choice if the data is too large or there are too many variables.

A recurrent neural network can also be trained with reinforcement learning, allowing the parameters of the model to learn from experience. As with predictive models, this allows us to train a recurrent neural network to play a game such as Space Invaders or Pacman – or to predict what behavioural or EEG data might look like if certain parameters or features were adjusted. Of course, the best way to show the combined power of behavioural, computational modelling, and neuroimaging techniques is by following a real set of experiments!

Cultural context

Brain science has a long and terrible history of supporting racist ideas. Stephen Jay Gould in his book *The Mismeasure of Man*, describes some of this 'science'. For example, Paul Broca (he of Broca's area) believed that brain size was an indicator of intelligence and set out to show that the brains of eminent men were bigger than those of others, that the brains of men were bigger than those of women and that the brains of white people were bigger than those of black and brown people. This ambition was symptomatic of many of the neuroscientists of the time who are still lauded today, and we all need to be mindful of this racist context.

4. EXAMPLE RESEARCH STUDY: EPISODIC MEMORY

Horner, A. J., & Burgess, N. (2014). Pattern completion in multielement event engrams. *Current Biology, 24*(9), 988–92.

Horner, A. J., Bisby, J. A., Bush, D., Lin, W. J., & Burgess, N. (2015). Evidence for holistic episodic recollection via hippocampal pattern completion. *Nature Communications, 6*(1), 1–11.

4.1 Introduction to the piece of research

In human episodic memory (our memory for events in our lives), it is thought that the retrieval from memory of one element of a particular lived experience will trigger the memory of other elements of the same experience. That is, if I recall the movie that I watched at the cinema last year on my birthday, that will trigger the recollection of who I was with, where we were sitting in the cinema, and what snacks we were eating. Or I might recall where we were sitting, and that would trigger the recall of the people that I was with, the snacks we were eating, and when we went to the cinema. Either way, the recollection of one element of the experience would trigger the recollection of the entire experience, including elements that were incidental to the event. The retrieval of all elements of an experience from just one partial cue is called 'pattern completion' in the episodic memory literature – if one element is successfully recalled, the rest of the experience can also be recalled – the memory 'pattern' is 'completed'. The recollection of entire events or experiences is one of the reasons that episodic memory is so different from other types of human learning and memory.

From a neuroscientific point of view, the pattern completion theory suggests that when a memory is being formed (in the literature this is known as encoding), different elements of an experience that are processed in different brain areas are bound together into a cohesive memory in the human **hippocampus** (which is involved in episodic memory encoding and retrieval, amongst its other duties). However, even more interestingly, if one element of an event is cued to a participant (for example, who you were with when you went to the cinema, triggering the recollection of the event), the hippocampus will trigger the pattern completion process, which should manifest in the brain as activity similar to when the memory was formed. That is, when a memory is recalled there should be activity in areas of the brain related to people, locations, etc., just as there was when the memory was formed … even though that event isn't currently being experienced, only recalled.

4.2 Aims of the study

Aiden Horner and his colleagues, while working at University College London, wanted to show direct evidence of such pattern completion (Horner & Burgess, 2014; Horner, Bisby, Bush, Lin, & Burgess, 2015). They designed their experiments in such a way that they could use behavioural, modelling, and neuroimaging techniques to provide strong converging evidence of pattern completion.

The first main prediction of the pattern completion theory that the researchers tested was that the retrieval of different memory elements from the same remembered event would be statistically related – that is, if the participant was presented with a cue of one element of a memory, they could recall the experience, and if they were presented with a different memory element cue from that same experience, they could also recall the experience. That is, all of the elements of the recalled event are related.

This prediction can be tested in the memory recall performance behavioural data collected from the participants, and from computational models of memory performance that either predict pattern completion is how memory works, or that pattern completion is not how memory performance works. That is, the computational models were created so that in one model the researchers built in a statistical relationship for the retrieval of memories of the same event given different cues, and in another model, there was no such statistical relationship built into the model. So, if pattern completion is how recall from memory works, then the performance of participants should resemble that of the model with the built-in statistical dependencies, but if pattern completion is not how recall from episodic memory works, then the performance of the participants should resemble the model that does not have the built-in statistical dependencies.

The second main prediction was that all elements of the event would be recalled given a memory cue and successful recall performance, even those elements that were incidental to the event being remembered, and that the neurons and areas of the brain that were active in encoding the memory in the first place would be reactivated during recall. To test this prediction, the researchers used functional magnetic resonance imagine (fMRI).

Ethel ethics

Neuroimaging experiments come with a number of unique ethical challenges. Informed consent is particularly important – it is important that your participants are competent enough to fully understand the risks involved in the experiment. Stimulation techniques can be quite frightening, so it is important to be very clear with your participant about the physical sensations that they will experience. Other techniques, such as fMRI have a number of additional things to consider: the MRI scanner can induce a feeling of claustrophobia in some participants, so it is important to have, and to train the participant to use, an emergency alerting system so that the experiment can be aborted and the participant removed from the scanner. Another, more troubling, ethical concern is that scans of a participant's brain might reveal a medical issue that the participant is not aware of, and that you, as a researcher, are not qualified to deal with. There is a lot to consider when using neuroscientific approaches in your research!

4.3 Design

The design of the experiment is reasonably straightforward but very clever, and suitable for participants to complete while in an MRI scanner. A single group of participants learned associations between locations, people, objects, and animals. They were later tested on their recall of the full association after being presented with a cue of one of the elements.

In more detail, there were two memory conditions. In one condition, participants were separately presented with two of the elements (say, a location and a person) on a given trial. They were instructed to try to remember the two elements together by imagining the two elements interacting together in a vivid way. On another trial, one of the elements was presented with a third element (say the person and an object).

Finally, on a different trial, the remaining association was presented (the location and the object). This created a 'closed loop' where each of the three elements were presented with each other. In the other condition, the elements were presented in a way to create an 'open loop': one element was presented with another (say, a location and a person), then on another trial the person was presented alongside an object, and on another trial the object with an animal. There were still three presentations, but the memory loop was not closed – each element was not presented with each other element.

Since the experiment was done in an MRI scanner, proper experimental design for the scanner had to be kept in mind. In the encoding phase (the learning phase), each pair of elements to be remembered was presented for six seconds – this ensured that the relatively slow haemodynamic response (see the discussion about the poor temporal resolution of fMRI earlier) has been captured by the scanner and the activity has returned to baseline between trials. The same six seconds was allowed for each retrieval trial.

On the retrieval trials, the participants were shown one element from a memorised association, and a set of six elements to choose from. For example, say the cued element was the location, then there were the names of six people presented. Each of those six people was associated with a location in the encoding trials, but only one of them was associated with *this* location. That is an important part of the experimental design – think about why, or refer back to the chapter on the Experimental method. Each element from each association was presented to the participants an equal number of times.

The experimenters hypothesised that memory performance for the closed-loop associations would resemble the model with the built-in statistical dependency. For the open-loop associations, the experiments hypothesised that the memory performance would resemble that of the predictions from the model without statistical dependency built in. The fMRI results should show reactivation of the same brain areas used during encoding when the associations were being recalled, and that those activations would be stronger for the closed-loop condition.

Note that there has to be a contrast – a difference – in the design of neuroimaging research. In this, and any experiment, there will be all sorts of brain activity, for example, relating to hearing the sound of the scanner, seeing things on a computer screen, and pressing buttons on a response box. All of this activity is expected to be the same between the two conditions. So (and this is absolutely critical) a properly planned neuroimaging experiment keeps all things equal between conditions in an experiment *except* the mental process being investigated. That way, when you subtract the imaging data of one condition from the other, the results can only be explained by differences in the mental process that is being investigated. In this case, the pattern of brain activity during memory recall.

4.4 The findings

The researchers compared the memory performance of the participants to the performance predicted by the computational models. The results were in line with their hypothesis. The data generated by the participants and the predictions of the model were not different (in the first of the two papers) when the closed loop performance was compared to the model with statistical dependency, but was different from the predictions of the model without statistical dependency. To be clear, the statistically significant result was that the participant data was different from the model without dependency. It was also not different from the model with the statistical dependency. This suggests that there is a statistical dependency, as the pattern completion theory suggests. Similarly, the open-loop association participant data was no different from the model without statistical dependency, but statistically significantly different from the model with statistical dependency. These were the results that the researchers had hoped to see.

For the fMRI results, the researchers examined the areas that were active during encoding, identifying locations specific to encoding locations, people, and objects/animals (there was a reason why the researchers chose these different elements for memory associations – they are encoded in different areas of the brain!). Then, during recall, they examined the difference in the activity in those three areas and the hippocampus between the closed-loop and open-loop conditions. Recall how the retrieval phase of the experiment worked: on a single retrieval trial, one element was presented (say, a person), and a list of six elements of the same type were presented (say, objects).

The participant had to identify which object had been presented with that particular person during the encoding phase. But surely we would see activity in brain areas that process people and objects, because we are presenting the participant with a person and a list of objects! Of course, the researchers were examining the brain activity at the processing site of the third element: the location. If the pattern completion theory was true, we should see activity at the brain area processing location information, even though there is no location information presented to the participant in this trial. And similarly, if a trial presented a location, and the participant had to choose the person that was associated with that location, the researchers would be examining the area of the brain that processes objects. And the results showed exactly what the researchers were hoping to see: significantly different brain activity in the area of the brain that was incidental to the retrieval trial for the closed-loop trials compared to the open-loop trials.

Ig Nobel Prize

Something fishy here

In 2010, Craig Bennett and his colleagues published a paper called 'Neural Correlates of Interspecies Perspective Taking in the Post-Mortem Atlantic Salmon: An Argument For Proper Multiple Comparisons Correction' in the *Journal of Serendipitous and Unexpected Results*, for which they won the 2012 Ig Nobel Prize in Neuroscience. The researchers had set up an experiment that presented people in social situations with a specific emotional valence. The plan was to present those situations to human participants and ask them to identify the emotion the person in the situation was experiencing. However, before doing the experiment with human participants, they needed to test the experimental set-up and scanning equipment. In order to do so, they enlisted the help of a large Atlantic salmon.

The salmon was given the task instructions, put in the fMRI scanner, and completed the experiment – watching the photos and determining the emotions presented. Afterwards, the experimenters analysed the data and noticed that an area of the salmon's brain showed significantly different activity between when the photos were shown versus when the salmon was at rest (with $p < 0.001$).

This is surely a very surprising result! It should probably be pointed out that the salmon was dead. How is this possible? You may have heard about something called corrections for multiple comparisons. A researcher does this when performing multiple statistical comparisons. This is because there is always a chance for a false positive with many standard statistical tests, and the chance of there being at least one false positive increases when multiple statistical tests are performed. In the case of fMRI research, the scanner is imaging the brain as a three-dimensional object with 130,000 (on even older scanners) three-dimensional voxels (think pixels, like on a computer or television screen, but in three dimensions). Statistical tests are performed on *each* of these, leading to a very high chance of a statistical difference just by chance alone. This makes this study a great case for why corrections for multiple comparisons is important in science, and in particular, in neuroimaging research.

4.5 Reflections

These very well designed and executed experiments show the power of using neuroscience methods in addition to experimental behavioural data. Without the computational models to compare the behavioural data there could be no way to answer the question of whether pattern completion was how human episodic memory retrieval worked. And without the neuroimaging, the evidence would have been much less sound. Together, these approaches provide very strong evidence in favour of a popular theory of human memory retrieval. Also, and very importantly, the researchers carried out this work in two steps: the first was an experiment that compared the behavioural data to the models. The second was the same again but done in the MRI scanner. That is, rather than do the experiment only once, using the MRI scanner the first time, the researchers replicated their own work and extended it by doing the experiment a second time. You may have heard about the importance of replicating work in science, and so had the scientists involved in this series of studies!

LEARNING OBJECTIVES

Now that you have read this chapter you should ...

1. Be able to describe the varying techniques in cognitive neuroscience.
2. Be able to consider how to investigate human perception and cognition.
3. Be able to describe how behavioural experiments, brain imaging data, and computational models can be used to better answer research questions.

FURTHER READING

Carlson, N. R. (2018). *Foundations of behavioral neuroscience*. Pearson Education.

This book is a great introduction to the investigation of the human brain with regards its function. This book is more about the biological basis for perception, cognition and action – from the level of the neuron, to the level of the cortex.

Seth, A. (2021). *Being you: A new science of consciousness*. Penguin.

This book is looking at the brain from another angle, with regards to how all of those neurons and connections come together to create the concept (or the hallucination) of being you.

Kurzweil, R. (2013). *How to create a mind: The secret of human thought revealed*. Penguin.

Interested in computational neuroscience? This book looks at the theoretical basis of artificial intelligence.

LINKS TO USEFUL RESOURCES

Allen Brain Atlas – https://portal.brain-map.org

BrainFacts – www.brainfacts.org

Neuroscience Crash Course –www.youtube.com/playlist?list=PLOA0aRJ90NxuIgOC9YGRUT4Y-CsP12bsS

Exploding Brain Myths – http://explodingbrainmyths.weebly.com

Brain Terms Glossary – www.dana.org/explore-neuroscience/brain-basics/key-brain-terms-glossary/

TED Talks on understanding the brain – www.ted.com/topics/neuroscience

2-minute neuroscience –www.youtube.com/playlist?list=PLNZqyJnsvdMqFNFyHvMFrF-nlXLosnwwB_

a video explaining the role of a neuropsychologist and how they conduct research using neuroscience methods

https://sk.sagepub.com/video/neuropsychology

5

RANDOMISED CONTROLLED TRIALS

JANET VOUSDEN AND ANNA CUNNINGHAM

1. INTRODUCTION TO RANDOMISED CONTROLLED TRIALS (RCTs)

An RCT is a way of conducting a fair comparison between two or more interventions. RCTs have been used as a methodology for trying new treatments since the middle of the 20th century and have become almost the universal methodology for medical and health research. Since the first published study in 1948, trying a new treatment for tuberculosis ('Streptomycin in the Treatment of Pulmonary Tuberculosis,' 1948), the number of RCTs used in medicine has rapidly increased. Their benefits have been harnessed commercially as well, with household names using the RCT methodology to test how to maximise fund-raising, or which website designs are best to convert page visits to sales (refs). Over the last few decades, in partnership with the UK government, the Behavioural Insights Team have been busy testing the impacts of national policy change using RCTs. For example, a notable trial of theirs demonstrated that sending people who had failed to pay their court fines personalised text messages increased the amount paid by over 30% (Haynes et al., 2013). Similarly, there has been an increase in the use of RCTs to test the effectiveness of educational programmes as a way of increasing evidence based practice in schools. In the UK, the Education Endowment Foundation (EEF; https://educationendowmentfoundation.org.uk/) acts as a 'What Works Centre for Education' by conducting large scale education focussed RCTs in Primary and Secondary schools.

Interesting fact

The first RCT

The first published Randomised Controlled Trial in medicine appeared in a 1948 paper on the treatment of tuberculosis. One of the authors of that paper was Austin Bradford Hill, who is credited as having conceived the modern RCT and who also demonstrated the link between smoking and lung cancer.

The use of RCTs as a methodology is on the rise because it is the best way to compare interventions. This is important because we need to know what does not work as well as what does work. If a treatment is ineffective, it may not only save money not to implement it, but also prevent people suffering harm. No one wants their child to receive an intervention that delivers worse outcomes than standard teaching practice, but in other areas such as medicine, failing to understand the impact of treatments can be a matter of life and death. For example, it was once thought that treating people for head injuries with steroid injections was an effective treatment. However, an RCT showed the opposite – more head injury patients died if they had received the steroid treatment (Edwards et al., 2005). Thus, RCTs are rapidly becoming the methodology of choice when comparing two or more interventions, or a new intervention against standard practice.

1.1 The gold standard

RCTs are often thought of as the 'gold standard' for evaluating the effectiveness of interventions because they remove many of the biases (unfairness) in making such comparisons. RCTs achieve this by:

1. Dividing a population into two or more groups by random allocation
2. Giving different interventions/business as usual to each group
3. Measuring a pre-specified outcome for each group after the intervention

This is illustrated in Figure 5.1., below.

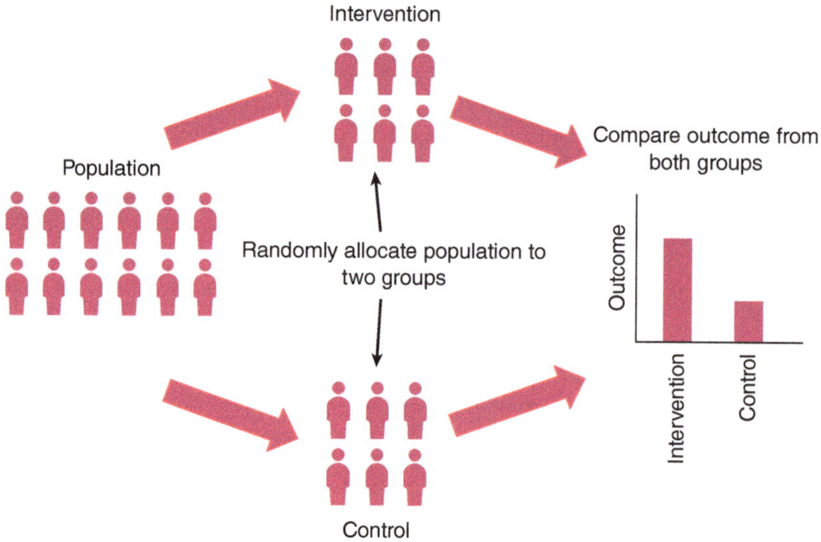

Figure 5.1 The basic structure of a randomised controlled trial comparing an intervention against a non-intervention control group

For example, suppose a researcher wanted to evaluate a new programme of teaching reading to beginning readers. The researcher might simply advertise the programme and ask schools if they would like to try the new programme. The schools that volunteer implement the new reading programme at the start of the academic year, measure the reading ability of the children at the end of the year, and then compare the results to last year's results. If this year's results are higher than last years in participating schools, then the new method of teaching reading is a success. However, perhaps reading ability only increased in some schools that tried the programme, so a survey was administered that showed overall the children and teachers really enjoyed the programme and read more books with the class than usual. Was the new reading programme a success or not?

1.2 Selection bias

Perhaps this year's intake of children were naturally better readers than last year. What we really need to know is how well this year's intake of children would have done if they had not received the new method of teaching reading. Without a comparison group of children that did not use the new programme, it is hard to tell. This is just one problem that erodes our confidence in the success of the new programme, but there are other problems too.

Suppose the schools that volunteered to try the new reading programme had consistently poor reading results at their school, or perhaps they had a higher than average number of disadvantaged children at their school. Thus, the schools that volunteered to try the new programme might be systematically different in some way to those schools that chose not to participate, and this is a form of **selection bias**. For example, perhaps the schools are located in areas of deprivation and stand to gain much more from intervention. If so the relative higher performance of these children at the end of the programme might also be due to these external factors. This would exaggerate any effects of the reading programme, which may not replicate in a different school.

Which measure should we take most notice of? The measure of reading ability or the survey results showing more reading and better enjoyment of reading? All of these issues make it difficult to interpret the results of the trial, as we cannot be sure what the effects are, or whether they are down to the reading programme itself, or some external factors beyond the researcher's control. While there are some sophisticated statistical techniques that can be used to 'fix' some of these problems in a mathematical sense, they do not fix the underlying problem.

1.3 The value of an RCT

The benefit of an RCT is that these problems can be overcome. At the beginning of the trial the researcher can declare what the outcome measure will be, and how it will be measured. Success will then be judged by whether this measure has changed in a specified way after the programme has finished. For the reading programme, the outcome might be a standardised test of reading. Once the researcher has a sample of schools that are happy to try the programme, they can be randomly allocated to two groups – schools that try the programme, and schools that do not. Schools that do not try the programme are called a **control group**, and they carry on 'business as usual', i.e., they carry on teaching reading as they normally would. The key here is that the schools are allocated to each of the groups randomly, and ideally by a third party who has not recruited the schools and is not involved with the reading programme. This way, there can be no bias or unfairness in who gets to try the programme and who doesn't. At the end of the programme, if the scores on the standardised test of reading are higher in the participating schools than in the control schools, the researcher can have some confidence that the reading programme is effective.

2. EXAMPLE STUDY: YEAR 1 READING PROGRAMME

2.1 Introduction

The trial we will describe in this chapter is a reading programme for Year 1 children in UK Primary schools. In the UK, although a main focus of primary education is literacy, by the end of the first three years of schooling, only 75% and 69% of children achieve at or above the expected standard in reading and writing respectively (Department for Education, 2019). While schools focus on decoding level skills (Rose, 2006), there is less of an emphasis on text comprehension, even though these skills form part of national assessments early in primary education (Department for Education, 2018), and comprehension is a basic requirement for accessing secondary education.

The trial presents the results of using a balanced reading programme that teaches primary aged children (aged 5–6 years) reading comprehension skills as well as decoding level skills. The main aim was to determine whether children completing the reading programme would have better reading ability, and be more likely to achieve at or above the expected standard in national teacher assessments in reading and writing. The trial also compared two different delivery methods for the programme: an ICT and a non-ICT version to see if both were equally effective.

The trial was funded by the EEF, who fund large scale RCTs of education programmes. The EEFs use a robust model for conducting RCTs which involves separating the delivery team (these are the people who recruit schools and train them to deliver the programme), from the evaluation team (these are the people who govern the trial to make sure it is run according to robust principles, including the randomisation process and analysis and reporting of the outcomes). Although the two teams worked collaboratively they each reported directly to the funder, thus maintaining independence of each other.

2.2 The study and the teams

Johnson, H., McNally, S., Rolfe, H., Ruiz-Valenzuela, J., Savage, R., Vousden, J., & Wood, C. (2019). Teaching assistants, computers and classroom management. *Labour Economics*, *58*(February), 21–36. https://doi.org/10.1016/j.labeco.2019.02.006[1] [2]

Delivery team

Dr Janet Vousden is a Senior Lecturer in Developmental Psychology at Nottingham Trent University. She led the delivery team, and continues to run RCTs in literacy education.

Dr Helen Johnson was a member of the Literacy Research Group at the Centre for Research in Psychology, Behaviour and Achievement at Coventry University and is a qualified Educational Psychologist.

Professor Clare Wood is Professor of Psychology in Education at Nottingham Trent University.

Professor Robert Savage is a qualified Educational Psychologist and Head of the Department of Psychology and Human Development at University College London.

[1]Note: in *Labour Economics*, authors are listed in alphabetical order.

[2]See also (McNally et al., 2016) for the full version of the report.

Evaluation team

Professor Sandra McNally is a Professor of Economics at the University of Surrey.

Dr Jenifer Ruiz-Valenzuela is a research economist at the Centre for Economic Performance, London School of Economics.

Dr Heather Rolfe leads the research team at Demos, a leading cross-party think tank which focuses on improving democratic processes and public engagement.

2.3 General aims and background

Typically, researchers choose to conduct an RCT when they want to compare some intervention against another. The goal is to measure change in a particular outcome and attribute the change to the intervention being tested. In the field of psychology and education, this might be to test if a new intervention improves, e.g., reading ability. The desired comparison might be, for example, to test a new intervention against standard practice, but might also be driven by a desire to pit two interventions against each other to see if one is better. The interventions are usually driven by theory, and often aim to fill a particular need, for example, to raise standards in literacy.

Whoa there!

One potential limitation to RCTs is that they can be costly and logistically challenging to implement. This is especially the case if the effects of the treatment are likely to be small because much larger sample sizes are required to detect small effect sizes. Sample sizes for small effects can often run into the hundreds or even thousands, which increases the cost of administration and presents more logistic challenges to manage. Proof of concept or pilot studies are usually undertaken before moving to the RCT stage.

RCTs in education often build on previous research. It is usual for a new intervention to go through several stages (eg., proof of concept, pilot studies) before it is taken to RCT stage because of the cost and effort involved with large scale trials. Often funders want some tangible evidence in the way of published pilot studies that the intervention is worth trialling with an RCT before funding can be secured.

The trial we describe here had a main aim of improving reading ability in primary school children in a cost-effective and scaleable manner. The research literature on the components of reading and the skills and knowledge necessary to obtain them is vast, but two prominent components are decoding and comprehension. There is a large literature on phonics showing that teaching the systematic relationship between print and sound and the associated skills necessary to convert the sounds into words is an effective method to teach most children to read (Castles et al., 2018; Ehri et al., 2001). These skills and knowledge include knowing which sounds each letter typically makes (letter sound knowledge), and how to 'blend' individual sounds to make a word (phoneme awareness) – both skills are associated with reading (Hulme et al., 2012).

Much of early literacy instruction focuses on phonics because children need to read words to know what they mean. Although reading comprehension skills form part of national assessments even in early readers, there is less focus on comprehension in the early years. This is partly because children need some decoding skills before they can complete reading comprehension measures. Research on reading comprehension is equally vast, and shows a diverse range of skills that are associated with comprehension outcomes (National Institute of Child Health and Human Development, 2000). Much of the literacy intervention research focuses on either decoding or comprehension, and few studies consider both aspects simultaneously. One aim of the trial was to assess whether combining both decoding and comprehension instruction in the same programme would benefit reading comprehension ability for beginning readers, relative to children who receive 'business as usual' literacy instruction. We were also interested to see whether any effects would still be apparent a year after the programme had finished.

Another aim of the study was driven by a desire to compare different delivery methods. The use of ICT in schools to deliver or supplement teaching is ever increasing, however, there is a body of research that suggests that ICT-delivered language teaching is not effective (Bulman & Fairlie, 2016; Slavin R. E. et al., 2011). More recent research has suggested that poor outcomes for ICT-based programmes may stem from how well trained and supported staff are to deliver them (Archer et al., 2014) suggesting that the content of ICT programmes may not be problematic if staff are well trained and supported to deliver them. This observation is further supported by a number of studies that use an ICT toolkit for delivery literacy instruction called *A Balanced Reading Approach for Canadians Designed to Achieve Best Results for All* (ABRA; Abrami et al., 2010). ABRA is a free-to-access web-based suite of activities for beginning readers. The activities cover decoding, reading fluency, comprehension and writing (although we did not use the writing activities). ABRA has a long development history by a multi-university team in Canada and has been developed from developmental theory and a large evidence base on effective reading interventions (Savage et al., 2009). The ABRA software has been extensively evaluated by RCTs in Canada and beyond and shown to be an effective tool in improving literacy outcomes (Abrami et al., 2020). We therefore decided to use ABRA to implement the ICT version of our reading programme. However, ABRA had never been used in the UK and required adaptation to the UK education context.

Cultural context

Using educational programmes in a different context often requires them to be adapted to the particular cultural context they are going to be used in. Just because they work in one country does not mean they can be exported without adaptation elsewhere, where the education system may be very different. For example, we adapted how we used the ABRA software for use in the UK because the way literacy is taught in Canada (where much of the ABRA research had been conducted) is different to the UK. At the time in Canada, primary school teachers had complete freedom in how they taught literacy, whereas in England it was compulsory for schools to teach literacy using phonics.

A further aim of the study was to compare the efficacy of the reading programme for certain subgroups of pupils that we know to be disadvantaged. This aim was driven by the funder because they are interested in improving the educational attainment of the poorest pupils in English schools. A standard method for selecting pupils that are economically disadvantaged is to use eligibility for Free School Meals (FSM) as a proxy measure for disadvantage. We also decided to examine whether the programme was efficacious for those children who start the programme with lower ability than average.

2.4 Research questions

1. Do the programmes have an impact on the treatment groups relative to the control group on outcomes within one academic year? Do any effects persist one year later?
2. How do the programmes compare to each other in terms of effectiveness?
3. Are the effects of the programmes different depending on: free school meal status; gender; above median attainment on pre-test?
4. Is there any evidence of **spillover** effects on the control group?

2.5 Design

In agreeing the research aims and questions, we will know what intervention we are testing, and how many **arms** (conditions in experimental terminology) the trial has. For example, if we are testing to see if a reading intervention is better than 'business as usual' this will normally entail a two-arm trial: the reading intervention group and a 'business as usual' control group. Alternatively, we might be testing more than one intervention or programme, either against each other or against business as usual, which might entail a three-arm trial: reading intervention A, reading intervention B, and business as usual.

We also need to decide what outcome we want to measure to see if the programme is effective. This will be our **primary outcome** and is something we can measure quantitatively like a score on a standardised reading test. If there are other variables that we think might also be affected by the programme under test, we can declare these as **secondary outcomes**. Declaring our primary outcome means that we reduce the risk of i) **type 1 errors** (finding effects that are not true effects) because the overall result of the trial depends only on the primary outcome, and not any other measure that we might retrospectively like to test, and ii) **type 2 errors** (failing to find a true effect that is really there) because we use the primary outcome to calculate how many participants we need to detect a change or difference in the primary outcome (Andrade, 2015).

Once we know how many arms the trial has and what our outcomes are, we need to decide who our participants will be and how we will allocate them to the arms of the trial. In order to make this decision, we need to know whether they naturally occur in clusters. For example, if we are testing a literacy intervention for beginning readers, our participants could be children in schools. In this case, they are clustered by school because multiple children attend the same school. This will help us decide whether we randomly allocate *individuals* to the different arms of the trial, or whether we randomly allocate *clusters* of participants (e.g., schools) to the different arms.

2.6 Randomisation

When participants are clustered (e.g., schools, clinics, villages) there are a number of reasons why researchers randomly allocate clusters to each arm. It is often the case that the intervention naturally applies at the cluster level. For example, schools usually teach the whole class the same way. It can be administratively simpler to randomise by cluster; in a school setting it is easier to teach the whole class the same way rather than split the class into groups who each receive a different type of instruction. There may be ethical issues to consider as well; it may be unethical to give an intervention to raise literacy to half a class and not the rest, for example.

Ethel ethics

Sometimes it can seem unethical to give treatments that are thought to improve outcomes to some participants and not offer the same chance of improvement to other participants. This is especially the case when we think that RCTs often test treatments that are designed to support vulnerable groups, and it seems unethical to only offer that support to part of the group that needs it. However, although RCTs are often conducted with treatments that have some evidence that they work, there are many examples where RCTs have shown treatments to be no better than existing practice, or in some cases, even to be harmful (compared to best current practice). So, we cannot assume that the treated groups will be better off until we know that the treatments work, and the benefits of having gold-standard evidence that a treatment is effective outweighs the disadvantages brought by selecting a control group. Furthermore, there are ways to combat these disadvantages, for example by having a wait-list control group, who are offered the treatment at the end of the trial.

However, there can be other practical reasons why randomising by individual is preferred, even when participants are clustered. For example, fewer participants are required with individual randomisation, and this can reduce the cost and administrative burden of the trial. Yet another factor to think about when deciding how to randomise participants is that of **contamination**. If participants are naturally clustered (e.g., by school class), then randomising by individual means that the children who do not receive the treatment risk becoming contaminated by the children who do. Consider an intervention in secondary schools to test a new sex-education programme – if only some of the class receive the programme there is a high risk they will talk to those who do not receive the programme and thus contaminate the control group. Thus, clustering and contamination need to be carefully considered when choosing how to randomise participants.

When choosing how to randomise participants, we need to decide *who* will randomise them. It is really important that an independent person, who is not part of the research team, conducts the randomisation. **Selection bias** is possibly the most damaging artefact if it occurs in an RCT (Schulz et al., 1995) because it undermines the randomisation process and admits the possibility that participants can be allocated on a systematic basis. For example, if a researcher is aware that certain schools have made it clear they will only participate if they get to do the intervention, they may be tempted to fix their allocation rather than lose them from the trial. Independent randomisation can be achieved by recruiting a separate organisation to conduct the randomisation, such as a clinical trials unit.

2.7 Power and effect size

Once we have decided how many arms our trial has, our outcomes, who our participants are and how we will allocate them, we then need to decide how many participants we need in the trial to be sure that we will have the power to detect if the programme works. Researchers use specialist software, such as Optimal Design (Spybrook et al., 2011), or Stata (StataCorp, 2019) to calculate sample size because the calculations are often complex. When we design an RCT, we often have a good idea of the likely **effect size** of the programme being tested. When deciding how many participants are needed, we need to ensure we have at least enough participants to have the power to detect an effect this size. This is called the **minimal detectable effect size (MDES)**.

Sample size calculations require the researcher to specify the level of power, the significance level, and the MDES as a minimum. Conventionally, power is set to 80% or above and the significance level is set to 5% ($p < 0.05$). Other factors also affect sample size and must be specified, including the unit of randomisation and cluster size, and if a baseline pre-test measure is used, how strongly it correlates with the outcome variable. When participants are clustered, as in schools, how similar participants are to each other within a cluster also affect the sample size calculation because the participants are not truly independent. This can be measured (or estimated from previous studies) by the intra-class correlation (ICC). The ICC is often around 0.1–0.2 for education studies, where zero indicates no similarity between participants, and 1 indicates that they are identical.

Baseline pre-tests are a good idea if they are feasible to collect because they increase the power of the trial (or alternatively mean that fewer participants are required). For a baseline pre-test to be effective, it must correlate, preferably strongly, with the outcome measure. A common strategy for pre-test is to use the same test as the outcome measure. For example, in a trial where the outcome is reading comprehension, we might use the same comprehension test at pre-test. If this is not possible, it is perfectly acceptable to use a different measure at pre-test, as long as there is a good correlation between it and the outcome measure. For example, we could use an different comprehension test, or a measure or reading ability, as long as it correlates with the outcome. But how do you know in advance whether a pre-test will correlate with the outcome measure? This can be answered by consulting the research literature for previous studies or RCTs that have used the outcome measure(s) in the current design. Additionally, sometimes it is possible to use data from a pilot study to answer this question. Pre-tests need to be collected before randomisation occurs, to prevent biasing the outcome of the pretest.

Skoolkid errors

It can be tempting to collect pre-test data after randomisation has occurred, perhaps because of time constraints or the logistics of collecting the pre-test. However, this should be avoided because it can introduce bias into the pre-test scores. Suppose a school discovers it has been allocated to the intervention group before the pre-test has been collected. They may feel really excited and pleased to be receiving the intervention and put extra effort into preparing their children for the pre-test because they want to show their pupils' abilities in the best possible light. However, in doing this they are influencing the pre-test scores.

Once the design is decided, the trial should be registered with an official RCT registry. These can be found online, for example, with the International Standard Randomised Controlled Trial Number Register at www.ISRCTN.org. Trial registration makes the full details of the trial publicly available. Trial details are also often published in the form of a trial protocol (eg., by the funder) which is a document that specifies the full details of the trial, similar to trial registration. Making the details of the trial public is considered good practice because it prevents trial researchers making unjustifiable changes to the trial during or after it has finished.

2.8 Procedure

For the Johnson et al. (2019) trial, we tested two different delivery methods of a balanced reading programme for Year 1 children in the UK against 'business as usual'. We therefore had three arms in the trial: an ICT reading programme; a non-ICT reading programme; and business as usual (the control group). We were testing whether the reading programme improved reading ability in beginning readers, so the primary outcome was the Progress in Reading Assessment (PiRA; McCarty & Ruttle, 2010). This is a reading test that assesses both phonic skills and word reading, but also reading comprehension.

There were also several secondary measures, as we expected that the programme would improve several component parts of reading. Phonological awareness was measured with PIPA, letter sound knowledge was measured with Pre-Reading Inventory of Phonological Awareness (Dodd et al., 2000) and Letter Sound Test (LeST; Larsen et al., 2015), word reading was measured with Diagnostic Test of Word Reading (DTWRP; Forum for Research in Literacy and Language, 2012), and vocabulary was measured with British Picture Vocabulary Test (BPVS; Dunn & Dunn, 2009).

All of the primary and secondary measures were measured at pre-test, and were collected **blind** by independent researchers who had no knowledge of the study or group membership. Other secondary outcomes were national teacher assessments (Key Stage 1 teacher assessments in reading and writing) that were collected a year after the reading programme had finished. An additional pre-test measure was the Early Years Foundation Stage Profile (EYFSP), a teacher assessment of 17 early learning goals. Pre-test data was collected prior to randomisation.

2.9 Participants

Participants were Year 1 pupils in primary schools in the West Midlands region of the UK. An effort was made to recruit schools from disadvantaged areas, as this was a main focus of the funder. To increase the power of the trial, pupils were randomised individually within schools. First, schools were matched in pairs based on the size of the cohort, average academic ability of the preceding year, and the number of pupils eligible for free school meals. Then, schools from each pair were randomly allocated to either a control group or a programme group. Pupils in the control group continued business as usual. Pupils in the programme group were further randomly allocated within their school to either: i) the ICT programme; ii) the non-ICT programme; or iii) a control group. However, as pupils were naturally clustered in schools this risks contamination if the teaching staff in the programme groups inadvertently used strategies from either programme to teach the children in the control group (they might do this consciously if they think a strategy is particularly effective, or unconsciously through a general improvement to their skill set through teaching the programme). Contamination was assessed by comparing the outcome from the control group pupils in the programme schools to those of the pupils in the control group of schools (where no programme delivery occurred).

The reading programme was delivered in schools by their own teaching assistants (TAs) who were trained by the delivery team. Importantly, the TAs delivering the programme were also randomly allocated to deliver either the ICT or non-ICT programme. Randomisation was conducted by an independent evaluation team at the London School of Economics, who were not involved in recruitment or the delivery of the programme. A sample size calculation was carried out using Optimal Design (Spybrook et al., 2011), assuming randomisation at the school level, using 80% power, a 5% significance level, an MDES of 0.2, a pre-test to primary outcome correlation of 0.7, and an ICC of 0.2. Note that the actual trial included individual-level randomisation, so in practice would have the power to detect smaller effects. The result of the calculation was 60 schools. The delivery team initially recruited 58 schools to the study but seven dropped out before randomisation, leaving 51 schools who were randomised. The trial was registered with the ISRCTN (www.isrctn.com/), and the protocol was published online by the EEF (McNally, 2014).

3. FINDINGS AND REFLECTIONS

3.1 Analysis

As can be seen above, the design of an RCT must be carefully thought through and there are standards that must be followed in, eg., recruiting and randomising participants. There are also recommendations for how an RCT should be reported. The Consolidated Standards of Reporting Trials (CONSORT; www.consort-statement.org/) is a set of recommendations for reporting RCTs in a complete and transparent way. It covers the design, analysis and interpretation of the trial and has been endorsed by many journals as a way to improve the quality of research based on RCTs.

The recommended analysis for RCTs is an **Intention to Treat** analysis. This is where we leave all participants in the condition to which they were randomised, regardless of whether they completed the intervention or not (**non-compliance**). This may sound harsh as it could dilute any effects if many participants in the intervention group do not actually complete the intervention. While this may indeed be true, and produce a conservative estimate of the effect, this estimate will nevertheless be unbiased. Participants who do not complete the intervention are likely to be different from those who do, and thus simply removing them from analysis introduces bias, which is what we are trying to avoid by conducting an RCT. There are advanced statistical techniques that can be employed to assess the effect of non-compliance, such as Complier Average Causal Effect (CACE) analysis (Gerber & Green, 2012).

The impact evaluation is quantitative and focused on comparing outcomes from the different arms of the trial. This will tell us whether the intervention worked, but not why. The process evaluation looks at qualitative data, and focuses on *how* and *why* the intervention worked. The impact evaluation can use any method that is suitable for comparing two means, but usually this is complicated by the presence of clustering of the participants, and covariates (i.e., the pre-test). More often than not, a statistical analysis called Analysis of Covariance (ANCOVA) is conducted using a regression-based approach to take account of the clustering and to add known covariates. It is important that any clustering of the participants is taken into account at the analysis stage because otherwise the estimates will be biased, specifically the analysis is more likely to find an effect that isn't truly there if clustering is not acknowledged during analysis.

Schoolkid errors

In research

Analysing the data by ignoring any clustering will yield biased results. This is because ANCOVAs assume the data are independent. If the participants are clustered (e.g., by school) then their data will be correlated and no longer independent. The standard errors of the estimates, therefore, need to reflect the fact that the effective independent sample size is smaller when participants are clustered, which will *increase* the standard errors. This has the knock-on effect of increasing the p-value of the estimate. There are techniques available using regression to account for this (e.g., multilevel modelling or using Huber-White standard errors). An alternative approach is to use data aggregated at the cluster (e.g., school) level.

Analysis should also consider any known covariates where possible, not limited to just the pre-test. Including known covariates that are strong predictors of the outcome will improve the precision of the estimated effect by removing variance due to the covariates.

Lastly, the analysis plan should be determined at the design stage, and published within or alongside the trial protocol.

3.2 Analysis of the example study

For the Johnson et al. (2019) trial, we started with 51 schools (pupils: N = 2241) randomised into the trial with 26 schools allocated to the programme group (pupils: ICT N = 360, Non-ICT N = 350, Control N = 373) and 25 schools allocated to the control group (pupils: N = 1158). Unfortunately, five schools in the programme group dropped out; however we were able to collect the primary outcome data from four of them. As the analysis was an intention to treat analysis, we included them in the analysis. The one dropped out school that we could not collect primary outcome data from was dropped from analysis, along with its matched randomisation pair. One school in the trial was an independent school, this was also dropped from the analysis (this school did not have a matched randomisation pair). This left 48 schools for analysis, 24 in the programme group, and 24 control schools. 220 pupils were also lost to analysis because they were missing either pre-test or primary outcome data (or both). There were many reasons for this, but most commonly they had either left that school or were absent at the time of testing. This left 1901 pupils for analysis, 877 in the programme group (ICT N = 240, non-ICT N = 277, Control N = 310), and 1024 in the control group.

A regression approach was used to test the effect of the ICT and Non-ICT programme against the control children by including group membership as a dummy variable. Several covariates were included in the analysis. The pre-test and EYFSP data were included because prior academic performance (both generally and specifically) are strong predictors of later performance. Gender was included as attainment has been shown to differ according to gender, and disadvantage is also strongly associated with school attainment. Disadvantage was measured by proxy by a variable indicating whether each pupil was eligible for free school meals (FSM).

3.3 Findings

1. Do the programmes have an impact on the treatment groups relative to the control group on outcomes within one academic year? Do any effects persist one year later?

The results showed that pupils who received either the ICT or the non-ICT programme performed significantly better than the control children on the PIRA at post-test. This was true whether the control group included both the control group schools *and* the control children in the programme schools, or just the control group schools. One year later, there was no longer an effect of either programme on the PIRA, but the pupils in the non-ICT programme were significantly more likely to achieve at or above expected levels in the Key Stage 1 teacher assessments in reading and writing.

2. How do the programmes compare to each other in terms of effectiveness?

In all cases, there were no significant differences *between* the two programmes indicating that both were equally effective.

3. Are the effects of the programmes different depending on: free school meal status; gender; above median attainment on pre-test?

In terms of FSM, both programmes were significantly more effective for pupils in the FSM category; both programmes were equally effective for boys and girls; the non-ICT programme was equally effective for pupils above or below median ability on pre-test, and the ICT programme was more effective for pupils below median ability on pre-test.

4. Is there any evidence of spillover effects on the control group?

Yes. The control children in the programme schools performed significantly better on the PIRA than the control children in the control group schools, and they also performed equally as well on the PIRA as the children in the ICT programme in the programme schools. Spillover effects disappeared one year later.

3.4 Reflections

The aim of an RCT is to test the effectiveness of an intervention or policy of some sort, with a longer term objective of making that intervention or policy widely available if it is shown to be effective. However, the findings from an RCT should not be taken as the endpoint of that research programme. We can never really rule out the possibility that the results occurred by chance. Therefore, findings from an RCT, although considered the 'gold standard' by many, should only ever be considered in conjunction with other studies in that area. In this way, researchers can assess the converging evidence for a particular intervention. For our reading programme, the findings are consistent with a body of research showing that teaching decoding (ref) and comprehension (ref) skills can improve reading ability. We add to this body of research by showing both sets of skills can be effectively taught to beginning readers in the UK by improving national literacy assessments.

Ig Nobel Prize (in the post)

Do you really need that parachute?

Yeh R. W., Valsdottir L. R., Yeh M. W., Shen C., Kramer D. B., Strom J. B. et al. (2018). Parachute use to prevent death and major trauma when jumping from aircraft: Randomised controlled trial. *BMJ, 363*, k5094. https://doi.org/10.1136/bmj.k5094

This paper has not been awarded an Ig Nobel prize yet, but we think it is just a matter of time. The title tells the story. Yeh and his team used an RCT to see whether using a parachute when you jump out of a plane has any benefit in terms of death or injury, and remarkably they found that the parachute did not significantly reduce death or major injury. How can this be you ask yourself? The study was rigorously controlled as you would expect from an RCT but … I recommend you read the study to find out. It raises some issues about the way that RCTs are reported and how much weight is put on this design. And our tip is to still use a parachute if you are offered the opportunity to do so.

www.bmj.com/content/bmj/363/bmj.k5094.full.pdf

Sometimes the findings from the impact evaluation are not positive, telling us that the treatment didn't work, but not why. The process evaluation can be a helpful guide here to understand issues such as **compliance** with the treatment, and barriers to compliance. For the Johnson et al. (2019) trial, the findings revealed evidence of spillover, but the data cannot tell us *why* spillover occurred. We prefer an explanation based on the idea that through completing the training to deliver the reading programme, TAs increased their theoretical knowledge about literacy as well as their skill set, and therefore became 'better' teachers of literacy. As many of the TAs in the programme group of schools also helped the control children with literacy during the normal course of the day, the control children would also likely benefit from having 'better' instruction. We favour this explanation because the process evaluation revealed, through a focus group with the TAs, that many of them had increased both their general theoretical knowledge of reading, and become skilled in effective delivery strategies.

Care should be taken before embarking on rolling out treatments to the population on the basis of positive findings from RCTs. Positive findings are no guarantee that the treatment will generalise to a wider population or apply in different contexts. The reading programme RCT described here was carefully designed to fit with the UK teaching context, but may well not work in the same way if adopted elsewhere. A second RCT of the same programme in Johnson et al. (2019) is currently underway to investigate if it still works when: i) it is delivered in different regions across the UK; or ii) the training the schools receive on how to deliver the programme is delivered by a third party rather than the research team. These seemingly small changes to enable scale up cannot be assumed to be insignificant until tested, again with an RCT design.

LEARNING OBJECTIVES

You should now know,

- the main components of an RCT
- how to design a basic RCT
- what the standards of reporting RCTs are
- how to assess the quality of published RCTs
- how to understand and interpret the findings of published RCTs

FURTHER READING

Haynes, L., Service, O., Goldacre, B., & Torgerson, D. (2008). *Test, learn, adapt. Developing public policy with randomised controlled trials*. Cabinet Office Behavioural Insights Team.

This paper is aimed at a non-specialist audience and sets out the rationale for using RCTs to inform evidence-based practice. It is easy to read and contains a step by step guide of the RCT lifecycle, as well as many interesting real-life examples.

Torgerson D. J. (2008). *Designing randomised trials in health education and the social sciences*. Palgrave McMillan.

This book is authored by David Torgerson, an authority on RCTs, especially in education research. This book focuses more on design rather than a statistical treatment of RCT data, and is great reading if you want to know what underpins a rigorous design in RCTs.

Torgerson D. J., & Torgerson C. J. (2013). *Randomised trials in education: An introductory handbook*. Educational Endowment Fund.

This is a more technical go-to guide for conducting RCTs if you want to find out more about the technical details of each aspect of an RCT, e.g., how to randomise or conduct an analysis of RCT data.

CONSORT website: www.consort-statement.org/

The CONSORT website contains a wealth of information on how to report RCTs to an increasingly accepted standard. There is a checklist that can be consulted as a quick check of whether the standards have been followed, as well as a more comprehensive section-by-section guide on how to report an RCT.

LINKS TO USEFUL RESOURCES

Gorard, S., See, B., & Siddiqui, N. (2014). *A randomised controlled trial (or 'fair test'): Evaluating an educational innovation*. SAGE Research Methods Cases. https://dx.doi.org/10.4135/978144627305013514714

National Foundation for Educational Research (2014). *How to … Run Randomised Controlled Trials (RCTs): An introduction (How to Guides)*. Slough: NFER.

6

INTERVIEWS

DAVID WILDE, BETH JONES, JENNIFER MACKAY AND LISA SANDERSON

1. INTRODUCTION

Within qualitative research, the interview is the most common method of data collection. Most interviews are carried out face-to-face. However, as technology has advanced, the possibilities for alternate means of collecting interview data have broadened: interviews can be carried out synchronously (e.g., both parties conversing in real time) via telephone or online video communication software (e.g., Skype, Zoom, Teams), or asynchronously (e.g., with questions being asked at one time point, and answers given at a different time point) via email or a plethora of social media messaging platforms. This technological flexibility proved to be incredibly valuable and convenient in enabling research to continue during the recent pandemic, which would otherwise have surely limited this kind of data collection.

1.1 Basics

Before deciding to use an interview, the researcher should carefully consider *why* they would use one. It may be that a researcher has an **ontological/epistemological** position about what knowledge is and how it can be considered legitimately as data. For example, some qualitative researchers view what people say (discourse) as central to social and **self-constructions**, forsaking the exploration of the inner life of the mind in favour of examining psychological phenomena as things that are constructed via talk-in-interaction between people (see Chapter 8), other researchers focus on lived experience, how people make sense of their experience, and how they attribute meaning to their **lifeworld** both individually and socially (Smith, 2017). It may be that a researcher wants to see through the worldview of their participants, or consider contextual factors in-depth, or examine the process of social change, i.e., 'how do things come to be'.

As with all good research, an interview study must be planned out thoroughly before submission for ethical approval. All research starts with an appropriate research question. The design of the study must be able to robustly answer that question, pragmatic and logistical factors need to be considered, for example, how and where will participants be recruited from? What sample size is appropriate for the methodology you are employing? Where will the interviews be conducted? What ethical factors come into play? Do you (or the person who collects the data) have the appropriate listening skills required to carry out an interview, particularly if the topic is a sensitive one? How will issues of power be handled? How will you ensure a suitable rapport can be built with your interviewee? How will the data be analysed, and the findings disseminated? All of these will be covered in later sections but we note them here to highlight that conducting interview-based research requires a lot of preparation and thought before its execution.

There are several core features that constitute the interview method. The foundational element of what Kvale (1996, p. 2) terms an 'interview' is that it involves a reciprocal, conversational, exchange of knowledge about a topic of shared importance. The aim of the interview is to freely explore the topic of interest with a participant in a fluid and flexible way as one would if they were to engage a person in everyday conversation. The conversational style employed in an interview is somewhat informal and relaxed, compared to the more formal wording style of questionnaire items, yet is deployed with a specific focus and purpose – this is research after all, and interviewers are investigators who seek to understand! Therefore, the knowledge generated from an interview is both situated (in time and space) and contextual (historically and socially). It follows then that the interpretations, understandings, and meanings that arise in an interview are viewed as co-constructions between the interviewer and interviewee, rather than the interviewer simply mining the participant for information (Kvale & Brinkmann, 2009).

There are different forms of interviews, and in the next section we will cover the four main types: (i) structured; (ii) semi-structured; (iii) unstructured; and (iv) narrative (or biographical) interviews.

1.2 Structured interviews

In a structured interview, the power and control lie with the interviewer and they dictate the line of questioning. In these interviews, there is little or no space for the interviewee to expand on their responses.

Cultural context

Power asymmetry

Power asymmetry refers to the disproportionate power dynamics that can materialise in research interviews. An interview is a conversation between a researcher and a participant. From a **humanistic** standpoint, there should exist an **egalitarian** status between those involved in the dialogue generated in an interview. However, several power imbalances can arise in interviews. Interviewers can limit how participants express their views (Wang, 2006), for example, by interrupting the flow of the conversation with more questions, thus controlling the structure of the interaction, favouring the use of 'yes/no' questions rather than the more exploratory Wh-questions (e.g., when, where, etc.), or by interjecting with their own experiences/perceptions on the topic, which can leave the participant feeling they have nothing of importance to contribute. Power can take the form of coercion and manipulation (Lukes, 2005). Whilst Lukes referred to this power being wielded intentionally (covertly or overtly), this can happen unintentionally as well, whereby an interviewer, strongly pursuant of elements of the topic that they deem interesting or important, can essentially set an agenda through a line of questioning that can unwittingly restrain a participant from telling the story they want to tell, and in the process, limiting the collection of novel data. Power exercised in these ways can ultimately dominate the interpretations and worldviews of the participant (Anyan, 2013).

Power relationships also exist in the wider society and these are inevitably brought into the interview. For example, our society privileges white, male, heterosexual views and individuals over others. The interview situation does not take place in isolation from these societal understandings and so the interviewer has to acknowledge and respond to these power relationships that exist in their encounter with their interviewee.

Interviewer countermeasures can be employed to take a less powerful stance, such as being aware of the dynamics of the unfolding interaction (monitoring facial expressions and body language for sign of uneasiness), asking open-ended questions and using minimal prompts, being mindful of limiting the number of interruptions or keeping interjections brief and minimal. However, these countermeasures can also be interpreted by a participant as the interviewer attempting to gain power through covert control techniques. Thus, when planning an interview study, a researcher must familiarise themselves with these issues, how they can arise, what they might mean and how they can be avoided. It is worth remembering that, whilst the researcher may be very knowledgeable about a topic from an academic point of view, the participant is the *experiential expert* in their own life and how the phenomenon under investigation has affected them.

Neither will the interviewer use prompts to elicit further detail from their participants. In duration, structured interviews tend to be shorter (e.g., 20 minutes) than unstructured, semi-structured or narrative interviews that typically last for about an hour. They can be seen to be similar in content to a questionnaire that we would use in quantitative work. In this type of interview, the interviewer does not necessarily need to be present and could ask the interviewee to respond to the questions (e.g., by writing their responses down) in their own time. **Rapport** is still important to ensure you are obtaining reliable responses from your participants. In psychology, structured interviews are commonly used to collect information to inform a decision around diagnosis of a mental health condition. In research, such tools may be used to collect information on **incidence** of a diagnosis in a given population. For example, they might be used to help for a diagnosis such as the Adult Asperger Assessment (AAA; Baron-Cohen et al., 2005).

1.3 Semi-structured interviews

Described as a 'conversation with a purpose' (Burgess, 1984, p. 125), the semi-structured interview is probably the most popular qualitative data collection strategy and occupies the middle ground between structured and unstructured interviews. In a semi-structured interview, the interviewer will use a pre-planned interview schedule which consists of either a number of open-ended questions or a list of topics they wish to cover. Thus, the researcher has more control over the topics that are discussed than in an unstructured interview. However, in contrast to a structured interview, the interviewer has more flexibility in how they respond to the participant; they can follow up answers with further questions, or use prompts if they think there is more to be said, and the interviewee is free to answer the question in any way they wish.

Semi-structured interviews may be particularly useful when the research question addresses concepts that are relatively well understood. However, the interviewer needs to have a good knowledge and understanding of the topic under investigation in order to develop the interview schedule (the design of interview schedules is discussed in detail later in this chapter). Knowledge of the topic will often come from the literature, however, in a qualitative research interview, the participant is often perceived as the expert due to their lived experience and therefore novel findings not yet explored within the literature are likely to emerge from the interview data. However, having a schedule can help the interviewer feel more prepared for the interview, and provides some structure to the interview, which may make the interviewer (particularly those who are inexperienced) feel more confident. This could also be advantageous on research projects when data is being collected by more than one interviewer and can provide a comparable dataset.

The interviewer may decide to send the schedule to the interviewees ahead of the interview to give them additional time to think about the questions beforehand. This is more commonly done when the topic of the interview is of a sensitive nature, for example if you wanted to ask an interviewee about their experiences of a traumatic event. Giving the interviewee the opportunity to see the questions ahead of the interview affords them the opportunity to reflect on their experiences and may make it easier for them to talk about the topic being examined. Additionally, the interviewee is afforded more power and control with this kind of interview than they would have in a structured interview.

1.4 Unstructured interviews

When conducting an unstructured interview, the interviewer will have selected a general topic of interest that they would like to explore with the interviewee but wouldn't necessarily have a fixed interview schedule (see section on interview schedules below). Unstructured interview schedules tend to have fewer questions than structured or semi-structured interview schedules, and the questions are generally broader in scope. When starting an unstructured interview, neither the interviewer nor interviewee are sure on where the interview will go, with each interview seen as a unique journey. It is open to the interviewee to tell their story, how they see it, how they feel it and how they experience it with no constraints in terms of content or duration. For this reason, the difference between unstructured, semi-structured and structured interviews comes down to the aforementioned power relations between the interview and interviewee and hence, control over the interaction that takes place during the interview (for further details see Corbin & Morse, 2003, pp. 339–41). Within an unstructured interview, the power and control over the course of the interview very much lies with the interviewee.

For topics that are of a sensitive nature or are not well understood, having the power and control lie with the interviewee can be beneficial as it allows them to tell the stories and experiences they want to be heard. This type of research tool is often used when the researcher wants to give 'voice' to their participants and empower them in doing so. Some have argued that unstructured interviews, because often used to explore sensitive topics, may increase risk of harm to the participant and additional ethical procedures should be put in place to mitigate this (Corbin & Morse, 2003). However, it can be argued that giving the interviewee control over the course of the interview allows them to decide which topics they feel comfortable raising, and the level of detail they wish to provide. Any aspects they feel uncomfortable discussing or find too distressing, they can omit from their narrative.

As mentioned at the start of this chapter, when interviewing, the skill to build a rapport with an interviewee is important but especially so when conducting unstructured interviews. When rapport is built, the interviewee is likely to feel more relaxed and provide a more detailed and personal account of their experience (Davies, 1999). Therefore, you might for example use this type of interview to follow-up topics covered in semi-structured interviews once a rapport has been established. The location of the interview is also important – people may divulge different stories when they feel relaxed, for example at home, compared to a research laboratory.

1.5 Narrative interviews

Particularly popular in health research, the narrative interview is an approach similar to unstructured interviews in that the control largely rests with the interviewee, who dictates the content, pace and direction of the interview (Anderson & Kirkpatrick, 2016). Narrative interviews typically use interview schedules that are structured to some extent like a semi-structured interview schedule but focused more on inviting the interviewee to tell their life story. So, asking the interviewee to consider their life in stages (almost like 'chapters' in a book), focusing on key events (e.g., highs and lows, turning points, earliest and most recent memories), and their future 'scripts' (i.e., what are the interviewee's plans for the future) (Crossley, 2000), but the questions asked are broader in nature, more like what would be seen in an unstructured interview schedule. As in all types of interviews however, it is a good idea for the interviewer to build up good knowledge of the topic area prior to the interview.

The aim of the narrative interview is to encourage the interviewee to narrate their experiences to the interviewer and to this end the interviewer is likely to begin with an open-ended question which invites the interviewee to summarise their experiences of an event. For example, following introductions and rapport building, a researcher interested in the career experiences of school teachers could start the main section of a narrative interview by asking, 'Reflecting on your teaching career up until now, please tell me about the professional training you have received that has been the most and least valuable in terms of influencing student outcomes in the classroom?.' There are three phases to a typical narrative interview with this first one being referred to as the narrative phase. The ability to build trust and rapport at the beginning of the interview is especially important here as rich data is more likely to be obtained if the interviewee feels comfortable in sharing their stories with the interviewer. Telling stories is a way in which people make sense of their lives and by conducting a narrative interview the interviewer can understand how the individual has ordered the events and experiences of their lives to give them meaning.

Once the interviewee has begun telling their story the interviewer should refrain as much as possible from interrupting unnecessarily until the story is finished. In this way, the interviewee has complete freedom to construct their story in any way they see fit, focusing on their own priorities and perspectives, and using language and terms that are natural to them. By not interrupting and asking questions the interviewer is not exerting any influence on the story. This may be challenging when the interviewee says things that the interviewer is particularly keen to follow up on. However, it is a good idea to encourage the interviewee to talk freely by intermittently using non-verbal signs of encouragement such as smiling and nodding and make either a real or mental note of anything they wish to follow up on. Once the interviewee has finished their story, the interviewer can engage in the second phase of the narrative interview which is referred to as the narrative follow-up. In this phase the interviewer asks the interviewee to expand upon certain elements of their story, again without interruption. An example of such a follow up question could be, 'can you tell me a bit more about ...?' Finally, there is an optional third phase which is to conduct a second interview, usually semi-structured, to ask any additional more specific questions which the interviewer thinks will further illuminate the research topic.

There are some disadvantages in using the narrative interviewing technique. First, some interviewees may find telling their stories in this way particularly challenging rather than being asked a series of questions such as in a semi-structured interview. For example, when faced with a broad open-ended question, the interviewee might be perplexed as to where to start their story. Realising this, interviewer can prepare a set of short prompt words to stimulate the start of the conversation. Second, the quality of the data that is obtained may depend upon the active listening skills of the interviewer and the verbal abilities of the interviewee.

Now we have explored some of the advantages and disadvantages of the four different interview types, we have summarised the key points in Table 6.1.

Table 6.1 The advantages and disadvantages of the four different kinds of interview

	Structured interview	Semi-structured interview	Unstructured interview	Narrative interview
Advantages	Useful for collecting diagnostic information	Gives a transparent purpose to the interview	Participant can dictate the course of the interview	Participant fully empowered to tell their story
	Can be a quick method of data collection	Interviewer can follow up points of interest with further questioning	Sensitive narrative can be avoided as the participant has control	Participants may feel more comfortable relating their experiences as a story than answering a series of questions
	By using predetermined, meaningful response categories these types of interview may be more efficient than other types of interviews	Having pre-prepared questions aids in guiding the conversation and keeps participants on topic	High degree of flexibility regarding questioning and probing	This is particularly useful when the research aims to consider experiences in a biographical context
	As every participant answers the same questions it may be easier to compare responses during analysis	More freedom for the interviewer to follow up on things which the participant identifies as being important to them		
Disadvantages	Interviewee cannot expand on any points they might want to	Might not allow for consistency across different researchers on the same project	Difficult to use with children	May be more difficult to conduct with participants of low verbal ability
	Interviewers less free to explore any unanticipated or interesting topics that arise during the interview	Can be time consuming and challenging particularly for novice interviewers	Participants may be more likely to go off topic	Some participants may find telling a story about their experience more challenging than being asked a series of questions about it

(Continued)

Table 6.1 (Continued)

	Structured interview	Semi-structured interview	Unstructured interview	Narrative interview
			This might be the most demanding for the interviewer as they have to ensure that the interviewee remains on topic	
Power dynamics	Very little power beyond consent to take part/withdraw. Power rests mostly with the interviewer.	Power is more balanced in favour of the interviewee than in a structured interview as they are viewed as the *experiential experts* of the phenomenon under investigation.	Power is mostly in the control of the interviewee as they are again seen as experts in their own life experience	Very similar to the unstructured interview, except the interview schedule will generally be more structured, almost like a semi-structured interview, so there may be less flexibility in terms of how the interviewee can direct the interview.
		Interviewees can see the questions in advance, although this is at the discretion of the researcher	As with the semi-structured interview, interviewees can see the questions in advance, although this is again at the discretion of the researcher	
		Interviewee is more able to control the direction of the interview and how much information is given	Interviewee is much more in control of the direction and content of the responses to the interview questions	

<table>
<tr><th></th><th>Structured interview</th><th>Semi-structured interview</th><th>Unstructured interview</th><th>Narrative interview</th></tr>
<tr><td></td><td></td><td>However, the interviewer does have a structured schedule of questions/topics that they have deemed important to research.</td><td>Interviewer still has a set of interview questions prepared but these are broader in nature and allow for far more flexibility in how the interviewee responds.</td><td></td></tr>
<tr><td>Rapport building & active listening skills</td><td>Generally, very little to no rapport is generated with this type of interview. Minimal active listening involved.</td><td colspan="3">With these types of interview, the researcher should allow for and take the time to get to know their participant before the interview starts. Rapport building, alongside the deployment of active listening skills, is key to getting rich data from an interview. Conducting unstructured interviews usually requires an interviewer to have more developed active listening skills and so may not be suitable for novice researchers.</td></tr>
</table>

2. INTERVIEW STRUCTURE

2.1 Interview schedules

In this section, we focus on the development of a semi-structured interview schedule as this is the most common form of interview conducted in psychological research. We will then consider how a schedule may be different for an unstructured and structured interview.

When thinking about the types of questions you want to be asking in an interview schedule, you will want to consider the topics or areas of knowledge that will help you answer your research question(s). These often come from the literature and you will often have an idea of what they are even before you start putting the schedule together. You can also draw upon your own experiences where relevant (yes, depending on the topic, you can be an experiential expert, too!). One good way to start is to list the domains of experience that you wish to investigate. For example, an undergraduate student supervised by the first author carried out some research looking at how fellow students had experienced studying at university during the Covid-19 pandemic. The student began by reviewing literature that discussed how people's working and studying lives had been affected in previous similar crises. They then considered their own experiences of studying during this time. From this they built a list of what were the key areas of student life that were most likely to have been affected. This list contained (but was not limited to), student background information (e.g., were students studying at home, on campus, etc.), wider university life (limits on socialising, access to library resources, etc.), effects on teaching (e.g., online vs. face-to-face, use of technology), student use of social and news media, etc. The student then set about drafting questions that would tap into the lived experiences within these domains.

Once these areas have been identified, you can start to develop interview questions that tap into these areas of experience or expertise. When doing so, there are a few things that you need to consider along the way. Below, we will discuss each of these considerations. It is also worth bearing in mind that the development of a good interview schedule will take several drafts and it is always a good idea to obtain feedback before conducting the interview with a participant.

2.2 Open-ended questions

Questions in a semi-structured interview should be open-ended (i.e., questions which enable participants to share their opinions, thoughts and ideas in depth) such as 'How is your relationship with your parents?' and not constrained to a set number of responses like we might see in a quantitative questionnaire (e.g., Do you get along with your parents?). The response to this question would most probably be 'yes', 'no', 'sometimes' and would not tell us anything about the participants experience and why they may or may not get along with their parents, which is typically what we want to hear about when conducting a semi-structured interview. To ensure questions are openly phrased it is a good idea to start them with 'How', 'What' or 'Can you tell me …'. Try and avoid questions that start with 'Why' as some interviewees may become defensive when such lines of questioning are used.

2.3 Leading questions

Through personal experiences, extensive review of the literature or a combination of both, we might have an idea as to how we expect our participants to respond to the questions we put to them. This, often without us even realising, can affect how we phrase questions. For example, I have read the literature around the impacts of the Covid-19 pandemic on mental health. The literature tells me that the pandemic has worsened mental health and consequently I expect my participants to tell me about their experience negatively. Therefore, I ask my participants: 'Can you tell me why the pandemic has had a negative effect on your mental health?' While this initially looks like a good question, it leads the participants to tell us about the negative impact and we lose all possibility of our participants telling us about any positive experiences they may have had with regards to their wellbeing. In this way, we are limiting the possibility of undercovering novel findings not before realised within the literature. Instead, we should be looking to phrase questions neutrally when constructing an interview schedule: e.g., 'Can you tell me about how the pandemic has affected your mental health?'

2.4 Double-barrelled questions

It can be tempting to ask multiple question in one go, especially when questions feel connected. We often do this as we do not want our participant to feel as if we are repeating ourselves. However, when asking two (or more) questions in one go, we run the risk of gathering a partial response. If I asked a participant, 'Can you tell me about your first job and also why you choose that line of employment?' they will tend to answer the first part of the question and forget about the second. The second part of the question is equally as important if not more so and therefore it should either be included as a follow-up prompt or as a question in its own right.

2.5 Prompts

You will also want to think about prompts when designing your schedule. These are used to elicit further detail from your participant. Some prompts can be very minimal and general, consisting of simple utterances, for example, 'uh-uh', 'yes', 'right', 'that's interesting'. These help the keep the conversation flowing and let your participant know you are listening intently and should flow naturally. However, other prompts you want to be more specific in order to go deeper into a line of questioning. To develop these, you will need to anticipate how your participants may respond to your questions and consider how you may want to follow these responses up to obtain a richer account. For example, if I ask: 'How did you get into playing basketball at University?' I might follow this up with 'Did you have any experience of playing before you came to university?' 'Did level of experience matter when joining the university team?'

2.6 Jargon, technical language and acronyms

Avoid using jargon, technical language (e.g., specialist language not used in everyday circumstances) or acronyms when asking participants questions. In qualitative work, we tend to recruit participants because they are perceived to be a 'expert' in the topic under investigation. For example, if as a researcher I was interested in learning what it was like to be an Olympic athlete, I would invite Olympic athletes to take part. These participants will have relevant lived experience but might not necessarily be familiar with terminology that is used within the literature, or in some circumstances may even find the terminology offensive. By using jargon or acronyms you run the risk of your participants not understanding the question. Many participants may feel reluctant to ask for the meaning behind jargon or acronyms as they wouldn't want to be perceived to be unknowledgeable in a topic you have invited them to talk about. Any language that isn't accessible can be corrected by getting feedback on your schedule and having a dummy run before data collection with your participants begins.

2.7 Structure of the schedule

Once you have developed interview questions and prompts that address your research question, you will want to consider the order of the questions. You will want to begin with a question that is 'easy' to answer for your participant, as you will see with the example schedules below given in Figure 6.1 and Figure 6.2. The questions may or may not relate to the topic of enquiry. So, for example, you might ask your participant how their day has been. This can facilitate with rapport building which will help put your participant at ease and generate a richer account. In some cases, topics may be sensitive, and you will want to leave sensitive questions until later on in the interview to give you the opportunity to build rapport. However, in a semi-structured interview, you can be flexible with the ordering of specific questions; i.e., you do not have to ask questions in the order they are listed on your schedule. Within a semi-structured interview, you are also free to ask questions that aren't on the schedule to follow up interesting discussions so long as they are within the remit of the topic of inquiry and are sensitively phrased. For this reason, active listening skills are really important when conducting semi-structured interviews. Finally, you will want to round off by asking the participant whether they have anything that they would like to add. In a semi-structured interview, this gives the power and control back to your participants and can be an empowering way to finish the interview.

---

1. **Please tell me a bit about yourself?**
   Prompts: Age, hobbies, interests. Are you working, studying?
2. **What is it like being part of the Non-Offending Minor Attracted Person (NOMAP) community?**
   Prompts: Socially? Emotionally? From a mental health point of view?
3. **Who else are you able to talk to about your sexual preference?**
   Prompts: Friends? Family? Partner? Other NOMAPs?
4. **What stigma do you feel is associated with being a NOMAP?**
   Prompts: What makes you say that? How does this make you feel? To what extent have you personally experienced stigma related to being a NOMAP?
5. **What is your view of the process for NOMAPs of accessing Mental Health Services?**
   Prompts: What makes you say that? Can you give me an example of that?
6. **To what extent do you trust Mental Health Services and professionals?**
   Prompts: What makes you say that? Can you give me an example of what you mean?
7. **How do you feel about the cultural competence and knowledge of the mental health professionals regarding NOMAPs?**
   Prompts: Why do you think this? Can you give me an example of what you mean?

---

8. **How does the idea of engaging with a Mental Health Service make you feel?**
   Prompts: Positive? Negative? Why do you say that?

9. **To what extent have you personally engaged within Mental Health Services?**
   Prompts: What was your experience of it? What was good about it? What was not so good about it? What could have been better about it? Can you give me an example of that?

10. **How do you think services could cater for the needs of NOMAPs?**
    Prompts: Social needs? Mental health needs? Tailored support and interventions?

11. **To what extent do you think that the Mental Health Services offer support and guidance for NOMAPs?**
    Prompts: What makes you say this?

12. **Given your experiences and what we have discussed in this interview, if another NOMAP were to ask your advice about approaching a Mental Health Service in relation to their sexual preferences, what would your advice be?**

That is the end of the interview

Thank you for taking part

Figure 6.1 Examples of interview schedules

Section 1

1. Tell me a bit about yourself
   (Age? Ethnicity? Highest qualification? Family? Where from? What do you enjoy?)
2. Who are the important people in your life?
3. Tell me how long you have been in prison for, how you came to be here and offending history
   (Not specific offence details, but what in for, what sentence, whether first time in prison, other sentences)

Section 2

Timeline (flipchart paper and different coloured pens)

Now going to create a timeline of your life. Starting at the beginning, will take our time and talk through key experiences in your life. Can jump around as much as you need to. Timeline will start at birth and end at where we are now.

Section 3 (Time periods in life)

Early childhood, approx. 0–10 (timeline to be a prompt for each question)

4. Who did you live with growing up?
5. Early childcare and schooling?
6. Relationships with friends?
7. Relationship with parents/caregivers?
   (Discipline? Play? Time spent?)
8. Relationship with siblings?
9. Significant events during this time?

(Continued)

Figure 6.2 (Continued)

Adolescence/Early adulthood, approx. 10–18

10. Who living with at this point?
    (Who else in family home? New siblings? How many house moves?)
11. Schooling? Or possibly employment?
12. Relationship with family (parents and siblings) and significant others?
    (Discipline? Time spent?)
13. Relationships with friends?
14. Romantic/intimate relationships?
    (Discuss any use of violence and/or abuse)
15. Significant events during this time?
16. Substance use
17. Physical and mental wellbeing

Adulthood, 18+

18. Who living with at this point?
    (Who else in family home? New siblings? How many house moves?)
19. Schooling or employment?
20. Relationship with family (parents and siblings) and significant others?
21. Relationships with friends?
22. Romantic/intimate relationships?
    (Discuss any use of violence and/or abuse)
23. Significant events during this time?
24. Substance use
25. Physical and mental wellbeing

Section 4

Offence chain

Think of current IPVA offence that sentenced for or a significant other IPVA related offence – whichever is more prominent in your memory and that you can talk through in some detail.

- Describe the relationship you were in (with the victim)

Presenting problem

- Describe the offence
  - Describe exactly what you did
  - Describe exactly how you were feeling and thinking at the time
  - Describe the intensity of the feelings

Predisposing factors

(factors that made the person vulnerable to committing the offence)

- What else was going on in your life at that time?
  - Stressors
  - Physical and mental wellbeing
  - Emotional management
  - Substance use

Precipitating factors

- Describe the chain of events that led up to the offence
- What exact event started the whole chain of events? What was going on at the time the problem started?
- Why did it happen on that day and not on other days?
- What happened next?

Perpetuating factors

- What were the consequences of the behaviour? Immediately after? Later?
- How did people around you act immediately after? Later?
- How did you feel, think, behave immediately after? Later?

Protective factors

- Go back through the chain of events – if you had not used violence, what would have been different? What would have to change?
- What coping strategies or skills could you have used for a different outcome?
- When have there been similar situations in which you didn't use violence? Why is that? What was different?
- If this situation was to happen again in the future, what would need to be different in order for you not to become violent?

End

- *Thank you*
- *Debrief (if not returning for further interview)*

Figure 6.2 Interview guidelines

2.8 Interview schedule for a structured interview

In a structured interview, the questions, the way they are worded, and the order of questions are set prior to the interview and, the exact same questioning is used with all participants.

The questions will mostly be closed, and the interviewer will not deviate from the schedule. The standardised structure of the questions and responses requires less use of active listening skills on behalf of the researcher, so this kind of interview can be done by relatively novice interviewers. Unlike structured or semi-structured interviews, the schedule may have undergone reliability and validity testing to ensure it is robust like you would with a questionnaire.

2.9 Interview schedule for unstructured interviews

When developing a schedule for an unstructured interview, you may develop a couple of questions to begin the interview and may also have some prompt to maintain the conversation. This can be especially useful if you are a novice interviewer. As the interviewee takes the lead on the direction of the interview, you don't need to develop a set schedule of questions that you would ask of all your participants. Like in a semi-structured interview, some of your questioning (i.e., prompts) may serve to add clarity to what the participant has said. Here, well-developed listening skills are important so you can respond with relevant and useful follow-up questions

Regardless of the type of interview you are conducting, it is always a good idea to conduct a mock interview and revise your schedule accordingly. This can also help you becoming more familiar with your schedule before data collection starts.

3. CONDUCTING INTERVIEWS

Conducting interviews is not as easy as you might think, they require a number of skills and generally a lot of practice to perfect. However, a successful interview starts long before meeting the participant to ask any questions, at the planning stage. During your project planning, you should have considered the ethical aspects of the work you are going to be doing. Research in psychology (unless you are doing comparative psychological research with non-human animals) can be seen as a continuum of human-to-human interaction. Near one end of this continuum there is survey/questionnaire research, where participants fill in items and scales and return the data while remaining completely anonymous to the researcher. Interviewing is towards the other end of this continuum, where the researcher and the participant meet and interact with each other, either in a real world, face-to-face scenario, or perhaps in a digital meeting space using cameras and microphones. Given the additional complexity of such a social event between relative strangers, some serious thought must go into how this event is to be staged. A well planned and executed interview can be a fruitful and rewarding experience for both parties. However, a poorly conducted interview can be at best awkward for both parties and at worst distressing for the participant. Some things to think about are considered below.

3.1 What makes a good interview?

Informed consent

Your participants must know what the study is about, what is expected of them, what they can expect of the researcher, how will their anonymity be assured, and what the limits of confidentiality are. Typically, quotes are used from interviews in the findings of research outputs, so full confidentiality cannot be assured. Anonymity beyond the research team should be guaranteed, however, full anonymity cannot be guaranteed because the researcher will almost certainly know who they are interviewing. We never use deception in qualitative research when interviewing.

Venue and timing

Expectations about this must be outlined in advance on information sheets and arranged in practice to suit the convenience of the participant. Each meeting space has its own idiosyncrasies, and this must be accounted for in relation to the sensitivity of the topic, privacy, level of noise, etc. Both participant and researcher safety must be thoroughly risk assessed, especially when both parties are meeting face-to-face. Where possible, ask your participant if they can meet at your institution. Consider allowing plenty of time to carry out the interview. Most interviews are scheduled to last for an hour but allow time either side to set up and set down. Arrive early, be prepared, take time to get to know and build rapport with your participant, and afterwards to spend some time with them, particularly if the interview has traversed some sensitive areas, as Kvale (1996) said, to leave them feeling safe and whole.

Ig Nobel Prize

Never read the instructions

Thea Blackler and her team used interviews and diary studies to examine how people deal with instruction manuals. They found that people commonly do not read the instruction manual for products they buy and hence never use many of the features of that product. This effect was particularly pronounced in young people and educated people. For this insight Blackler's team were awarded the 2018 Ig Nobel Prize for Literature.

Blackler, A. L., Gomez, R., Popovic, V., & Thompson, M. H. (2014). Life Is too short to RTFM: How users relate to documentation and excess features in consumer products. *Interacting with Computers*, *28*(1), 27–46.

Recording

Most researchers audio record the interviews they conduct. Some may want to use video, although there should be a sound academic rationale for doing this. Security of the recordings must be considered paramount and a strategy in place for this. From a purely pragmatic point of view, if you are recording an interview in a venue such as an office or someone's home, consider any background noise that may be present. Certain frequencies of sound can be picked better than the frequency of the human voice, so you want the interview space to be as quiet as possible.

This list is not exhaustive, and each project will have its own ethical and procedural considerations.

3.2 The interview

It is important that the interviewer invests some time at the start of the interview to establish rapport and gain the interviewee's trust as this will likely result in obtaining much richer, better quality data. Gaining an interviewee's trust is important in all research interviews but particularly in instances where the research is investigating very personal or sensitive issues such as an individual's experiences of trauma or mental health difficulties. The absence of trust in the research interview may mean that the interviewee provides short and superficial answers to the questions rather than engaging in an in-depth exploration of the topic under investigation. Therefore, it is a good idea to start by explaining to the interviewee what the interview is about and what they can expect. You might want to ask your participant if they have read the information sheet and what they understand the study is about – you will be surprised how many participants cannot do this or have an inaccurate notion of what it is you are doing – this is *informed* consent. Similarly, it is unlikely that the interviewee will open up about their experiences if no sense of rapport or **affiliation** exists between themselves and the interviewer.

3.3 Active listening skills

The ability of the interviewer to use good, active listening skills throughout the interview is also crucial to its success. Active listening skills, defined as 'Involved listening with a purpose' (Barker, 1971, p. 9), refer to a set of strategies which ensure that attention is focused on the interviewee and includes both non-verbal and verbal communication. Non-verbal strategies include such things as the interviewer looking at their interviewee, orientating their body towards them and nodding and smiling when appropriate. The importance of really listening to what their interviewee is saying cannot be underestimated as without this the interviewer will be unable to probe the interviewee to provide deeper and more meaningful information. In addition to probing other key verbal active listening skills include paraphrasing, emotions labelling and summarising (Kvale, 1996):

- Paraphrasing is where the interviewer restates what the interviewee has said in their own words, for example, 'so if I have understood correctly ....'
- Emotion labelling (sometimes called 'reflecting') attempts to articulate feelings and can help interviewees view situations more objectively, for example, 'I'm sensing that you are feeling ...'.
- The interviewer should guard against the continual use of summarising but periodically it is a good idea to sum up what your interviewee has said, for example, 'so it sounds to me as if...'. Following the summary, you and your participant may then discuss what to talk about next.

There are many other techniques you can use. There are numerous websites nowadays that give further information on how to develop these skills and you can access example videos on video hosting websites such as YouTube. Try searching for these resources with terms like 'active listening skills' or 'interviewing skills'. These strategies not only help the interviewer check their own understanding of what is being said but also help rapport building as they signal to the interviewee that the interviewer is listening and is genuinely interested in what is being said. Lastly, the use of silence, strictly categorised as a non-verbal listening strategy, can be a very powerful tool in an interview (see also the Interesting Fact section below).

Interesting fact

Silence of the interviewer

Well-crafted questions are key components of an interview, but one of the most powerful and valuable techniques an interviewer can employ is silence. Skilled interviewers know when awkward pauses occur in conversations, one person is usually compelled to begin talking. They judiciously employ silent pauses to encourage the participant to self-explore, to make connections, to make sense of words and mental imagery, and to open up and choose what they will share next. Silence also allows time for the interviewer to collect their thoughts before continuing. So, next time you are interviewing someone, try inserting the occasional silent pause after a question or when a participant stops talking. Who knows, maybe your participant will give you your best data when you are saying nothing at all!

3.4 Background and aims

As noted at the start of this chapter, for the purpose of research, interviews will only ever be as good as the research question they are trying to answer. Like a quantitative study, one that is using interviews as a way of gathering data still needs to be conducted with a clear research question (or questions) in mind. This will usually follow a review of the literature, or it may be that a real-world organisation wants to know more about a certain topic or group of people. It is most likely that, when a study uses interviews for its method of data collection, this means it is a qualitative study. Therefore, the research question is usually of an exploratory kind, such as that trying to understand people's experiences of, or the way they talk about, a particular phenomenon.

Skoolkid errors

Bias

Interviews are largely exploratory in nature, which is to say that as researchers we interview our participants in order to gain knowledge about their thoughts, feelings, experiences of particular events and how they make sense of the world they inhabit. it is generally considered a good idea to have a sound knowledge of the interview topic prior to the interview, although proponents of some variations of Grounded Theory prefer to leave their background research until after data collection so that this prior knowledge has less chance of 'contaminating' the data collection process. Whichever methodology we employ, we must be extremely careful not to use this knowledge to prejudge what our interviewee is going to say. Similarly, we must guard against doing anything during the interview process that can affect the participants' responses and thus introduce bias into the data we collect. Therefore, throughout the interview the interviewer should make every attempt to remain neutral, such as in the way they ask the questions, react to a response or even the tone of their voice, as all of these factors can potentially affect the interviewees answers (Leedy & Ormrod, 2001). As we know from social psychology, people will often tell you what they think you want to hear (Bergen & Labonté, 2020).

Once a research question is developed, unlike with experimental studies, no hypothesis is stated. This is because interviews are not used to make predictions about how people will behave or what their attitudes are. However, even though there is no hypothesis to be made, the researcher still needs to be clear what the purpose of the interview is, who they want to interview, and why. For example, if the study wanted to find out about people's experiences of their children starting school, who would need to be interviewed? Clearly, we would want to interview parents or those with caregiving responsibilities, for example, in order to best explore this topic. This is because we would want to find out more about this phenomenon from the people who have experienced it (i.e., individuals who have children that have started school). However, it may be that our aim is to understand more generally the experiences of starting school, in which case perhaps we would consider interviewing teachers or maybe even the children themselves.

It is also important to think carefully early on how the data that is being gathered from the interviews will be analysed. This would also follow from the research question; if you wanted to look for patterns or themes across interviews with different people, then you might consider **Thematic Analysis**, or if you wanted to gain in-depth understanding of someone's personal experience of a phenomenon, then you would use **Interpretative Phenomenological Analysis** (IPA). Knowing early on how the data will be analysed, is crucial for understanding how to format the interview in order to get the most useful data possible.

Finally, thinking of the study holistically, the researcher should also consider what kind of knowledge is being generated, what are the potential implications and impact of this, and who would be interested in this knowledge, so a plan for **dissemination** should be developed (e.g., scientific journals, public lectures, etc.).

3.5 Design

We introduced you to different types of interviews earlier in the chapter, but this is only the first step in thinking about how to design an interview study. Broadly, there are two important points to consider here: 1) how much input the interviewer will have in the actual interview, i.e., a consideration of the balance of power between interviewer and interviewee (see earlier sections on different types of interviews); and 2) how much the design of the interview will be influenced by existing theory. A researcher might want to understand a phenomenon through the lens of a certain theoretical stance, and therefore they can design their interview with that theory in mind. There are no rights or wrongs here, but whatever decision is made needs to be justified in the write up.

Regarding the input of the interviewer, there are certain things to consider when writing the interview schedule, including:

- How to build rapport with participants.
- How many questions will be asked and so the length of the interview – individuals may find it tiring answering questions and talking intensely for long periods of time (although interviews can be split over more than one occasion).
- How sensitive the topic is – the interview may need to be led more by the interviewer if the topic is one that may be difficult for people to talk about.
- How people will be prompted to talk if they give answers to questions that are too short or do not know how to answer questions.

Whether any tools will be used to aid the interview – for example, you could make use of timeline techniques (Adriansen, 2012 and also see Chapter 9 in this book) to encourage people to talk about their life histories. Timeline techniques work well with the aforementioned narrative style of interview.

Whoa there!

Who is taking part and what might it mean for the research findings?

Interviews rely on how much the interviewee is, a) willing to share, and b) able to recall. This may sound obvious, but it is important to remember that people who are willing to take part in an interview for research probably already feel they have a story to tell and are happy to share it. They also will be those who are able to articulate their experiences and have the time and space to do so. This is important to be aware of when interpreting findings, and a good researcher will offer an interpretation of the findings in the context of the people who declined to be interviewed or who the researcher recruited, as they may have a different story to tell.

There are also many practical considerations to be thought about when carrying out interviews.

Where to interview

It is important to consider where to interview people:

- Is it comfortable enough?
- Is it private enough?
- How will the participants and the researcher be kept safe if it is a sensitive topic being talked about?

Considerations of risk

Some research is carried out on populations that have been convicted of violent offences, for example in prisons; the researcher needs to consider if there are any risks associated with these kinds of interviews.

Considerations of power

Or, is the 'space' where the interview is taking place in conflict with the research? For example, if you wanted to interview people about negative experiences with their GP, choosing the GP surgery might not help participants to feel comfortable enough to share their experiences openly.

Virtual interviews

It may be that you decide to conduct your interviews 'virtually', that is, via an online forum like a video call. In these circumstances, careful thought needs to be given to all the points above in order to get the most out of a virtual interview.

Capturing the data

Lastly, it is vital to know how the data is going to be captured during the interview. It is likely that the interview would be audio or video recorded. A researcher may just decide that taking notes is enough, however it is more normal to record audio so that this can be transcribed **verbatim**.

3.6 Findings

Once interviews have been completed, the hard work continues! Now is the time for researchers to listen back to their audio recordings and transcribe what has been said. Depending on the type of analysis being done (demonstrating again why it is important to know this early on), then transcriptions of interview data can look different. Whilst transcribing, it is important to anonymise to protect the identity of participants. Then comes the task of analysis!

Just like with a quantitative study, analysis of interview data should be transparent so that others can understand how it was carried out and how decisions were made, even if they might not agree with them. It should be clear whether analysis of data was **inductive** or **deductive**, and how that impacts the findings drawn from the data. There are varying types of analysis which can be conducted on interview data, including, but not limited to, Thematic Analysis, Interpretative Phenomenological Analysis (IPA), **Discourse Analysis**, **Conversation Analysis** and **Grounded Theory**. Remember, researchers will not use this analysis to draw conclusions about predictions of behaviour or make statements about causal inferences. However, this analysis will be used, for example, to theorise about a certain behaviour, to examine patterns across what participants say or to learn about how language is used to talk about experiences. How to conduct your analysis is a crucial element to understand for the qualitative researcher; each qualitative **methodology** has its own way of analysing data, therefore, the conventions and procedures of that methodology should be followed.

3.7 Reflections

We need to consider what the implications of our findings are. This means getting to grips with what the findings, i.e., the data, are telling us about the phenomenon that we have been examining. How do the findings fit with existing theory? If we were led by theory in the design of our interview schedule and analysis of our data, then it would be expected that we would make some comments about how our findings relate back to this theory now. It may be that the interviews revealed information that does not fit with existing theories, and therefore this paves the way for the development of a new or slightly different theory. Further research would then be able to test new theories and build on its development.

It is likely to be important to also reflect on the interviews themselves. Carrying out research of this kind can be emotionally taxing; when participants are willing to be interviewed by a near stranger, it is not unusual for them to open their hearts and tell you things that they may not have told others before. With particularly sensitive topics, the researcher needs to protect both the participant and themselves, during and after the process. This means doing two types of reflection – in-action and on-action reflection (Schön, 1983). In-action reflection is the process of reflecting in the moment, so in this case, whilst an interview is taking place. This would require the interviewer to be tuned in to the body language, mood and behaviour of the participant, in order to make sure the participant leaves the interview in a positive state of mind, not being negatively affected by the interview. Reflection on-action happens after an incident. In this case, the interviewer would therefore be reflecting how the interview went, what they learnt from it and whether they need to adapt their practice going forward.

Ethel ethics

When participants are interviewed for a study, quite often their exact words will be used in the write up of the findings. If so, it is really important for researchers to make sure they have properly anonymised the data. This means doing more than just removing their name from the transcripts. For example, someone from a particular area of the country might use a **colloquialism** that could identify where they are from, or say the name of a building that hints at their location. It is vital that the researcher is sensitive to this and pays close attention to transcribing to make sure they protect participants' identities as best they can. Participants should be made aware of this when they sign up for a study using interviews. This means an explicit statement within information sheets and consent forms highlighting to participants that their exact words are likely to be used in papers (and possibly conference presentations). They must be made aware that whilst the researcher will do everything possible to anonymise the transcript, there is still a chance (albeit a small one) that their words could be recognised.

4. EXAMPLE STUDY: FINDING MEANING IN NEAR-DEATH EXPERIENCES

4.1 The study and the researchers

Wilde, D. J., & Murray, C. D. (2009). The evolving self: Finding meaning in near-death experiences using Interpretative Phenomenological Analysis. *Mental Health, Religion and Culture*, *12*(3), 223–39.

Dr David Wilde carried out this research as part of his PhD at the University of Manchester. David now holds a senior lecturer position at Nottingham Trent University and continues to teach and research anomalous phenomena.

Dr Craig Murray was David's PhD supervisor at the University of Manchester. Craig is now a senior lecturer at Lancaster University specialising in health psychology and qualitative methods.

4.2 Background and aims to study

The Near-Death Experience (NDE) has been defined as 'a profound subjective event with transcendental or mystical elements that many people experience on the threshold of death' (Greyson, 1994, p. 460). Research over the last 40 years has mainly tried to ascertain the underlying physiological and psychological processes associated with the NDE, for example, using clinical research (e.g., Blanke et al., 2004; Van Lommel et al., 2001), or profile the personality of the experient using questionnaire surveys (e.g., Gow et al., 2003). Findings have established the NDE as a phenomenon that can happen to anyone during their lifespan (Holden et al., 2009) and experients as well-adjusted, psychologically healthy people (Greyson, 2000). Although these findings provided researchers with considerable understanding of NDEs and the people who have them, there was little research at the time that examined psychological life of the experient. No studies had considered the temporal, social, and psychological factors that impinge on the integration of the experience alongside any health issues that may have led the person to the point of NDE occurrence, or what effect these might have on the experient's sense of self or identity. This study was designed to address these shortcomings by taking a qualitative approach using Interpretative Phenomenological Analysis (IPA) (Smith et al., 2009) with the aim of exploring in-depth the lived experience of having a NDE and what meaning experients attribute to that experience.

4.3 Design

IPA is a methodology that privileges the experiential accounts of a small sample of participants therefore the interview is an ideal tool to explore the nuances and fine details of individual lived experience. Data were collected using face-to-face, semi-structured interviews with three participants.

Interviews were participant-led with the interviewer taking a non-directive role in proceedings. Building a rapport with the participant was key to the success of the interviewer gleaning rich, in-depth data, so it was important that the researcher took an empathic, non-judgmental attitude when interviewing, trying as far as possible to put the participant at ease and facilitating an open, accepting atmosphere in which the participant felt comfortable disclosing intimate experiences. This is very important for near-death experients as the circumstances of their NDE occurrence are likely to be traumatic (e.g., a cardiac arrest) and their initial construal of the experience very confusing. It is perfectly plausible that they may not have reached any resolutions as to what the NDE is or why it happened to them, even after a long period of time. At the same time, the researcher maintained a certain critical distance as they listened attentively; consciously aware of interesting and unusual instances in the accounts as they happened, which when followed up, 'facilitated fruitful diversions from the interview schedule' (Wilde, 2012, p. 127).

The interview was conducted using a pre-prepared schedule of questions organised under several topics of interest covering the background to the experience, what happened before, during and after the NDE, and questions probing the participant's understanding of the experience and their life post-NDE. The design of the schedule was crucial in order to obtain information about the biographical context of the NDE, instead of exploring the NDE in isolation as previous research had done, and to also investigate the meanings the participant held about the experience.

4.4 Findings

Interviews were transcribed and analysed using IPA according to the guidelines set out by Smith and Osborn (2007, pp. 66–75). The analysis yielded three overarching themes. The theme '*The day I nearly died: Considering NDEs biographically*' captured the NDE as an experience inextricably embedded in the flow of a person's life with 'overtures and after-effects ... which serve as wayfinders and indicators to how a person might interpret and find meaning in the experience' (Wilde & Murray, 2009, p. 228). '*New understandings: The roots of development and growth*' described how each participant reached novel understandings about their lives post-NDE. No causal links were attributed between the NDE and life decisions or changes described by participants. However, it was clear that the NDE forced them to think very deeply about the nature of themselves and their reasons for being, which once integrated, allowed them to meaningfully plan future personal development and growth. '*Being and becoming: Life post-NDE*' highlighted the struggles each participant faced trying to integrate their NDE. Psychological and physical and factors related to the NDE occurrence either aided or obstructed this process in the intervening years and challenged how well the person managed to maintain and develop their sense of self.

4.5 Reflections

Interviews allowed the researchers to deeply explore individuals' NDEs, which were unexpected and confusing. Findings revealed that the participants' lives were not affected by just having an NDE per se, rather certain prominent motifs that were more personally meaningful for them became fundamental constituents of their evolving self-identities. Participants were able to express how they were able to make sense of their NDEs, from early bewilderment about the veridicality of the experience to resolving them as positive life-affirming incidences.

LEARNING OBJECTIVES

After reading this chapter you should be able to:

- Understand what an interview is, what the four main types of interview are, how they can be used and when to use them.
- Describe what basic skills an interviewer needs to carry out a successful interview.
- Be able to consider the key design points in the development of an interview-based piece of research.

FURTHER READING

King, N., Horrocks, C., & Brooks, J. (2018). *Interviews in qualitative research* (2nd ed.). Sage.

A great foundational text for those wishing to design, plan and execute qualitative interview research. The book covers interviewing from a range of different epistemological and ontological positions.

Kvale, S., & Brinkmann, S. (2009). *Interviews: Learning the craft of qualitative research interviewing* (2nd ed.). Sage.

For novices and seasoned researchers alike, this book provides a broad but in-depth treatment of qualitative interviewing. Deals clearly and coherently with many difficult concepts, as well as providing a useful appendix of learning tasks.

Adriansen, H. K. (2012). Timeline interviews: A tool for conducting life history research. *Qualitative Studies*, *3*(1), 40–55.

An example of a specific, visual interview tool that can be planned into the design of an interview.

Magnusson, E., & Marecek, J. (2015). *Doing interview-based qualitative research: A learner's guide*. Cambridge University Press.

An in-depth guide to each stage of interview-based research, including planning, data collection and data analysis.

LINKS TO USEFUL RESOURCES

https://methods.sagepub.com/video/researching-nurse-educators-lessons-learned-from-a-phenomenological-approach?seq=3&fromsearch=true.

https://methods.sagepub.com/video/skills-for-conducting-a-semi-structured-interview.

https://methods.sagepub.com/book/the-active-interview?fromsearch=true.

7

FOCUS GROUPS

LYDIA HARKIN AND FRANCESCA CHLOE RYDING

1. INTRODUCTION

1.1 What are focus groups?

A focus group is 'a research technique that collects data through group interactions on a topic determined by a researcher' (Morgan, 1996, p. 130). This is a qualitative method designed to elicit spoken word, talk, and group interaction. Focus groups can shed light on both individual and group perceptions, views, and attitudes on a focused topic. Key components of a focus group include one shared space, a group of participants, and a **moderator**.

Focus groups are a versatile method of data collection. After the advent of widespread internet use in the 2000s, focus groups have also developed to take two styles: the traditional face-to-face focus group and the online focus group. We will explore these two different designs using real research examples in this chapter and consider their relative strengths and limitations.

Interesting fact

Psychology at the movies

You might recognise the term 'focus group' from TV and films such as *Mad Men* (2007–2015), *Parks and Recreation* (2009–2015), *The Thick of It* (2009–2012) and *Vice* (2018). In popular culture, focus groups are associated with marketing and politics. However, focus groups have been embedded in social science research from their inception. Researchers Merton and Kendall in 1946 used focus groups to understand the social effects of wartime propaganda. More recently, focus groups have found a home in social, health, and clinical psychology research, as the group interactions and social data they produce can work well with ideas of **Social Constructionism**, commonly applied in these areas of psychology.

1.2 What data will be produced?

Focus groups are often viewed as the sister to interviews. Interviews and focus groups both involve a researcher speaking to the participants and recording their views for qualitative analysis. However, focus groups contain a different dynamic to interviews. A focus group rarely involves an interviewer asking individual questions to individual participants in the group. The focus group interviewer is known as a moderator. The moderator's role is to help participants speak to one another. As a focus group unfolds, participants are encouraged to interact with one another; they may discuss shared views, disagreements, challenge one another, and alter the focus of the conversation. As such, focus groups stand apart from interviews with their dynamic group setting.

1.3 Why are focus group interactions important?

Kitzinger (1994) suggested five main advantages that researchers gain from facilitating interactions in focus groups. The interactions:

- Highlight attitudes, priorities, language, and group level understanding;
- Encourage a variety of communication from participants (including non-verbal cues of agreement and disagreement such as nodding, tutting, as well as verbal interjections and arguments);

- Help to identify group norms (i.e., what groups consider normal and abnormal attitudes, behaviours, and perceptions);
- Provide insights into the operation of social processes when particular knowledge is discussed (e.g., by showing what is censured within the group);
- Encourage open conversation about embarrassing subjects and facilitate the expression of ideas that might be left underdeveloped in an interview.

Participants are likely to consider the presence of the other people in the focus group before giving their answers in an unfolding conversation, which is difficult to stage or predict. This means that focus groups have a huge potential to produce diverse views according to who is recruited and how they are put together. Due to these sensitive social dynamics, the data produced may not be exactly **replicable**. For this reason, focus groups have attracted criticism for producing **subjective** data. Indeed, this method would not be suitable if a researcher were searching for **objective** data, for instance, to objectively categorise people's attitudes. However, some research aims require us to understand differing subjective views and different interactions that occur amongst groups.

It must be recognised that focus groups may be designed to elicit conversation and social dynamics, but they do not produce '**naturalistic**' data. The researcher(s) select participants who often (but not always) do not know one another, place them in a room or online space of their design, with the purpose of recording a conversation on a topic of the researcher's choosing. This remains a 'false' situation if you compare this with real world conversations that you will have unprompted and uncontrolled amongst your friends and family.

1.4 Summary

In summary, a main strength of the focus group is its ability to capture individual perspectives, group level agreement and disagreement, and interactions about a topic. Looking at it this way, a focus group is more than the sum of its parts; more than just a collection of views on a topic; it allows researchers to observe the topic of discussion in a social space.

Cultural context

Is this a good method for seldom heard voices?

The research setting can be intimidating or inaccessible for populations who are not familiar with researchers, or who may have had negative experiences with research and the concept of being studied and recorded by others. For example, research studies in the UK are commonly conducted in English with written English language components. Linguistically diverse groups may not be able to complete written English language surveys or experiments. Fortunately, verbal focus groups do not require a level of English literacy to be eligible to participate. This can make focus groups a good method for populations who are seldomly heard in research. The group setting also means that the participants outnumber the researchers, which can implicitly offer safety for participants who might feel less comfortable being examined one on one by a researcher. However, it is important to note that simply holding a focus group does not put culturally and linguistically diverse groups at ease. Halcome et al. (2007) highlighted that adaptations to the research process are sometimes required if a researcher is to respectfully research specific populations. For instance, in a study of Diabetes in Canadian first nations people, Berthelette et al. (2001) identified that audio recording and note-taking was inappropriate and intrusive to this group who placed great importance on their oral histories. The researchers altered their method of recording data by following each focus group with a one-to-one meeting between the moderator and a community elder to confirm the perspectives shared in the focus group and used this meeting to write up the study findings.

2. FOCUS GROUP BASICS

2.1 Aims in focus group research

Considering the relative strengths and weaknesses of focus group research, this method is suited to studies which aim to understand the following:

- A phenomenon under investigation that is socially constructed;
- A topic involving group processes;
- How people think and act in social settings;
- How topics or concepts are contextualised both within and across research settings;
- Areas where little is known in the literature about the topic of interest. (Cyr, 2019)

Focus group aims are usually non-directional, exploratory, and direct the study to *understand* the views of the participants. The focus group will generate interactional data, and so it is best suited to aims which are focused on social and interactional topics.

Exploratory research aims mean that researchers do not approach focus group studies with hypotheses. A hypothesis is an explicit statement, based on literature, that outlines how the researcher has made sense of a topic before consulting with participants. On the contrary, in focus group research, we give a topic to a group of people participants and ask them to make sense of it.

This style of research is known as **emic** rather than **etic** research (Cyr, 2019). This means that participants' views of a subject are given priority over the researcher's view of a subject. In practice, it is unlikely that a researcher will be naïve to the topic. All research methods should be supported by a good knowledge of the literature. However, the evidence base for a qualitative topic may overlook or underrepresent the views of the participants. For this reason, the researcher must acknowledge that there may be gaps in their own understanding of what the participant knows.

Ig Nobel Prize

Crazy cat ladies?

In 2013, researchers analysed the health records of over 750 people who have visited their doctors with a bite from a cat (Hanaur, Ranakirshnan, & Seyfried, 2013). They found an increased statistical likelihood that these patients would have been diagnosed with depression *at some time in their lives* – and this likelihood was higher for women than for men. The researchers went on to suggest that women with cat bites should be screened for depression.

We think that there is not enough evidence to understand why there might be a high likelihood of these phenomena occurring together. If we think there might be a relationship between mental health and pet ownership, why don't we ask cat owners about pet ownership and mental health? There may be a diverse range of reasons to explain why people own cats and what role pet ownership plays in mental illness and mental wellness. To address this, a focus group of pet owners, with a heterogenous mix of genders, age, mental health diagnoses, and living status (alone or with others) might help to collect a more nuanced picture of what pet ownership means to individuals who may have had a mental health diagnosis in their lifetime.

2.2 Focus group design

There are various ways to design a focus group. The design decision should be driven by the best way to elicit group interactions. In other words, the correct combination of features must allow people to comfortably discuss the chosen topic. There are few hard and fast rules about focus group designs, as settings will influence groups of people differently. However, there are general recommendations, and strategic differences between offline and online focus group design features, which we will discuss in this section.

2.3 Face-to-face focus groups

All focus groups take place in spaces which are selected and organised by the researcher. In a physical or face-to-face focus group, the venue should allow participants to comfortably share eye contact with one another, and this often results in a group of participants sat in a circle or around a table. Physical focus groups are typically one to two hours in length. A researcher will usually run several focus groups with different participants in order to ensure that a range of viewpoints have been recorded.

The benefits to this face-to-face approach are that the in-person connection should allow the groups to quickly establish interpersonal connections, allowing them to communicate with one another more easily than when compared with the online versions of the focus group. However, attending a physical focus group can be very time consuming for the participants. They are required to travel to the chosen location at a fixed time, which may not be suitable for all potential participant candidates.

2.4 Online synchronous focus groups

Synchronous focus groups are those which occur online at a set time, and the conversations unfold between participants with real-time responses. These focus groups are the closest online version to the traditional focus group. Participants are invited to an online space and the moderator facilitates interaction between a group of participants. This may involve video communication, or text-based communication, or both.

An advantage of an online synchronous approach as opposed to the traditional focus group is that it may be more convenient for participants to attend. There are no transport costs and the participant can join from any location, provided they have suitable equipment and internet access to participate. However, even with video technology, it is not possible for participants to establish eye contact, and so turn-taking within the conversations may be more difficult to establish within the group conversations. Visual conversational cues provide some of the richness of conversational interaction, and so there is some argument that this form of focus group may be more task-focus and less flexible in contrast to a face-to-face style (King, Horrocks, & Brooks, 2018). Additionally, some participants have reported struggling with synchronous focus groups which use text as a primary tool of communication (Williams, Clausen, Robertson, Peacock, & McPherson, 2012). The text communication style requires fast and confident typing skills to contribute to a current conversation, and this can feel chaotic to individuals who might be slower to read and respond to text conversations.

2.5 Online asynchronous focus groups

Asynchronous focus groups are spaces which are set up for focus group discussion, but the participants can access the conversation and post their responses at any time during a long set period, such as over the course of several hours or days. This can work like an email chain or a discussion forum. This format necessitates the focus groups to be largely text based, though the platform might allow people to share images or emojis.

Asynchronous focus groups can be convenient for participants who are typically too time poor for a traditional or synchronous focus group, or individuals who are living in different time zones. Less data may be produced in this type of focus group, which is to say that text-based communication is often shorter than verbally communicated conversation. Additionally, this conversation poses challenges for detecting when participants are distressed and may wish to withdraw. However, asynchronous communication may allow people to feel less judged by the other members of the focus group, and this might enable people to share views which might be too taboo or stigmatising to share in a face to face conversation. As such, for some topics, asynchronous focus groups might be richer in terms of what views are shared (Williams et al., 2012).

2.6 Sampling participants

When selecting participants for focus groups, researchers need to sample from participants who have views or experience of the chosen topic.

Whoa there!

OK, so we just put people together who have the same experience of a phenomena?

The researchers will also want to consider what level of diversity they want to reflect in their focus groups, in order to facilitate discussions that have depth and variety. If participants are all too similar in terms of their views (also known as **homogenous** groups) then the conversations may quickly form strong norms, and it may be difficult for anyone with a different view to share amongst the group. Alternatively, if the participants are vastly different (or **heterogenous**) then the group may struggle to find common ground and the participants may not feel comfortable interacting with one another.

This is a tricky balance, and indeed, there is some disagreement in the literature about this approach. On one hand, Gibbs (1997) recommended that focus group researchers should strive to represent diversity, e.g., in terms of gender, age, socio-demographic background, ethnicity, and education in each focus group, and that participants should ideally be strangers to one another before the focus group begins. On the other hand, Paolo Freire (from Kamberelis & Dimitriadis, 2011) believed that a homogenous group of people can be extremely valuable for capturing insight into individuals who share common experiences, and who may know one another through friendship groups, political debating clubs, shared illness groups and other defining shared characteristics.

So which is the correct approach? Well, it all comes down to the study aim. If the researchers are trying to understand or explore a tight-knit community or concept within a seldom heard group, then it may be appropriate to hold more homogenous focus groups. Alternatively, if the researchers are exploring a cultural phenomenon which is known by a diversity of individuals, a more heterogenous style may be more suitable.

2.7 Group size

Face-to-face and synchronous online group size

Morgan (1996) advised 6–10 participants would form an ideal sized offline focus group and this recommendation is often replicated for synchronous focus groups online. This may be because the interactions offline and in online synchronous focus groups are similar, and so the groups are designed similarly. As focus group data relies on participant interactions, focus groups need to be an optimum size for managing a discussion. A group too small might not generate ample discussion, whereas a group too large may be difficult to manage.

Asynchronous online group size

Asynchronous focus groups have commonly been successful with between 12–14 participants in a group (Williams, 2009). There have even been reports of much larger focus group studies which have been successful, notably an asynchronous focus group of 57 people in a study of inflammatory bowel disease patients (Stewart and Williams, 2005). Asynchronous focus groups can recruit more participants than their counterparts because they run for a longer time and tend to have less communication activity at any one time point. In fact, this longer time frame can lead to participants dropping out from the conversations, and so larger samples within the focus groups can buffer for some of this loss of participants.

Skoolkid errors

Small sample size

It is very common in student reflections on focus groups to see the method criticised for a small sample size. Often, a small sample within focus groups is necessary for creating a dynamic conversation. If a focus group contained a room of 100 people, it would be unlikely that all individuals in that room would speak to one another and so the data needed for the study would not be as in-depth. Instead, let's remember that small focus group samples are required to elicit in-depth interactional data about a topic. For some topics, this can be the necessary route for furthering understanding.

2.8 The moderator

Interviewing skills covered in the previous chapter are important for focus groups; active listening, ethical sensitivity, and the ability to probe for more in-depth answers are all important interviewing skills. Uniquely in focus groups, the researcher present also acts as a moderator to manage the group, their interactions, and the direction of their group conversations.

Moderators in face-to-face and video/verbal online focus groups

The twofold aims of the moderator are to ensure a group keeps up a flow of conversation, and to ensure that the discussion focuses on the research topic (Wilkinson, 2004). King, Horrocks and Brooks (2018) suggested key types of interjections that moderators can make to group discussions which can help to facilitate view sharing:

- Non-reflective listening: Moderators illustrate that they are listening in face-to-face settings by nodding along to responses, and in video or audio call focus groups by minimal responses (such as mm-hmm sounds). These non-verbal sounds of acknowledgement are non-judgemental, minimal, and can simultaneously help verbal participants to feel acknowledged whilst building a positive environment for more reserved participants to join in.
- Reflective listening: Moderators can show that they are listening in a non-judgemental way by using techniques such as asking for elaboration. They can mirror back the views of one or more speakers by reflecting back phrases or feelings conveyed, and summarising key points and differences of views.

Moderators in text-based synchronous and asynchronous focus groups

Moderators for text-based focus groups face a greater challenge when trying to convey active listening. After all, non-reflective active listening often involves remaining quiet and interjecting only where conversation may not flow or stall. It is challenging in a text-based environment to convey a sense of presence and a sense of quiet listening. Im, Guevera, and Chee et al. (2007) used moderation techniques in their asynchronous focus group study which were guided by the aim of ensuring adequate participation. They contributed to their own focus group only to ask participants to remain on topic. They asked participants to ensure they visited their focus group at least twice a month, and emailed those who had not contributed.

2.9 The schedule

Regardless of the style of focus group, the schedule of the focus group should be designed and prepared in advance. It should help the group to discuss in and around the topic of focus. Furthermore, research papers reporting focus groups should detail what the schedule contained. Focus groups typically have a beginning, a middle, and an end:

The beginning of a focus group should be designed to help the participants to relax and open discussions in an ethically sensitive way (Barbour, 2007). It is important to set ground rules at this stage, including explaining the ethical issues involved with the research participation, explaining how the focus group will run, how it will be recorded, and the role of the moderator. The researchers may also run an ice-breaker task to encourage participants to become acquainted with one another and to ease them into the unusual situation of sharing their views in a group-based research session.

Much of the guidance on good interview schedules applies to focus group schedules. This includes designing questions which are opening, rather than leading. Questions may be accompanied by prompts which encourage the moderator to actively listen and probe for more information from participants. King and Horrocks (2010) suggest that focus group questions should be short and aimed at a group, rather than at individuals. Some focus groups utilise ***discussion stimuli*** such as images or text, or use exercises (Kitzinger, 1995) to give participants insight into the chosen topic and prompt a discussion. News excerpts, advertisements, stills or clips from television, or images are some examples. These resources are paired with open-ended questions which stimulate discussions about the research topic.

It is imperative that moderators leave enough time to debrief participants at the end of the discussion. Discussions may have been sensitive or divisive, and this may result in concerns after the focus group about how the researcher and fellow participants may then utilise the discussions they shared. As researchers, we do not want to compromise the wellbeing of our participants in the name of collecting data. Thus, a debrief often involves reiterating the ethical information shared at the beginning of the focus group.

2.10 Analysing focus groups

A transcript for a focus group gives researchers a word-by-word account of the discussion. It is this transcript that the researchers use to find meaning from the data. As a transcript is much too long, often meandering, and complicated, the researcher must find a way to break the transcript down and rearrange it into meaningful data. The data are often (but not always) rearranged into themes with subthemes, and example quotations are used for these themes in publications. This way, a researcher can examine what is said in a focus group and frame the most important findings for a wider audience.

In qualitative analysis, we rely on set styles and standards to help this analysis process be applied logically and rigorously. Before data collection begins, the researcher(s) identify what **methodology** will be most suitable for the research question. While **methods** are the ways in which we collect data, the term methodology captures our entire approach to the research. This approach includes what we believe about the nature of research, what we believe data can capture, and that we believe about how methods capture data. The methodology provides rules for data analysis which match the researcher's aim. There are lots of different methodologies, such as Grounded Theory, and Phenomenological, or Discursive approaches. It is not the purpose of this chapter to describe those methodologies in depth (for an overview see Willig, 2013). However, it is important that the researcher selects the appropriate methodology and applies the analysis according to the methodology. The methodology can change the type of data examined during the analysis and turned it into themes.

3. EXAMPLE STUDIES: SMARTPHONES AND BODY IMAGE

To provide you with working examples of focus group research, we will present you with two studies, taken from the same research group, which utilise two different styles of focus groups.

3.1 The authors

Dr Lydia Harkin is a Psychology lecturer at Nottingham Trent University, and has been researching the role of digital technology in social support and health since 2013. She has used a range of methods in her career, but primarily identifies as a qualitative researcher, utilising a range of qualitative methods and methodologies to understand the interaction between digital technologies and health.

Francesca C. Ryding is currently a PhD candidate at Nottingham Trent University researching the influence of social networking sites on wellbeing, body image and body dysmorphic disorder. Within her research, she has employed both qualitative and mixed-method designs to help further understand the relationship between social networking sites and wellbeing.

Dr Daria Kuss is an Associate Professor, a Chartered Psychologist and a member of the International Gaming Research Unit and the Cyberpsychology Group at Nottingham Trent University. She led the two studies described in this chapter and is a leading international researcher in the impact of smartphone and internet technology on wellbeing.

3.2 Study 1: A a face-to-face focus group

Harkin, L. J., & Kuss, D. (2020). 'My smartphone is an extension of myself': A holistic qualitative exploration of the impact of using a smartphone. *Psychology of Popular Media*. Advance online publication. https://doi.org/10.1037/ppm0000278

Why do we use our smartphones habitually, in inappropriate settings, and when we believe that our use is causing us harm? A rapidly developing body of research in the field of CyberPsychology is exploring smartphone use and its impact on wellbeing. There are numerous survey studies in this field that focus on the concept of smartphone 'dependence' (Billieux, 2012). Smartphone dependency is often discussed in terms of overuse, pathological use, obsessive use, symptoms of impulsivity and lack of control (e.g., Laconi et al., 2018). However, these analyses are often based on negative symptoms, and don't account for the growing role the smartphones play in everyday life, for instance when facilitating social connections and workplace use. Moreover, as the apparent integration with smartphone technology and society increases, the line between 'overuse' and 'necessity' use may become blurred. Understanding the social importance of smartphones and apps might give us a more holistic, rounded perspective of how the devices interact with wellbeing.

Study one aimed use face-to-face focus groups to understand the social importance of smartphone use, and the role that the device plays in the lives of the users.

3.3 The design of the face-to-face focus groups

We selected face-to-face focus groups to benefit from the increased opportunities for interpersonal connection that can be found in traditional focus groups. In a dedicated university research room, participants could share eye contact and non-verbal cues, as well as discussing the content of the semi-structured schedule. Three focus groups were scheduled for 90 minutes each.

The face-to-face level of connection was important to our study, as we opted to recruit participants to two heterogenous focus groups (Group 1 n=9 participants, Group2 n=6 participants). We diversified these groups in terms of age and gender. We also recruited one homogenous focus group of participants who were friends. The same schedule was used in all focus groups. In this way, we took the best of both worlds in terms of diversified views shared in the heterogenous focus groups, while established group dynamics explored in the homogenous focus group (group 4 n=6).

Our focus groups were designed to explore participants' views of smartphone use in different elements of every day life. Therefore, we designed open ended questions for the groups, and paired these with static images of smartphones being used in a situation which corresponded with our open-ended question. The images corresponded with our open-ended questions, and are summarised in the table below:

Table 7.1 A focus group schedule using discussion stimulus

Open-Ended Question	Discussion stimulus image
What do people think about the amount of time spent on a smartphone?	Smartphone in a hand;
How do smartphones contribute to the ways you communicate?	A romantic couple embracing while looking at smartphones;
Can you discuss places where mobile phones should not be used? What are the norms?	Commuters using smartphones; smartphone user in a library and cinema;
What might be risky about smartphones? How might smartphones influence safety/security?	Smartphone user crossing the road; Smartphone user exercising.

3.4 Study 2: The online focus group study

Ryding, F. C., Kuss, D., Kanjo, E., & Harkin, L. The impact of social networking site-use on body image and body dysmorphic disorder, PhD Thesis in preparation.

The premise for Study two:

Applications used within smartphones may have an interactive relationship with individuals' social worlds and their sense of self. One aspect that has gained attention over recent years is the influence of social networking sites (SNS) like Instagram on body image satisfaction; the evaluation of one's appearance. Self-report measures have shown us that app use and body image dissatisfaction might be related, and experimental research has shown that certain features of SNS, such as likes and comments, may cause appearance comparisons and lower self-esteem (Tiggemann & Zaccardo, 2015; Tiggemann, Hayden, Brown, & Veldhuis, 2018). Passive SNS use (i.e., scrolling) has been linked to body image dissatisfaction due to users comparing themselves to others on the same SNS platform. However, previous studies do not offer insight into how wider social elements like self-promotion and learning about others play a role in the way that people engage with Instagram and how they reflect this back on their own image. We need to explore social attitudes to Instagram to develop a greater understanding on the interaction between SNS, our body image, and well-being.

Study two aimed to use online synchronous focus groups to explore SNS (Instagram) users' perceptions of SNS and to understand how SNS platforms influence body image.

3.6 Conducting the online focus group

Synchronous text-based groups were chosen to explore how SNS platforms influence body image. This approach was selected due to the ability to be involved in a real-time conversation, allowing interaction and discussion between participants. A text-based approach was used for the focus groups using a platform that enabled both instant messaging, and the ability to see when participants were typing. As the participants were existing SNS users, this was a convenient and familiar method for their participation.

Five focus groups were conducted consisting of three female groups (group one n=4; group two n=3; group 3 n=4) and two male groups (group 1 n=4; group 2 n=3). Single gender groups were formed as we wanted to explore how perspectives of SNS and body image satisfaction may be discussed amongst male and female users. We also anticipated that participants might be more comfortable discussing body image issues amongst groups of their own gender. All participants were users of the Instagram so that we could gain insight into body image influences in regard to this platform.

When preparing the semi-structured schedule, the introduction to the study, ground rules of the online discussion and the main questions for discussion were written clearly and in full sentences. When conducting the online groups, we loaded the focus group schedule in a separate window to the focus group discussion. This allowed us to copy and paste longer pieces of text (e.g., the introduction to the study) and the questions efficiently. We used a platform where we could see participants' typing and this helped to observe who was participating and when the moderator was needed to facilitate the discussion or move onto the next question. Probes were also used to reassure participants that their contribution to the discussion was valuable (e.g., 'you're drawing on some really interesting points here') to validate participants' contribution and encourage further.

Ethel ethics

Protecting participant identity

In face-to-face focus groups, researchers protect participant identity by asking the participants to keep one another's participation and comments confidential, and by removing identifying information from transcripts and publications. Virtual focus groups pose an additional challenge to maintaining participant anonymity. Existing social media platforms that enable instant messaging often require respondents to log in using a name to join a chat. If participants already have an account registered in their name with the platform you are using, or if participants input their full name when logging into the online chat, they can compromise their own identity and anonymity. When planning the group, it is therefore important to consider whether the platform you use can enable use of pseudonyms or alternative names, and to make sure participants are aware that the name they choose will be available to be seen by others within the group discussion.

3.7 Analysing the focus groups in study 1

In study one, we used the methodology constructivist grounded theory (Charmaz, 2006) which posits that communication reflects shared meanings, interactional processes, and social roles within groups (driven by principles symbolic interactionism, see Blumer, 1986). This allowed analysis of the way individuals framed their own smartphone use, and the way they positioned and analysed the smartphone use of others in the focus group discussion.

Focus groups revealed that participants placed a great importance on the role of smartphones in their lives and the lives of their friends and families. Smartphones were framed in these focus groups as practical, social, and enhancing the ability of human begins to connect. We named this theme *an extension of the self*. We also formed subthemes from the data to explain the various ways the participants believed the devices interacted with themselves and with others' sense of self. Firstly, smartphones and apps were highly customisable, proving a space for *externalising identity*. Secondly, a *constant connectivity* made smartphones seem like an important presence in their social world. Thirdly, the devices were utilised in romantic and friendship connections, acting to *mediate intimacy*. Fourthly, device use and social media sharing was framed as a way to *authenticate experiences*. Finally, when device use was automatic and habitual, groups believed that people had *forfeited agency*.

Looking at this theme structure, you can see that the group conversation has been analysed to represent how individuals are influenced by smartphone devices. For instance, the central category (which is a word for theme used in Constructivist Grounded Theory) is named 'an extension of the self' which reflects inwardly on the individual. However, the focus group method used to obtain this data means that the themes reflect shared meanings, rather than simply individual feelings. This means that participants constructed this idea that themselves and others were extended by smartphones. Similarly, the subcategories reflected examples the groups used to justify and explain this perception. We should leave this analysis with the impression that the groups of participants believe smartphones to be powerful and essential devices with a range of influence over people.

3.8 Analysing the focus groups in study 2

In study two, we analysed our data using thematic analysis, informed by social constructionism (Braun & Clarke, 2006; Burr, 2015). Social constructionism states that knowledge and meanings are developed in coordination with others. Synchronous focus groups were suited to this method, as the online discussions allowed for group interactions between individuals and the ability to see how each group member narrated their perceptions of SNS.

The focus group analysis revealed four themes illustrating the integration of SNS sites in participants' daily lives. One theme, *Staying cautious on SNS,* revealed the group expectations of how to manage the impact of SNS on body image, including two sub-themes; *agency and awareness of SNS* and *Development of SNS use:*

Take a look at this short summary of the theme *Staying cautious on SNS.*

Focus groups understood negative impacts of SNS through the lens of information they had witnessed in the news media and news outlets. In response to news media, the group discussions emphasised the importance of being cautious when using SNS. Participants framed SNS use to be an integrated behaviour within daily routines and agreed that it was the user's responsibility to be aware of how SNS content may impact body image satisfaction, and to take control of viewing content to mitigate these impacts. When discussing this *agency and awareness,* participants referred to actively unfollowing content that may influence the user to feel negatively about their body image. This conscious engagement with SNS was also regarded by participants as a way of *developing SNS use*, by providing the ability to see what type of content was most beneficial to user's wellbeing.

With this theme, you can see that we have analysed the group discussion to reflect the groups' shared understanding of using SNS. Here, the theme and subthemes represent knowledge that has arisen from the interaction between participants during conversation. In the subtheme Agency and Awareness this was a group expectation; the analysis revealed that there are social expectations for individuals to have vigilance in their SNS use. Moreover, these social expectations are derived from a wider media climate of negative news stories. Through this analysis, we have been able to see that staying cautious is an individual state, created by a social climate of group and wider societal expectations.

4. REFLECTION AND SUMMARY

So, considering what we have learned about focus groups in this chapter, how do we reflect on what we learn from a piece of focus group research?

4.1 Focus group evidence can extend understanding of current theory

Focus group research should not be conducted to simply confirm an idea or knowledge which is established. After all, if you already have evidence that a social process exists, you can test for this using quantitative methods. Focus group research is often conducted to illuminate on processes that we don't have in-depth empirical evidence for. This means that focus group findings should then be discussed in terms of how they provide extensions for theory or how they change what we understand in the existing literature.

4.2 Focus groups can be handy in mixed-methods studies

Focus groups are favoured by mixed methods researchers as they can be a time-efficient way to collect qualitative data, when compared to interview studies. A researcher can conduct 18 individual interviews over 18 hours, or they can conduct three six-person focus groups in six hours. This efficiency can be particularly practical for mixed-methods studies which often aim to collect a diverse range of evidence to be integrated with different types of data.

4.3 Focus groups pose unique challenges for privacy

All studies post unique ethical challenges that researchers must be aware of and protect against in order to produce ethical research which respects the participants and produces findings that will offer an honest impact on knowledge. Focus groups have a unique ethical challenge in maintaining the privacy of participants (Barbour, 2007). This is because participants in a focus group will see and interact with one another, and therefore participation cannot be truly confidential, unlike almost all other forms of methods. For online versions of focus groups, researchers must also consider the potential privacy implications of where the focus groups are being hosted. If a focus group is hosted through a third party company server, for instance via Skype, or via a social media instant messenger, then the third party company could potentially access this data. Researchers need to be aware, and need to inform participants, that full confidentiality on such websites is not possible because the networks are not in the control of the researcher.

LEARNING OBJECTIVES

So what have you learned?

- Focus groups are a versatile qualitative research method that can take place face to face, online in real time, or online in discussions over days or weeks;
- Focus groups can capture individual and group views on a focused topic;
- Focus group ideal participant samples vary, and researchers decide to hold heterogenous or homogenous focus groups;
- Focus groups require a moderator who uses a semi-structured topic guide and help the groups to interact;
- Focus group analysis is guided by the overarching methodology, which should be suitable for the study aims;
- Focus groups are often combined with other forms of data collection in mixed methods study because they are an efficient way of collecting multiple participant perspectives.

FURTHER READING

If you are interested in doing online synchronous focus groups, the following article provides some considerations:

Fox, F. E., Morris, M., & Rumsey, N. (2007). Doing synchronous online focus groups with young people: Methodological reflections. *Qualitative Health Research, 17*(4), 539–47.

For somemore information and reflections on online asynchronous focus groups, read:

Williams, S., Clausen, M., C., Robertson, A., Peacock, S., & McPherson, K. (2012). Methodological reflection on the use of asynchronous online focus groups in health research. *International Journal of Qualitative Methods, 11*(4), 368–83.

If you are preparing to run focus groups, the following book offers a thorough practical guide to focus groups and to remote group interviews:

King, N., Horrocks, C., & Brooks, J. (2018). *Interviews in qualitative research*. SAGE Publications Limited.

To understand a little more about the philosophical positioning of focus group methods in social science research, read:

Willig, C. (2013), From recipes to adventures. In C. Willig, *Introducing qualitative research in psychology: Adventures in theory and method* (pp. 1–13). Open University Press.

LINK TO USEFUL RESOURCE

Look up SAGE's case study online for a detailed summary of the practicalities and challenges of conducting race-based focus groups, i.e., **homogenous** focus groups with people of the same race, ethnicity, and culture, as a way to better understand groups' perspective of healthcare: Harder, B. M., & Adams, C. (2020). Conducting race-based focus groups on health issues: Confronting challenges in design, implementation, and analysis. *SAGE Research Methods Cases*. https://dx.doi.org/10.4135/9781529743630

8

NATURALLY OCCURRING DATA

ANASTASIA ROUSAKI, EVA PRIKRYLOVA, KRISTINA NEWMAN AND SARAH SEYMOUR-SMITH

1. INTRODUCTION TO NATURALISTIC DATA

Within psychology, qualitative research tends to be associated with collecting interview or focus group data. In contrast to this, in this chapter we focus on what is termed **naturally occurring data**. Naturally occurring data are often referred to with a number of terms; you may encounter expressions such as 'transcripts of naturally occurring interactions' 'natural conversational materials' 'natural conversation' 'naturally occurring talk in interaction' and even 'actually occurring data' (Speer, 2002). These terms often refer to similar types of data. They describe textual, audio or video recordings of naturally occurring interactions; conversations which unfold in everyday life, or in workplace interactions, and would have occurred without being a direct result of a researcher's actions (Taylor, 2001). The naturalness here does not necessarily imply that the participants are acting in a calm, comfortable manner. It suggests that the interactions in question would have taken place even if the participants were neither recorded nor observed. Thus, these interactions would be authentic, original, and would not be influenced by the presence of the researcher or the recording equipment (Taylor, 2001).

Interesting fact

The dead scientist test

As Potter (2002) stated, to understand whether data are naturally occurring, we should subject them to the 'dead scientist test': would the interactions take place (and would they have taken place in the exact same form), even if the researcher died this morning while they were driving to work? For example, a research interview would not exist without a researcher setting up and conducting the interview. However, a doctor/patient consultation would remain the same.

To further explain naturally occurring data, we will contrast them with their counterpart, known as **contrived or researcher generated data**. Such data are the direct result of the researcher's design and are deliberately generated by a researcher for the purpose of a study. An example of that would be a researcher deciding to conduct focus groups to discuss men's perceptions of feminism. The data produced in these remits demand a high level of involvement on the researcher's part and would not exist apart from of their research project activities (Speer, 2002). Thus, in the aforementioned example, the researcher would have to design the focus group study, arrange the time and place they will take place, discuss the participants' availability, and come up with a focus group schedule of topics to discuss.

1.1 A critique of interview data

Within psychology, proponents of the move towards naturally occurring data stem from researchers whose focus is on social interaction, notably discursive psychologists. In their critique of interviews, Potter and Hepburn (2005) highlighted a number of problems with interview data. Here we highlight a few of those issues. One key concern was that more attention was needed to acknowledge the interviewer's role in the production of the data (Potter & Hepburn, 2005). For example, they claim that interview questions are full of social science agendas and categories and argue that researchers are steering the participants in a particular direction. For example, Sarah Seymour-Smith was interested in studying men's health and masculinity. The interview schedule she created was influenced by research in the area and specifically asked questions such as 'it is often said that a lot of men find it difficult to talk about their health. Is this true of your experience?'. Thus, a focus on masculinity was already presented rather than this topic rising naturally as it might on, say, a health support forum.

This leads to another point about the '**footing positions**' of both interviewer and interviewee and the various categories that each represent. If we contextualise this, sticking with the masculinity and health example above, Seymour-Smith was the interviewer as well as the researcher in the study, and also the ex-partner of somebody who had testicular cancer (a point that she made the interviewees aware of). The interviewees were recruited to the study because they were men who had either prostate cancer or testicular cancer. Yet, at times they were asked to speak from the category of a man. With the latter category, the researcher is effectively treating the participant as somebody who can offer valid scientific explanations and theories regarding the category of people (men in this instance) that they represent.

In qualitative research papers, Potter and Hepburn (2005) also note that authors often delete the interviewer's input, such as their questions or comments. This results in the participant's answers being treated as independent statements which are taken out of context. This misses the co-constructed nature of such interactions – participants' react to specific questions they are asked thus a 'proper' analysis needs to include these or the analysis could be misleading. In addition, Potter and Hepburn (2005) urge researchers to try to capture the delivery of the interaction in the transcription process.

Typically, research papers present a verbatim record of what was said (i.e., a simplified account which does not include things such as laughter, pauses, overlaps and non-verbal interaction). However, this misses things of possible interest in the analysis. To remedy both these points, the interviewer's input (such as questions, prompts) should be included in data excerpts and a Jeffersonian (Jefferson, 1985) transcription system employed. We discuss the **Jefferson transcription** later in this chapter, but it captures most of hearable and visible conversational features and uses line numbers so any analytical claims can be evidenced by specific line/lines within the transcript (see example below). Potter and Hepburn (2005) concluded that naturally occurring data should be used for data collection where possible.

Whoa there!

The distinction between contrived and naturally occurring data, and the preference towards the latter with discursive approaches, has received substantial criticism. Speer (2002) raised a number of points, suggesting it is an unsustainable distinction. It is quite common for researchers to audio or video record data, and one of the bedrocks of the BPS code of ethics is to obtain informed consent from the participants. These two preconditions constitute a practically impossibility to collect data 'even if the researcher was never born'. Moreover, it is quite difficult to conduct qualitative research without a recorder that the participants are not aware of. When taking these factors into consideration, all data can be considered contrived (Speer, 2002). There is also an implication that naturally occurring data are better precisely due to the lack of researcher presence. This suggestion paints the researcher in the light of a contaminating element to the dataset (Speer, 2002). However, interviews and focus groups also contain spontaneous interactions (Griffin, 2007).

1.2 When are naturally occurring data used?

Only a few analytic traditions appear to show a preference towards naturally occurring data. Namely, some of the most prominent are discursive psychology, conversation analysis and membership categorisation analysis (Seymour-Smith, 2015; Stokoe, 2012). This particular preference is due to the focus on social interaction, the sequential elements of talk, and perception of the function of language as action. What we mean by this last point is that talk is not perceived as a transparent medium and a neutral resource through which information is just transmitted. These approaches treat language as action; talk can 'do' things (such as justify, blame etc.) in the context it is produced.

In the following sections, we illustrate how one might conduct a study that uses naturally occurring data. To do this we draw upon three discursive studies in various stages of completion to illustrate our points. The first study is currently being conducted by the first author, Anastasia Rousaki and focuses on adolescent sexting and is at the stage where data collection has not yet commenced. The second is appropriately from the second author, Eva Prikrylova, based on completed but yet to be disseminated research about infertility treatment. Finally, we provide a case study of published research from the last author, Sarah Seymour-Smith, about gendered online support.

1.3 Background and aims

As with most research, those using naturalistic data start with a research question that needs answering identified from a gap in the literature. However, as the data is not contrived in the way that experiments or interviews are, we often need to be flexible as what we want to explore might not end up being present in the data. This may seem like a risk but the **inductive** nature (meaning grounding the analysis in what is actually present in the data) of the qualitative approaches employed means that there will always be something of interest and it is possible to reframe the research question post analyses to better reflect the new focus. For example, Eva Prikrylova, was interested in the role of gender identities within infertility treatment for heterosexual couples. The existing literature review revealed that, due to traditional ways of being masculine, men found it difficult to participate in discussions and decision-making regarding the treatment and felt marginalised by the clinical staff (Culley, Hudson & Lohan, 2013; Malik & Coulson, 2008). However, in contrast to this, the analysis of video recorded infertility consultations revealed that to overcome the issue of excluding men, the clinicians employed the generic term 'people' (and other specific interactional devices) in order to include and address the men even whilst they were explaining medical procedures aimed at the female body. This meant that the original wide aim of research was gradually refined during the analysis, where the final research questions were only established after the analytical findings.

Cultural context

The digital world is immense and presents the opportunity to explore numerous communities, many of which have unique participatory elements or even rules. Such communities often have their very own culture, means of expression such as a specific discursive constructs, slang, media they prefer or even means of communication such as **memes** (Wiggins, 2019). Other (often political) communities form their own version of online activism; for example, feminists tend to perform cyber-activism in order to tackle the normalisation of rape culture, e.g., the recent #MeToo movement (Mendes, Ringrose, & Keller, 2019). These can provide rich and often contextual naturally occurring data.

2. EXAMPLE STUDY: TESTICULAR IMPLANTS

2.1 Study and researcher

Seymour-Smith, S. (2013). 'A reconsideration of the gendered mechanisms of support in online interactions about testicular implants: A discursive approach.' *Health Psychology*, *32*(1), 91–99.

Sarah Seymour-Smith is a discursive psychologist at Nottingham Trent University, whose main research focus is masculinity and health.

2.2 Background and aims of the study

Men who have testicular cancer may need to undergo a procedure named orchiectomy, during which one (or both) of the testicles are surgically removed. Yet testicular cancer affects primarily young males, at a time when the loss of a testicle can significantly affect how they perceive themselves, their sexuality and masculinity. To combat such feelings, the insertion of testicular implants may improve the patients' perception of their body, sexuality and quality of life. Research focused on the result of men's decisions to have, or refrain from having, testicular implants are sparse and contradictory. On the one hand, some studies indicate that post surgery men were pleased with their body image and comfortable in sexual relationships. On the other hand, others were more concerned about having surgery. Moreover, some men who were not offered surgery expressed an interest in having it. Adshead et al. (2001) concluded that all men should be offered a choice of prosthesis, preferably at the time of their initial surgery.

How do men make such a decision though? Especially, despite men needing time to make a decision, the doctors typically need to perform the orchiectomy (and consequently along with it, the implant surgery) in the 24 hours following the patient's diagnosis. Furthermore, academics have highlighted that men are reluctant to talk about health (Seymour-Smith, Wetherell & Phoenix, 2002).

In the current study, online support groups were chosen due to the anonymity they offer and that the format potentially empowers users to feel more informed and help each other. However, men are less represented in these online spaces. Additionally, men use forums differently than women do. For example, a number of researchers have argued that women post more emotional messages in online support forums than men do (Blank et al., 2010; Lieberman, 2008; Sullivan, 2003; Zakowski et al., 2003). However, some mixed gender support sites failed to support these findings of gender differences, instead demonstrating similarities in the communication styles of men and women (Mo, Malik, & Coulson, 2009).

In the current study, the author decided to explore the men's decision-making process regarding testicular implants. Doing so also afforded the opportunity to provide a more nuanced understanding of what kind of support men employed during this process.

2.3 Design

With the focus of the study set, the next thing to consider is how to go about designing the research. Returning to our case study, what Internet support groups should fall into the remit of the study? How much data is needed? What restrictions might be placed on the type of data to be collected? In order to answer such questions one must consider the purpose of the study and the claims you want to make from the resulting analyses. Before we reveal our case study design, there are a number of issues to consider at the design stage.

On a practical level, collecting naturally occurring data can be significantly time-intensive and obtaining access to, for example, institutional settings can be challenging. You might encounter potential **gatekeepers** (doctors, practitioners, corporations, school principals, etc.) who are hesitant to provide you with permission to record their everyday or work related activities (Kiyimba, Lester, & O'Reilly, 2018). Thus, you might be required to contact a plethora of gatekeepers and institutions, until you find those willing to grant you access. Even in cases where you have access to a setting, you might need to dedicate a substantial amount of time in order to create a data set that is directly relevant to your research questions (Kiyimba, Lester, & O'Reilly, 2018). For example, Anastasia Rousaki planned to examine how sexuality is discussed in sex education classes; however, it is likely that schools will be hesitant to provide her with access to record the sessions due to the sensitivity of the topic. Several schools might need to be contacted before they eventually grant her permission to conduct the study. Moreover, once you get access, you might discover that only five minutes of said education classes discuss sexting, and the vast majority of the class materials are dedicated to discussing how to avoid STIs and using contraception. Therefore, you might need to collect more data and to record more sex education classes in order to create a rich data corpus. These parameters can result in further time restrictions to your assigned schedule.

Skoolkid errors

Generalisation is the act of drawing conclusions about a big group of individuals from one's results, usually emerging from a relatively smaller study sample. It is a crucial concept in the social sciences and often mentioned in quantitative studies (Polit & Beck, 2010). However, in qualitative research we *typically* do not consider our results generalizable (see Smith, 2018 for a detailed review). We are more interested in obtaining a rich, contextual understanding of a participant's (or a small group of participants') perception of reality or experiences (Polit & Beck, 2010). Thus, we often employ smaller sample sizes which do not permit us to make claims for the wider population but we do sometimes use the concept of **saturation**. This refers to the point at which no more patterns or themes are evidenced in your data (Braun and Clarke, 2019).

Recording can become complicated when collecting naturally occurring data. Sometimes you won't be able to record the data yourself; you might have to assign the task to someone else. For example, if a medical consultation needs to be recorded and your presence is not allowed, you have to ensure that the doctor in question will indeed record the sessions. You may even have to teach them how to use the necessary equipment. You might need to additionally think about logistics and practicalities of how to fit your research around the real-time events you would like to record, e.g., treatment procedures of your participants, or consultations of your medical staff. For example, how does one monitor treatment progress of participating patients, how to regularly access the internal administrative systems to be alerted to the dates and times of further appointments and consultations. It needs to be noted that most of the collaborating organisations do not benefit directly from research and can be very busy. Researchers need to be therefore considerate of the time and pressure they put on the organisation and to be creative in their research procedures not to obstruct the running of these establishments. Additionally, the researchers will be dealing with sensitive data specifically in medical environments and it is therefore imperative to follow all the ethical considerations of the involved organisation and address protection of all participants and collected data.

Finally, the collection of naturally occurring data often poses a variety of ethical considerations. Within private settings such as infertility treatment, you may encounter extremely sensitive personal information. Normally, people might be hesitant for their data to be used in research, which could render obtaining informed consent exceptionally difficult.

Furthermore, data are subject to legislative rules and regulations. For these reasons, you should always consult the appropriate code of ethics (such as the most recent BPS Code of Ethics and Conduct) and strive to conduct research with integrity and respect towards your participants. You should anticipate potential ethical issues and additionally ensure you have considered and studied any potential legislative concerns regarding your topic of choice (Kiyimba, Lester & O'Reilly, 2018). Next we return to our case study.

2.4 Design

The author Sarah Seymour-Smith searched testicular cancer sites on Google. Afterwards, she searched for any posts within these sites that related to testicular implants. These resulted in four sites with a total of 129 posts regarding prosthetics, one of which openly suggested that individuals should not have implants. The rest of them provided places where people could post their thoughts and be advised by the other forum users. She then selected and analysed the four longest threads regarding the topic of testicular implants.

Seymour-Smith then employed discursive psychology (Wiggins, 2017) to analyse the data. While coding, she emphasised in the rhetorical organisation of the posts, how participants negotiated issues of stake and interest (analytic terms associated with discursive psychology about how people attend to issues that they have a vested interest in). When examining the interactions taking place in these fora, the author focused in the discursive features of support and emotion.

Past studies explored how the new fora users try to fit in the norms of the online communities to become their member. To enrich the analytic output, Seymour-Smith examined the next turn proof procedure – meaning she explored how the responses to the original post indicate how it is perceived and interpreted by the other forum users. To ensure that the research results were thorough, she presented and discussed her research and received feedback by other discourse-oriented scholars.

Ethel ethics

Internet research poses unique ethical challenges. Namely, what is considered private and public in cyber-space is open to discussion. Where blogs, posts and vlogs are accessed via a private forum, explicit permission is needed to analyse them. Hookway (2008) suggested that as the content of numerous blogs are available to the general public, obtaining consent is not a necessity. However, the BPS Ethics Guidelines for Internet-Mediated Research (2017) cautions that despite being publicly available, bloggers, support forum users and vloggers might not anticipate their online contributions being used for research. The best practice is to always try to seek informed consent. However, obtaining informed consent can prove complex. You may try to seek permission but receive no response.

2.5 Data

Our case study consisted of posts from an Internet support forum, hence the data did not need transcribing. However, one of the immediate steps post data collection is usually transcription. Transcription is one of the fundamental pillars of qualitative research. It refers to a transition of medium; by transcribing, we convert speech to text. In simple words, to transcribe is to write down what is being said in an audio or video recording. Yet it is particularly challenging to turn audio and video into a written record, as it is difficult to depict its richness and complexity in a text format.

For example, some forms of transcription might not be able to represent elements which can be crucial to the researcher, such as intonation, sarcasm, laughing and pauses (Poland, 1995). An example of that is what Henderson (2017) refers to as the 'tidy' transcript; this type of transcript is simple and focused on the content/meaning of the data. It does not take into consideration any changes in the voice tone or pauses.

The majority of qualitative researchers uses a verbatim record (a repetition of what was said during the data collection using the exact same words) as this is fit for their purpose. Yet, discursive approaches (such as the case study) employ an analytic approach which focuses on the **micro, sequential analysis** of talk. This means that they explore the sequential organisation of how individuals' talk is structured. Due to this emphasis they use a more nuanced approach – the Jefferson transcription system. Jeffersonian transcription was named after its pioneer, Gail Jefferson (Jefferson, 2004). Jefferson developed a system of transcription which is easy to use, as it employs a number of common, familiar keyboard symbols such as the dot, underlining, etc. (Jefferson, 2004; Wiggins & Potter, 2013. As such, the Jeffersonian transcription captures in textual form both speech and other non-verbal cues which often accompany it, such as laughter, pauses, or verbal expressions or overlapping talk (Hepburn & Bolden, 2013).

A Jefferson transcription provides the most information possible about the transcribed audio and its detailed nature can effectively capture the rich nature of naturally occurring data.

2.6 Extracts

The next extracts capture the same interaction however, extract one employs an **orthographic transcription**, while extract two is an example of the Jefferson transcription system.

Both extracts are from the research on infertility treatment conducted by Eva Prikrylova, Sarah Seymour-Smith, David Wilde & Maria Kontogianni (Prikrylova, 2019).

Transcript 1: Orthographic extract

Researcher: So now I would like you to think back these nine years when you decided to have a baby. How did you decide to have a baby?

Jo: We have got married, have not we? We have got married in 2008.
Ste: The next step buying.
Jo: We had got our own house and it was just natural next step.

Transcript 2: Jefferson transcript

```
Res:  so (.) now (.)I would like you to think back the£se hah nine ye£ars
      .hhhh when you decided to have a baby * how did you decide * to have
      a baby
Jo:   (.) we'd got married >haven't we we'd got married< in two thousand
      and eight↓
Ste:  next step (buying)
Jo:   we'd got our own house and it was just natural
Res:  [uhm]
Jo:   [the] next
Ste:  [step]
Jo:   [the] next step
```

3. ANALYSIS AND FINDINGS

3.1 Analytic findings

In qualitative research, the analytical procedure and consequently the findings are highly dependent on the method and approach you adopt. A key step across all qualitative approaches is familiarization with the data; the researcher has to read, listen or watch their data sets multiple times, to become familiar with them. Another step is coding. Coding is the process of labelling the data, their content and characteristics by prescribing them a word or a short phrase – through coding findings are generated (Saldaña, 2015). Our case study adopted a discursive psychology approach to analyse the data, thus during coding Sarah focused on how the data were organised rhetorically to explore how forum members were navigating issues of stake and interest. When coding the data Sarah became interested in how men supported each other and discussed their emotions. These are supposedly practices that men are not great at doing. Therefore, a collection of all such instances were collated and analysed in more detail.

During the analysis, researchers who work with naturally occurring data should avoid cherry picking phrases or extracts that fit solely their own narrative. Instead, they should actively engage with the discourse and the organisational element of the conversations. Moreover, they should explore the data with curiosity and avoid deliberately spotting discursive patterns that fit their pre-existing beliefs (O'Reilly et al., 2020).

After the analytical phase, qualitative researchers employ multiple means to ensure that their findings are rigorous. One of these means is to present parts of the data in their manuscript (word count permitting) so the reader can form their own opinion on the analysis. Another step to ensure rigour is the process of **triangulation**. There are numerous forms of triangulation, yet in the present study Sarah adopted a process called investigator triangulation; after the initial analysis, two or more researchers gather to contribute their perspectives and approaches to the data set. For the novice researcher, such perspectives can be incorporated in the form of feedback, which they might receive from their supervisory team or other experienced researchers and academics.

3.2 Findings

Overall, the analysis found that men were able to 'do' support and also 'do' emotion. These points are illustrated in the analysis section through the use of posts and how other men on the support site respond to them.

For example, one of the posts submitted by Mark requests advice from the other members of the forum, regarding his decision of whether to get a prosthetic testicle (a fake testicle). His post highlights that he was offered a prosthetic testicle but displayed an uncertainty about this choice. He then paints his diagnosis and treatment as difficult, using emotive words. Yet the way he does this protects his masculine identity as he frames it as indicating that everyone would feel a similar way. In his post then Mark displays concern about his health and emotions to this, something that other researchers argue men do not do. So, the analysis then moves on to consider how others respond to this.

Responses align with Mark's concerns. For example, Dave assesses Mark's dilemma and concurs that it is indeed a difficult one. He thus validates Mark's right to be feeling like this. Dave also makes a joke, a common mechanism for men to perform support in such spaces. Another way that other users support Mark is to tell their own stories. This effectively empowers Mark via providing him with information.

In summary, the way the forum users respond to Mark relates to the accountability and initial concerns he touched upon in his original post. The way that his emotion is expressed, which could potentially be labelled as problematic, seems to be further perpetuated and normalised by other men. This can be indicative of how performative the masculine identity is in relation to emotion.

3.3 Reflections

Collecting naturally occurring data tends to be characterised by numerous advantages, which might sound tempting to the novice researcher who wishes to conduct qualitative studies. A key advantage of choosing to gather naturally occurring data is their applicability to a range of topics. Furthermore, they are useful ways of reaching topics and participants which undergraduate students might struggle securing ethical approval for. For example, a recent graduate student studied a support forum for partners of sexual offenders due to the difficulty in accessing and gaining ethical approval to interview such participants. However, the decision to collect naturally occurring data is not to be taken lightly. If one decides to collect naturalistic data for an assignment or thesis, you should do so only after careful consideration about the practical and ethical complications outlined in the design section above.

With the above considerations in mind, before you start collecting data contemplate the feasibility of the project. There may be time constraints – such as course imposed deadlines – you need to plan in advance. You may not be able to obtain the **data corpus** (the collection of data) you desire, you need to come up with an alternative plan or even study approach. Before deciding whether to collect naturally occurring data, realistically consider the chances of key stakeholders granting you access. Finally, to ensure that the project is ethically reasonable, it would be wise to discuss it with your supervisor, and potential risk assessment/data storage officers or other academics responsible for similar projects with experience in qualitative research.

Some of the external establishments might also be rightly protective of their treatment ideas and their reputation. To follow ethical requirements, we as researchers need to be always respectful of our participants. This sometimes means a type of agreement needs to be put in place regarding publishing of the research outcomes. In Prikrylova's research, this resulted in the inability to have her thesis publicly available in the university depository where a permission must be sought from the collaborating clinic for all publications. Since gaining access to specific NOD might be very difficult, the benefits of obtaining and studying these data often outweigh the problems. However, these issues need to be carefully considered and negotiated before the start of the research.

3.4 Summary

To conclude, in this chapter we have introduced the use of naturally occurring data – recordings of authentic, day-to-day or institutional interactions. Such interactions get straight to the heart (hopefully!) of the phenomena you might be interested in exploring rather than seeking retrospective accounts in the form of interviews or focus groups. They are characterised by a number of benefits and are uninfluenced by the power dynamics the presence of the researcher imposes. Naturally occurring data can be contrasted with contrived data; these are data collected as a result of the study design of the researcher (e.g., interviews and focus groups). They can be highly beneficial in exploring and solving problems of the everyday life. Their data collection can be conducted in a variety of institutional and everyday contexts and they can provide us with simple, yet effective, solutions.

LEARNING OBJECTIVES

By now you should have learned how to define naturally occurring data and how to differentiate them from contrived data. You should be able to identify the methods advocating their use.

You should also have some insight regarding the debates in the field such as the critique of interviews, the arguments towards and against the use of naturally occurring data, as well as the complexities of their distinction. You should be aware of what is the most appropriate transcription style for this type of data and why it is important. By reading the practical analysis of naturally occurring data when exploring the psychology of testicular cancer, you should have a brief idea of their applied aspect. Finally, you should be aware about the ethical and practical issues which might emerge when collecting naturally occurring data.

FURTHER READING

Potter, J., & Hepburn, A. (2005). Qualitative interviews in psychology: problems and possibilities. *Qualitative Research in Psychology*, *2*(4), 281–307.

This is useful if you want to understand the critique about interview data better.

Kiyimba, N., Lester, J. N., & O'Reilly, M. (2018). *Using naturally occurring data in qualitative health research: A practical guide*. Springer.

This is useful if you want to learn more about naturally occurring data applied to health research.

Stokoe, E. (2013). The (in)authenticity of simulated talk: Comparing role-played and actual conversation and the implications for communication training. *Research on Language and Social Interaction*, *46*(2), 1–21. https://doi.org/10.1080/08351813.2013.780341

If you want to read about practical applications of naturally occurring data research and how they can ameliorate our everyday life.

Smith, B. (2018). Generalizability in qualitative research: Misunderstandings, opportunities and recommendations for the sport and exercise sciences. *Qualitative Research in Sport, Exercise and Health*, *10*(1), 137–49.

This is useful discussion of how generalisability in qualitative research can be applied.

LINKS TO USEFUL RESOURCES

Jefferson's transcription annotation can be found here https://ugc.futurelearn.com/uploads/files/47/8b/478b50f3-890e-4f15-9f6b-b30563b1229d/Jefferson_transcription_symbols.pdf

A discussion of contrived versus naturally occurring data can be found here www.research.manchester.ac.uk/portal/files/33172197/FULL_TEXT.PDF

9

VISUAL METHODS

DAVID WILDE AND AMANDA EDMONDSON

1. INTRODUCTION

When asked to name a 'visual method' used in psychology, you might immediately think of the traditional formats researchers use to represent their data, such as graphs or charts (Banks, 2008). Perhaps with good reason, as historically there has been a tendency in psychology to privilege verbal and numerical data (Frith et al., 2005), yet we are very visual beings, we 'see' a lot of our world, every day we are surrounded by pictures, videos, and artworks, we imagine what things are to be throughout our waking lives, and even when we sleep, we dream in images (Brunsden et al., 2009).

1.1 Visual data

Our social lives are dominated by the visual, perhaps most notably by the popularity of social media platforms that encourage and facilitate the sharing of pictures and video clips. Behind most images there is usually an associated story – something to tell, often using visually related metaphors – and images are frequently accompanied by powerful emotions, for example, tears well up when we reminisce over pictures of a deceased loved one. So, for psychological researchers, the visual is a rich, largely untapped, gateway into the human condition.

There is a wealth of data in the real world that is visual in nature, whether these images exist already independent of research, or are created by participants within research studies, the visual presents an investigator with a plethora of opportunities to explore the lives of people in novel and stimulating ways. Visual research methods as part of qualitative research are now gaining more traction in psychology (Pain, 2012). Increasingly, researchers are finding the deployment of a visual method in their studies allows them to innovatively investigate their subject by fruitfully augmenting traditional data collection methods, such as interviews and focus groups.

Whoa there!

Are visual methods accessible to everyone?

Some people may be more receptive than others to a visual way of working. It can take a while for researchers and/or participants (whoever is responsible for creating the images that are being used in the research) to produce the images, which suggests it is not an approach that comes naturally to everyone, despite the visual world we live in. Perceived creative ability can have an impact on willingness to participate and participants may feel the need to produce images of great interest which can hinder the research process. Taking pictures of difficult experiences is also less familiar and participants may require guidance and support (Edmondson, 2013).

The use of visual methods is increasing apace and there are numerous reasons why a researcher would wish to employ visual methods. For example, engaging difficult to reach participants, giving 'voice' to those who find it hard to express themselves verbally (Pain, 2012), and assisting with the development of rapport and engagement with the research itself (Rhodes & Fitzgerald, 2006). However, visual methods also pose some challenging methodological and ethical dilemmas. There are a wide variety of visual methods on offer to the researcher (see Bravington & King, 2019 for a more detailed review). In this chapter, four visual methods will be explored: the Pictor Technique, Rivers of Experience, Image (Document) Analysis, and Photo Voice/Elicitation.

1.2 The Pictor Technique

The Pictor Technique was developed by Professor Nigel King specifically for investigating '**collaborative working**' in the fields of health and social care, although it has been applied in other settings (see Terry, 2019). It is a visual research tool that is employed as an adjunct within interviews to inspire deeper exploration of the roles, relationships and identities participants find important when talking about specific cases of working with others. Pictor is derived from a social network method developed by Hargreaves (1979) and used in family therapy. Hargreaves method involves providing a client with a stack of plain arrow-shaped cards, upon which they were asked to write the names of their family members. The next step of the process was to ask the client to organise the cards such that they depicted the 'story' of the family's relationships and interrelationships. This constructed visual representation served as the basis for therapeutic exploration of family dynamics.

Theoretically, Pictor has its underpinnings in **phenomenology** and **personal construct theory** (PCT, Kelly 1955a, see also Chapter 11 in this text). Kelly's conceptualisation of the human being is that of the 'informal scientist', formulating and testing personal hypotheses to construe their world. The person is seen as an active agent in engaging with the world, revising and amending their extant **construct** systems when they are disputed or discredited (King et al., 2013). However, much of this interpretation and meaning making happens naturally without much conscious attention to the process, meaning that when questioned about their construed world, a person may find it hard to describe things they do that have become habitual. The Pictor Technique was developed to help participants make sense of the routine elements of their daily working lives (King et al., 2013).

Practically, the Pictor Technique requires the participant to create a chart that stimulates discussion in an interview (Hardy et al., 2012). Figures 9.1 and 9.2 are examples of Pictor charts. King and colleagues (2017a) argue that there is no predetermined way of composing a Pictor chart and the researcher should consider the context of the study they are designing when deciding how to implement Pictor during data collection. The following guidelines should therefore be considered as the basic steps of the procedure. The materials needed to create a Pictor chart are a stack of multi-coloured arrow-shaped adhesive notes, a large plain sheet of paper, a felt marker pen and a digital audio recorder and camera.

To begin, the participant is asked to bring to mind a case they have been involved in (e.g., a nurse managing a patient) and think of all the people, services, or other important factors related to that case. The participant then jots these onto the adhesive notes, one note per person, service, or factor, using pseudonyms where appropriate for anonymity. The participant then arranges the notes on the paper to tell the story of the case with respect to the nature of the relationships involved.

Clarification of the relationships in the case can be visually enhanced in three ways: 1) the colour of certain arrows can be used to represent something significant (e.g., all

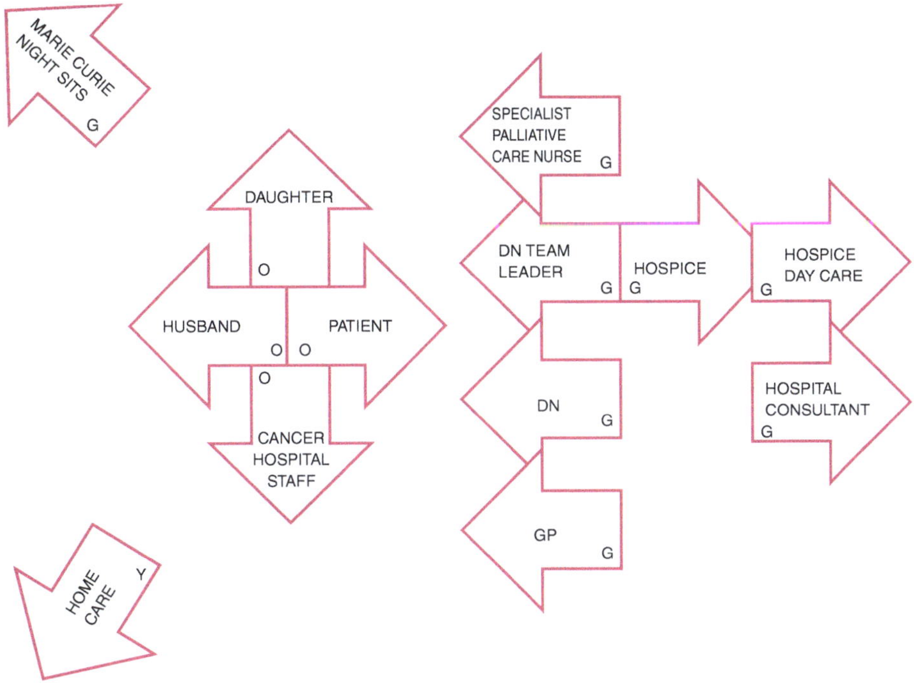

Figure 9.1 Pictor chart from a district nurse, pseudonym, 'Fiona'. See King et al. (2017a, p. 3) for further details of this chart.

professionals involved); 2) the proximity of the arrows relative to each other can indicate geographical or emotional distance or closeness between people or places; and 3) the points of the arrows can be used to indicate things like directions, timelines, stages or processes. There are no fixed rules for how this is done, and the participant can be as creative as they like. Once completed the participant talks through their chart while the interviewer probes and follows up interesting leads, referring to the chart to seek clarification where necessary. Arrows can be moved, removed or added, as the participant develops their account. Once the interview is finished, the interviewer draws around the arrows with the felt tip pen and takes a digital photograph of the chart.

Despite its PCT and phenomenological foundations, King et al. (2013) argue that Pictor is a theoretically and methodologically flexible technique. This applies to the analysis of the data, where a range of methods can be employed to explore the biographical and experiential elements of the case story. Both visual and textual data are generated and therefore the analysis should be carried out by considering both together. It is beyond the scope of this chapter to consider analysis in detail, so the reader is directed to examples of published works that have used the Pictor Technique by King et al. (2017b), Gillespie et al. (2018) and Bulk et al. (2020).

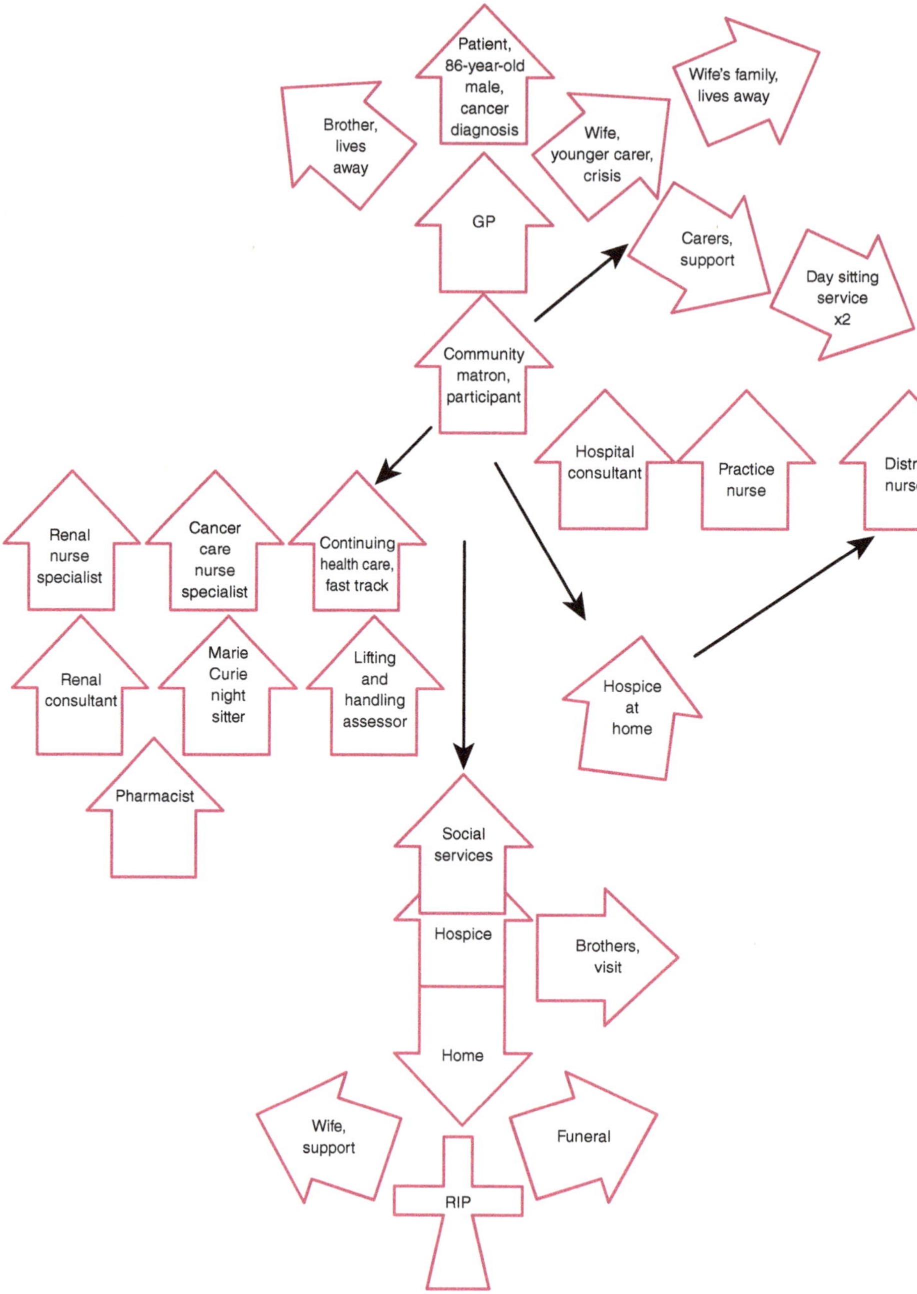

Figure 9.2 Pictor chart from a community matron, pseudonym, 'Janine'. See King et al. (2013, pp. 1142–44) for the analysis of this chart.

1.3 Rivers of Experience

The Rivers of Experience (RoE) method (Iantaffi, 2011) is a relatively recent enhancement to a long-standing technique called the 'Snake technique' (Denicolo & Pope, 1990, p.158). Using the 'Snake technique' Denicolo and Pope asked participants to consider their pasts chronologically, imagining the significant events, people, places and times that made up their life as laid out along the back of a snake, with each bend in the snake's torso representing a '**critical incident**'; a point in time when there was a change of direction in a person's life (Hodges, 2010). Iantaffi (2011) revisited this method for his PhD work by asking participants to imagine instead the timeline of their past as if travelling along a winding river. The river metaphor gives this method a distinct advantage in that journeys along rivers characteristically involve encounters with a greater number of geographical and environmental features that can serve as allegories to real life experiences, all of which take place within temporal and historical contexts. For example, an immediate crisis can be portrayed as like going over a waterfall, or long periods of stress or anxiety could be symbolised as struggling through rapid waters. The RoE is a very useful participatory tool to provoke more in-depth reflection than a traditional verbal interview.

Like the Pictor Technique, PCT theoretically underpins the RoE method. PCT (also known as Personal Construct Psychology) views human beings as actively engaged in making sense of their everyday experiences. As they do so they build up a dynamic, constantly evolving system of constructs organised around specific themes, for example, what is it like to be a doctor in a local health service? Constructs comprise thoughts, feelings, attitudes, beliefs, and decisions, which can be verbal labels, or images, or symbols, and are essentially how we come to know the world around us, and reciprocally, how others come to know us. Thus, interviewing participants about their RoE engages a multi-sensory reflection on the construct system, in terms of the chronological and sequential elements as voiced in the story they tell, and in terms of the conceptual and relational components of the visually mapped **timeline** they produce (Hodges, 2010).

As with many creative methods, there is some degree of flexibility in how a RoE can be deployed in an interview scenario. The rudimentary materials needed are a large sheet of plain paper (A3 or A1 ideally) and a collection of coloured pens, pencils, or crayons. Participants are free to add their own materials, for example, pictures or sticky notes, to form a collage (see Hodges, 2010, pp. 189–95). The interviewer begins by asking the participant to think of their life as a journey along a river, as shown in Figure 9.3. Every bend in the river represents an occurrence, person, time, or object in their life that had some influence on whatever the topic of the interview is (e.g., becoming a student in higher education, Iantaffi, 2011). It is important to emphasise to the participant that their RoE can be as complex or simple as they like.

The interviewer should not lead the participant as to what to draw on their RoE, but suggesting some examples of the kinds of features intrinsic to most river journeys

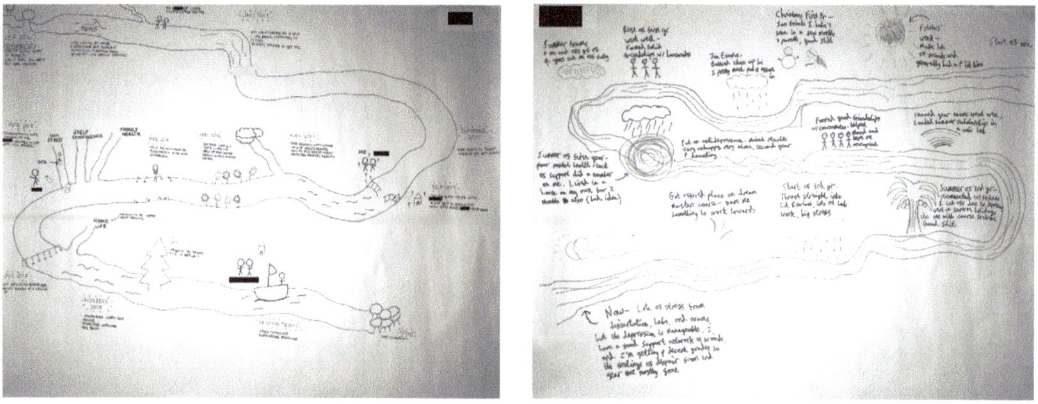

Figure 9.3 Two Rivers of Experience from a student project investigating final year undergraduate student mental health supervised by the first author. Participants took part in interviews lasting approximately one hour during which they also constructed a RoE of their experiences of their mental health trajectory over the preceding three study years. Note: Segments blacked out to cover up personal names.

(e.g., rapids, tributaries, etc.) can assist the participant to envision their journey. Once the participant has drawn their RoE, they are asked to talk the interviewer along their river 'journey'. As the story progresses, the interviewer inquisitively probes the participant about certain features and inclusions on their RoE. The participant is free to add further embellishments as the discussion continues. When the interview is over, a good quality digital picture should be taken of the final RoE.

As with many visual methods used in interviews, there are two tranches of data to analyse, the RoE itself, and the associated **interview transcript**. Similar to the Pictor Technique, although the RoE is theoretically underpinned by PCT, a number of alternative theoretical and methodological positions can be adopted in practice. Therefore, the data can be analysed using a range of methods. Transcript data can be analysed, for example, using **Narrative Analysis** (examining the content, tone and structure of the told story, see Sutcliffe, 2018), **Grounded Theory** Methodology (exploring trends and patterns in the data), and **Thematic Analysis**.

1.4 Image (document) analysis

In the same way researchers might gather and analyse a set of 'documents' to conduct a 'documentary analysis' defined as 'a systematic procedure for reviewing or evaluating documents, both printed and electronic material' (Bowen, 2009, p. 27) the same can be done with a collection of images, printed or digital. Like document analysis, image analysis can also be conducted as a stand-alone study or as part of a larger study using qualitative or quantitative methods. For example, Edmondson (2013) conducted an analysis of images of self-harm posted in blogs tagged as self-harm to expand on findings from a qualitative study which used photographs with people to explore their reasons for self-harm (see case study for further details).

This sort of data is referred to as '**extant material**, created independent of any intervention, influence or prompts by the researcher; the researcher has no direct contact with the users' (Salmons, 2017, p. 182). Image analysis of extant (visual) material has been used to research a diverse range of topic areas. For example, learning disabilities (Gleeson, 2011), funeral or commemoration practices (Gibbs et al., 2015) and electronic cigarette use and promotion (Laestadius et al., 2016). There are lots of ways a researcher could gather images for analysis. For example, some researchers have used social media platforms such as Instagram, while others have used printed images from calendars (Gleeson, 2011).

Ig Nobel Prize

Recognising our mates

Images can be used in so many ways in research but this is one of the more surprising.

2012 ANATOMY PRIZE: Frans de Waal and Jennifer Pokorny won the 2012 Ig Nobel Prize for anatomy for discovering that chimpanzees can identify other chimpanzees individually from seeing photographs of their rear ends.

de Waal, F. D. M., & Pokorny, J. J. (2008). Faces and behinds: Chimpanzee sex perception. *Advanced Science Letters*, *1*, 99–103.

Like any other type of research, when conducting an image analysis there is a need to clearly report the method used for gathering the images and the systematic steps/stages of the analysis in order to provide a robust, thorough and comprehensive answer to the research question, and demonstrate trustworthiness in the research. To demonstrate trustworthiness in research, Lincoln and Guba (1985) set out four important criteria: dependability, credibility, transferability and confirmability, the criteria are comparable to validity and reliability, concepts more aligned with a quantitative research approach.

Dependability is about transparency. Providing a detailed account of the research method of data collection and analysis to enable a future researcher to repeat the work, if not necessarily to gain the same results but to assess the extent to which proper research practice(s) have been followed.

Credibility is the fit between the image and the interpretation – it must be clear how the researcher reached the interpretation.

Transferability is to consider if the findings could be applied to other situations/ settings.

Confirmability is whether the findings are free from researcher bias? A report of the detailed steps taken to ensure, as much as possible, the findings are the result of a transparent and systematic analysis of the images, rather than characteristics of the researcher.

Remember, 'all images are regarded as polysemic (having many possible meanings)' (Prosser, 2006, p. 2). So, dependability, credibility and confirmability are critical in image analysis – researchers must be transparent and clearly show how they arrived at the findings, whilst accepting others may arrive with different findings.

1.5 Analysing visual methods

Researchers have employed different methodology or methods of analysis when working with images, such as **Grounded Theory** (Gibbs et al., 2015), **Content Analysis** (Smith & Sanderson, 2015) and **Polytextual Analysis** (Gleeson, 2011). Gleeson provides a very detailed, step by step guide to conducting a Polytextual Thematic Analysis of two calendars containing portraits of people with learning disabilities.

Finally, a word of caution. Although images feature prominently throughout the internet and more and more researchers are turning to the internet and/or social media platforms to conduct their research, there are some important ethical issues to consider. When conducting an image analysis, consent to use images perceived to be in the public domain, issue of authorship verses protecting anonymity, and complex issues surrounding ownership, require careful ethical consideration. There are a number of useful guides available, such as 'The Ethical Guidelines for Internet Mediated Research' (British Psychological Society, 2017), and 'Social Media Research: A Guide to Ethics' (Townsend and Wallace, 2016). The Sage Handbook of Social Media Research (Sloan & Quan-Haase, 2017) also features some useful best practice tips for conducting research using Instagram (Laestadius, 2017), and a chapter on social media users' views on the ethics of social media research (Beninger, 2017).

2. USING PHOTOGRAPHS IN RESEARCH

> When two or more people discuss the meaning of photographs, they try to figure out something together – this is, I believe, an ideal model for research. (Harper, 2002, p. 23).

Photographs have been used in research for many years in disciplines of **anthropology** and **sociology**. Sarah Pink, a Professor of Social Sciences, Design and Media Ethnography known internationally for her **ethnographic approaches** to research, talks extensively about the use of photographs in her research, see various books for further detailed information (Pink, 2006, 2013). Using photographs in psychology research is said to have 'crept in' during the 1990s, but it was treated as a 'waif on the margins' compared to other '**traditional' research methods** (Harper, 2002). Since then it has grown in popularity. For example, Visual Methods in Psychology, edited by Paula Reavey (2016) a Professor of Psychology and Mental Health, features a collection of research which has used photographs (and other visual methods) to research a diverse range of topics including gender, embodiment of pleasure, cancer, and relationships and marriage. Two of the most common research methods to use photographs are 'photo-voice' and 'photo-elicitation'.

Interesting facts

Estimates suggest we take more than one trillion photos in a year and share a staggering 730 billion images a year on Facebook alone. Since the invention of the camera in the 19th century, people have been taking more and more pictures. In the 1880s one of the most popular subjects to photograph were family scenes that included the bodies of recently deceased family members. Although this seems quite macabre now, it was a way to record the memory and physical appearance of the deceased loved one.

Source: Expert Photography, https://expertphotography.com/photography-facts

2.1 Photovoice

Photovoice is a community-based participatory research method developed in the late 1990s by Wang and Burris (1997). A group of participants take photographs to document their experiences and identify issues in their community. They describe and discuss the photographs as a group to help them think critically about their community and the different influences in relation to a particular issue. The group then exhibit the photographs and narratives (their stories) to inform social action. For example, Cabassa and colleagues (2013) used photovoice with people living with **serious mental illness** (SMI) in two supported housing organisations in New York. The aim of the study was to engage participants in conversations about their physical health to inform the development and implementation of health interventions for people living in supported housing. The photovoice groups enabled participants to use photographs to help them voice their preferences for any health intervention and critically discuss what mattered most to them. One participant took a picture of a bike rack and used the photograph to express the problem of weight gain from years of taking psychotropic medication; the bikes represented a desire to increase her physical activity and return to her former self. The participant gave it the title 'my old self back'.

2.2 Photo-elicitation

Photo-elicitation, put simply, is defined as 'inserting a photograph into a research interview' (Harper, 2002, p.13). A technique was first put to use by John Collier, an anthropologist who used photographs to research environmental sources of stress in the 1950s. The photograph(s) can be generated by the participant and/or researcher and used as a stimulus or guide throughout the interview. Collier (1957) found using photographs within an interview elicited longer and more comprehensive interviews, reduced fatigue and misunderstanding during the interview, and enabled the participants to discuss more of the emotional aspects of their life, compared to interviews without photographs.

As the use of photographs in research grows, further benefits and challenges are being noted and shared, together with comparisons with other more 'traditional' research methods. For example, Edmondson and Pini (2019) discussed the pros and cons of using photographs in research and compared how the key objectives of qualitative research, such as establishing rapport, engagement with the research, can be met using interviews with and without photographs.

Some of the key benefits included how photographs served to 'build a bridge' and reduce the gap between the researcher and participant, which helped establish a rapport (Drew et al., 2010; Packard, 2008). The photographs also enabled participants to express more meaningful data. For example, the photographs can take the researcher into different environments with different people, adding layers of data that may be difficult to introduce and verbalise (Balmer et al., 2015).

A lot of the challenges when using photographs centre around ethical issues such as consent, anonymity and copyright (Edmondson & Pini, 2019). For example, participants usually own the photographs they produce for participation in research; they own the copyright. The researcher must therefore obtain consent to use and store the images; this is particularly important for when researchers are ready to share and disseminate the findings. However, participants may use images from internet-based image banks, magazines, or they may take photographs of artwork. In such cases, it can be difficult or even impossible to ascertain the copyright owner (Edmondson, 2013).

To get a better idea of how photographs are used in a research project, the next section provides a more detailed look at a study which used photographs to explore the reasons why people self-harm.

3. EXAMPLE STUDY: USING PHOTO-ELICITATION TO UNDERSTAND REASONS FOR REPEATED SELF-HARM

3.1 The study and the researchers

Edmondson, A., Brennan, C., & House, A. (2018). Using photo-elicitation to understand reasons for repeated self-harm: A qualitative study. *BMC Psychiatry, 18*(1). https://doi.org/10.1186/s12888-018-1681-3

Dr Amanda Edmondson is a Lecturer in Psychology at Nottingham Trent University. She is also an experienced mental health services researcher with an interest in qualitative approaches to mental health and wellbeing.

Dr Cathy Brennan is an associate Professor of Psychological and Social Medicine at the University of Leeds. Cathy's PhD utilised visual and creative methods to explore the experiences of families with a child with a life-limiting illness.

Professor Allan House is Emeritus Professor of Liaison Psychiatry in Leeds Institute of Health Sciences, in the School of Medicine. His research interests cover several aspects of liaison psychiatry – especially psychiatric co-morbidity complicating physical illness, medically unexplained (functional) presentations and self-harm.

3.2 Background and aims of the study

Self-harm is a major public health concern (Tsiachristas et al., 2017). One of its most problematic features is the high rate of repeated self-harm, especially in younger people (Hawton & Harriss, 2008). There is also an increased risk of eventual suicide for people who repeatedly self-harm (Hawton et al., 2012). Treatment approaches have faced criticism from people who self-harm because they fail to understand the reasons why people self-harm (Hunter et al., 2012).

A challenge for research in this area is the difficulty experienced by people in verbalising reasons for their self-harm (Adshead, 2010; Pembroke, 1994; Spandler, 2001). For example, when asked why they have self-harmed people often report feeling unable to put it into words (Spandler, 2001).

Research into self-harm may therefore benefit from using a visual approach. Using photographs during an interview, for example, is said to promote expression, communication (Drew et al., 2010) and more of an emotional response than verbal questioning alone (Harper, 2002). The benefits of using a visual approach to research sensitive subjects are well documented (Harrison, 2002; Pain, 2012; Pyle, 2013; Whitehurst, 2006). For example, photographs are helpful in introducing difficult subject matter (Lachal et al., 2012) and creating a sense of distance between the participant and their experience (Balmer et al., 2015).

This research aimed to explore the reasons why people self-harm using photo elicitation, a method in which photographs are used as a stimulus or guide during an interview (Frith & Harcourt, 2007).

3.3 Method

Participants were asked to take photographs over a two-week period of anything that would help them describe their experience of self-harm. All participants were offered the use of a digital camera, although some chose to use their own equipment.

Ethel ethics

Due to ethical concerns and principles of **consent**, participants were asked to avoid taking pictures of others. Pictures can be depicted in ways that the person photographed may be unhappy with, which is an ethical concern.

Also, given the sensitive nature of the topic and the novel technique being used, clear **safety and wellbeing** procedures were in place to protect the participant and the researcher.

Once the participants had taken their photographs, arrangements were made to meet and discuss the images.

In this approach a prior topic guide is not used by the researcher but the participant 'drives' the interview by choosing which pictures to discuss, in what order and how they talk about the pictures. The researcher adopts the role of 'active listener' (Heisley & Levy, 1991). Prompts were used to explore thoughts and feelings about presented images and how they represented the participants' experiences. Each participant was asked how they felt about using the method at the end of each interview.

3.4 The choice of analysis

This study performed a Polytextual Thematic Analysis (Gleeson, 2011) on both the visual and textual data. Given that images were felt and reported to be as much of an integral part of the research process as the verbal dialogue it seemed wrong not to include them in the analysis. However, there is little guidance on how to analyse combined visual and textual data (Frith et al., 2005; Gleeson, 2011) which led Kate Gleeson to develop polytextual thematic analysis (Gleeson, 2011).

3.5 Findings

Eight adults, two males and six females, aged between 21 and 65 years, participated in the study. Many of the participants reported experiencing adverse events throughout their lives, such as sexual abuse, death of significant others and bullying. One participant represented the impact of her experience of adverse events through an image of a shattered window with glass which had not yet fallen apart. She described feelings of vulnerability and how she felt shattered on the inside but never actually broken. They left her internally damaged but she needed to present herself as someone who would never break and self-harm enabled her to 'stay upright', see Figure 9.4.

> Stay upright, stay together and not cross those boundaries so people would find out what was going on because that was something that I couldn't do so I had to internalise it. (Participant 4)

Figure 9.4 Shattered glass

Feelings of control (or a lack thereof) were experienced in different and complex ways as a function of self-harm. Fundamentally, control was something participants felt they lacked. For some, it was being controlled by another. Participant 4, a young woman who had a long history of self-harm described feeling controlled by 'evil' inside her and self-harm was a way to exert control over 'the evil' and feel a sense of mastery, see Figure 9.5.

> I had so many times where I was like, I need to cut because I need to, I can't stop the evil, I can't stop it taking over and putting all these pictures in my head and I thought ultimately it was going completely take over my personality and I was going do all these horrible pictures that I was seeing in my head to other people. So, I needed to slow it down so it was very logical of ok how do I slow down something that's in my blood would be to cut cos I'm releasing the blood therefore I can slow down the evil. (Participant 4)

Figure 9.5 An evil inside

The range and number of photographs facilitated detailed discussions about self-harm. The absence of pictures of actual injuries that are frequently present on internet sites and accessible via social media was notable. Since the purpose of the study was to explore the reasons why people self-harm, participants may have chosen images that enabled a discussion of the purpose it served for them, rather than the end result.

The images were readily incorporated into the interviews and there were many occasions where seemingly mundane images, such as a road works sign, unveiled complex narratives relating to self-harm; the interaction between image and narrative was important in understanding what was being communicated.

Participants described using photographs as 'helpful', 'a good thing' and 'interesting'. For the most part they felt able to capture photographs which represented their experience of self-harm, although finding images to express emotional states was described as difficult by one participant who then came up with her own solution:

> I don't understand how I can take a picture of anger, like I guess I could take a picture of something that causes the anger, which I did. (Participant 1)

Some participants appeared to lack confidence when showing their photographs and perhaps felt under pressure to produce images of great interest, which may have inhibited their ability to express their experience of self-harm.

Ethel ethics

Protecting participants **anonymity** is crucial. When using visual methods, the researcher needs to ensure none of the quotes or images are directly attributable to an individual. BUT achieving complete anonymity of a picture of a place is difficult. (e.g., one participant included a picture of a local school). In some cases, **photo-editing software** can be used. Where it is not possible to achieve complete anonymity, those photographs should be textually described only.

4. REFLECTIONS ON VISUAL METHODS

4.1 Background and aims

Every study requires an appropriately focused research question if it is to fully address its research aims. Otherwise, unusable (and unethical!) data may be collected. For more about the development of research questions for interviews and focus group studies, see Chapters 4 and 5. Whilst it might seem exciting, novel, even edgy to include visual data collection methods, the researcher must ask themselves, 'what will the inclusion of this kind of method bring to the research that using a more traditional method alone would not bring?' If no good rationale can be evinced for including a visual component to the study, then one should critically reconsider why they want to proceed with it.

Once a method has been chosen, then the type of data to be collected also needs to be established, for example, are participants going to 'make' data (**respondent generated data**) as in Pictor or RoE studies, or are the data going to be produced by the investigator (**researcher generated data**) for instance, mapping public use of places and spaces, or are the data going to be culled from an extant data pool (**'found' or naturally occurring data**) such as, collections of images from social media or a website?

Further key practical design questions need to be addressed, for example, how has this method been used in previous studies? Who will form the sample, what size of sample will be recruited? How will the method be administered? What will be the number and frequency of the data points to be collected? What special or unanticipated practical or ethical challenges may arise? How can these be resolved? Answering these questions can be very useful when designing any study, but particularly so where a relatively novel component is being introduced.

Finally, it is important, even at the earliest stages of study conception to consider how the data are to be analysed. Most visual research studies generate both textual and visual data, yet authors have noted a preference to privilege textual data in analysis (Rose, 2000, as cited in Frith et al., 2005), but both components deserve detailed attention. This will be dealt with in more detail later in this chapter.

4.2 Design

The design of a visual method study requires a great deal of thought in terms of its overall execution, timing and presentation of the visual method within the data collection phase, and how the data are to be analysed and presented in research outputs.

Skoolkid errors

Before starting any research, the whole project needs to be carefully thought through from start to finish; from **epistemological/ontological** approach, to thinking ahead about what analysis will be applied and, beyond that, how the findings will be disseminated. This is particularly important when including a visual component to ensure that all elements of the data are analysed and incorporated in the latter stages of the study. Sullivan et al. (2012) have helpfully conceptualised the planning of a project in the form of a 'methodological kite' (p. 12), where each point of the kite (i.e., each key methodological decision) must be soundly and coherently coupled to each another. Just like a real kite, if the connections are loose or poorly linked, the kite (project) will not fly!

The choice of visual method will depend on the nature and aim of the research question. Ultimately, a technique should be chosen that will generate data that will answer that research question. One key consideration is sensitivity of the topic and how vulnerable the participant sample is when asked to reflect on potentially emotionally troubling life events (Sheridan et al., 2011). An additional consideration is the relative **homogeneity** of the sample to be recruited (Bravington & King, 2019). If a study has a biographical nature to it, a technique that captures a timeline of some kind would seem appropriate (e.g., a RoE, or participant generated photographs covering the life cycle of a phenomenon, such as attending a residential training course). However, some authors (e.g., Ancona et al., 2001; Bagnoli, 2009; Orland, 2000) have criticised using timelines with samples of participants that either have difficulty cognitively construing time in a linear fashion, or culturally conceptualise time using different geometric properties (e.g., time as a spiral).

The number of visual artefacts the participant is asked to provide is also important to consider. Some participants can get anxious when asked to draw a picture or create a chart because they feel they suddenly have to be an 'artist' (Scherer, 2016) – in fact, participants do not have to be artistic at all to provide good quality visual data. Participant fatigue needs to be factored in, too. In a Pictor project that the first author was involved in investigating collaborative working between health care professionals (HCPs), each HCP was asked to construct two Pictor charts, each one focusing on a different case management scenario. The timing of when the visual method is to be presented to the participant is also crucial, particularly in studies where the collection of sensitive information is anticipated. In several RoE studies conducted by the first author's students, interviews began with three or four less emotionally difficult 'lead in' questions. The construction and discussion of the RoE formed the centrepiece of the interview. The interviews ended with two or three questions designed to ease the participant out of the interview into a safe space.

4.3 Findings

Analysis and presentation of findings is something to be considered at the outset of a project. Most researchers and students are familiar with how to write a report or paper containing data in verbal and tabulated/graphical formats. Incorporating the visual element often bestows novice visual researchers with presentation and ethical dilemmas (ethics will be covered in further detail in the next section. See also the 'ethel ethics' sidebars in the case study in this chapter). Both visual and textual data should be thought of holistically, as Frith et al. (2005) note 'the verbal and the visual are integrally intertwined in representing scientific theory, method and data, and in enabling the expression of everyday experiences' (p. 187).

Unlike text, images are usually encountered in their entirety almost immediately (Hustvedt, 2005). Visual artefacts therefore stimulate interesting interview discussion at the time of their creation, but further sustained engagement permits a deeper, more intimate encounter with a phenomenon (Boden & Eatough, 2014). Images can speak to the researcher and the research audience on literal and figurative levels, invoking tantalising ambiguity that requires a greater commitment from the analyst and reader to critically divine their interpretation. On the other hand, as Bravington and King (2019) highlight, images can bring clarity into meaning-making as they condense broad swathes of complex data.

Presentation of visual data therefore should involve the judicious choice of images and accompanying text. The findings section of the case study in this chapter illustrates how single pictures and quotes coupled with a nuanced interpretative analysis can reveal penetrating psychological insights into the lived experience of self-harm. Where larger scale drawings and charts have been constructed, a similar approach can be used – a good example of this is the presentation of Martha's case in King et al. (2017a, pp. 227–29). Alternatively, the whole chart/drawing can be inserted in the method section, and in the findings section illustrative segments of the chart can appear as a picture along with accompanying analysis and participant quotes.

4.4 Reflections

Augmenting a research study with a visual data collection component can enhance participant involvement, expand a study's reach to difficult to recruit populations, facilitate communication, particularly to those who find it hard to verbalise feelings and thoughts, and result in deeper and richer data being gathered (Pain, 2012). Participants creating visual artefacts can feel empowered to engage in ways that allow them to think and reflect beyond providing verbal responses to questions (Guillemin & Drew, 2010). However, it is important to consider the ethical challenges involved, which can go beyond the more usual considerations of minimising harm that one might face in carrying out social research (Glegg, 2019).

Several authors have raised issues about potential participant safety because of how visible people can be in things like photographs (e.g., Black et al., 2018; Holtby et al., 2015), particularly when those pictures appear 'unmanaged' online (Creighton et al., 2018), or divulging personal disclosures that could open them to criticism or even ridicule (Cox et al., 2014). Langmann and David (2014) warn that, whilst public interpretation of data is invited, sometimes misinterpretation (unintended or otherwise) can lead to the creation or perpetuation of negative stereotyping. This has been emphasised with regards to several groups of people who find themselves marginalised, for example, sexual minorities, refugees, and people living with HIV or a disability (Teti, 2019), leading for calls that researchers consider 'special protections' (p. 2) for samples taking part in visual research.

There are a number of strategies researchers can employ to mitigate potential ethical problems. For example, the possibility of **confidentiality** being breached exists should someone be inadvertently recognised by the context of a picture or the surrounding environment in which the photograph was taken. Here risk can be reduced by blurring faces and incorporating a detailed consent process whereby people are made aware of the wider risks of taking part and must give explicit permission for each picture used (Drew & Guillemin, 2014). Participants should be guided to anonymise names of people, organisations, places, etc., during the construction of drawings and charts. Upon completion, the researcher should scan the created artefact for anything potentially compromising. Where visual methods are being used in certain environments, such as a theatre or school, third parties appearing incidentally in any images most likely will not have given consent. Again, obscuring parts of the images may help to minimise risks in this case (Cox et al., 2014).

LEARNING OBJECTIVES

After reading this chapter you should now have:

- An understanding of some of the key visual research methods used by psychologists. Why and how they might be used, instead of, or to supplement some of the more well-known research methods of data collection.

- An awareness of the different ways visual data might be analysed.
- An awareness of some of the benefits and challenges, including ethical challenges, when using visual methods.

FURTHER READING

Reavey, P. (Ed.). (2011). *Visual methods in psychology: Using and interpreting images in qualitative research*. Psychology Press.

A great book for realising the potential of visual methods. Chapters include examples of research using static media (photographs) and video, and Rivers of Experience. Ethical and methodological reflections are also featured.

Sloan, L., & Quan-Haase, A. (2016). *The SAGE handbook of social media research methods*. Sage. https://dx.doi.org/10.4135/9781473983847

Great chapters for those interested in using visual methods online, including ethics of social media research from the perspective of the social media user.

Clark, A., Prosser, J., & Wiles, R. (2010). Ethical issues in image-based research. *Arts & Health, 2*(1), 81–93. https://doi.org/10.1080/17533010903495298

This paper discusses informed consent, anonymity and confidentiality, specifically in relation to how they may differ in image-based compared to word-based research.

King et al. (2017). The Pictor technique: Exploring experiences of collaborative working from the perspectives of generalist and specialist nurses. In: J. Brooks & N. King (Eds.), *Applied qualitative research in psychology* (pp. 221–34). Macmillan Education/Palgrave.

This chapter gives a broad overview of the Pictor Technique, covering the underlying assumptions of the technique, practical advice and an illustrative findings section.

Harper, D. (2002). Talking about pictures: A case for photo elicitation. *Visual Studies, 17*(1), 13–26. https://doi.org/10.1080/14725860220137345

This is a great article to help you understand photo elicitation and a history of its development.

Edmondson, A., & Pini, S. (2019). Visual methods in health research: A literature review of the pros and cons of using photographs. *Nurse Researcher*. https://doi.org/10.7748/nr.2019.e1620

A useful summary of the pros and cons of using photographs in research, including a comparison of conducting interviews with and without photographs.

LINKS TO USEFUL RESOURCES

https://methods.sagepub.com/book/the-sage-handbook-of-qualitative-research-ethics-srm/i1259.xml?fromsearch=true

'Using visual methods in qualitative psychology research' by Dr Jo Brooks: www.youtube.com/watch?v=9mw2cFtjvY4

Morgan Centre for Research into Everyday Lives: series of useful toolkits and The Real-Life Methods Working Papers: Researching with visual images. John Prosser offers some useful key points and a glossary of terms for those starting out with visual methods. www.socialsciences.manchester.ac.uk/morgancentre/research/resources/toolkits

10

COMBINING TWO METHODS: INTERVIEWS AND PSYCHOMETRICS

ROWENA HILL, LISA SANDERSON AND BETH JONES

This chapter introduces you to combining two methods and what this typically looks like by looking in depth at one study. Using two of the approaches you have read about previously in this book (surveys and interviews) and a published paper as an example to explore how they can be combined to gain a fuller understanding of a research question. Normally, this approach is used by students undertaking larger pieces of academic work where there is enough time and space to do the approach well, as it takes a lot of time and an in-depth understanding of more than one method as well as knowledge of how to combine methods appropriately.

1. INTRODUCTION TO MIXED METHODS

A healthy approach to thinking about mixed methods is how two methods can be used together to understand a phenomenon of interest in more depth. The way not to think about mixed methods is that it is simply answering the same research question twice in two different ways. A mixed methods approach typically uses the structure where one method is used, then another one is used afterwards *in sequence* in an explicitly interrelated approach. Put simply, the methods are not completing different jobs, but building together to inform the same question. Robson (2011) highlights that qualitative and quantitative approaches should not be pitched against each other as an 'either/or', but can be used usefully together to compliment, rather than oppose, one another. This chapter will explore a mixed methods approach using two methods that are presented elsewhere in this text. The first method sits within the interview approach presented in Chapter 6. The second method included in this worked example sits within the quantitative approach and uses psychometric scales as described in Chapter 3.

1.1 Sequential exploratory design

Sequential exploratory design (Robson, 2011) builds these two approaches together to jointly answer research questions. It takes the synthesised findings from both qualitative and quantitative methods to provide more insight and an understanding of the research question. Denscombe (2008) defines the approach as having four defining characteristics:

- quantitative and qualitative methods should be within the same research project;
- a research design that clearly specifies the sequencing and priority that is given to the quantitative and qualitative elements of data collection and analysis;
- an explicit account of the way in which the quantitative and qualitative aspects of the research relate to each other; and
- a practical approach to conducting the research.

The way that sequential exploratory design uses the qualitative and quantitative approaches is to use one method to understand the topic in a different way than the other method is able to understand the phenomenon. For example, qualitative approaches seek to scope the complexity and how people understand the topic and to suggest relationships and patterns. While a quantitative approach seeks to understand how common the phenomenon is experienced across populations and tests out these relationships and patterns to see if they hold against statistical significance.

Differences can occur in the design and point at which the data are collected. A sequential design means one data collection method follows another. A convergent design means that the methods collect their data at the same time. We will talk more about these designs later in the chapter.

Skoolkid errors

The mixed method approach is sometimes misunderstood and underused. It is misunderstood by some researchers as just putting two methods together in the same study to broadly address similar research questions. This is not what mixed methods is. If a study was designed with two methods from very different epistemological and ontological positions, it is hard to integrate their findings. This is because the methodological approaches are trying to do very different things. Experimental designs typically try to isolate and then manipulate part of a phenomena to test difference. Survey and qualitative designs usually try and understand the breadth or depth of a phenomenon in context, and so are similar. The methods have to work together by combining their findings to answer the research aims. They shouldn't be able to fully answer the research question on their own (more about appropriate research question formulation later), instead they should complement each other with different pieces of the answer which is brought together in the discussion. Or the findings of one method should inform the content of the next method so that the research question is fully answered by combining the findings from the two methods.

1.2 A brief introduction to the qualitative data collection method of interviews

The most common form of qualitative data collection in mixed methods are interviews. These can be face-to-face, or online, but typically they involve one-to-one interviewing by the researcher with the participants. This is because the aim is to create a representation of the participants' understanding of the phenomenon they share. They are invited to participate based on their inclusion criteria aligned to the research questions. For example, if the research question was to establish the nature and prevalence of the impact from lockdown measures on those attending training for their A levels during the Covid-19 pandemic, we would need to find participants who were in that position at that time. Those who are not in that situation cannot offer an understanding of that experience. However, before the data are collected, the qualitative analytical method should be selected based on the research question.

The two most typical qualitative methods in mixed method studies are the approaches of Thematic Analysis and Grounded Theory. This is because of the flexibility of Thematic

Analysis to generate data that focuses on an individual's understanding of their world and experiences, and Grounded Theory because of its unique ability to generate models of the phenomena being explored (Willig, 2013; Charmaz, 2008). Grounded Theory can generate an explanation of the phenomena, which can then be tested as a model or theory using psychometrics within a mixed methods approach.

Ensuring a robust qualitative analysis concerns academic rigour of qualitative methods. The first aspect to this is the development of the interview schedule. The chapter on interviews addresses this in detail but ensuring that your interview schedule will unpack your participant's understanding of the topic is essential. One-to-one interviews are typically chosen in mixed methods approaches over things such as focus groups due to their flexible and thorough exploration of the phenomenon with the participant. The key factors to consider when choosing a qualitative method include: the nature of data sought, the subject matter/phenomenon and the research participants (Ritchie & Lewis, 2003). The interview schedule is developed once the method is selected.

1.3 Reflections on robustness of a mixed method design

One thing that shouldn't get missed just because a qualitative method is being used within a mixed methods design is ensuring academic rigour, quality and validity as would be usual practice with a quantitative analysis. This includes the interviewer's practices of reflexivity, in other words, an honest awareness of how the data are being co-constructed between the participant and the researcher. The quality and validity processes should include techniques such as establishing the quality of data and analysis (e.g., Mays & Pope, 2000; Patton, 1999; Barbour, 2001), ensuring the removal of bias within interview schedules, the transcription and full analysis of every interview (rather than the analysis of one interview serving as the framework for subsequent transcripts). The definition and action of reflexivity is central to sound research interviewing (Silverman, 2011; Ritchie and Lewis, 2003; Smith, 2003) and tries to capture the explicit role and cultural knowledge of the researcher (Charmaz, 2014). This includes the positions and assumptions taken by the researcher, their research experience, decisions and interpretations.

1.4 A brief introduction to the quantitative method: Surveys

Surveys are used frequently in mixed method designs as they align with qualitative approaches well. They use batches of questionnaires to explore a topic in its context. There is more about this in Chapter 3 on surveys. But essentially the method involves breaking the research question down into aspects of the phenomena, then matching questionnaires (also known as 'measures') to gather quantitative, and/or qualitative data, which is then analysed to provide an answer to the research question from a large number of participants. It is an effective way of gathering similar, targeted data from a large participant pool. These can be numerical in design, or they can be qualitative, open-ended questions. The typical data collection method for use in surveys is to use pre-validated scales. This means they have been designed and tested by someone else and then published in a journal. Each potential measure is reviewed against a range of evaluations such as how much it fits with the theories being used to contextualise the topic, and how strong the evaluation indices such as reliability and validity statistics and overall scale performance (Furr, 2011). Then it is put together in an order which makes sense to the participant and the collection of questionnaires then becomes a survey.

Whoa there!

Sometimes we see researchers make mistakes because they don't acknowledge that prediction and measurement are not foolproof methods and contain error in them. By this we mean that any understanding inferred from questionnaire results are purely based on the scores someone provides. If we think about what this means for depression, for example, the survey simply measures the symptoms of depression, depression itself cannot objectively be measured. So, the scores on questions about a range of symptoms indicate a person may be experiencing depressive symptoms. The mistake people make is to make the unsupported leap and assume that the measurement of variables is actually measuring the phenomena, rather than being simply an indication. So, you may see studies using language such as 'the mean scores for the depression scales indicate a higher score of depressive symptoms are endorsed by participants'. This is basically saying the scores are reflecting an endorsement of the symptoms of depression, not endorsing depression as it is not directly measured.

2. MAKING THE FINDINGS DANCE TOGETHER RATHER THAN SITTING ALONE IN SEPARATE CORNERS

Whether the design is to use surveys first to gain understanding about the patterns of the phenomena, then use interviews to gain an in-depth understanding of the phenomena in context, or the other way round, the challenge of a mixed methods design is to ensure that the findings are integrated. *Integration* is essential for research to be considered mixed methods and involves using the qualitative and quantitative approaches to inform and build on one another to provide a nuanced understanding of the phenomenon in question (e.g., Creamer, 2017). Integration of methods is employed as it is acknowledged by the researcher that such insights that are gleaned from a mixed methods approach would not be available if qualitative or quantitative methodology were adopted in isolation (Moseholm & Fetters, 2017). The limitations of one method are often seen to be outweighed by the strengths of another (DeCuir-Gunby & Schutz, 2017; Moseholm & Fetters, 2017). However, combining methods doesn't signify high quality research and therefore critical evaluation is still imperative. While conducting high quality qualitative and quantitative work is important, how the researcher(s) goes about combining and integrating these methods is also a sign of quality.

2.1 Integrating at the design and method level

Successful integration of the methods can be achieved by the way the study design is built and the methods used. **Building** is the term used to describe the aspect of sequential design where the findings from one method inform the specifics of data collection for the other method, therefore building on the findings of the first method (Moseholm & Fetters, 2017). For example, in an exploratory sequential design interview data and participants words or quotes would be used in the development of scale items within a survey. In an explanatory sequential design, findings from a quantitative survey would be followed-up with interviews to understand the relationships found in the quantitative phase (Creswell, 2015).

Merging data means that both sets of data are designed, collected and analysed in a way that means they can be contrasted or brought together as one large dataset for comparison (Moseholm & Fetters, 2017). For example, I may conduct a survey and at the same time, interviews with participants to explore the same or similar constructs. Findings are then integrated through themes in the discussion of the results. This usually happens after analysis of each dataset and requires a deep understanding of the boundaries of how and what can be compared. This is referred to as a convergent parallel mixed methods design (Creswell, 2017).

2.2 Embedding

Embedding is when data collection and analysis are linked throughout the design by using combinations of *connecting*, *building*, or *merging* (Moseholm & Fetters, 2017). Here, one method will be embedded within a larger study that is contrasting in method (Creswell, 2015). It is very common for embedding to be used when running and evaluating a health intervention. For example, if I am conducting a study that shows an intervention is effective from quantitative measures, I would want to also understand why the intervention was effective by conducting interviews with those that ran the intervention (i.e., a process evaluation).

2.3 Connecting

Connecting the data by using the same participant pools for both the survey and then a selection of that pool for the interviews is one way to add another layer of integration into the research (Moseholm & Fetters, 2017). *Connecting* can be used in a sequential, explanatory of convergent design. Having a clear idea about the desired outcome of the study will help inform these design choices. Regardless of the type of mixed methods design that has been used, it is important to communicate to the reading which design has been used and why.

While here we have explored some different ways, mixed methods research can be design, the researcher can be flexible so long as they ensure their design includes the following four characteristics (Halcomb, 2019):

1. The researcher needs to be clear about the interaction (or independence) between the qualitative and quantitative components of the research. For example, is the interview data used to inform the self-report questions for the quantitative phase?
2. Will data from both the qualitative and quantitative strand be collected simultaneously or concurrently?
3. Will priority be given to the qualitative (such as in an exploratory design) or quantitative strand (such as in an explanatory strand).
4. When in the research process will integration occur? Will it occur at multiple time points?

2.4 Techniques for integrating data successfully

A joint display is 'a table or figure that can be used for organising mixed data collection and analysis' (Fetters, 2019, p. 194). The main purpose of a joint display is to facilitate the integration process and consequently communicate to an audience how the findings from the methods have been integrated (McCrudden, Marchand, & Schutz, 2021). When collecting data, a joint display can be used to facilitate purposeful recruitment participants for the next study, design interview schedule items, and facilitate with self-report measure development. There are also several ways a joint display can be used when analysing the data. Some have used it formatively with quantitative data to help make decisions on how to proceed with the subsequent analysis or next study (i.e., what topics should be explored in the interviews). They have also been used to compare findings from each method in a merged design by presenting the qualitative and quantitative findings side-by-side in the table to enable meta-inferences from both sources of data (McCrudden, Marchand, & Schutz, 2021).

2.5 Writing-up mixed methods research

When the findings are written up in a report or output, there are recognised ways to present the integration to the reader. In a mixed-methods output or report, authors will usually be expected to separately present the findings from both the qualitative and quantitative strands separately and then include a third mixed-methods finding section which explains how the findings have been integrated. Like the structure of essays, the comparison of approaches could lead to the discussion of one approach, then the discussion of a second approach followed by a summary and conclusion section. Alternativity, in one source of data, you may find a result that you wish to follow-up or explore with another source of data. For example, I may find a significant association between two variables in my quantitative dataset and want to better understand this association by looking for discussion of it in my qualitative interviews. However, a more complex way to structure an essay of this kind is to compare and contrast on a concept-by-concept basis. In this way it is how the different findings relate and integrate at the level of the phenomena, rather than the structure implicitly bringing out the contrast and differences of the approaches of data collection.

2.6 Summary of integrating mixed methods research

The two methods are very different in how they collect and interpret the data, they are like two separate entities that on the face of it do not feel like they are very similar, and they are not. However, a sound researcher will respect their differences and understand that they offer different insights to the phenomena. So, whilst their approaches are different, the findings they generate should talk and dance with one another. The researcher should be looking for the following things:

- consistent messages between the findings that infer the same interpretation of the situation
- complementary messages that finish the sentence that findings from the other method started to explain
- contrasting interpretations of the situation, where the researcher can make an inferred explanation about why that difference has occurred (and this should not simply be a critique of one of the methods)
- is there suggestion that the findings are providing evidence of different expressions of the phenomena?

Once the researcher engages with these types of questions about their findings, they should be starting to integrate the findings, understanding how they interplay, and explain parts of the other methods' findings. The approach should be to try and sit them alongside each other and find ways in which the findings are telling different parts of one story. It is the overall dance we're interested in, not the individual steps each method is striking on the dance floor.

Interesting facts

One of the most respected authors on mixed methods research is Vicki L. Piano, who has published frequently alongside other authors highlighting leading practice in mixed methods research. She has also been interested in establishing how young females can be inspired and supported to consider careers in science. Her paper in 2008 highlights what young females need in order to have positive influential science role models which in turn would support their consideration of a career in science. The paper also highlights the ways in which cultural contexts should be considered throughout a research process. To read about their findings, or the ways in which they safe guarded their research from just capturing the most rehearsed, loudest voices of privilege, look up the paper: Buck, G. A., Clark, V. L. P., Leslie-Pelecky, D., Lu, Y., & Cerda-Lizarraga, P. (2008). Examining the cognitive processes used by adolescent girls and women scientists in identifying science role models: A feminist approach. *Science Education*, *92*(4), 688–707.

Ig Nobel Prize

Pandemic? What pandemic?

It is very telling that there are few examples within the Ig Nobels of designed award-winning research that have used a mixed method approach. Most of the award-winning research has been completed using experimental approaches. However, the mixed method approach is seen in the write up and documented evidence cited by the Ig Nobels for lots of naturally occurring award winners. For example the following award winners:

2020 Ig Nobel Award Winners for the MEDICAL EDUCATION PRIZE [BRAZIL, UK, INDIA, MEXICO, BELARUS, USA, TURKEY, RUSSIA, TURKMENISTAN] Jair Bolsonaro of Brazil, Boris Johnson of the United Kingdom, Narendra Modi of India, Andrés Manuel López Obrador of Mexico, Alexander Lukashenko of Belarus, Donald Trump of the US, Recep Tayyip Erdogan of Turkey, Vladimir Putin of Russia, and Gurbanguly Berdimuhamedow of Turkmenistan, for using the Covid-19 viral pandemic to teach the world that politicians can have a more immediate effect on life and death than scientists and doctors.

This award is written up in many different newspaper reports and the inference is founded on data collected within each of these countries which inform the assessment of politicians influence survival chances within a pandemic more than scientists and medical professionals can. The data are typically self-reported infection rates, self-reported trust in government indices, death rates attributed to Covid-19 within the countries, and interviews with emergency management and public health experts exploring the effectiveness of strategies and decision-making on survival rates within those countries.

Cultural context

There is a risk that mixed methods are used negligently across cultural contexts. Some researchers who use mixed methods make the assumption that pre-validated scales can be used to establish a common understanding of a phenomena of interest across cultures, and then the interview method can be used to articulate and nuance the phenomena of interest within each of those cultures. This should be carefully tested and considered as there are many risks involved.

Firstly, this assumes that within each of those cultures (be they different organisations or different cultures across a large geographical area) the phenomena of interest exists in similar ways across those cultures. This is not always the case. Culturally the phenomena of enforcement of the law is constructed very differently in the police service in the United Kingdom, where we have the notion of policing by consent, contrasted to the phenomena of enforcement in the police service in other cultures where the law is enforced. In the United Kingdom, the legitimacy of the police to be able to do the actions of 'policing' come from the consent of the public, in the UK policing is not a power of the state. This means the construct that sits behind the word enforcement is quite different. So, when selecting a survey or scale to measure policing and enforcement between cultures should make sure that any scale has taken account of this in the theoretical development of the survey.

The assumptions that cultures experience or define phenomena in a similar way (be that cultural differences between occupation, place or peoples) is something that can be addressed through introducing more reflexivity and feedback points within the research design. This is so any assumption of similarity can be

(Continued)

explored before the research is actioned. This can be achieved through consulting on the formulation of the research questions, materials, the full piloting of both the survey and the interview schedules, making sure that the findings and inferences are quality assured through published process checklists and other such steps to ensure that those informed in the cultures have the ability to voice any concerns and safely challenge the assumptions of the research. This is to ensure that the researchers are not neglecting cultural contexts or, in the case of global cultural contexts, imposing Western norms on other cultures.

3. EXAMPLE STUDIES: FIREFIGHTERS

These two examples are taken from two of thc author's PhD thesis, Hill (2015) and Sanderson (2017). Both of these explore the occupation of firefighting and use mixed methods to try and understand areas of under-researched phenomena surrounding the occupation.

3.1 Example 1: Post-traumatic growth in firefighters

This research developed from the discussions contrasting the theoretical models of post-traumatic growth (PTG). PTG is the experience of positive impacts from a traumatic event such as an increased engagement with life (wanting to live life each day to the full), increased appreciation of family and friends (wanting to love and cherish loved ones to the full), increased spirituality (things happen for a reason, this doesn't have to be religious but should be spiritual), increased desire to grow and learn from the experience (there are things to learn and change as a result of that experience). PTG is relatively new as a psychological concept and therefore the research evidence base is still being established. One occupation who do experience traumatic events as part of their daily working activities role is the fire and rescue service, and so this research aimed to use a population which is known to have exposure to traumatic events, to develop and inform the competing theoretical models of PTG.

3.2 The researchers

Dr Lisa Sanderson is a Senior Lecturer in psychology at Nottingham Trent University, she researches wellbeing and impacts of traumatic events within occupations such as the military and the fire and rescue service.

3.3 PTG in firefighters: Why were mixed methods the best option?

A sequential mixed methods design was used in this research which is characterised by an initial phase of qualitative data collection and analysis followed by a phase of quantitative data collection and analysis (Cresswell, 2003). This design was chosen because it enables an in-depth exploration of the phenomenon under investigation, which in this case was PTG. An in-depth exploration of PTG was needed because this is a relatively under-researched area of psychology and despite several models of PTG being developed in the last twenty years it was still somewhat unclear why some individuals experience PTG following trauma whilst other individuals do not. Additionally, the development of existing theoretical models of growth had been undertaken using general population samples and very little work had been undertaken with the emergency services.

Thus, using this mixed methods design allowed us to start with a qualitative study. Data was collected using semi-structured interviews to explore firefighter's experiences of dealing with traumatic events and their subsequent negative and positive reactions (PTG). The resulting data was analysed using grounded theory which enabled us to build a model of PTG to compare with the existing theoretical models of PTG. One of the strengths of mixed methods research has been identified as the ability to generate and test a grounded theory model (Johnson & Onwuegbuzie, 2004). Whilst the grounded theory model allowed us to see how this subset of firefighters were experiencing trauma and subsequent PTG we were interested in seeing if we could generalise this to a bigger sample. Thus, undertaking a subsequent quantitative study enabled us to operationalise this model and test it on a very large sample of firefighters.

3.4 Design: How the psychometrics were chosen, the interview schedule considerations

The interview schedule was developed to explore firefighter's experiences of dealing with the traumatic incidents they encounter as part of their daily working lives and their subsequent reactions to this. Grounded theory is sometimes criticised for being subjective because the researcher decides which questions to ask in the process of data collection (Willig, 2013). However, using a semi-structured interview schedule, designed with a conversational tone ensured that the firefighters perspectives became the focus of the interviews, with the interviewer using prompts and probes to encourage them rather than explicitly direct. There is more detailed information provided on the things you need to consider when designing an interview schedule in Chapter 6.

Once we had used our qualitative data to develop our theoretical model of PTG we wanted to test this in a large sample of firefighters. In order to do this, we needed to operationalise our theoretical model, which means that we needed to identify scales, which we could use to measure each of the constructs that had been identified. These scales would then be combined into a survey. One example of this is coping, identified as one of the key constructs within our model and considered to be very important in the process of PTG. Thus, the literature on coping was searched and all the scales used to measure coping were identified and an appropriate scale was chosen for inclusion in the survey. Whilst psychometric evaluations, i.e., validity and reliability data were the primary factor in scale selection there were some additional considerations such as the length of the scale and whether it had been previously used within the area of PTG research. It's always worth considering the length of a scale if you are going to be administering multiple scales as too many items and participants may get fatigued.

3.5 The findings: The type of data analysis, the results and interpretation

The qualitative phase of our research enabled us to develop an in-depth understanding of how our sample of firefighters' cope with the traumatic incidents that they attend as part of their daily working lives. For example, the most frequently cited coping strategy was talking to colleagues, which in the majority of cases, ensured that the negative reactions which they experienced when they attended traumatic incidents were short-lived and did not lead to any negative long-term effects.

Collecting survey data in the quantitative phase of our research provided the opportunity to see whether our theoretical model of PTG was applicable to a larger firefighter population. This data was analysed using structural equation modelling which allowed us to test the relationships between these multiple factors.

3.6 Reflections: On the findings, the usefulness of mixed methods and ethical considerations

Taken together the findings of both studies suggests that the process of PTG is a complex one and involves the interplay of many factors. Combining both qualitative and quantitative methods within the same study enabled us to further our understanding of these factors. If we use the example of coping again, analysis of our qualitative data revealed several coping strategies used by firefighters following traumatic incidents. Building on this the quantitative study illuminated the relationship between these coping strategies and PTG. For example, the use of emotional social support, active coping and positive re-interpretation were all found to be positive and significant predictors of PTG. This formed evidence-based recommendations about how procedures in the workplace could be strengthened to ensure that firefighters would not suffer long-term negative consequences from dealing with traumatic incidents and how PTG could be promoted.

Thus, we can see that mixed methods can be extremely useful in answering complex research questions. However, mixed methods research is not easy, not least because the researcher must have sufficient knowledge of both qualitative and quantitative approaches, to enable them to carry out the research effectively. Also, as a mixed methods project is using both qualitative and quantitative approaches it is likely that there will be multiple ethical issues to be considered.

3.7 Worked example 2: Occupation related consequences for relatives of firefighters

In the first worked example, we saw that the mixed sequential method was selected in order to inform the competing academic theoretical models of PTG. In this second example, we see the same occupational context as worked example one (the UK Fire and Rescue Service), and a similar mixed method design was chosen, but for very different reasons. This design of mixed methods was selected to explore and establish a concept and develop a model where there were no pre-existing theoretical concepts or model. So, the reasons for the design are very different, but there are similarities in the context and practical applications of the work.

3.8 The researcher

Dr Rowena Hill is an Associate Professor at Nottingham Trent University. She works alongside the emergency services and also in disaster and emergency management. She was seconded during 2020 to the Covid-19 National Response as an embedded scientist in a cross-department governmental group to look at the long-range predictions of Covid-19 and its impacts across society. You can see some of the outputs from this group here: www.ntu.ac.uk/about-us/nottingham-civic-exchange/c19-national-foresight-group

3.9 Why look at families of firefighters?

Previous literature looking at how firefighters are supported and show resilience throughout their challenging occupation has identified their colleagues as one of the main sources of support (Neale, 1991; Bacharach, Bamberger, & Doveh, 2008; Regehr, 2009; Schumm, Bell, & Resnick, 2001). This has been demonstrated by most firefighters through an increase in peer support and shared coping strategies between individuals (Hill & Brunsden, 2003; Hill & Brunsden, 2009; Hawker, Durkin & Hawker, 2011; Pietrantoni and Prati, 2009). Firefighters describe their immediate team members (their 'watch') as a second family because of the large amount of time spent and shared experiences they have together.

The other biggest source of support identified throughout the literature is the family. If the Fire and Rescue Service has a set of unique stressors and impacts on the employee, then their family is supporting them and experiencing the impacts of those unique stressors. Therefore, the relatives of firefighters are helping to maintain their firefighters resilience and well-being and should be supported too.

3.10 What did the study aim to do?

The study aimed to develop a theoretical framework of how threats to well-being and resilience are experienced and responded to by families of firefighters. The study was a sequential mixed methods design where families of firefighters were interviewed and from the analysis of that data a bigger quantitative survey was designed. This was needed as there was no theoretical models in the previous literature. With no evidence to guide further study, the qualitative data and analysis enabled the development of a model, which the quantitative survey was then designed to test. The findings suggest that the impacts on the family included sacrifice and spillover between work and home and so the firefighter became a 'satellite' family member in order not to disrupt the family routines due to their changing duty systems. Also, family members had secondary traumatic reactions and perceived danger and harm within the occupation. The support offered to deal with these impacts included positive growth, resilience, well-being and family structures. This formed evidenced-based recommendations to support both firefighters and their families across the firefighting occupation in the UK.

3.11 Choices of instruments

The interview schedule was developed in order to try and get the full range and scope of families' experiences of having a family member in the fire and rescue service. The interview schedule asked about their perception of what the firefighting occupation was, the kinds of demands that has on their firefighter family member and what impacts that had on the wider family. This was completed as a one-to-one interview for ethical reasons (see below).

Ethel ethics

What happens if you gain consent from a participant to take part in an interview and then decide you wish to collect data via both an interview and a survey? Can you simply send the participant the survey to complete? Or do you need to revise your original ethics submission? Or add a correction? Can you think of any issues with combining data from a qualitative study with a questionnaire study? Ethical issues? Methodological issues? (or are these the same)? Indeed, there is a conflict between the two data collection methods which is commonly resolved by collecting ethics consent for each part of the study separately (and preferably as two parts of the same ethics application), integrating the two approaches into one argument.

Once the findings of the qualitative study was completed, this then provided a structure with which to guide the survey study. The process of selecting appropriate scales began with mapping the conceptual model developed in stage one on to an operational model, which means that variables were identified from the conceptual findings of the qualitative model and mapped to aligned literatures (such as the literature on resilience, wellbeing, risk perception, traumatic reactions). Questionnaires which measured these variables such as resilience, wellbeing, risk perception and traumatic reactions were then sought within the literature to measure the constructs. Different possibilities were then reviewed against each other on their psychometric properties. In some areas, such as resilience there were lots of questionnaires to choose from. In other areas, such as risk perception, there were significantly fewer to choose from as most of the questionnaires are focussed on an individual's perception of their own risk, rather than the family members perception of risk to their firefighter family member. This was harder to address and risk perception of families of the firefighting occupation was broken down further in to three variables; perceived physical danger, risk perception, and trust in procedures and occupational safety.

3.12 The findings

The analysis of the qualitative study shaped the quantitative study, but the findings of both studies were combined to inform the research aim. This is where the real challenge of mixed methods comes in, integrating two sets of findings is challenging and poorly conducted mixed methods studies sometimes analyse them separately without then making sense of them together. These studies were able to present the developed model of impacts on families of the firefighting occupation, identify the factors which impact the most from that model, as well as the strength of those relationships.

3.13 Reflections

Mixed methods are hard to do well, but their ability to inform more complex and demanding research questions is worth the challenge. The key to doing mixed methods is to give careful thought to how the methods combine and speak to one another. Leaving them separate is like having two people talking out loud to themselves instead of speaking to each other in a conversation. Enabling a design where the methods combine and complement each other ensures a conversation which can inform the research question to much greater depth. The ethical considerations they carry are dependent on the methods selected to include and combine, so it is best to refer to the specific ethics challenges in other relevant chapters according to the qualitative and quantitative methods chosen.

LEARNING OBJECTIVES

You should now know the following things about mixed methods:

- The typical methods selected for mixed methods
- How to think about sequencing or combining the methods in the study design

- How to think about integrating or combining the findings of the methods in the write up
- The necessity of maintaining robustness for each method within mixed method design

FURTHER READING

Some good examples of mixed methods studies include a paper by Côté-Leclerc, Duchesne, Bolduc, Gélinas-Lafrenière, Santerre, Desrosiers, and Levasseur (2017) who completed a mixed method study with people with mobility limitations to explore how playing adapted sports affects quality of life.

Côté-Leclerc, F., Duchesne, G. B., Bolduc, P., Gélinas-Lafrenière, A., Santerre, C., Desrosiers, J., & Levasseur, M. (2017). How does playing adapted sports affect quality of life of people with mobility limitations? Results from a mixed-method sequential explanatory study. *Health and Quality of Life Outcomes*, *15*(1), 22.

Also, have a read of the paper by Isaacs, Roman, and Savahl (2019) to see how relatively unexplored cultural contexts can be significantly informed by a mixed methods sequential exploratory design, in this case exploring the family resilience needs of a rural community in South Africa.

Isaacs, S. A., Roman, N. V., & Savahl, S. (2019). An exploration of the family resilience needs of a rural community in South Africa: A sequential explanatory mixed methodological study design. *Current Psychology*, *38*(6), 1634–48.

To see a mixed method study where the researchers needed to design their own survey would be Wariri, Ajani, Raymond, Iliya, Lukman, Okpo, and Isaac (2020) who explored the experience of caregivers on their disclosure of HIV status to infected children in their care in Gombe, north east Nigeria.

Wariri, O., Ajani, A., Raymond, M. P., Iliya, A., Lukman, O., Okpo, E., & Isaac, E. (2020). 'What will my child think of me if he hears I gave him HIV?': A sequential, explanatory, mixed-methods approach on the predictors and experience of caregivers on disclosure of HIV status to infected children in Gombe, Northeast Nigeria.*BMC Public Health*, *20*(1), 1–13.

LINKS TO USEFUL RESOURCES

Colin Robson's Real World Research has some great resources to look at the practical aspect of mixed methods in contexts outside of university research laboratories and participants who are not recruited from a student population. His book about research methods is written for researching practitioners who are mostly working within organisations. He is clear, well balanced and informative.

11

REPERTORY GRIDS

NICHOLAS BLAGDEN AND
ROSIE KITSON-BOYCE

1. INTRODUCTION

The **repertory grid** is a research/assessment method that is rooted in Kelly's (1955a) Personal Construct Theory. Personal Construct Psychology (PCP) is a psychology of human concern, it attempts to understand people's construing and how they make sense of the world (Shotter, 2007). Kelly's central epistemological position was '**constructive alternativism**', which asserts that people construe reality in different ways. People make sense of their social worlds by forming hypotheses about the world and putting them to the test of experience. There will be commonality amongst people's construing as well as individuality and the emphasis on 'constructive alternativism' is because we can always construe things differently (Walker & Winter, 2007). As Kelly (1955b, p. 937) argues 'there is nothing in the world which is not subject to some form of reconstruction'.

Originally, Kelly developed the Repertory Grid as a way to understand his clients' psychological difficulties, and to enable them to gain insight into their construing and the implications this was having for them (Burr, King & Heckmann, 2020). The repertory grid (rep grid) has since become the most widely used technique of personal construct theory and has been applied to thousands of different studies in diverse settings (Neimeyer, 2004). From counselling (see Proctor, 1985), education and social work (see Borell, Espwall, Pryce & Brenner, 2003), social identity (Burr, King & Heckmann, 2020), immigration (Mancuso, 2003), clinical and forensic settings (Blagden et al., 2012; Horley, 2008; Houston, 1998). In basic terms, the repertory grid allows for the assessment of **personal constructs** and allows an understanding of the individual's unique world view. The repertory grid is thus a method for studying personal and interpersonal systems of meaning (Neimeyer, 2004).

Interesting facts

Make believe is essential for science

According to George Kelly, make-believe is an essential feature of science. Indeed, in his 1964 article 'The Language of Hypothesis', Kelly explains that without make-believe, neither scientists or novelists would be able to come up with anything new. For more about Kelly's argument about how much novelists and scientists have in common, please see Kelly's (1964) article. Enjoy!

The repertory grid is a form of participant-led structured interview which utilises a card sorting task to elicit personally meaningful constructs (more detailed focus on the process of this is covered later in this chapter). Data are collected and analysed both qualitatively and quantitatively; this mixed method approach helps the researcher to develop an understanding of the way a participant makes sense of their world and interprets their experience (Neimeyer, Bowman & Saferstein, 2005; Mason, 2003).

Cultural context

One of the advantages of personal construct psychology and the use of repertory grids is that, unlike some psychometrics, pcp privileges the individual's own culture and psychology and attempts to understand their world rather than trying to impose one on them. Repertory grids can be seen as an 'empty' method rather than a 'psychological test' and it depends on the context, purpose and culture of the individual. Personal construct psychology is a way of understanding clients' idiosyncratic beliefs and is a position that acknowledges that we all construe things (people, situations, events) differently in accordance with our own life

(Continued)

experience (Kelly, 1991; Blagden et al., 2012). The heart of personal construct theory is a focus on how people make sense of their lives and how they construct social reality, rather than moving them towards a kind of uniformity that reflects the culture and backgrounds of most psychologists. According to Kelly (1991), a person's view of the universe is construed 'through transparent patterns or templates which he creates and then attempts to fit over the realities of which the world is composed (Kelly, 1991, pp. 8–9). Although we cannot ever fully understand an individual's construing, we can seek to understand their world view and help them to reveal their own ways of making sense to us (Shotter, 2007). PCP research has previously focused on culturally sensitive research topics such as immigration (Manusco, 2003), citizenship and national identity (Kalekin-Fishman, 2009), resettlement of refugees (Naffi & Davidson, 2017), and terrorism (Canter, Sarangi, & Youngs, 2014).

1.1 Design

A basic repertory grid consists of **elements**, **constructs** and **ratings** with each **grid** being conducted in relation to a particular **topic**. Over the last 50 years, more than half of the published empirical studies using the repertory grid method have been in the field of psychology (Saúl, Lopez-Gonzalez, Moreno-Pulido, Corbella, Compan, & Feixas, 2012). With this methodology growing in popularity (Hardison, & Neimeyer, 2012), it is unsurprising that it is used to explore topics in many areas of psychological research and practice, including clinical, forensic and occupational psychology. Indeed, given that one of the primary aims of using repertory grids is to make underlying patterns of individuals thinking more apparent, one can see the clear benefits this may have for research and clinical practice (Leach, Freshwater, Aldridge, & Sunderland, 2001).

1.2 Elements

The elements of a repertory grid usually take the form of people with whom the participant has either a positive or negative relationship. It is recommended that no more than 12 elements are used. These can be supplied to, or elicited directly from, the participants. As Jankowicz (2004) states, using the correct (that is, appropriate) set of elements is crucial as it indicates the realm of discourse and enables the person's constructs to be discovered (more detail on this in the next section in this chapter). Within psychological research it is often useful to ask the participants to consider how they compare to the person they have been previously and to their ideal self in the future. Elements such as 'past self', 'self now' and 'ideal self' are, therefore, often supplied as elements to participants.

Supplying elements in this way enables different grids, from different time points or participants, to be compared and, therefore, may provide a greater statistical comparison (Tan & Hunter, 2002). The drawback is that supplied elements may not be personally meaningful for the participant, working against the method's concern with how the participant construes their world (Blagden, Winder, Gregson, & Thorne, 2014). Indeed, the elements need to provide representative coverage of the participant's experience of the topic. Participants can therefore be asked to think specifically of a 'friend', 'past partner', 'someone they do not like' etc., so that the elements represent meaningful people in their life, either positively or negatively.

1.3 Constructs

Next, and possibly most important within a repertory grid, are the **constructs**. These can be defined as the psychological mechanism used by individuals to make sense of the world around them and, in the case of the repertory grid, interpret the elements chosen (Mason, 2008; Tan & Hunter, 2002). Constructs are bipolar; that is, they have two poles that are contrasts rather than diametric opposites (Horley, 2008). Traditionally within the repertory grid, the constructs would be elicited entirely from the participants, enabling the researcher to explore more deeply the way in which the participants construe their social world (Bell, 2005; Borell, Espwall, Pryce, & Brenner, 2003). Although the process of eliciting a meaningful grid is not standardised, the main method is the triadic one. This involves the participant being presented with three elements and being asked to identify how two of them are alike and in what way they are different from the third, e.g., my father and brother are 'ambitious' whereas my best friend is 'easy going'. The aim in doing this, is for participants to identify two contrasting constructs, which make up both the implicit and emergent poles of the repertory grid.

This triadic process of elicitation, however, is a complex one requiring participants to provide logical opposites rather than opposites of meaning, e.g., 'ambitious' versus 'does not trample on colleagues' as opposed to 'ambitious' versus 'not-ambitious' (Easterby-Smith, 1980). Another issue with the triadic method is the increased likelihood of it producing 'bent' constructs, that is two entirely different constructs within a single dimension, e.g., 'ambitious' versus 'athletic' (Neimeyer et al., 2005). In research, involving individuals with intellectual disabilities in particular, some acknowledge that participants struggle to consider the differences between people and are only able to think of the similarities (Mason, 2003; Kitson-Boyce, Blagden, Winder, & Dillon, 2018). In cases such as this, a simpler dyadic elicitation method may be used whereby only two elements are presented to the participant, who is asked to describe two ways in which they are similar, e.g., how are your brother and father similar. Following this, they are asked to consider the contrasts of these constructs, representing the alternative of how they currently view the world and, therefore, the implicit pole of the construct, e.g., what is the opposite of 'ambitious'? The resulting opposite pole may be, for example, 'lazy' (Walker & Winter, 2007).

Both elicitation methods facilitate communication, and a laddering process can be used, whereby participants are asked which construct they prefer, which they associate themselves with and why. This enables higher order constructs to be explored and elicited (Hardison & Neimeyer, 2012).

A clear benefit of the repertory grid is its flexibility; the process can be adapted to a format best suited to the individual needs and abilities of the participant. It is vital, however, that the researcher suspends their own view of the world and instead accepts the construing of the participant, thus enabling them to get as close as possible to the experience of the individual being questioned (Butler, 2006). In doing this, 'good' constructs can be elicited, which convey the participant's meaning appropriately. The process, however, can involve hard work on the part of the participant and this should be managed sensitively by the researcher, allowing breaks and thinking time where necessary.

Skoolkid errors

Taking the person out of a person-centred method

A school child error is, in trying to standardise or generalise repertory grid data, the researcher creates all the elements and constructs. This may be tempting for the reasons just stated (the capacity to generalise across participants) but this should be avoided since it undermines the very ethos of the methodology. By doing this, you will miss out on the individual construals and lose much of the potency of this method. Where researchers are keen to make some comparisons, they may wish to predetermine some of the elements and constructs, but ideally these should be kept to a minimum.

1.4 The rating process

Once the elements and constructs have been either supplied or elicited, the rating process is commenced. A semi-structured interview procedure is used to ask participants to evaluate quantitatively the degree to which each element can be characterised according to their own personal constructs (Borell et al., 2003). This involves the elements being rated against each pair of constructs using a **Likert Scale**. A 7-point Likert scale arguably provides a meaningful rating scale for statistical analysis (Tan & Hunter, 2002) but other variations can be used. Each pole of a given construct can be seen as a logical boundary with every rating indicating the element's degree of membership towards that pole (Horley, 2008). For example, on a scale using constructs 'lazy' versus 'ambitious', a rating of 1 would indicate they were perceived as lazy 100% of the time, and a rating of 7 would indicate the element (i.e., person) in question was perceived by the participant to be 100% ambitious and a rating of 4 would indicate the element/person was perceived as lazy and ambitious in equal measures.

As with eliciting constructs, the rating process is not always an easy task. The process can often be quite abstract, requiring participants to quantify the extent to which people in their life, past or present, fit certain constructs. To ease understanding, visual aids may be used. For example, each point of the scale can be written on pieces of cardboard and laid out in order (1–7) with each pole of a construct written down and laid at either end of the scale, i.e., *trusts others easily* would be placed on a piece of card at on end with *untrusting* placed at the other.

Ig Nobel Prize

Observations of everyday life

This prize-winning work has absolutely nothing to do with this chapter but we wanted to include it in the book so here it is. John Trinkaus is a giant in observational research. When something annoys him enough he takes the time and trouble to categorise and record it. He has published nearly 100 brief reports of observations of everyday life. For example, one study in 1993 looked at the number of shoppers in the express checkout line who had more than the permitted number of items. In his 1990 paper 'Exiting a Building: An Informal Look' he calculated the percentage of people who chose a door that was already open rather than one that was closed. In his 2003 paper, 'Snow on Motor Vehicle Roofs: An Informal Look' he calculated the percentage of drivers who don't bother to brush the snow off their cars. For his careful appreciation of the little things in life, Professor Trinkaus was awarded the 2003 Ig Nobel Prize for Literature.

Additionally, gentle probing of the participant's decision process can be used by the researcher to explore why certain ratings have been given. For example, if the element 'self in the past' was given a 1 on a 'selfish/generous' construct, but the 'present self' was rated a 5, the researcher may want to explore with the participant why they believe themselves to be more generous now and what happened to initiate this change. This exploration enables any gaps in understanding to be identified and produces qualitative data that can be analysed alongside the quantitative data.

2. TYPES OF ANALYSES

On completion of the repertory grid, there are many types of analysis that can be performed on the data. In the next few sections, we will take you through the most commonly used analyses, with detailed examples included as case studies in this chapter.

2.1 Eyeball analysis

The first step on completion of a repertory grid is to review and familiarise yourself with the data collected. Jankowicz (2004) provides a detailed step-by-step guide for how to carry this out. The first consideration, however, is how did the participant find the elicitation process of both the elements and constructs, i.e., did they find it difficult? How long did it take? The same applies for the rating process; did they struggle to rate a particular element? Did they rate certain elements exactly the same, use the extreme ratings or go for the middle ground repeatedly? It is important to draw conclusions from the questions considered and, as the researcher, you now begin to make interpretations.

Descriptive statistics: The mean, standard deviation and skew can be produced for the entire grid, element and/or constructs. In addition, the extent to which the participant may be using the extreme ends of the ratings, e.g., repeatedly choosing 1 and 7, can be determined via an extremity analysis.

2.2 Bivariate statistics

As we move towards more detailed analyses, it is worth acknowledging that statistical software programmes can be used to aid the analysis of repertory data. Although there are resources available to conduct such analyses manually, programmes such as **Idiogrid** can uncover the structural features of construing that manual analysis alone would arguably fail to reveal (Mason, 2003). Bivariate statistics can be produced for both the element and constructs. Some of the statistics often used are **Pearson correlations** and **Euclidean distances**. These enable the relationships between pairs of constructs, pairs of elements, and the relationship between a construct-element pair to be assessed (Grice, 2002).

2.3 Principal component analysis

A structural measure often used when analysing repertory grid data is the **Principal Component Analysis** (PCA). The PCA provides a two-dimensional graphical display of the components of a participant's construal system, where the elements are represented as points and the constructs are represented as lines from the origin. This visual output enables the participant's internal relationship between people who are, or have been, significant to them and the way they construe them to be presented.

The more 'fanned' the lines or vectors are, typifying a spoke-like PCA output, indicates a more elaborate construct system with the constructs being more meaningful (Fransella, Bell, & Bannister, 2004). In contrast, a polarised PCA output may indicate 'tight' construing, which alone, is maladaptive in a changing world and can be characterised by 'all or nothing' thinking (Houston, 1998; Winter, 1992). This can be explored further by examining the percentage of variance accounted for by the first factor (PVAFF) of the PCA: this information is available from the PCA output from Idiograd. An over-reliance or high loading on to the first component is interpreted as an indicator of a tightly organised construct system (Fransella, Bell, & Bannister, 2004; Winter, 2003). Ryle and Breen (1972) found, using relatively large grids, that typically, the mean variance accounted for by the first principal component was 39.4%. Whereas where the first principal component accounts for a higher percentage of variance, e.g., 56% (see Garcıa-Mieres et al., 2016), this was indicative of tight construing.

2.4 Self-identity plots

These are a graphical method, which use any combination of two elements to form a two-dimensional space (Norris & Makhlouf-Norris, 1976). The standardised Euclidean distances between the elements in the grid are plotted in this two-dimensional space providing a summary of the relationships among the elements (Grice, 2002). In doing this, a self-identity plot shows the relationship between those elements a person views as important and meaningful in their world and highlights the way they construe the self and others.

2.5 Implicative dilemmas

Implicative dilemmas arise due to an awareness of discrepancies between a person's actual self (self now) and ideal self (self in the future) (Dorough, Grice, & Parker, 2007). These cognitive conflicts can be identified within some individuals' repertory grids and are based on correlations between congruent and incongruent constructs (Feixas & Saul, 2004).

2.6 Qualitative analyses

As mentioned previously, the structured interview used to elicit the elements and constructs, as well as structure the rating process, can be recorded and transcribed. This data can be analysed via qualitative methods, such as Thematic analysis and Interpretative Phenomenological Analysis. Indeed, the blending of IPA alongside the quantitative data produced from the repertory grid arguably provides a rigorous exploration of participants' meaning making (Blagden et al., 2014; Yorke & Dallos, 2015). It has been argued that repertory grid interviews have been neglected as a source of meaningful data with grid analysis weighted too heavily on the content of the grid (Fromm, 2004). The extracts below are examples of repertory grid interview data (see Blagden, 2011).

Extract 1

Participant: [moves cards]
Interviewer: OK in what way are those two similar?
Participant: We both look for hidden meanings in what people say
Interviewer: OK, so what kind of …
Participant: Meanings define people's words; it's not what people say it's what they don't say.
Interviewer: Ok, looks for hidden meanings in what people say, can you elaborate on that a little bit, what does that mean for you?
Participant: They're looking for motivation and evidence
Interviewer: Ok, so what is the opposite of someone who looks for hidden meanings
Participant: Erm an optimist.

Extract 2

Stef: You see I [points to me now me card] I used to be pretty outgoing … but now it's all changed
IV: That's interesting, how has that changed?
Stef: I'm not happy now I'm not outgoing anymore
IV: How would you describe yourself now?
Stef: I've boarded up the windows, all the doors are shut, I'm like a tortoise aren't I (.) I've retreated inside me shell for safety. I can't let err apart from a few people that are there already, I can't let any other people near me or close to me … they've trampled all over me and my family and my life and I've had enough, end of and that's how I am …

Traditionally, these extracts would not make it into the final analysis or discussion of repertory grid data, and we have argued previously that repertory grid interviews can be a source of clinically rich data (Kitson-Boyce, Wheatley, & Blagden, 2020). The extracts here highlight how the participant is making-sense and how he construes himself as a pessimist, and as someone who seeks out people's motives and looks for their hidden meanings – he cannot take things at face value. This seems to point to their struggles to trust within interpersonal relationships.

3. EXAMPLE STUDY: PRISONER REINTEGRATION

3.1 The study and the researchers

'This Time It's Different': Preparing for Release through a prison-model of CoSA: A phenomenological and repertory grid analysis.

Rosie Kitson-Boyce, Nicholas Blagden, Belinda Winder and Gayle Dillon

3.2 Background and aims of the study

Desistance research seeks to understand the processes involved that lead individuals towards becoming a productive member of society and a new life away from crime (Willis, Levenson, & Ward, 2010). **Circles of Support and Accountability** (CoSA) is a community-based programme that supports this desistance journey by working with individuals with a sexual offence history to reduce their risk of harm and safely reintegrate into society. The prison-based CoSA model begins prior to the prisoners ('core members') release from prison and continues with them on release into the community. The research question was to consider how the prison-model of CoSA relates to the desistance of crime. Repertory grid data were collected at two different time points; prior to starting the CoSA in prison (T1) and just before release from prison (T2). A case study will now be discussed from this larger study to illuminate the use of the repertory grid over different time points.

3.3 Design

To achieve the aims of the research, the elements of the repertory grid were both supplied and elicited. From the elements presented in Figure 11.1, the 'self in the past', 'self now' and 'self in the future' were supplied with the rest elicited. This enabled the researcher to explore the participant's (Nigel's) relationships with both his past and future self, as well as any other relationships he deemed meaningful.

As with the elements, a mixture of both supplied and elicited constructs were used. The supplied constructs were given after the rest of the constructs had been elicited so as not to influence the type of constructs the participants thought of themselves (Easterby-Smith, 1980). These consisted of 'socially supported'/'socially isolated'; 'trusts others easily'/'untrusting'; 'intimate and meaningful relationship'/'the opposite was elicited from participant'. Supplying these constructs ensured that the topic of social networks around the participant had complete coverage. The same constructs were used at each time point to enable a comparison between grids. The supplied elements equally remained the same, however, the elements elicited came freely from the participant, which enabled insight into any shifts that may have occurred.

In the rating process, time was spent explaining what the scale meant in detail and Nigel's understanding was checked at various points throughout the rating process. The completed grid involved each element having been rated by Nigel against each pair of constructs (see Figures 11.1 and 11.2), which could be analysed.

3.4 Findings

An initial eyeball analysis of the elicitation process highlighted the construct 'genuine' as being important to Nigel at both time points. Nigel elaborated on this further, explaining that he himself had previously never been genuine but since going into prison and joining the CoSA he had made a considerable effort to change this, with positive results.

> because I've never been me before, I'm always somebody else and for people to know who I am, what I am and my history, erm it's wonderful.

	Self in the past	Self now	Self in the future	Someone you don't like 1	Someone you don't like 2	Someone convicted of a sex offence 1	Someone convicted of a sex offence 2	Ex-partner 1 (Ex-P 1)	Ex-partner 2 (Ex-P 2)	Prison officer 1	Prison officer 2	Non-offending person	
Deceitful/manipulative	6	2	2	7	7	2	2	1	1	2	2	1	Pleasant/likeable
Doesn't want to know	4	1	1	7	7	2	2	4	4	1	1	1	Helpful/honest
Dismissive	7	1	1	7	7	1	1	1	1	1	1	1	Accepting of people
Nasty/vile	5	1	1	7	7	3	3	1	1	3	3	3	Friendly
Judgemental/criticises people	3	2	2	7	7	3	1	1	1	1	1	1	Trustworthy
Doesn't talk about anything	6	2	1	7	7	2	2	1	1	1	1	1	Open
Control freak	6	1	1	7	7	1	1	1	1	1	1	1	Genuine/nothing to hide
Untrusting	4	1	1	7	7	3	3	1	3	3	3	1	Trusts others easily
Socially isolated	6	1	1	7	7	2	2	1	3	2	2	2	Socially supported
Untrustworthy	4	3	1	7	7	3	3	3	3	3	3	2	Meaningful relationships

Figure 11.1 Nigel – pre-CoSA grid. A completed repertory grid for Nigel at T1

	Self in the past	Self now	Self in the future	Someone you don't like 1	Someone you don't like 2	Someone convicted of a sex offence 1	Someone convicted of a sex offence 2	Ex-partner 1 (Ex-P 1)	Ex-partner 2 (Ex-P 2)	Prison officer 1	Prison officer 2	Non-offending person	
Liar/interfering	5	1	1	7	7	1	1	1	1	1	1	1	Genuine/honest
Evil people	4	1	1	7	7	2	2	1	2	1	1	1	Happy
Haven't got time for you/too busy	2	1	1	7	7	2	2	2	1	1	2	1	Will talk to you
Manipulate you	5	1	1	7	7	2	2	1	1	1	1	1	Genuinely helpful
Selfish	5	1	1	7	7	2	2	1	2	1	1	1	Passion to help
Controlling	5	1	1	7	7	2	2	2	2	2	1	1	Being able to laugh
Self-centred/think they know best	5	1	1	7	7	2	2	2	2	2	2	1	Listens to you
Socially isolated	5	1	1	7	7	2	2	1	1	1	1	1	Socially supported
Untrusting	6	1	1	7	7	2	2	1	1	1	1	1	Trusts others easily
Lonely/suspicious	4	4	1	7	7	2	2	1	2	1	1	1	Intimate/meaningful relationships

Figure 11.2 Nigel - pre-release grid. A completed repertory grid for Nigel at T2

> it's just new people cause I've always been suspicious and I've always disliked men and knowing people, being honest and talking to them in a genuine way makes you feel so much better, makes you feel so easy inside.

During this part of the repertory grid, the researcher used probing, questioning and laddering to attempt to explore a wider range of the participant's construct system. Nigel became very emotional at this point, specifically when talking about the 'people he did not like' elements. These individuals had caused Nigel significant trauma in his past and he found talking about them emotionally draining. This highlights the need for compassion as a researcher, whereby the offence is separated from the individual, who is a fellow human being with real emotions. It also highlights the importance of transcribing the interview that facilitates the repertory grid. The reasons behind the constructs given, and the importance attributed to them can be captured, and included within the analysis.

When reviewing the rating process, it was apparent that Nigel construed himself now to how he would like to be in future on all constructs except 'meaningful and intimate relationships'. Although Nigel felt he had made positive changes whilst in prison, he had not, unsurprisingly, established any intimate or meaningful relationships with other prisoners. He construed his self in the future, however, as having achieved this and could not foresee any negative connotations that may be related to this. Whilst it is positive that Nigel was optimistic about his upcoming release from prison, those convicted of a sexual offence often face significant issues and stigma when trying to reintegrate back into the community (Tewksbury & Lees, 2006). Nigel may have, therefore, experienced this period as more problematic than he thought, making CoSA support even more essential.

Whoa there!

Limitations

Like all methods/methodological approaches it has limitations. Repertory grids are useful for illuminating an individual's underlying thinking, but it is important that they are not mistaken for a sort of psychic x-ray, which offers privileged access to the exact workings of a person's mind (Butt & Burr, 2004). Kelly (1955a) views individuals as a 'form of motion' (p. 48) thus one's thinking does not remain static, people are always engaged in something, the outcome of which may elaborate or amend one's construct system. The aim of personal construct psychology is not to arrive at tightly defined constructs, like traits, in order to infer meaning (Butt & Burr, 2004). Rather personal construct psychology is interested in how they construe, meaning is approached through investigating the relationships between constructs, elements and their implications for each other. Thus, meaning of any construct can be recognised in terms of its relationships with others (Butt & Burr, 2004). The caveat of using repertory grids is not to see the grid as a hard and fast 'mental map', but instead something that is more tentative, that allows one to make predictions about individuals construing. The idiographic emphasis is often seen as a limitation due to it not being generalisable. The process can also be time consuming and complicated and, at times, needs to be adapted for those who have intellectual or learning difficulties (see Kitson-Boyce, Wheatley, & Blagden, 2020).

Within this part of the process, Nigel has also rated both the 'someone you don't like' elements the same at both time points and assigned them a 7 regardless of the construct (see Figures 11.1 and 11.2). It was apparent that Nigel construed both individuals as 'horrible people' and 'evil' and had no ability or desire to construe them in any other manner.

3.5 Structural analysis of the grid

In order to make sense and understand the relationships within the grid, a structural analysis of the repertory grid is needed. Whilst other software programmes can be used, the researchers in this study used Idiogrid to analyse the grid data. There are different forms of statistical analysis that can be performed on grid data including correlational analysis, cluster analysis, principal component analysis (PCA) and self-identity plots (Blagden et al., 2012; Jankowisz, 2004). We will use PCA and self-identity plots to further make sense of Nigel's grid.

A principal component analysis (PCA) of Nigel's repertory grid offers insight into how Nigel construes himself over time. A PCA plots the constructs and elements in the same two-dimensional space and shows the internal relationship between elements and constructs regarding the people important in Nigel's world (Blagden et al., 2012; Mason, 2003). Figures 11.3 and 11.4 highlight how Nigel construes his 'self in the future' as diametrically

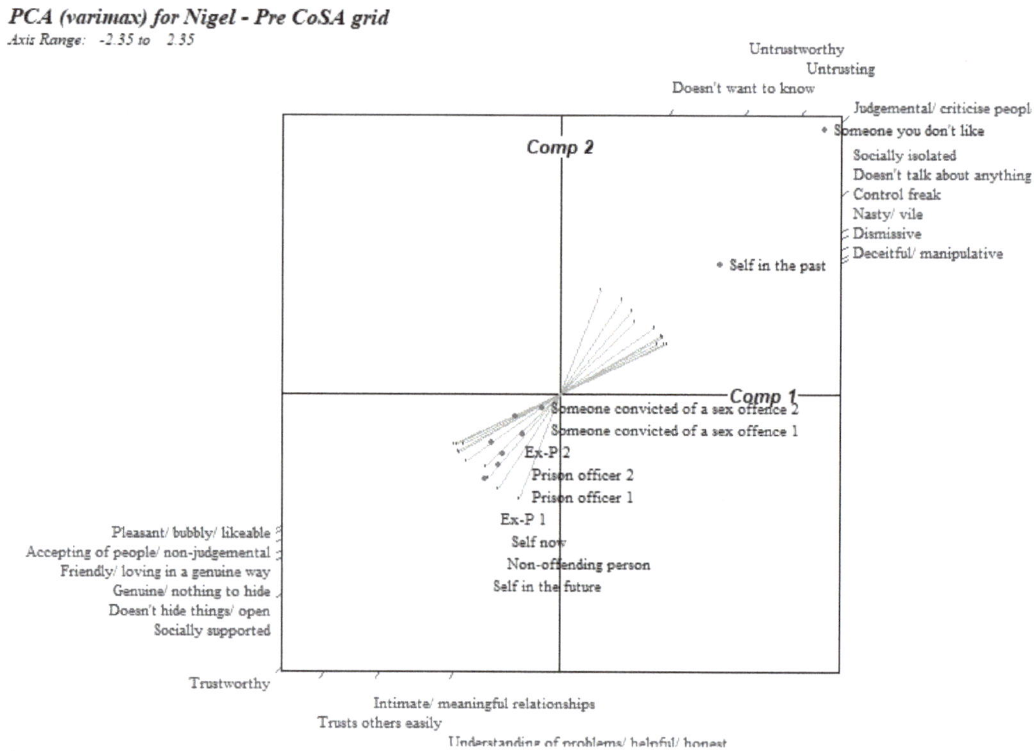

Figure 11.3 Principal Component Analysis (PCA) for Nigel at T1

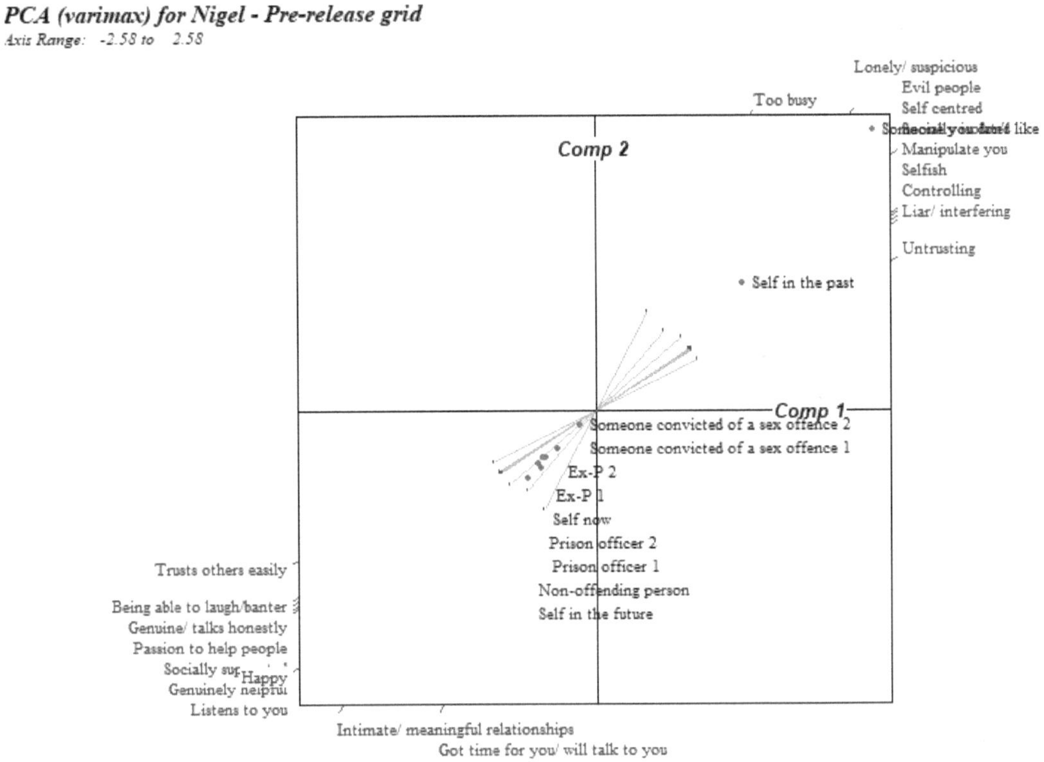

Figure 11.4 Principal Component Analysis (PCA) for Nigel at T2

opposed to his 'self in the past', which is located among the constructs of 'deceitful', 'manipulative' and 'nasty' at T1 and 'liar', 'controlling' and 'untrusting' at T2. This is in contrast to his 'self now', which, as previously discussed, he construes as being genuine.

Pro social support, and the subsequent sense of belonging, is considered as vital in the desistance process (Weaver & McNeill, 2015). It is positive, therefore, to see Nigel's construal of his progression towards the 'socially supported' construct between the two timepoints. Although this change is small, the benefit of the repertory grid is that these can still be presented graphically. However, this may represent a naïve optimism regarding his life after release from prison, considering the social stigma and barriers to reintegration, individuals with a sexual conviction face (Willis, Levenson, & Ward, 2010).

The final point of interest to note from Nigel's PCA grids, is that, at both time points, the vectors form two tight groupings of constructs, which fall within only two of the quadrants. This can represent tight construing, characterised by an 'all or nothing' type of thinking (Houston, 1998; Winter, 1992). If over-relied on, this could result in Nigel's predictions about the world becoming unvarying (Winter, 1992) and possibly hinder his progression towards a more pro-social self. Indeed, Nigel has been in prison for several years, meaning life in the community is new and outside what he has previously been used to. The PCA grids indicate that he will need the support of the CoSA volunteers to loosen his construct system. In doing this, he will be able to take on the new concepts encountered as he enters the community as this true and genuine 'self'.

A self-identity plot can document an individual's different selves in the process of change and desistance from crime. At T1, the element 'self in the past' is diametrically opposite to the 'self now' (see Figure 11.5) but by T2 the same element is almost at the origin of the plot (see Figure 11.6). If an element falls within the centre in what is referred to as the 'zone of indifference', as is the case here, then it suggests that the element has not been given much consideration. This indicates that Nigel, as he prepares for release from prison, is no longer associating himself with the person he was in the past and views this element worthy of very little thought, thus explaining the shortening of the Euclidean distances between the two time points. In addition, the plots show visually that how Nigel construes his 'self now' compared to his 'self in the future' remains stable and similar throughout the time periods. This absence of change between the two plots could be due to the extensive therapy and offending behaviour work Nigel had undergone prior to beginning the CoSA. For example, he may have addressed his offence-related thoughts and behaviour to such an extent prior to meeting the volunteers that in terms of cognitive change, the role of the CoSA was to support and encourage this rather than help develop it in the first instance. This is in of itself still noteworthy, the progress Nigel had made in prison appears to remain consistent right up until the point of release, a point where some of the other core members began to develop underlying anxiety (see Kitson-Boyce et al., 2018 for more detail on this).

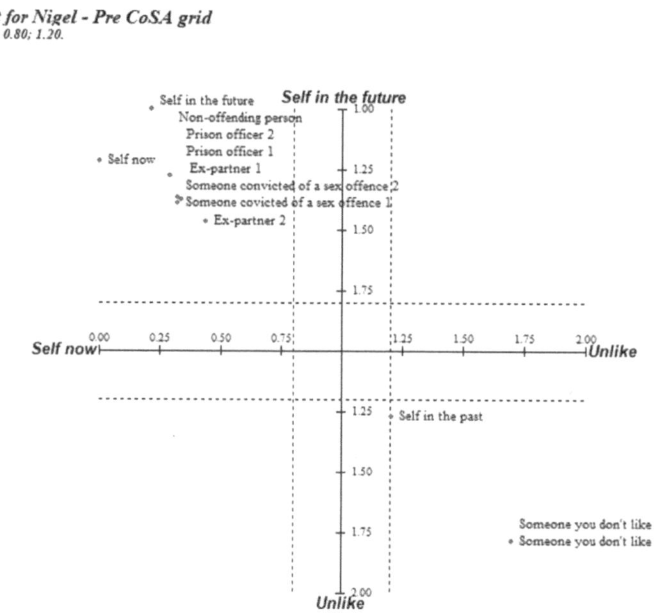

Figure 11.5 Self-identity plot for Nigel's 'self-now' and 'self in the future' at T1

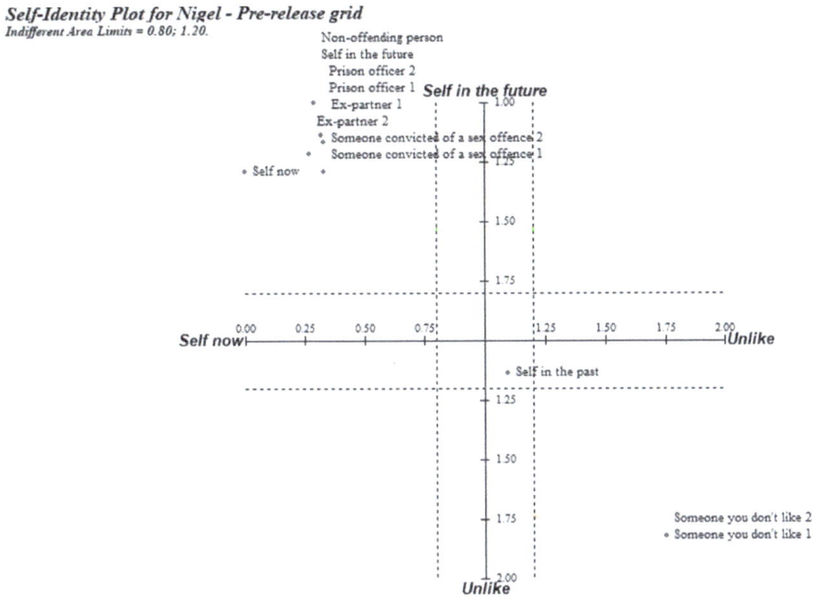

Figure 11.6 Self-identity plot for Nigel's 'self-now' and 'self in the future' at T2

The final point of interest to acknowledge is the distance between Nigel's 'self now' and 'self in the future' to individuals convicted of a sexual offence. This initially appears to contrast with the analysis, however, the qualitative data captured enables Nigel to explain his relationship with these individuals.

> Cause he's a sex offender, he had problems I had problems and we both seen the light and we talk to each other and encourage each other and it makes us feel stronger, you know, telling the truth and not hiding anything.

This extract explains how the 'individual convicted of a sexual offence' element was a positive relationship in Nigel's life, whereby they encouraged and supported each other on the desistance journey. Without this interview data, it is likely that the similarity with this element may have been interpreted differently and this highlights the importance of transcribing and analysing interview data collected in the repertory grid process.

3.6 Discussion

Desistance from crime is rarely instantaneous, with time needed instead for individuals to gradually commit themselves to their new pro-social lifestyles (Serin & Lloyd, 2009). Repertory grids enable this process to be explored with participants; the reflection on how they construe the person they were in the past, compared to how they are now, enables positive (or negative) change to be acknowledged. Similarly, participants are able to reflect on the constructs that are important to their self-definition and the traits in other people that they value or dislike.

In addition, a repertory grid enables an exploration of participants' relationships with meaningful individuals in their life. This in turn can highlight how the participants construe their future desistance from crime. McNeill (2006) has argued that desistance can only be understood within the context of human relationships between the person convicted of an offence and those who are important to them. The repertory grid process can encourage participants to reflect on the empathic and sustained support they have around them. This can involve identifying any potential negative relationships they would like to move away from and positive relationships they would like to invest in further. Finally, repertory grids are able to encourage participants to reflect and consider how they construe their ideal future self. This can be used to create goals for the individual, which will encourage them to continue their desistance journey.

Ethel ethics

The aim of eliciting elements is to determine the people the participant perceives themselves to have meaningful positive or negative relationships with, either in the past or present. People convicted of a sexual offence, however, often report having very small support networks (Tewksbury & Copes, 2013) and have typically suffered adverse childhood experiences (Levenson, Willis, & Prescott, 2016). Taking part in the repertory grid process may highlight a lack of social relationships to the participant or bring negative experiences back to the forefront. This needs to be managed ethically and sensitively by the researcher, including a detailed debrief process containing further avenues of support.

4. REFLECTIONS

The repertory grid method allows individualised data to be collected in relation to how that individual construes a certain part of their world (Bell, 2005). There are numerous advantages to this when considering understanding individual experiences. An additional benefit of using repertory grids as a data collection tool is that the process has been described within the literature as opaque. This means that the overall aim of procedure is unclear and difficult to see through, thus socially desirable response sets are likely to be reduced (Blagden, Winder, Gregson, & Thorne, 2012; Mason, 2003).

One further reflection for these authors is the applicability of this methodological approach to challenging populations. We have argued previously that repertory grids can be an important approach for research and practice within forensic psychology (see

Kitson-Boyce, Wheatley, & Blagden, 2020). However, there is still a limited amount of personal construct work applied to forensic settings, which is surprising given that such an approach can aid in identifying, exploring and formulating issues relevant to offending behaviour and idiosyncratic beliefs of individuals (Horley, 2008; Mason, 2003; Houston, 1998). Needs (1988, p. 495) comments that in using grids with people with sexual convictions 'an important aim of mine has been [the] facilitation of communication and understanding in clinical work'.

LEARNING OBJECTIVES

You should now know:

- What a repertory grid is
- What constructive alternativism
- What elements, constructs and ratings are
- The two methods of eliciting constructs
- How repertory grid data can be analysed quantitatively and qualitatively
- The strengths and limitations of the repertory grid technique

FURTHER READING

Blagden, N., Winder, B., Gregson, M., & Thorne, K. (2012). The practical utility of using repertory grids with sexual offenders maintaining their innocence: A case study. *The British Journal of Forensic Practice*, *4*(4), 269–80.

Case study using repertory grids highlighting the method's utility in research and practice settings.

Capuit, P., Viney, L., Walker, B., & Crittenden, N. (2012). *Personal construct methodology*. Wiley-Blackwell.

This book places the repertory grid method in the wider Personal Construct Theory, exploring the assessment of constructs in considerable detail.

Jankowicz, D. (2004). *The easy guide to repertory grids*. John Wiley & Sons Ltd.

This does what it says on the tin and offers a detailed step-by-step guide to conducting a repertory grid.

Kelly, G. (1991). *The psychology of personal constructs*. Norton.

The condensed version of Kelly's work from the man himself. Detailing his underpinning theory in good detail – a key read.

Kitson-Boyce, R., Wheatley, R., & Blagden, N. (2020). The application of the repertory grid in forensic practice. *Journal of Constructivist Psychology*.

Detailing the applicability of personal construct psychology in forensic practice and highlights its utility through three case studies.

Idiogrid.com

This resource provides a free download for the software along with a detailed list of the possible analysis functions the software offers.

LINKS TO USEFUL RESOURCES

Here are links to two lectures on personal construct psychology, the basis upon which the rep grids method is based
www.youtube.com/watch?v=SeRv62ugJFc
www.youtube.com/watch?v=yaiv8UVLiQo

12

CASE STUDIES

RUSI JASPAL, CAROLINE FLOWERS AND MELINA THROUVALA

1. INTRODUCTION

1.1 What is the case study approach?

Broadly speaking, the case study method in psychology refers to the systematic study of a single individual, group, event or community (Miles et al., 2014). It does not refer to a single approach but, like many other methods in psychology, is characterised by significant diversity. The case study focuses on the in-depth study of a singular phenomenon. To this extent, the case study approach is **idiographic**. However, there is much variation in the type of data that can be generated and the ways in which the data can be analysed. The approach actually has a long-standing history in psychology and one of the most famous early proponents of this approach was of course Sigmund Freud with his in-depth analyses of his patients, Anna O and Little Hans (Freud, 1909a, 1909b). Case histories, a type of case study, remain common in psychiatry where relevant aspects of an individual's life narrative are invoked in order to provide an overall understanding of their psychiatric state.

In psychology, it is relatively common to use the case study approach with a single research participant to provide a detailed, rich and in-depth exploration of a particular experience, event or condition in their life. In order to construct the case study, the researcher may interview the individual participant several times and, in addition to the interview material, draw upon other relevant sources of data, such as a personal diary that the participant may have kept and observational data relevant to the participant's life. Other material, such as letters, personal notes and photographs, may also be used as part of case study research. These distinct 'datasets' can then be brought together and analysed collectively in order to provide a nuanced, holistic case study.

Case study data tend to be primarily qualitative but it is also possible to incorporate quantitative data into the broader dataset. Case study research can be conducted using a variety of methods of data generation (e.g., interviews, diaries, photographs) and data analysis (e.g., thematic analysis, interpretative phenomenological analysis, discourse analysis). In this chapter, we acknowledge these distinct approaches to case study research but focus mainly on case studies using qualitative interview data given that this approach is most common (Schoch, 2016).

Interesting facts

One of the most cited case studies in psychology is that of Phineas Gage who was a railway worker in the US in the mid 19th century. An industrial accident sent a large tamping iron through Gage's head removing a significant portion of his brain. He survived this but the story goes that he was a changed man. Most famously it was reported that his friends said that Gage '*was no longer Gage*'. When he recovered, he appeared for a while in fairgrounds displaying the tamping iron that gone through his skull (see Figure 12.1). The story had such an effect on our view of the relationship between brain and personality that it is still written about today (see Kean, 2014).

Figure 12.1 A daguerreotype of Phineas Gage with the rod believed to have penetrated his skull

Like any other method in psychology, there are advantages and disadvantages associated with case studies. The advantages include the in-depth, rich understanding of a person or phenomenon that the approach can yield, its ability to address topics and constructs that are not easily quantifiable or for which there might not be easy access to a larger sample, and the exploratory nature of the approach which can help the researcher to design larger, more generalisable studies (e.g., qualitative or quantitative studies with larger sample sizes). Possible disadvantages of the approach include the lack of generalisability of case studies given their idiographic focus, researcher subjectivity which may be understood as researcher bias, and the challenges associated with managing and analysing large quantities of qualitative data. The researcher has to consider these and other possible advantages and disadvantages and take an informed decision about which methodological approach to use.

As mixed method researchers, we believe that the case study approach has much to offer the study of psychological phenomena. In this chapter, we provide insight into the key issues that researchers using the case study approach ought to consider.

1.2 Ethical considerations

Conducting case studies can bring significant value to under-researched areas and can have important implications for practice. Nonetheless, as with all research methods, conducting case studies presents key ethical considerations for the researcher. Crucial ethical aspects of conducting case study research are: **Consent**, **Confidentiality**, **Transparency** and **Competence**. The topics and themes discussed may be sensitive, and the researcher may need to encourage the participant to share personal information about themselves, their views, and their life experience. There is the possibility that participants may not have discussed, divulged, or shared such detail with others previously. Engaging in such research, participants need to be made aware of how such personal information will be used. For example, that the information they disclose will be written up as a formal research report, who will get access to this, and that there is a likelihood that paper may be published in journals or books. To this end, a critical ethical factor is confidentiality which means that the researcher must ensure the protection of all participants. Given that case studies often focus on individuals and provide detailed insight into aspects of their lives, it is important that the researcher puts into place steps for ensuring the participant's confidentiality. This may be challenging but is necessary.

Depending on the nature of the case study, the issue of labelling is an ethical issue which warrants consideration. For example, case studies that include participants from forensic or clinical settings for studies which seek to explore issues such as domestic abuse, rare medical conditions, or personality disorder, may increase the risk of a negative emotional response from the participant. Therefore, strong interviewing and interpersonal skills are needed to ensure the researcher is working within the remit of their professional competence. This is a critical ethical issue underpinning case study research, as the researcher must possess the awareness and skills to be able to identify these issues, engage effectively with participants, and have the competence to address any personal or emotional impact that conducting case studies may bring.

2. HOW TO DO CASE STUDY RESEARCH

Conducting case study research can be a rewarding experience for researchers, generating valuable insight and rich data, especially in understudied areas. The case study research design can also be challenging and, as with any other research design, requires robust research, interviewing and interpersonal skills. Furthermore, undertaking case study research requires a considerable amount of background work. As we will see as we go through the process of conducting case study research, effective planning increases the likelihood that the researcher will achieve their objectives and produce high-quality research output. Indeed, each stage of the research process requires effective planning – that is, from the early stages of identifying a gap in existing knowledge and development of an important research question, through to ensuring data collection and ensuring that the entire research process is underpinned by a strong understanding of ethical issues. The final report reflects a clear story of the process and research cycle, highlighting the overall contribution of the research – both to addressing your research questions and to filling a gap in the literature.

Ig Nobel Prize

Farting as a defence against unspeakable dread

Psychoanalyst Mara Sidoli was famous for her willingness to deal with difficult cases. She took on a severely disturbed boy who frankly didn't smell too good. According to Sidoli (1996), 'Peter held loud conversations with imaginary beings and made loud anal farts as well as farting noises with his mouth whenever he became anxious or angry.' He also tended to soil himself when anxious. After a year of therapy that seemed to be having little effect, Sidoli took the nuclear option and started to make farting noises herself. This so surprised Peter that it finally broke through the defences and he was able to express his dread, affection and humour about his parents in a less noxious way. For this report and for her courage and tenacity Mara Sidoli was awarded the1998 Ig Nobel Prize for literature.

Sidoli, M. (1996). Farting as a defence against unspeakable dread. *Journal of Analytical Psychology*, *41*(2), 165–78.

The following section outlines the key steps for conducting a case study, from formulating the research question to producing the research report. The list of steps is intended to be neither prescriptive nor exhaustive and each researcher will develop their own way of conducting case study research. However, following these steps is recommended for beginners in case study research. Throughout this chapter, reference is made to key ethical issues that should be considered during the research process. With this in mind, we then look at three real-world examples to demonstrate how empirical research using a case study design has had value for informing theory and practice.

2.1 Key considerations when conducting case studies

In this section, we outline various aspects that we see as being central to research using case studies. We focus on planning, case study design, personal skill development, research material development, data collection, data analysis and the formulation of your research report.

2.2 Planning

This is a crucial first step of any research project and will shape the subsequent stages as well as the final research product. Case study research requires robust and methodical planning through all the stages. You will have identified a broad topic that you wish to research. The next step is to determine the focus of your research and, more specifically, the research questions that you want to address using a case study approach. This can be achieved through considering the following questions:

- Why is this topic an important area to explore?
- How will an in-depth exploration of this area increase understanding of a particular psychological phenomenon?
- What are the unanswered questions in this topic area?
- What do I actually want to find out?
- How will I collect data?
- What is my chosen method of analysis?
- How will this research fill a gap in existing knowledge?
- How will the research inform theory and real-world issues?

At this stage it is useful to make a mind-map of these issues so that you can identify how these issues are interlinked. It is also beneficial to begin to highlight key ethical issues that you will need to address. For instance, at this stage, you may realise that some of the questions that you will need to pose are actually quite sensitive and could cause psychological distress in your participants. How would you reduce the risk of distress to your participants and how would you support those who become distressed?

Conduct an early review of the existing literature in the area that you have identified. This will illuminate what research has been conducted to date in your area of interest, which research questions have already been addressed, and will highlight any gaps in the existing literature. Add any ideas this generates to your mind-map. Review key papers in more depth. The recommendations sections may highlight ideas where authors suggest future research should be conducted. Reading with purpose and drawing on your analytical thinking skills here will enable you to consolidate your understanding of the research area and stimulate questions or thoughts. This process will in turn move you closer towards identifying concrete research questions that can be addressed using the case study approach. The development of research questions for case studies is one of the most important phases of the research design. Taking time to refine this is crucial.

2.3 Research questions addressed using case studies

Previous research using the case study approach have asked the following questions:

- What are the sources of stress among music teachers at a high school? (Scheib, 2003)
- How is Parkinson's disease experienced? (Bramley & Eatough, 2005)
- What is the experience of being Muslim and lesbian in Scotland? (Siraj, 2011)
- What does it feel like when a person's meaning-making in life breaks down? (Eatough & Smith, 2006)

All of these research questions could be addressed using other qualitative approaches, such as semi-structured interviews with large samples. The case study method would enable the researcher to provide detailed insight into an individual. This precludes the need to generalise across participant accounts, arguably facilitating a richer account of just one individual.

2.4 Designing case studies

Consider whether your research is going to include a single or multiple-case studies. Your case study may be focused on an individual participant or on several participants experiencing a particular event, for instance. Even in the latter case, researchers tend to focus on four–five participants as this sample size is deemed to be more manageable in view of the aim of the case study researcher to generate rich and detailed empirical insights into the phenomenon under study (Patton, 2002). It is important to consider the scope of your study and, in doing so, defining the parameters of the study and setting the inclusion and exclusion criteria (that is, who is your intended population). This should be driven by your research question. Having conducted your literature review, you will know which have been the dominant methodological approaches in your area of study. You need to formulate a strong rationale for conducting a case study. Ask yourself what your study would add. You then need to make a decision about the participant sample. Will this be an individual? If so, how will they be selected? Write all this up in your research protocol.

Whoa there!

Whose story is it anyway?

Case studies provide some of psychology's best stories. Stories like Little Hans, or the Two Faces of Eve or the memory of HM appear in most introductory texts. There are, however, concerns about ownership of the story. If my life story was going be told in a book or a scientific paper then I would like to have some say in it. Apart from anything else it is my story and I ought to be able to tell it. This apparent basic is not granted to all our case study stars. Christine Sizemore (Two Faces of Eve) found that her attempts to tell her own story were impeded and discouraged by her therapists who had authored papers and a book about her. In this, and many other cases, the therapists took control of their patients' life stories and in some cases made money out of it.

At this early stage it is important to consider how you intend to select the case(s) for your research based on your research question. Considering this early will ensure that have thought through any potential setbacks and ensure that you have sufficient data for your potential case.

2.5 Develop your skills

Strong research skills and robust knowledge of research ethics are central to conducting high-quality research using the case study approach. Ensuring that you have the competence and skills to undertake the proposed research is important. This may involve the need to conduct background reading or to engage in training to develop your skills. For instance, a researcher with expertise in conducting cross-sectional survey research may recognise the value of conducting a research study using a case study approach. In addition to reading this chapter, they may decide to attend a workshop on the case study approach and collaborate with a researcher with greater experience of using this approach.

This will enable the researcher to acquire the necessary skills to carry out this research independently in the future.

One of the most common methods of data generation using the case study approach is the semi-structured interview. The ability to build rapport is a key element of successful interviewing. Your aim is to encourage participants to feel safe and at ease in the interview so that they can tell their story in an open, honest and detailed manner. This is about developing trust, demonstrating empathy and patience, transparency, genuine curiosity, and having an open mind, essentially drawing on ***motivational interviewing*** and ***active listening*** skills. It is vital to have a non-judgemental stance (see Jaspal, 2020b). Knowing when to prompt and dig deeper can open up interesting new avenues during data collection. The richness of your data will be dependent, in part, upon the quality of your interviewing skills.

2.6 Develop your research materials

Key research materials include consent forms, the participant information sheet, interview schedule, and debrief sheet. The researcher should design a broad semi-structured interview schedule. The interview schedule is essentially a framework to guide the interview, providing a flexible data collection tool. It is good practice to conduct a pilot interview to enable you to reflect on how useful the interview schedule was and whether you need to refine questions or the ways in which you pose your questions to the interview. It is also important to reflect on the process and to seek feedback from participants. Addressing issues at this stage increases the reliability of case studies. This process is also useful for identifying any practical or ethical issues that may have arisen. If your initial pilot interviews have gone to plan, there is no reason per se why they cannot be included in your overall participant sample.

The participant information sheet should outline fully to participants what taking part in the research will involve. It should clearly specify the rationale and aims of the research. It sets the scene for participants and provides key information relating to how their data will be used and stored, limits of confidentiality, and sources of contact should they have further questions. The debrief sheet should thank participants for taking part in the research and importantly it allows for the researcher to check-in with participants how they are feeling having taken part in the research. This should also include signposting to relevant sources of support. Consent forms are a key requirement for undertaking research. They should be written and formatted clearly and concisely. The researcher must be certain that participants have the capacity to give informed consent. Keep all documentation for participants simple so that they are accessible.

Consider the possibility that not all participants will be confident in articulating a narrative of their story or opening up about their experiences. This is especially true of research into topics that are deemed to be sensitive, such as mental health, sexuality and substance misuse. To assist with this, you might wish to consider providing stimulus material to act as a prompt to encourage participants to talk through specific areas. For example, this could take the form of timelines, key words, or a mind-map.

2.7 Data collection

Case study data are often gathered in the form of in-depth interviews. It is advisable to record the interviews in some format, subject to your participants' approval, as this will enable you to focus fully on your interaction with the interviewee, rather than taking notes. Note-taking during data collection may adversely impact the development of rapport and there may be a consequential loss of richness in the data. Considerations should also be given to the location of the interviews – some participants may wish to be interviewed at their own home, while others may wish to be interviewed in a public place. It is important that both you and your interviewee feel safe and comfortable in the context in which the interview is being conducted. A critical interviewing skill is being responsive to the individual needs of your participant. Use your motivational interviewing skills to guide the interview.

Prepare beforehand and ensure you are confident in how you will approach the interview. Ensure you review consent prior to beginning the interview. Participants should be debriefed following the interview and provided with follow-up contact information and sources of support. This is particularly necessary if the interview is of a sensitive nature so that participants have someone to contact should they have any concerns after the interview. As noted earlier, case studies involving a single participant sometimes rely on other datasets, such as diaries, personal letters and artefacts, photographs and other material. Think carefully about how you will gather these additional datasets, what the inclusion/exclusion criteria will be and, importantly, how the distinct datasets will fit together. They need to create a coherent whole and ultimately enable you to address your original research questions.

Consider using techniques to enhance the interview experience for participants. Encourage them to identify key emotions, thoughts, and responses to jog their memory.

Cultural context

Even the rat was white

In 1955, when Robert Guthrie enrolled in a master's program at the University of Kentucky, he was the only black face in a sea of white. 'I remember one of my white professors eyeing me as if I were an anthropological specimen and remarking, 'You are from one of our Negro schools,' Guthrie recalls (APA website).

After serving in the US army Guthrie returned to psychology and wrote the classic text *Even the rat was white*. In the book, he describes the role of racial bias in the history of psychology, in the development of divisive theories and also in the failure to value the work of black psychologists. The book describes the biographies of early African-American psychologists and their scientific contributions, as well as their problems, views, and concerns towards the field of social psychology offering case studies of these individuals. He uses research documents that are not often found in the mainstream by referring to journals and magazines such as the *Journal of Black Psychology*, the *Journal of Negro Education*, and *Crisis*.

The second edition of his book, published in 1998, reviewed the progress of the next 25 years and discussed the new challenges for black psychologists. Guthrie argued that the 'myth of mental measurement' and eugenicist philosophy continue to exist and create negative stereotypes of oppressed peoples.

2.8 Analysis of case study data

Conduct your analysis in line with the chosen method. There are many different approaches that can be used to analyse qualitative data using a case study design, such as content analysis, thematic analysis, discourse analysis, interpretative phenomenological analysis and grounded theory. The choice of analytic approach will depend largely on the research questions that you have formulated. For example, if your research questions focus on exploring the phenomenological world of the participant, interpretative phenomenological analysis may be an appropriate approach while a research question focusing on the social construction of the participant's experience may lead you to consider discourse analysis as a potential analytic approach.

Jaspal (2020a) describes an overarching generic framework for conducting content analysis, thematic analysis and discourse analysis which consists of nine stages. Three especially important stages for the analysis include: developing and applying your **coding scheme**, identifying patterns of meaning in the data and, for the purpose of case study research, how patterns of meaning can be pieced together to construct broader themes, content categories or discourses (depending on the analytic approach you use). This guide could be used in the context of data analysis for case studies.

An essential part of the analysis involves documenting the process at each stage. For instance, keeping a reflective journal or diary outlining the steps taken in analysis and how the analysis is unfolding. Consideration should be given to capturing your reflections and the development of the themes (Silverman, 2013). Through the process of reflexivity, understanding the role of the researcher within the research process is crucial for considering how this shapes the findings (Yardley, 2000). Personal reflexivity involves reflecting upon the ways in which the researchers' own experiences, values, knowledge, interests, and identities have shaped the research (Robson, 2002).

2.9 Reporting your case studies

There is no prescriptive way of reporting case studies. The key is for the reader to acquire a clear understanding of the data analysis and, crucially, how your analysis addresses the research questions. Researchers tend to represent the qualitative analysis of their case study as a series of themes, content categories or discourses (which are essentially patterns of meaning). Thus, each subsection in the Results section may refer to one of the overarching patterns of meaning that you have identified during the course of the analysis. For instance, imagine you were doing a case study on the experience of a person recently diagnosed with HIV and that, using thematic analysis, you had found the following three themes: (1) initial shock at diagnosis; (2) social and psychological adjustment to diagnosis; and (3) positive construal of diagnosis. Each of these themes could be presented as a subsection within the Results section. Sometimes it can be helpful for each theme to be broken down into subthemes in which case you may present these as additional subsections within your Results section. In addition to text, consider using tables, figures, or other creative approaches to present the findings.

Focus should be given in the discussion section to highlighting the significant contribution to knowledge and wider application of the research to policy and practice. Think of the writing-up process as narrating a story about how the research unfolded and what the main findings were. Bearing in mind your target audience, adapt your writing style appropriately in order to communicate the key messages within the report. Note the strengths and limitations of the research.

3. EXAMPLES OF CASE STUDY RESEARCH

3.1 Example 1: 'You want to catch the biggest thing going in the ocean': A qualitative analysis of intimate partner stalking

Flowers, C., Winder, B., & Slade, K. (2020). 'You want to catch the biggest thing going in the ocean': A qualitative analysis of intimate partner stalking. *Journal of Interpersonal Violence.* https://doi.org/10.1177/0886260520958632

3.2 Background

Stalking perpetrators present with diverse characteristics and motivations. This presenting complexity bringing challenges in the identification and clinical management of perpetrators. (Nijdam-Jones, Rosenfeld, Gerbrandij, Quick, & Galietta, 2018).

3.3 Aims of the study

The study explores intimate partner stalking (IPS) through the eyes of the perpetrator using a phenomenological approach to capture the 'voice', experiences and perceptions of men who have engaged in stalking behaviour. The research question was: What personal meaning do men who have engaged in IPS attribute to their stalking behaviour?

The rationale for the study originated from the lead researcher's experiences and observations as a forensic practitioner working directly with men in a prison setting who had engaged in stalking behaviour. As with all research, the first step was to conduct a detailed literature review on the subject area, in this case on intimate partner stalking to establish the gaps in the research to date, and what was known about this group. This highlighted that no qualitative studies had explored the characteristics of intimate partner stalking from the perspective of the perpetrator, nor had studies been conducted in prison settings. Consequently, this was an unexplored area to date highlighting a clear gap in the existing literature. This was the starting point of the research and from this the research question was generated. The case study method was suitable as it provides a detailed, rich and unique understanding of how perpetrators attribute meaning to their behaviour, and illuminates the thoughts and emotions that play a role in their behaviour.

3.4 Method

The study employed a qualitative research design. Ethical approval was obtained. Semi-structured interviews were conducted with seven men with a history of IPS. Transcripts ere analysed using interpretative phenomenological analysis (IPA). IPA is an inductive qualitative method which seeks to understand individuals' experiences and how they make sense of the world (Smith, Harré, & Van Langenhove, 1995). IPA provided a flexible, rich and detailed insight into participants' psychological world, thereby providing an insightful exploration of participant's sense of self, cognitions, motivations, and feelings underpinning their experiences. Throughout the research process measures were implemented to ensure the validity and reliability of the research. Each individual transcript was analysed separately followed by an integration of cases. A table was produced presenting each superordinate and subordinate theme.

Ethel ethics

Full ethical approval was obtained. The research was conducted in line with the British Psychological Society's (2014) code of human research ethics and the Health and Care Professions Council's (2012) standards of conduct, performance and ethics. Informed consent is an essential requirement to participate in psychological research (British Psychological Society, 2014). Participants were serving a custodial sentence at the time of data collection, and as such were deemed a 'vulnerable participant group' (British Psychological Society, 2014, p. 31). Remember to fully anonymise your report, remember to remove all potential identifiers as any small detail has the potential to highlight the identity of participants.

Individual interviews offer the scope to elicit in-depth understanding and encourage personal disclosure by exploring individual experiences and reflections on behaviour, motivation, emotions, and thoughts underpinning their IPS behaviour. A semi-structured interview schedule was designed as a framework for the interview, providing a flexible data collection tool to capture the psychological/social worlds of participants. Participants were provided with stimulus material in the form of a visual timeline, presented on a flip chart to act as a prompt to narrate the pathway to IPS. This proved useful for participants as they chose to tell their stories as a chronological narrative of their pathway and key events relevant to their experience.

3.5 Findings

Five superordinate themes reflecting participants experiences were identified from the in-depth qualitative analysis of the interview data: 'The quest for attention and affection creating connection'; 'Conflicted identity and extremes of self', 'My life, a film set', 'Game-playing: 'One step ahead', and 'Severed connections, changing the gameplay'.

3.6 Contributions of the study: Implications for theory, policy and forensic practice

The study has contributed to the existing literature by further developing forensic understanding of the lived experiences of IPS perpetrators, and the factors that play a role in the pathway to stalking and stalking violence. The findings provide valuable knowledge which can inform the content of future intervention. Thus, having strong implications for international policymakers and informing guidance on the case management of IPS perpetrators.

Throughout the research process measures were implemented to ensure the validity and reliability of the research. Several verification strategies were employed to enhance the validity and reliability in line with those recommended by Braun and Clarke (2006, 2019). Throughout the stages of the research process a reflective journal was kept, strengthening credibility and capturing the analytical journey. Research questions were aligned with the chosen research method, data collection and analysis process (Morse, Barrett, Mayan, Olson, & Spiers, 2002). Credibility checks of the codes and themes were undertaken, thereby increasing transparency and providing evidence supporting the development of overall themes.

3.7 Example 2: Gaming disorder: An application of the case study method

In response to considerations for inclusion of gaming disorder to the International Classification of Diseases (ICD-11) by the World Health Organisation (*WHO*) and lack of valid diagnostic instruments to reflect the assessment criteria of gaming disorder, the World Health Organisation (*WHO*) *Collaborative Project on the Development of New International Screening and Diagnostic Instruments for Gaming Disorder and Gambling Disorder* was established in 2017. The purpose of the WHO collaborative project for the development of new instruments for gaming disorder involved partially expert consultation with the provision of clinical case studies. Clinical case studies of gaming disorder were submitted to the *Fourth Meeting on Public Health Implications of Addictive Behaviours* in Istanbul, Turkey, in 2017. Contributing countries were from Europe, the Middle East, Asia and Australia and provided clinical case studies of gaming disorder from an international perspective. Case studies provided an in-depth insight into the nature and consequences of excessive gaming and its clinical presentation from an international perspective and the conceptual and clinical validity of gaming disorder.

Clinical case studies can therefore broaden the understanding of the boundaries between normative and pathological addictive behaviours, to inform the provision of valid instruments for the assessment, screening and diagnosis of the disorder and to inform treatment and prevention initiatives but also contribute to a greater recognition of the phenomenology of the disorder. The clinical view is rather typical – those at risk are deemed to be highly intelligent young adults, usually of technological orientation, immersed in the world of gaming, withdrawn from everyday activities, with deficits in self and in relational capacities and with parents that express concern over the condition; they neglect their personal hygiene, obesity is a serious issue, due to poor dieting and lack of exercise (Throuvala et al., 2018).

Additionally, case studies may be used to demarcate differences in the context of a disorder and ensuing impacts for the individual. There are variables that influence online gaming behaviour. However, the role of individual context is of significance. For example, Griffiths (2010) provided case study evidence of two young men who spent an average of 14 hours a day playing massively multiplayer online role-playing games (MMORPGs) in order to emphasise that the context of the individual's life is an important factor demarcating gaming excess from gaming addiction.

The examples of Dave and Jeremy make a compelling case for how the same behaviour (namely regular online gaming for excessive periods of time) can have almost diametrically opposed consequences due to different individual contexts, with one experiencing gaming as pleasurable and ultimately beneficial and the other's entire life was negatively affected by his excessive gaming. Therefore, Dave's behaviour cannot be classified as a condition that would fulfil the requirements of a mental disorder classification as outlined in the Diagnostic and Statistical Manual DSM-5. Upon starting a new job and entering into a relationship with a woman he met in-game, his excessive gaming decreased significantly. Case studies have been highly relevant also to evaluate clinical outcomes when specialised psychological treatment has been applied (Torres-Rodríguez et al., 2019). Changes in clinical outcomes are evaluated pre-treatment, mid- and post-treatment and in certain cases a period of time following treatment.

> Alex is a 22-year-old student studying mathematics at university. He engages in excessive gaming for about 10–16 hours a day. He is a MMORPG player who had dropped out of university two years earlier and ever since the gaming has progressively become more intense. He has sleep problems. He takes breakfast and all his meals in bed. He started using technology when he was young at the end of primary school and use has been heavy since then with the permission of his parents, who did not place any restrictions. He has become irritable when unable to play – if asked by a family member to engage in a chore – spends time only with his online friends when gaming and has completely lost contact with the few childhood friends and friends he made in first year at university. He feels he cannot reduce his gaming activity as he already tried twice and failed. Alex dropped basketball a year ago which he used to enjoy and has not had a girlfriend for two years now. He mentions he is thinking of withdrawing completely from his studies and become a professional gamer.

3.8 Example 3: Understanding the barriers to HIV care

Jaspal (2018) developed the Health Adversity Risk Model to shed light on the social and psychological factors that lead some people to engage in behaviours that put them at risk of poor health outcomes. He focused on HIV acquisition among gay and bisexual men. Using a combination of research methods, including the case study approach, it was found that childhood experiences of trauma and abuse, prejudice on the basis of one's sexual orientation and emotional dysregulation, all appeared to be factors that increased the risk of engagement in sexual risk behaviours. The following case note exemplifies some of these issues:

> Juan is a 33-year-old gay man from Spain. He was diagnosed with HIV at a gay men's health charity in his hometown during the summer of 2014. As he did not view his sexual behaviour as risky, Juan expected to receive a negative test result and was thus shocked to learn that he was in fact HIV-positive. The gay men's health charity referred Juan to the local hospital to confirm the reactive test result. Although his CD4 count was still relatively high, Juan requested to initiate antiretroviral therapy (ART) immediately. Still shocked at his diagnosis, Juan viewed his medication as an unfortunate daily reminder of his HIV infection. Moreover, days after initiating treatment, Juan began to experience negative physical side effects. He discussed his side effects with one of the doctors at the clinic, who was dismissive and unhelpful. The doctor appeared to be suggesting that this is what life with HIV is like and that Juan should simply get used to it. Juan felt that the doctor was unsympathetic towards him because he was gay and living with HIV. This situation was further complicated by the fact that Juan had a very difficult relationship with his family. As a child, he suffered sexual abuse but felt let-down by his parents who never acknowledged this. He felt unable to disclose his HIV status to his family, with whom he was living at the time of his diagnosis. In fact, given his strict Catholic upbringing, he also felt unable to come out as gay, and thus, he felt that he had to conceal both his sexual identity and his HIV status from significant others. This made him resent his parents. Although Juan did have a small group of HIV-positive friends from whom he derived some social support, he viewed himself as different from them and implicitly stigmatised his own friends, whom he regarded as responsible for their infection. A year after his diagnosis, Juan decided to move to London to distance himself from his family and in order to 'be himself'. However, he felt lonely in London. Concerned about his declining health, Juan registered as a patient at his local sexual health clinic. His HIV consultant advised him to initiate ART immediately, reassuring him that he would be well looked after and that any side effects would be dealt with. However, Juan, still distrustful of medical professionals following his experience in Spain, initially refused treatment. This posed a dilemma for him because, on the one hand, he was well aware of his poor disease prognosis in the absence of medication but, on the other hand, he did not wish to think about his HIV infection and feared further side effects and indifference from his medical team. In view of a significant drop in his CD4 count, Juan reluctantly began ART. With his new drug regimen, he experienced no physical side effects but did continue to experience psychological adversity, including loneliness, depression, and shame. Juan decided not to attend support groups partly because he did not wish to disclose his HIV status to others and because he did not think he would have anything in common with other support group attendees. Indeed, he continued to deny that he had engaged in sexual risk behaviours in an attempt to differentiate himself from others living with HIV. As Juan's mental health has begun to deteriorate, he is missing doses of his medication, which has increased the risk of drug resistance and of onward

> HIV transmission to his sexual partners. He finds it difficult to discuss these issues with his doctor and has also started to miss appointments. To deal with his feelings of loneliness, Juan is meeting sexual partners online and in gay bars. After facing rejection from potential sexual partners to whom he has disclosed his HIV status, he feels more ashamed and distressed about being HIV-positive. He has started to attend chemsex parties in London because nobody asks him his status there, allowing him to forget about HIV and to experience a sense of connection and intimacy with other men. Juan now has a detectable viral load but is not consistently using condoms with sexual partners of unknown HIV status. (from Jaspal, 2018)

The case study enables the researcher to identify some of the key factors that may be driving sexual risk behaviour and also disengagement from HIV care among gay and bisexual men living with the condition. Results of the case study were shared with HIV healthcare professionals who were able to identify parallels with cases that they had observed in their own practice (see Jaspal & Bayley, 2019). This in turn led to the construction of a possible theoretical model based upon the case study which was concordant with the cases observed in clinical contexts. The model has come to be known as the Health Adversity Risk Model. Moreover, the case study enabled the development of larger-scale qualitative and quantitative studies which were able to confirm the major tenets of the Health Adversity Risk Model (Jaspal & Bayley, 2020; Jaspal et al., 2021). Thus, case studies can play a significant role in the construction of theory in psychology.

4. EVALUATING THE CASE STUDY APPROACH

Yardley (2000) has described four principles for assessing the quality of a qualitative analysis, which is also applicable to the qualitative analysis of case study data. These include:

sensitivity to context – the analyst must show that they are aware of the dominant theories, previous empirical studies, social context in which the research has been conducted, and of the participants' point of view when undertaking the analysis;

commitment and rigour must be discernible from research report. There should be evidence of in-depth engagement with the topic area and clear acknowledgement of previous research as well as a description of how one's own case study is positioned within that broader research literature. The case study approach should be clearly described and a strong rationale for using it should be presented.

transparency and coherence – the data collection, analysis and presentation of findings must be characterised by transparency and rigour. The researcher should present sufficient detail (i.e., extracts from the data) to demonstrate commitment and rigour. They should acknowledge the subjectivity that underpins qualitative research and acknowledge elements of their own identity that might have impinged on the data analysis.

impact and importance – the researcher must demonstrate the importance of the research questions and the impact of the research findings. The research questions must purport to fill a gap in knowledge that has been identified in the literature review. The research findings must have well-defined empirical, theoretical and/ or practical implications.

Paying attention to these four issues will enable the researcher to conduct high-quality research using the case study approach. They should therefore be considered during the research process.

4.1 Conclusion

In this chapter, we have described the major tenets of the case study approach in psychology. It has been shown that the approach is multifarious and compatible with many different methods of data generation and analysis. The approach is especially useful for providing in-depth rich analyses of psychological phenomena which have not been studied in-depth. It can generate novel insights into understudied phenomena, thereby paving the way for other methodological approaches. The case study approach is an important aspect of the methodological toolbox in psychology. Although effective and insightful as a stand-alone method, the case study in psychology is most effective when used in conjunction with other methods.

LEARNING OBJECTIVES

You should now know how:

- To understand the purpose, value and limitations of the case study approach in psychology
- To make an informed decision about the appropriateness of the case study approach for your particular area of research
- To understand the practical steps that are involved in the design and implementation of case study research
- To ensure a high-quality case study and to evaluate its significance for your area of research

SUGGESTIONS FOR FURTHER READING

There are other resources that can help crystallise your knowledge of case study research and complement the insights provided in this chapter:

Crowe, S., Cresswell, K., Robertson, A., Huby, G., Avery, A., & Sheikh, A. (2011). The case study approach. *BMC Medical Research Methodology, 11*, 100. https://doi.org/10.1186/1471-2288-11-100

Jaspal, R. (2020a). Content analysis, thematic analysis and discourse analysis. In G. M. Breakwell, D. B. Wright, & J. Barnett (Eds.), *Research methods in psychology* (5th ed.) (pp. 285–312). Sage.

Mills, A. J., Durepos, G., & Wiebe, E. (2010). *Encyclopedia of case study research* (Vols. 1–0). Sage. https://doi.org/10.4135/9781412957397

Schoch, K. W. (2016). Case study research. In G. J. Burkholder, K. A. Cox, & L. M. Crawford (Eds.), *The scholar-practitioner's guide to research design* (pp. 227–41). Sage.

LINKS TO USEFUL RESOURCES

There is also audio-visual material available online which can support you in your research using the case study approach:

Case Studies in Psychology pt.1 Dr Chris Moulin (YouTube) www.youtube.com/watch?v=Gu0Lr9uSrEY

Qualitative Case Study (YouTube) www.youtube.com/watch?v=ey4D5kKa4VY

Tips To Write An Excellent Case Study Report In Psychology (YouTube) www.youtube.com/watch?v=cW3TfQ1MkOg

Here are some links to famous case studies in psychology

Henry Molaison or H. M. to you and me: www.youtube.com/watch?v=SrmU8P3kBvM

Genie 'the feral child': www.youtube.com/watch?v=wqflmQ5TaFQ

13

BEHAVIOURAL OBSERVATIONS

EMMA J. VARDY, TRESHI-MARIE PERERA AND JAMES STILLER

1. INTRODUCTION TO BEHAVIOURAL OBSERVATION

We observe the behaviour of others all the time. You may call it people watching, watching the behaviour of others, making judgements, understanding the social world and building hypotheses from the observational data you are collecting from this simple act. This chapter is focussed on behavioural observations, this is a data collection approach used in psychology to explore and understand the social world. An observational study is the systematic examination of human and animal behaviour. When we mention behaviour, this is both **verbal behaviour** and **non-verbal behaviour** of humans and animals. There is a saying '*never work with children or animals*', in this chapter we discuss behavioural observations for both human and animal research.

When thinking about observing behaviours in animals as opposed to humans there are certain issues that arise, specifically we know how it feels for us to be human, but we cannot make such assumptions about animals. When we observe human behaviour, we tend to do this from our own perspective and understanding of the world and to a certain extent this can be useful in predicting the intentions and beliefs of others. This approach does create a bias in that we are projecting how we would behave onto others; this obviously is a bigger issue if we project these observational biases onto animals. With animals, it is arguably easier to distance yourself from this personal perspective as we can never truly know what it feels like to be another animal. Thomas Nagel (1974) argued that although it is possible for us to imagine what it would be like to be a dog, we would never actually know what it is like to be dog from their perspective and with their species-specific cognitive abilities. Therefore, when observing animal behaviour, it is important to not project human traits and feelings onto the animal being observed.

There are three questions to answer in animal observations and to some degree human observations; 'what do you classify as a behaviour?', 'What is the behaviour in response to?' and 'Does an observed behaviour have a function?'. Addressing the first question of what is classified as a behaviour, it is important to consider at what level you want to look at, arguably every action and thought is a behaviour, be that conscious or unconscious. However, as we are unable to know exactly what the internal mental states of an observed animal are, as researchers, we should always be very cautious and focus on behaviours that are measurable. For example, a behaviour observed in relation to a clear identifiable stimulus. This leads us to consider what the behaviour is in response to and therefore if it has a clear function; this is an important consideration for both human and animal behavioural observational studies.

2. FEATURES OF OBSERVATIONAL METHODS

An observational study can be described as an 'outsider looking in' (Hopkins, 2002, p. 49); as researchers are gaining access on how people behave. Do participants behave how they self-report to behave? The attachment between a parent and child is critical, parents want to have a positive bond with their child, thus if the study was based on self-report measures, parents may be inclined to respond in a certain way. In using an observational approach, the study was able to observe the relationship between the parent and child to determine attachment style. Observational methods enable you to observe behaviour in a naturalistic way, although there are caveats to this. In using a structured observational approach, the study was able to gain a better understanding of attachment than, say, by using self-report measures.

2.1 Design

Observational studies can be either structured or unstructured. For a structured observation, a clear code of what the behaviour that is be observed is needed and this is by having a clear operational definition for the observer to follow. This ensures data collected is of use. For example, if you think about the work of Skinner, the most common approach to studying animals is to adopt a stimulus and response approach to observing behaviours. If we cannot have a clear understanding of what it feels like to be a certain animal, we can still study via observations how animals behave in response to either an external or internal stimulus. Of course, we are still assuming that a particular stimulus is the cause of a behaviour and this has in the past resulted in many misinterpretations of animal behaviour.

It is important, however, to ensure you have a clear definition of what behaviours are going to be observed. If the observer is unsure of what they should be observing, then the data they collect will be of poor quality. The aims of the study need to be clear to ensure that the behaviour to be observed is constrained so that it is not open to interpretation. That is, unless the study is to take an unstructured observational approach, where the researcher produces field notes detailing the behaviour being observed.

2.2 Observing animal behaviour

There are four key approaches to consider when observing animal behaviour that can mitigate issues of identifying behaviours, which were proposed by Nico Tinbergen in 1963. Tinbergen suggested that researchers look at behaviour in terms of four key approaches or questions:

1. Survival value (why is the behaviour adaptive for the species?);
2. Evolution of the behaviour (Why or how has the behaviour arisen within a species?);
3. Ontogeny of the behaviour (How has the behaviour developed during the animal's lifespan?); and
4. The causation of the behaviour (How does the behaviour occur?).

In recent years these questions have been refined further to distinguish between the various types of mechanism (causes) and functionality (Bateson & Laland, 2013). For the purposes of observing animal behaviour the four approaches allow researchers to focus their research questions towards a specific approach. For example, for a field observation of young animals playing might be a useful way of looking at the ontogeny of a behaviour.

2.3. Behavioural checklist

A structured observation typically uses a checklist of behaviours to observe. These behaviours will be well defined, and observers will have a format to record the behaviours, i.e., rating scale. Structured observations are highly controlled compared to unstructured observations which can be defined as more descriptive observations. What unstructured observations do give is rich detail about the behaviour, thus alongside a checklist, a researcher may include a note section to report behaviours that are of interest, so that important detail of the behaviour or of the environment is not missed. For animal observations, the researcher needs to develop a list of discrete behaviours for the animals being observed and how these behaviours are utilised to achieve a goal or for a specific function. To do this the researcher can create an **ethogram**.

An ethogram is a list of observed behaviours that are unique to the animals being observed. A good starting point for creating an ethogram is to look at previous research on the species being observed. For example, if you are looking at the behaviour of spider monkeys in Mexico you would start by looking at the papers by primatologists in that field. Your next step would be to then directly observe the sample you want to study, this is where you have to habituate the animals to your presence so that your observations have the least impact possible on their behaviour and you can be confident that your observations are typical for the animal being observed.

When creating an ethogram, it can also be helpful to compare observations with a fellow researcher, i.e., there is some validation of your categorisation of behaviours. This helps to develop a clear protocol for sampling and observations. This can be done by preparing an observation sheet which has key behaviours listed that enable the researcher to quickly record any observations. Typically, on an observation sheet for observing animals in their natural setting you would also include times that the observations are being taken, the weather conditions, the time of year, and the layout of their habitat. If you are looking at a specific animal you would want to include on your observation sheet, the sex and approximate age of the animal. By including this information, the researcher has a record of various external (and possible internal) stimuli that might impact the observations.

2.4 Focus section on human–animal interaction

For many people the strongest relationship they have might be with a companion animal such as a dog or cat and within applied areas of psychology there has been a growing interest in human–animal interaction. For example, the use of dogs within classrooms or prison settings, the psychological benefits of disability support animals and the relationship between humans and animals in nature. When studying human–animal interactions there can be a bias towards looking at the animal from the utilitarian perspective and the function it performs to benefit the human. As mentioned previously this is ethically problematic as it excludes the motivations and the significance of the animal as part of the interaction. Therefore, when observing human–animal interactions and designing studies to do this it is important to consider the wellbeing of both the human and animal participant.

In recent years, there has been greater integration of observational and survey measures when looking at these interactions. For example, the Human Animal Interaction Scale (HAIS) devised by Fournier et al., (2016) requires the researcher to observe both the human and animal participants in affectionate/affiliative behaviours such as grooming, playing, unfriendly sounds, declining interactions or initiating interactions. The scale is used as an ethogram where the researcher during interaction can record the key behaviours observed, this can then be added to further by interviewing the human participant about the interactions. The importance of such approaches is that it acknowledges the animal and human as equal parts of the process, and from this can understand to what extent interactions are beneficial to each side of the equation. For example, when applied to educational interventions, it could be observed that there are lots of positive interactions and on the surface this intervention will look like a success. However, by adopting careful structured observations of both the animal and the child it might become apparent that the dog is showing more negative avoidance behaviours and if the intervention were to continue it may end with the dog hurting the child as a result of poor management of the intervention due to a focus on the human aspect.

Skoolkid errors

A common mistake is to think that an observational study is easy. It takes time to operationalise the area of interest and to turn that into a bulletproof checklist that limits variation in scoring. If executed robustly, an observational study takes time and dedication by researchers.

2.5 Observing human behaviour

The stages above are also important for human observations to ensure a checklist is fit for purpose. Once behaviours of interest have been identified, these require an operational definition, in other words, the specific actions that constitute the selected behaviours should be precisely and objectively outlined. It is important to set out, in the design stage, the parameters for the observation with a clear coding system so that the observer can discriminate between each item (Gridley, Bywater, & Hutchings, 2018). This is of importance because it results in observations not being biased by inferences and subjective judgements of the observer. Researchers typically develop coding manuals consisting of the operational definitions of the selected behaviours which are then used to guide observers when recording behavioural occurrences (Salkind, 2010).

For reliability in observational studies, where possible it is best to have at least two observers, so data collated can be compared and verified. This allows the researcher to ascertain consistency in behavioural recordings and ensure that a high level of agreement is maintained between the observers. For example, if two observers are completing a checklist of behaviours at playtime and one person is counting running as a game and the other person is counting it as a sport, comparing responses eliminates this discrepancy, and in comparing the responses can redefine the behaviours being observed. This is known as **inter-rater reliability** and is extremely important to support the credibility of your findings. In research involving only a single observer, reliability can be established by comparing the same behavioural ratings across separate instances.

2.6 Recording observations

Having identified an appropriate observation technique and clearly defined your behaviours to be observed (particularly in the case of structured observations), you need to select the method for recording these observations. Different approaches to conducting the observations will typically lend themselves to different types of questions. A good starting point is to consider if you want to do **continuous recording** or **time sampling**. Continuous recording involves recording all the behaviours of a group or an individual continuously without interruption. This technique is particularly useful if you are attaching a camera to an individual and seeing with whom they interact throughout a day, remote sampling or perhaps if you are establishing some criteria for an ethogram.

Ig Nobel Prize

Observing glee

In case you think that psychologists only like to study negative behaviours like aggression, you might like to know that they also study happy behaviours such as 'glee'. A study of glee in small groups of children (Sherman, 1975) found that glee was characterised by joyful screaming, laughing and intense physical acts which occurred in all the children at the same time or spread in a contagious way from one to another.

In the lengthy observations Sherman found that glee occurs in nearly half the times that young children get together, it generally lasts between four and nine seconds, and it is more likely to occur in mixed sex groups than single sex groups. Among the things that can trigger glee are:

- simple questions; for example, 'Who wants to go out and get John?'
- funny words; for example, ya-ya or tat-tat,
- breaking taboos; for example, 'stinky poo'
- someone else's misfortune; for example, a child tripping over a milk carton,
- nothing at all; just gleeful about nothing.

For this pioneering work, Sherman was awarded the 2001 Ig Nobel Prize for Psychology.

Sherman, L.W. (1975) An ecological study of glee in small groups of pre-school children. *Child Development*, *1*, 53–61.

Time sampling is when the researcher records the behaviours occurring at regular time intervals. This method is useful when observing animals directly in their natural habitat as it allows the researcher time to record results and provides a snapshot of behaviour over long periods. Time sampling will often involve either instantaneous recording or one-zero sampling. With instantaneous sampling when the time interval has elapsed (usually signalled by a beep to remind the researcher it is time) the researcher will record whatever behaviour is occurring at that moment. With one-zero sampling the observer observes the behaviours during the time interval and when the interval is up using 1 or 0 will indicate on an observation sheet which behaviour or combination of behaviours has occurred.

Whilst there are a variety of different methods by which observations can be recorded, what guides the choice of sampling technique is the question you are intending to answer. We focus on a few of the most commonly used methods in this chapter. Researchers may opt to use one or multiple methods to record the occurrence of behaviours.

Table 13.1 Summary of key recording techniques

Tally method	This includes recording the number of times behaviours of interest are observed. The frequency of these behaviours is typically recorded in relation time, for example, the number of separate occurrences of a behaviour within 60-second periods. This allows computing the rate at which a behaviour occurs. As indicated by the name of this method, the frequency of behaviours is recorded by placing tally marks on paper and then obtaining the sum of the tallies over a period of time.
Duration recording	This includes recording the amount of time a behaviour of interest lasts within an observation period. Typically, a stopwatch is started at the beginning of a target behaviour and then stopped when it ends. Summing up these durations then provides the total amount of time the participant is engaged in a behaviour of interest. Researchers may also compute the average amount of time participants are engaged in a behaviour; this is achieved by dividing this total time spent on a behaviour by its total number of occurrences.
Interval recording	This method allows researchers to record the time interval during which a target behaviour occurred. Interval recording is particularly useful in situations where recording the frequency of a behaviour is not feasible. To implement this method, the researcher creates a grid of boxes with each box corresponding to a single interval of a specific duration (e.g., 30 seconds). If within an interval a target behaviour is observed, then the box representing this interval will be marked with an X.
Focal sampling	This is where the researcher would look at one animal at a time and record the behaviours and interactions that animal makes. For example, when looking at primate social behaviour and dominance hierarchies, you could observe individually each member of the troop and record who they are agonistic towards and who they are affiliative towards. When all the focal samples are analysed together you can then establish how these behaviours occur, the aggressive or passive connections between individuals and construct a clear picture of a primate social network and a dominance hierarchy of behaviours.
Event/ behaviour sampling	With event/Behaviour sampling you might be focusing on one specific type of behaviour, for example, aggression. With this approach the researcher would only be recording the instances when these behaviours occur and recording which animals are involved and the interaction between them.

2.7 Choosing the best recording technique

The design of an observational study needs to carefully consider the best approach to collate the data required that reflects the behaviour to be understood. Observations can either be designed with the researchers being present to observe the behaviour, or designed to use cameras to capture the behaviour. Cameras may be used when it is not possible for a researcher to be present, or their presence could be considered too intrusive. Without knowing, the presence of a researcher could affect the behaviour that is to be observed. For example, children may react to an observer in their classroom. This is known as **observer reactivity** and could be a threat to the validity of the observation, as the behaviour observed is different to the naturally occurring behaviour.

This is also true of animal observations. If the impact on the animal's wellbeing or day-to-day life is going to be severely impacted, then there must be some reconsideration of the approach used. For example, many species of animals are very sensitive to direct observation, some animals will see this as a threat or a confrontational signal, other animals may see this as predatory behaviour. It is important to consider how the animal behaves within their natural environment. This can be understood clearly if we look at the issue of human-animal interactions within zoos. Hosey (2008), identified that visitors to zoological parks can have either a detrimental effect on the animals whereby the animals are fearful of human visitors, a neutral effect, or even a positive effect whereby the animals want to interact with the visitors.

In terms of behavioural observations in both the detrimental and positive conditions, the animal's behaviour is a clear response to the observer and therefore it would be difficult to observe naturalistic behaviours. One potential way to overcome this is for the animals to become **habituated** to the observer. Habituation means that over an extended period of time, the animals are able to become used to the presence of the researcher and no longer perceive them as a threat or novelty within their environment.

Alternatively, video recordings are a strategy that can be used to capture behaviour without influencing the behaviour. With video recordings, the recording can be watched multiple times, the slowing of frames can give an in-depth broken-down account of the behaviour being observed. It can be deconstructed into minutes or even seconds to observe non-verbal and verbal behaviour. This in-depth analysis is not possible with real-time observations and can refine the observations. However, as the researcher is not there in person, they are not engaging in the environment being observed which may influence the understanding of the data collected. Importantly, for recordings the camera needs to be carefully positioned to record the behaviour to be observed accurately. Whereas with real-time you can capture the whole environment. Both approaches offer a way to capture behaviour to help understand the social world.

The best approach could be using a blended approach, known as a '**blended observational approach**' (Moors, 2020), the study design would incorporate both video and real-time observations. A real-time observation and video recording combined enhances the credibility of the data. The video recordings generate extra data that can supplement field notes, as videos can be re-watched to disentangle field notes or check whether any behaviour was missed. The video recordings can be used as a checker for field notes, with the researchers comparing their field notes with the recordings.

3. EXAMPLE STUDY: MOTHER–BABY ATTACHMENT

3.1 The study

Observing mother–baby attachment using Ainsworth's Strange Situation Procedure (Ainsworth and Bell, 1970).

To understand behavioural observations with human participants, the strange situation task will be used as an example, with information of animal observations interweaved into the sections. Observational approach is the gold standard method to assess parent–child behaviours (Gridley, Bywater and Hutchings, 2018). With one example being Ainsworth's Strange Situation task (1970), this classic **developmental psychology** study used structured observations to understand **attachment** in children.

Interesting facts

In 1951, John Bowlby completed a monograph for the World Health Organisation based on his research examining the effects of mother–infant separation on early life experiences. This work was responsible for changing the prevailing institutional practices for children and, importantly, allowed parents to visit their children in hospitals. This publication was, however, used as a source by governments at the time to prevent women from working and leaving their children in day-care services, with the aim of maximising job opportunities for returned or returning servicemen. This has had a long-standing impact in society and can be attributed to the gender inequalities still experienced in society today.

It is approximately around nine months, that babies begin to show clear attachment preferences for their primary caregiver. According to John Bowlby and Mary Ainsworth, attachment is a long-term emotional connection between people (Bowlby 1969; Ainsworth & Bell, 1970), which for instance, includes the bond between a caregiver and an infant. In the 1950s, John Bowlby highlighted the importance of early life experiences and attachment with a primary caregiver on children's later development. Bowlby suggested that separation or reduced opportunities to bond with caregivers influenced children's later development and manifested in the form of personality disorders such as delinquency, psychopathy and impeded cognitive and physical development. Bowlby's findings were, however, primarily based on observations of children in orphanages, and therefore should be interpreted with caution, as the findings cannot be generalised. Mary Ainsworth expanded upon Bowlby's research and ideas by designing a ground-breaking experimental procedure using structured observations called the **strange situation task** which explored the quality of the attachment between infants and their caregivers. This study was particularly used to examine patterns of attachment and separation anxiety between a mother (the primary caregiver) and the baby. It has since played an important part of developing our understanding of attachment in children and has contributed to attachment theories in developmental psychology.

3.2. Who is Mary Ainsworth?

Professor Mary Ainsworth (1913–99) was a developmental psychologist well known for developing the strange situation procedure, which has had a lasting impact on the field of developmental psychology. She worked at the Tavistock Clinic in England (with John Bowlby) followed by the East African Institute of Social Research in Uganda, exploring caregiver-baby attachment interactions. She was also the recipient of the Gold Medal Award for Life Achievement in the Science of Psychology, by the American Psychological Foundation in 1998. The task was developed alongside her colleague Silvia Bell, when we think about the strange situation task, the focus is on Mary Ainsworth casting a shadow over her colleague and thus little can be found on her.

3.3 Aims of the study

The aim of the study was to explore infant attachment. The strange situation task used structured observations to observe the relationship between the caregiver and child to determine the attachment style of the infant, overcoming the limitations of other research methods such as caregiver interviews and self-report measures which can be subject to **demand characteristics** and **response bias effects**.

3.4 Method

When exploring attachment behaviours between mothers and their babies using the strange situation task, Ainsworth and Bell (1970) employed a structured observational method by designing an unfamiliar setting in a laboratory room. What were the advantages of structured observation here? Well, exploring separation anxiety and attachment in a typical (naturalistic) setting such as at one's home environment poses a challenge, as researchers must wait for behaviours of interest under conditions of interest to occur (Ainsworth & Bell, 1970). These behaviours can also be infrequent (Salkind, 2010) which could prevent reliable data being obtained to establish specific behavioural patterns over observation periods. Therefore, by implementing the strange situation task under structured settings, Ainsworth and Bell (1970) were able to design situations that promoted behaviours of interest. This allowed the researchers to efficiently record behaviours of interest within a 20-minute testing period (Ainsworth & Bell, 1970).

Ethel ethics

With observational studies the approach provides researchers with what can be described as a 'backstage stage pass' to the participant's behaviour. It is therefore important you develop rapport and trust with your participants. This may be through the first visit, where the researcher would not observe but engage with participants and their environment, and from the initial visit plan the observations for research purposes. Furthermore, if gaining a true account of a person's behaviour deception is required, participants must be fully debriefed at the end of the study and the researchers should ensure no harm.

The strange situation procedure might be criticised based on present ethical codes for having potentially caused the infants distress following the brief period of separation from their caregiver. It should, however, be noted the episodes were curtailed in situations in which infants expressed high levels of distress. Indeed, Ainsworth et al. (1978) note that it was nearly always the researchers who initiated curtailing the procedures. Also, with animal observations, situations can be distressing.

Some studies, such as those looking at whether animals have a concept of self-recognition, using a mirror task will undoubtedly require some manipulation of their environment as the animals are being observed within experimental conditions. Within the mirror task, a dot is placed on the animal's forehead and the animal is presented with a mirror, if the animal tries to interact with the dot on their forehead or focuses specifically at the dot it could be suggested they have a concept of their own self. Guenther (2017) provides a comprehensive overview of this type of study on primates over the past 50 years. One issue that is apparent is that for some animals, seeing a reflection can be a distressing experience, while for others that have been living alongside humans, there can be issues with animals becoming encultured and not showing species-specific behaviours.

3.5 What was the setting of strange situation like?

In this procedure, the room or the 'strange environment' was standardised across participants and arranged to include a child's chair surrounded by toys for the infants to explore and play with, two chairs for the adults (i.e., the mother and stranger) to sit in and a door through which the mother and stranger entered and exited (see Figure 13.1).

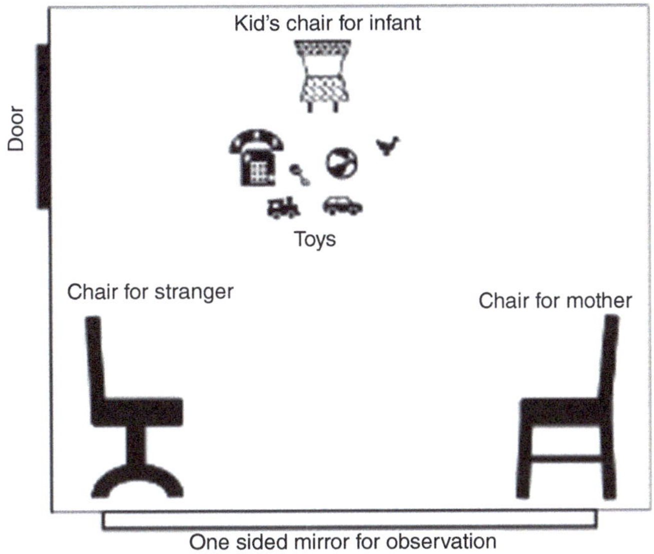

Figure 13.1 Example of a room layout in a strange situation paradigm

For the strange situation task, the researchers wanted to control the experiment, to do this they controlled the study environment by using a laboratory room. In the Strange Situation, infants' (aged 12–18 months) behaviours were observed in situations consisting of the mother's presence, her absence, in the presence of a stranger, and finally upon the mother's return. In designing this procedure, Mary Ainsworth expected that the strange environment, the presence of the stranger and separation from the mother would evoke attachment behaviours in children. Who was the stranger? The stranger was a role played by one of the female research assistants in this study. The structured nature of this study also meant, that both the mother and research assistant were briefed on their roles in advance, for example, mothers were asked to respond to their baby only in specific situations and to withhold initiating interactions except when needed. The purpose here was to minimise any potential influence from the caregiver on children's attachment behaviours.

3.6 Environmental control

The control over the environment and events in the strange situation task minimised the influence of external factors on the child's actions and behaviours, therefore ensuring consistency in situations across children (Lytton, 1971). In comparison, if the observations were to take place under naturalistic settings such as at one's home, the situation and physical setting will differ across participants thus attenuating control and increasing confounding effects.

Although structured observations offer greater control over the environment, it should be noted that an artificially designed environment does not adequately stimulate features of a naturalistic setting (Saini & Polak, 2014). Furthermore, as all participants were completing the same task in the same environment, some suggest that this imposed nature can reduce the spontaneity of the behaviour being observed (Gardner, 2000). These limitations can result in the observed behaviours being a consequence of the contrived nature of the setting (Salkind, 2010) and therefore, reduce generalisability of the findings. One way to overcome this would be how the task is presented to the participants, rather than be staged, it should be integrated into the research process. The controlled approach, however, enables researchers to compare across their sample the behaviour being observed, increasing the reliability of the findings.

3.7 Recording observations in the strange situation task procedure

Observers rated each infant's behaviour along two different measures:

1. The first of these included three types of exploratory behaviours (locomotor, manipulative, visual) and crying. Using the interval recording method, the occurrence of each of these behaviours was recorded in 15-second intervals for episodes 2 – 7 (see Table 13.2)
2. The second measure included four classes of behaviours that reflected infants' interactions with their mother and the stranger as well as the searching behaviours displayed by the infants upon the mother leaving the room. The occurrence of these behaviours was also recorded in 15-second intervals, additionally however, observers rated the intensity of these behaviours on a 5-point scale. These behavioural classes are listed below.
    i. Proximity and contact seeking
    ii. Contact maintaining
    iii. Proximity and interaction avoiding
    iv. Contact and interaction avoiding
    v. Searching behaviours

Table 13.2 Summary of observations for the Ainsworth study

Episode number	Persons present	Brief description of situation
1	Mother, baby and observer	The mother carried the baby into the room accompanied by one of the observers. This was an introductory episode – the mother was provided with information about where she should have sat and where to place the baby.
2	Mother and baby	The mother placed the baby in a specific location in the room (facing the toys) and sat quietly in her chair. The mother was instructed to only interact with the baby if they sought her attention.
3	Stranger, mother and baby	The stranger joined the mother in the room; she sat quietly for the first minute, in the second minute she engaged in a conversation with the mother and in the third minute approached and attempted to interest the baby with a toy. At the end of the third minute the mother left the room unobtrusively.
4	Stranger and baby	This was the first separation episode. The stranger geared her behaviour to that of the baby, she interacted or comforted the baby if they were inactive or were distressed. If the baby continued to explore the environment and play, the stranger did not interact with the baby.
5	Mother and baby	This was the first reunion episode with the mother. The mother re-entered the room and interacted with or comforted the baby. During this time the stranger unobtrusively left the room, while the stranger leaves the room. At the end of the third minute the mother left the room.
6	Baby alone	This episode included the second separation from the mother.
7	Stranger and baby	This episode continued the second separation from the mother, however, the stranger returned in this episode. As in episode 4, she geared her behaviour to the baby and interacted with it through play or comforted the baby if it was distressed.
8	Mother and baby	This episode included the second reunion with the mother. The mother re-entered the room, interacted with the baby and picked it up. During this time the stranger unobtrusively left the room.

Behavioural classes 1 – 4 were scored for interactions with the mother in episodes 2, 3, 5 and 8 while episodes 3, 4 and 7 were scored for interactions with the stranger. Searching behaviours were scored in separation episodes 4, 6 and 7.

Assigning a rating that reflects the intensity of a behaviour is another method by which observational data can be obtained. This is, however, not as straightforward as the recording methods introduced in this chapter. When rating the intensity of behaviours, a rating scale that clearly defines each point needs to be developed and this was indeed the case with the strange situation procedure. Observers were provided with detailed descriptors that corresponded to each point of the rating scale. Consider the behavioural class proximity and contact seeking for example, a rating of 7 for this measure reflected that the baby displayed an extremely active effort to approach and seek proximity with the adult. Conversely, a score of 1 represented no initiative to achieve contact or proximity, while points 2 to 6 indicated the different degrees to which the baby displayed initiative to seek contact and proximity with the adult (Ainsworth, Blehar, Waters, & Wall, 1978).

Cultural context

The strange situation was devised by Ainsworth and Bell in the US, and was initially carried out with American children. Attachment is dependent on cultural context, and the desirable attachment styles in the US may not be the same elsewhere in the world. Despite this, the task has been used to observe and rate infants' relationships with their caregivers in other cultures. A meta-analysis reported cross cultural variations with the strange situation task (van IJzeendoorn and Kroonenberg, 1988). When interpreting observational data, researchers need to be mindful of cultural differences.

4. ANALYSIS AND REFLECTIONS

4.1 Analysis

Once the observations have been conducted there is then the matter of how to analyse the data. When analysing observational data, the interpretation of data can be influenced by the researcher's biases and values. Observational researchers need to take special care to limit this. There can be a temptation when conducting observations to over-attribute value to one off events or to conflate a behaviour. It is therefore important to not over attribute the observations, the samples observed are specific to the environment and conditions that they are living in. For example, if you were to observe an animal within a zoo environment and identify increased aggression, this could be because of being within an enclosure and interacting with humans. Therefore, you could not state with confidence behaviours observed within a zoo environment are the same as observations from wild animals.

When analysing observational data, researchers need to be reflective and be aware of the influence of researcher bias and the impact the method will have on the environment being observed. An example of researcher bias, in some areas of research there is an extensive focus on human cognition and human behaviour being 'better' or 'superior' to that of other animals. This is obviously a bias due to us observing animals from a human perspective as a highly successful species. However, by taking a stance by which humans are perceived as the pinnacle of evolution and a dualistic view that humans are separate from nature there is a risk of trivialising the wellbeing and lives of the animals observed. Such human/nature separations also increase the risk of misinterpreting behaviours in terms of being 'primitive' or over-simplified or having no emotional content.

A healthier approach is that of an ecofeminist approach whereby the observer acknowledges that they are part of the ecosystem, and that the perception of human superiority is merely an illusion (Plumwood, 1992). For example, if you were a saltwater crocodile or great white shark a human being is just a potential meal, in this context human life is no more valuable than any other species and should be a vital consideration when observing such apex predators.

Video recordings can address questions of reliability, as the recordings can be re-analysed by multiple members of a research team. In the strange situation procedure, observations were recorded through a one-way mirror. Prior to recording observations, however, the observers familiarised themselves with the coding manuals dictating the behaviours of interest and ensured that they appreciated the distinctions between behaviours they observed (Ainsworth et al., 1978). Indeed, interrater reliability estimates between observers remained high indicating agreement and consistency in the recording of data.

You should now understand the design of observational studies using examples from human and animal contexts. For the strange situation you know the procedure, the behaviours of interest and how these were recorded. Let's now look at the key findings reported by Ainsworth and Bell (1970). They found infants' exploratory behaviours to increase in the presence of the mother but decline in the stranger's presence (e.g., episode 3) as well as in all episodes characterised by the mother's absence (e.g., episodes 4, 6 and 7). The depressed exploratory behaviours in the mother's absence were accompanied by increased crying and intense searching behaviours. In contrast, reunion episodes with the mother (e.g., episodes 5 and 8) were primarily characterised by heightened proximity and contact seeking and contact maintaining behaviours. Nevertheless, a few infants also displayed contact resisting and proximity avoiding behaviours in reunion episodes. Overall, these findings provide insight into how infants' attachment seeking behaviours are shaped by the presence and absence of their primary caregiver. Indeed, infants seem to display strong contact promoting behaviours (e.g., crying, searching) when the mother was absent, or in situations that might have appeared scary. We also see that infants engaged in reduced exploration in their mothers' absence, which might suggest that when exploring unfamiliar environments infants were using her as a secure base (Ainsworth & Bell, 1970).

For unstructured observations, at the findings stage, project field notes need to be written up systematically and quickly. This is because, quite quickly, notes can become difficult to decipher after the event. Unstructured observations need detailed notes that include but are not limited to reflections on the behaviour observed and a description of the environment. Like a method section of a report, if picked up by someone else, field notes should enable another person to visualise what was observed.

Whoa there!

One limitation of observational methods is when there is only one researcher and no supporting video evidence, as interrater reliability is not possible. Therefore, the results are questioned as to whether they are credible, are they an accurate reflection of the behaviour observed, as with this method, detailing a behaviour is open to interpretation and biases. You need to clearly operationalise the behaviour that you wish to observe.

Things to consider when designing an observational study:

1. It is a time-consuming method, especially in the data collection and analysis process;
2. Training is needed to undertake quality observations;
3. You need to clearly define the behaviour to be observed;
4. Incorporate validity checks, for example, using more than one observer.

4.2 Reflections

As you have now learnt, observational research methods allow researchers to collect data on behaviour with little or no interference from the researcher. As with all research however, when identifying the most appropriate research method – in this case the observational technique, researchers should first consider the nature of their research question(s) and identify the method which allows them to obtain data that best addresses their research question. To achieve this, you should consider the relative merits and limitations of the observational techniques introduced in this chapter and understand when they can be appropriately used.

Unstructured observations do not have a specific focus – this allows the researcher to document as much information as possible about an environment and participants' behaviour. This observational technique is therefore useful when researchers have limited knowledge in the area of interest and is typically employed in the early stages of a study.

It has potential to generate comprehensive datasets which can inform the focus of subsequent stages of a study, including the identification of behaviours of interest for structured observations. A major drawback of this method, however, is that observations can be biased as there is potential for observers to be selective of the behaviours recorded and how these are interpreted (Given, 2008).

Conversely, structured observations, rely on schedules or checklists of specific behaviours consisting of predefined criteria, and observers record the frequency, duration or intensity of these behaviours. This ensures consistency when recording data, as behaviours are not subject to the judgement and interpretation of observers. When employing structured observational methods, researchers also carefully construct or 'structure' their environment, for instance, they standardise the organisation of stimuli in the setting which offers greater experimental control across participants.

These structured settings are designed to evoke behaviours of interest within the scheduled observational period thus reducing the investment of time and other resources when collecting data. As we stated above, structured observations also include predefined observation checklists which focus on specific behaviours, this allows structured procedures to be easily replicated and its reliability tested. It should nevertheless be noted that the increased experimental control offered in structured settings reduces its ecological validity. Finally, unlike in unstructured observations, the narrow focus on specific behaviours in structured observations makes it unsuited for exploratory research studies.

When interpreting observational data, it can be difficult to examine objectively. There is always the temptation to **anthropomorphise** with animal observations, this is suggesting an emotional response has occurred that might not be appropriate and over attributing the significance of observations from easily accessible captive animals. This is a particular issue for psychologists that want to look at evolutionary explanations for human behaviours or personality traits in animals. There is evidence that different animals do have different internal states of mind and this indicates a personality, however, what is sociopathic to a human might be sociable to another species, so it is difficult to attribute too many human labels to animal behaviour. There can also be a danger of extreme behaviourism when examining observational data. For example, if the goals of the animal (purpose of the behaviour) are neglected in favour of only looking at a stimulus and response and assuming the animal is a total blank slate with no concerns apart from the current function.

Another issue particularly for psychologists is the assumption that for some reasons humans are more evolved and therefore the behaviour of animals are viewed in terms of their utilitarian value to people in term so their importance, e.g., a beetle might be seen as a mechanical feeding machine and not a caring mother (flesh eating beetles exhibit very strong maternal behaviours). Equally, there is a perception of superiority in that by researching behaviour the researcher is not part of the ecosystem when their presence (or even the presence of a camera) will change how a creature behaves and responds to their environment. Taking a psychological perspective on animal behaviour will always require some caution, however, it can be exceptionally rewarding when applied to real world settings and acknowledging human behaviours within the context of the wider behavioural ecosystem.

Observational approaches give you a way to understand social interactions and behaviours (Gardner, 2000), in a way that is not possible using other methods, such as self-report studies which are a person's perception of their behaviour. There are limitations to all methods, it is being aware of these, and in the design mitigating these where possible. For example, inter-rater reliability is an important part in designing observational studies, either by having two observers in a setting or an observer and a camera. Furthermore, in the design of observational studies you need to have clear operationalised definition of the behaviour. To support the credibility of findings, like in the Strange Situation Task, observational data can be triangulated with other methods to gain a deeper understanding of people's behaviours, for example, you could use interviews (see Chapter 6) or visual methods (see Chapter 9). If you want to understand the behaviour of humans or animals, observational studies give you the key to unlock and explore the behaviour of others.

LEARNING OBJECTIVES

You should now know:

- The stages to operationalise your behaviour; scoping observation, literature searches and piloting;
- Collect observational data based on the research question you have developed.

FURTHER READING

To find out more about the use of live or video observations, read this paper by Gridley, Bywater and Hutchings (2018):

Gridley, N., Bywater, T. J., & Hutchings, J. M. (2018). Comparing live and video observation to assess early parent–child interactions in the home. *Journal of Child and Family Studies*, *27*(6), 1818–29. https://doi.org/10.1007/s10826-018-1039-y

Want to know more about how to blend observational methods, this paper by Paterson, Bottorff and Hewat (2003) provides a how to guide and also the challenges:

Paterson, B. L., Bottorff, J. L., & Hewat, R. (2003). Blending observational methods: Possibilities, strategies, and challenges. *International Journal of Qualitative Methods*, *2*(1), 29–38.

For a good overview of qualitive methods in Psychology focusing on observational design in Chapter 4 read *Qualitative Methods in Psychology* by Banister et al. (2011):

Banister, P. (2011). *Qualitative methods in psychology: A research guide*. McGraw-Hill Education (UK).

LINKS TO USEFUL RESOURCES

Here is a video demonstrating the 'strange situation' observational method by Mary Ainsworth: www.youtube.com/watch?v=m_6rQk7jlrc

Here is a really useful and interesting video by an animal behaviour psychologist Dr Roger Mugford on human animal interaction: https://sk.sagepub.com/video/comparative-psychology-and-animal-behavior

GLOSSARY

Academic rigour Refers to a standard of excellence that is expected in academic work.

Affect Emotion or subjectively experienced feeling, such as happiness, sadness, fear, or anger.

Affiliation Being connected or associated with a person, community or organization.

Ambiguous questions Items that are not clearly worded and can be hard for participants to give a clear answer to.

Anonymity All identifiable information is removed from the data, and any data presented (i.e., participant quotes) cannot be traced back to an individual.

ANOVA An inferential statistic that can be used with interval-level data and that is capable of dealing with more than one independent variable at a time. The word is an acronym of ANalysis Of VAriance, and is conventionally written in capital letters. Probably the most widely used statistical technique in experimental psychology.

Anthropology Scientific study of humans, human behaviour and societies, past and present. The study of what makes us human.

Anthropomorphism The projection of human traits, personalities, and behaviours onto non-human animals (or even objects).

Arms A group of participants who receive a particular intervention; also, attached to shoulders, often in pairs.

Asynchronous online communication Online communication which takes place over a series of hours, days or weeks, in which individuals interact with posts shared to a discussion board at any time.

Attachment The bond between individuals, commonly between an infant and their caregiver.

Back-translation This method involves translating the instrument in the target language by group of translators. Translators then revert the survey instrument back to the original version using the translated version. In case of any discrepancy, translators along with the researcher make a decision with an overall consensus.

Banality of evil Coined by political theorist Hannah Arendt after watching the 1961 trial of Nazi SS officer Adolf Eichmann, this spare phrase captures the idea that evil acts are not necessarily perpetrated by evil people. Instead, they can simply be the result of bureaucrats dutifully obeying orders.

Behaviourism A psychological approach which emphasises scientific and objective methods of investigation. The approach is only concerned with observable stimulus-response behaviours, and states all behaviours are learned through interaction with the environment.

Between-groups design A research design in which different groups of participants are tested under different experimental conditions.

Blended observational approach observational approach that combines the two observational strategies of video recording and participant observation together.

Blinding When the allocation of participants to groups is kept from those involved in the trial.

Causal inference The process of concluding that one thing directly influences another, based on observed data.

Causality In an experiment, when manipulating the Independent Variable causes a change in the state of the Dependent Variable.

Causation The influence by which one event, process, or state contributes to the production of another event, process, or state.

Circles of Support and Accountability A 'Circle of Support and Accountability' is a group of Volunteers from a local community which forms a Circle around an offender.

Cognition The mental processes of thinking, knowing, and understanding.

Collaborative working Also known as joint or partnership working, collaborative working occurs when two or more professionals, teams, or organizations work together, either for a fixed term or permanently.

Colloquialism A word, phrase or expression that is not formal but is used is everyday language. For example, using the word 'cheers' as a less formal alternative to 'thank you'.

Colonialism Political oppression where one nation or culture dominates another one and, in particular, removes wealth from the dominated culture, believes it has a right of access into the dominated culture, and has a power base outside the dominated culture.

Comparable data set A data file (e.g., interview audio file or transcript) that is similar in content to others conducted (i.e., the same topics are explored). However, as each narrative will be different, data files won't tell the exact same stories.

Compliance The extent to which trial participants complete the treatment or intervention.

Computational modelling The study of complex systems using mathematics, physics and computer science.

Concurrent validity Established when participants' results from a survey are associated with participants' results of an existing survey measuring the same construct.

Condition(s) A sub-section of an experiment derived from the levels of the independent variable(s).

Confidentiality Linked with anonymity (see above). Confidentiality is difficult to guarantee in qualitative research because verbatim (word for word) quotes are very often used in the research outputs as evidence in the findings sections to support researcher claims. So, a reader/audience will know what was said by a participant, but should not be able to tell, if the data are anonymised properly, which participant any given quote came from.

Confirmability The findings are free from researcher bias and clearly derived from the data.

Confounding variable An improperly controlled variable that interacts with the independent variable(s) in a way that makes it impossible to determine their individual effects.

Consent An agreement to participate in research. It is a process, in which the participant has an understanding of the research and its risks.

Construct validity Established when participants' responses on a survey are associated with other constructs that you would expect to be associated based on existing theory.

constructive alternativism Reality is different for each of us. We see, intepret and construe things in different ways. What may be a stressful inquisition to one person may be construed by another person as a helpful or necessary fact-finding interview.

Constructs (personal constructs) (see also Personal Construct Theory) Psychologist George Kelly envisaged the human being as an informal scientist, who in their quest to understand and make sense of their world, does so by formulating constructs, much like hypotheses, about their world and 'testing' them in order to 'predict' how the world works and thus to make it actionable in real life.

Contamination Where participants in the control arm of a trial also receive the intervention.

Content analysis A method for identifying patterns in research data. It can be conducted quantitatively (e.g., summarizing data by counting and categorizing) and/or qualitatively (e.g., with a view to interpreting and understanding meaning in the data).

Continuous recording Is when the observed group or individual are studied continuously (usually recorded for accuracy) and this approach is often linked with event/behaviour sampling techniques.

contrived or research generated data Data are the direct result of the researcher's design and are deliberately generated by a researcher for the purpose of the study.

Control group A group separated from the rest of the experiment, where the independent variable being tested cannot influence the results. The participants in an RCT who do not receive the intervention being tested.

Controlled experiment A scientific test that is directly manipulated by a scientist, in order to test a single variable at a time.

Conversation analysis A highly technical qualitative method which began with the groundbreaking work of Harvey Sacks in the 1960/70s. Conversation analysis is literally the analysis of naturally occurring conversation which makes up social life and as such often employs 'naturally occurring' data. The main focus of the analysis is on sequence organization with the aim of identifying reoccurring patterns across interaction sequences.

Counterbalancing A method of controlling against potentially confounding variables in experiments. Typically, counterbalancing is seen in action in repeated measures designs in an effort to control against order effects, and characteristically involves alternating the order in which subjects do the conditions of an experiment.

Credibility Concerned with the truth-value of a research study's findings, the fit between the data and the interpretation.

Critical incident Developed by John Flanagan in the 1950s, the critical incident method (or technique) is a way of analyzing specific situations (incidents) with a view to understanding what actions and behaviours took place and what were the outcomes of the incident.

Cultural context The society individuals are raised in and at how their culture affects behaviour. It incorporates learned values and shared attitudes among groups of people.

Dangling alternatives Where items are worded in such a way that they give the participants the alternative answers before the participants are told the subject matter within the question.

Data corpus The collection of data you gather.

Deductive (see also Inductive). In relation to qualitative data analysis, this is sometimes known as theoretically guided analysis as the analysis sets out to explore a specific theory. Therefore, the researchers may be coding the data to answer a specific research question(s) and have pre-defined themes. Questions in the interview schedule are likely to closely align with the themes.

Demand characteristics Those aspects of a psychological study (or other artificial situation) which exert an implicit pressure on people to act in ways that are expected of them.

Dependability The degree to which the research procedures are clearly documented, allowing someone outside the research to follow and repeat the research process.

Dependent variable A variable which is expected to be influenced by one or more independent variables.

Descriptive statistics A set of summary statistics of a given sample that help describe the data.

Developmental Psychology Area of psychology that focuses on the development of humans across the lifespan from babies to teenagers to older people.

Diagnostic categories The limited set of descriptors that are used to categorise the experiences people describe. For example, the Diagnostic and Statistical Manual (DSM).

Discourse analysis A qualitative research method used across disciplines for studying written or spoken language in relation to its social context. Central to discourse analysis is the idea that the individual is always located in society and is at least partially within systems of difference and inequality.

Discussion stimulus Additional materials used in a focus group to facilitate discussion, such as exercises, images, or videos.

Dissemination The process of sharing research findings once a research project has finished. Ideally, research findings should be shared to a wide audience and in a way that is accessible to a range of people who would be interested in the findings.

Double-barrelled questions Items that ask about more than one thing in the same question meaning that it is hard to tell which part of the question participants are answering.

Double-blind control A form of experimental control which aims to avoid self-fulfilling prophecies, by ensuring that neither the subjects nor the experimenter who carries out the study are aware of the experimental hypothesis.

Ecological validity The extent to which the findings from a research study can be generalised to the 'real world'.

EEG (electroencephalography) A temporally accurate brain imaging technique that is based on the electrical discharge to the surface of the brain due to neuronal firing.

Effect size Image result for define effect size. 'Effect size is a quantitative measure of the magnitude of the experimental effect. The larger the effect size the stronger the relationship between two variables.'

Egalitarian Having the belief that all people should be treated equally and have equal access to opportunities and rights.

Electron microscopy The use of a microscope that uses beams of electrons to enlarge the image of an object. It allows for extremely small objects, even down to the size of large molecules, to be imaged.

Emic The viewpoint of the internal, emic research prioritises and is led by participant views of a subject, rather than researcher views of a subject.

Empirical evidence In research, evidence that is gained through concrete and verifiable research, rather than from postulating on theory or one's beliefs.

Empiricist A person who supports the theory that all knowledge is based on experience derived from the senses.

Epilepsy A neurological disorder marked by sudden recurrent episodes of sensory disturbance, loss of consciousness, or convulsions, associated with abnormal electrical activity in the brain.

Epistemological Epistemology is the branch of philosophy concerned with knowledge. Epistemologists study the nature of knowledge, epistemic justification, the rationality of belief, and various related issues.

Epistemology A branch of philosophy concerned with the study of knowledge, what constitutes knowledge, where it comes from, how it can be acquired, and what its limits are.

Ethics At its simplest, ethics is a system of moral principles. Ethics is concerned with what is good for individuals and society and is also described as moral philosophy.

Ethnography A systematic study of individual cultures where researchers observe and/or interact with study's participants in their environment.

Ethogram A list of behaviours that are characteristic of the species/individual being observed.

Etic The viewpoint of the outsider, etic research which prioritises and is led by researchers a priori understanding of a topic, usually led by the research literature.

Euclidean distance This is the distance between two points. Ignore the fancy name, it's simply something you measure. Preferably in Euclidean space with a glass of Andorian whiskey. But go carefully.

Event/Behaviour sampling This is when a whole group of animals are observed and when a key behaviour occurs, the individuals involved, and the interaction details are recorded.

Experimental method An experiment involves manipulating one or more variables to observe possible changes in one or more other variables. Commonly this method is used to test hypotheses.

Experimenter effect(s) When the experimenter's expectations regarding the study affects the participant's behaviour during the study, and/or how the experimenter interprets the data they obtain from the study.

Extant material Material(s) created independent of any intervention, influence or prompts by the researcher (see also naturally occurring data).

Extraneous variables In an experiment, variables which are not the Independent Variable, but which may also lead to a change in the state of the Dependent Variable.

Face validity Items within a scale are reviewed to ensure that they are measuring the same construct.

Feminist research Mary Gergen (1988) suggested the following as the main themes of feminist research: (1) Recognizing the interdependence of experimenter and subject; (2) Avoiding the decontextualization of the subject or experimenter from their social or historical surroundings; (3) Recognizing and revealing the nature of one's values within the research context; (4) Accepting that facts do not exist independently of their producer's linguistic codes; (5) Demystifying the role of the scientist and establishing an egalitarian relationship between science makers and science consumers.

Field experiment An experiment that is conducted outside of the laboratory in a 'real-world' location.

Florescent microscopy The use of a microscope that can detect fluorescent light emitted from an object when ultra violet light is directed onto it.

Focal sampling This is when the observer studies the behaviour of one animal/individual.

Focus group 'A research technique that collects data through group interactions on a topic determined by a researcher' (Morgan, 1996 p. 130).

Footing positions How participants speak from various categories that they represent.

Functional magnetic resonance imaging (fMRI) Functional Magnetic Resonance Imaging. This uses the magnetic resonance imaging (MRI) machine to measure function, i.e., activity rather than simply structure (as in MRI).

Gatekeepers Those bodies who determine whether or not research can go ahead (e.g., consultants if you want to video record infertility treatment consultations).

Gratuitous qualifiers Where items are worded in such a way that they present a rationale for a particular response.

Grounded theory Developed by sociologists Barney Glaser and Anselm Strauss in 1967. Grounded Theory is a systematic research methodology that aims to develop a substantive theory through the gathering and analysis of data. The methodology employs inductive reasoning as a counterpoint to the traditional hypothetico-deductive method, which aims to apply and test pre-existing theories of phenomena.

Habituation Over a period of time spent with the animal(s) being observed, the observer becomes accepted as a benign presence within their environment and neither a threat nor novelty.

Heterogenous Focus groups in which individuals are recruited to reflect a range of diverse backgrounds and perspectives.

Hippocampus Hippocampus is a complex brain structure embedded deep into temporal lobe. It has a major role in learning and memory. It is a plastic and vulnerable structure that gets damaged by a variety of stimuli. Studies have shown that it also gets affected in a variety of neurological and psychiatric disorders.

Homogeneity Homogenous sampling is quite common in qualitative research work, where the researcher seeks to recruit a small group of participants that are alike on certain key characteristics, defined by the research question and inclusion criteria, with a view to understanding and describing that group of people in fine detail and depth.

Homogenous Focus groups in which individuals are recruited because they share a number of similar characteristics or perspectives.

Human episodic memory The memory for events in our lives.

Humanistic A viewpoint that states the beliefs and views of humans are most important, above that of religion or other supernatural standpoints. Humanistic psychology focuses on understanding humans holistically and from the point of view of the person.

Hypothesis Experiments are designed to test one or more hypotheses. A hypothesis is a prediction of what will happen in an experiment. It is worded in such a way that the results of a well-designed experiment will clearly show whether the prediction is right or wrong.

Idiogrid is the name of a computer programme that allows you to analyse repertory grid data.

Incidence The rate of occurrence of a disease or behaviour within a population. This is different to prevalence, which measures the proportion of a population that has the disease or displays the behaviour.

Independent variable A variable that is manipulated by the experimenter in order to produce an effect on the dependent variable.

Individual differences Individual differences refer to enduring characteristics that distinguish one individual from another and that are stable over time and across situations. Commonly in psychology it is associated with the measurement of qualities through questionnaires and scales.

Inductive (see also Deductive). In relation to qualitative data analysis, theme or category development is driven by the data. Themes or categories will not align with the questions asked in the interview schedule and a pre-existing coding framework will not be used. This type of data analysis may be seen as exploratory.

Inferential statistics A way of using statistics to enable us to make inferences from data about relationships among variables, particularly with reference to cause and effect. This involves going beyond the data, hence the term 'inferential'. A contrast can be made with descriptive statistics.

Informed consent Where a participant is informed about all aspects of the research project in order to make a decision about their willingness to participate.

Intention to treat A type of analysis where all participants remain in the groups they were originally allocated, regardless of whether they completed the intervention.

Interrater reliability The extent to which independent raters agree with each other (for example, when they are categorising children's behaviour as aggressive or non-aggressive).

Interaction effect An effect whereby one independent variable is directly affected by one or more other independent variables.

Internal consistency If a test is internally consistent then the items in that test really are measuring the same thing (or same set of things). Note that this does not necessarily mean that they are measuring what they are meant to measure. In this respect, internal consistency has more to do with reliability than validity.

Internet-mediated research Any research involving data from or about human participants using the internet.

Interpretative phenomenological analysis (IPA) An idiographic qualitative methodology focusing on how people make sense of their personal and social worlds and the meanings they attribute to their experiences.

Interview transcript A typed text document that captures data from an audio or video recorded interview. The data captured is most commonly verbal in nature, although sometimes can include written summaries of body language, gestures and even facial expressions. Ultimately, what is to be included in terms of level of detail is dependent on what kind of analysis is to be performed on the transcript data.

Jefferson transcription A method of writing up what is said that captures most of hearable and visible conversation.

Lazy submitting Occurs when a participant may not be bothered to complete a questionnaire correctly so gives the same response for every question. For example, if there are 20 questions they simply select 1,1,1,1,1,1,1,1,1,1,1,1,1,1,1,1,1,1,1,1.

Leading questions Questions that encourage participants to respond in a particular way because they are given the sense that there is a 'right' answer.

Level The different values that can be taken by an independent variable, can be categorical, continuous, or binary.

Lifeworld From the German word Lebenswelt, the phenomenological concept of the lifeworld refers to the total world in which humans inhabit. It is made up of all the emotions we have, the events, objects and beings we encounter, and how these present themselves to our consciousness as we experience them.

Likert scale Widely used in questionnaire studies and attitude surveys as the means by which subjects give 'ratings' in response to closed questions. The scale can be any size (often it is from 1–5 or 1–7), and each point on the scale is assigned a verbal designation. For example, on an attitude survey using a 5-point Likert scale, a rating of 1 might represent 'strongly agree', a rating of 5 might equal 'strongly disagree', a rating of three might equal 'neither agree nor disagree', and so forth.

Manipulation checks A question or statement that is written in such a way that the answer indicates whether a participant has read and understood the information.

Matched-pairs design An experimental design where participants are matched on one or more key criteria, and then those individuals are randomly assigned to different experimental conditions.

Measurement error The difference between the true value and the measurement recorded through a particular technique.

MEG (magnetoencephalography) Magnetoencephalography is an imaging technique that relies on magnetic signals to image neural activity.

Memes concepts, ideas, pop culture references or jokes summarised in photo or video format, often circulated online.

Method This refers to the tools that the researcher uses to obtain data, for example, interview or survey.

Methodology A series of principles which guide the research process, including a coherent ontological framework, epistemology, theoretical perspective, and methods. Methodologies are usually published in a tradition and provide a set of rules for how to conduct qualitative research.

Methods The ways by which a researcher collects data.

Micro analysis Starting analysis from the bottom up (grounded in what participants say).

Minimum detectable effect size (MDES) The effect size below which we do not have the power to reliably distinguish it from zero.

Mixed-factorial A research design that involves two or more independent variables, of which at least one is a within-subjects (repeated measures) factor and at least one is a between-groups factor.

Moderator The individual who ensures the focus group schedule is adhered to, and who facilitates the focus group conversation.

Narrative analysis Not one but a genre of frameworks for conducting interpretative analysis on the stories that participants tell and share in everyday life. Rather than develop themes or theories from the data, narrative researchers are more concerned with things like story structure, the function and performance of stories and what the substance of a story is.

Naturalisitic Research and data which reflects 'real world' phenomena, rather than a false settings set up by a researcher.

Naturally occurring (found) data Information about a phenomenon that is produced without any intervention from a researcher (compare with researcher generated data and respondent generated data). This can be things like photographs or diaries that have been written by a person for the sole purpose of them documenting some interesting aspect of their lived world, without being asked to do so by a researcher.

Negatively worded questions Questions that are written in such a way that agreement or a response goes in the opposite direction to the other questions in the same survey.

Nervous system A system of the body that in vertebrates includes the brain, spinal cord, nerves, and sense organs and receives, interprets, and responds to stimuli from inside and outside the body.

Neural networks A system of neurons (artificial or organic) that can both simulate and predict data.

Neuroimaging Production of images of the structure or activity in the brain.

Neurology A branch of medicine that studies and treats disorders of the nervous system.

Neuron Specialised cells found in the central nervous system that are responsible for communication of information. Their distinctive shape relates to their function.

Neuroscience Study of the function and structure of the human nervous system and brain.

Non-compliance The act of not completing the intervention in an RCT.

Non-invasive stimulation techniques In neuroscience research a stimulation technique is considered non invasive if it does not involve invading the body for example with an instrument or by cutting or puncturing the skin.

Non-invasive techniques In neuroscience research and neurological treatment a practice is considered non invasive if it does not involve invading the body for example with an instrument or by cutting or puncturing the skin.

Non-verbal behaviour This includes facial expressions, body posture and eye contact, all forms of communicating without being verbal.

Objective The attempt to not be influenced by personal feelings, interpretations, or prejudice. Based on facts, unbiased; an objective opinion.

Observation In its broadest sense this is the core of psychological research. It is not just 'observational studies' that are based on 'observing'. On the contrary, all empirical work is by definition grounded in the act of observation. Experimenters observe the behaviour of their subjects, interviewers observe the spoken responses of their subjects, discourse analysts observe the texts with which they are working, and so forth.

Observational study A study which involves simply watching and recording what happens, rather than intervening and causing changes.

One-way translation Without any back translation, survey instrument is administered in the original language.

Ontology The philosophical study of the nature of being, whether things exist or do not exist, and the relatedness of things that exist.

Operational model This refers to the measures that are selected to test out a theoretical model.

Operationalisation A process in which the variables being manipulated and examined are defined and measured.

Optogenetics The manipulation of genes to produce light sensitive proteins within brain cells so that they can be detected and manipulated.

Order effects A set of confounding variables which must be controlled against in experiments that use repeated measures designs. In the simplest case of a two-condition experiment, if all the subjects do condition A first, then condition B, and (for the sake of argument) perform better in condition B, a sceptic can argue that this is nothing to do with the experimenter's manipulation of the independent variable, but is simply due to the subjects having practised on condition A, and improved by the time they did condition B (a practice effect, which is one kind of order effect). Counterbalancing, controls against this confounding variable by alternating the order in which subjects do the conditions of an experiment.

Orthographic transcription A style of transcription which uses the typical characteristics of a language (such as spelling, grammar); a simple approach to transcription which focuses on what the individual said, rather than how they said it.

Paradigm In science and philosophy, a paradigm is a distinct set of concepts or thought patterns, including theories and research methodologies.

Parallel-form reliability Established when two forms of a survey are developed at the same time and then when administered to participants there is a correlation between the participants' responses on both scales.

Pavlov's log Conditioned reflex action causing bowels to relax as soon as you see the toilet door.

Peer-support Support from those that have a similar lived experience.

Personal construct theory (psychology) A psychological theory or personality and cognition postulated in the 1950s by the psychologist George Kelly. Influential in the development of cognitive therapies, the theory focuses on psychological reasons underpinning human actions and decisions.

Personal constructs Individual ways of making sense of the world, which have been developed on the basis of experience. Personal construct theorists argue that getting to understand the personal constructs which someone applies to make sense of their experience is essential for effective psychotherapy, as well as for effective interaction in day-to-day living.

Phenomena of interest Refers to the topic that we want to research.

Phenomenological Concerned with the person's own perceived world and the phenomena which they experience, rather than with objective reality.

Phenomenology The philosophical study of the structures of consciousness, experience and awareness.

Photo-editing software Different software can be used to edit an image. For example, software that enables pixelation of images, to help anonymise the image.

Photo-elicitation A method in which photographs, taken by the researcher and/or participant are used during an interview.

Photovoice A community-based research method which uses photographs taken by the participant (or researcher) to enable them to think critically about their community and discuss the different influences on their lives, through a group process.

Polytextual (thematic) analysis The analysis of visual data that looks across sets of images and tries to capture the recurring patterns in the analysis both in terms of form and content.

Positron emission tomography (PET) This is a method of imaging that involves introducing radioactive isotopes into the body that are then detectable by the PET machine.

This technique is useful in neuroscience as it allows for measurement of glucose metabolism (and therefore neural activity) in brain and even more excitingly for mesurement of some neurotransmitters such as dopamine.

Positron Emission Tomography (PET) Uses radioactivity to label blood, blood sugars or important neurotransmitters such as dopamine. The labelled substance is then injected into mugs (sorry, volunteers) while they lie in the scanner and carry out mental tasks such as problem solving. The scanner picks up the gamma rays emission to find out where the labelled substances are active in the brain. This requires a fair amount of computer processing because the PET scanner has to sift through around 7–8 million gamma-ray signals per second. PET scanning is the most established of the brain imaging techniques but requires massive investment.

Post-hoc test A set of statistical comparisons between group means.

Practice effects When someone is asked to complete the same task more than once, their performance may change by virtue of being asked to the same thing again.

Predictive neural network This is a computational method that makes predictions about brain activity patterns based on past data.

Predictive validity Established when survey responses can successfully predict some future outcome.

Prestige bias When participants are asked to think about the views of others, the prestige of the person they are asked about may influence the response participants' give.

Primary outcome A measure used to decide the overall result of a study, and should be decided at the design stage. The primary outcome is also used to calculate the number of participants needed in the trial.

Priming Where the order of something influences responses on subsequent measures.

Principal Component Analysis Principal Component Analysis (PCA) is a multi variate statistical technique that will delight and please you. It finds patterns in data, reducing large quantities of data to (hopefully) meaningful units. Do try it it, you'll love it.

Psychometric properties This refers to the validity and reliability of the measurement tool(s) being implemented.

Psychometric tests Instruments which have been developed for measuring mental characteristics. Psychological tests have been developed to measure a wide range of things, including creativity, job attitudes and skills, brain damage and, of course, 'intelligence'.

Qualitative data Data which describe meaning and experience rather than providing numerical values for behaviour such as frequency counts.

Quantitative data Data which focus on numbers and frequencies rather than on meaning or experience.

Quasi-experiment An experiment in which one or more of the independent variables is not under the direct control of the experimenter.

Racism Steve Martinot offers a summary of racism that has four aspects. First, it insists that a difference exists, either real or imaginary. It can be something about our bodies or beliefs or cultural practices. Second, is the negative valuation on those perceived as seen as being different from the people who are making that valuation. Third, this negative valuation is applied to the whole group. Fourth, this negative valuation becomes the justification for hostility, discrimination and aggression.

Random allocation A method of controlling extraneous variables by assigning participants to different conditions at random.

Rapport If two people have a 'rapport' they have a good relationship in which they trust each other and understand each others' ideas or feelings very well. The idea of building rapport when interviewing a participant is crucially as important as building a relationship which has mutual trust and understanding will ultimately lead to richer data being collected.

Recurrent neural net This is a computational method that makes predictions based on sequential or time series data.

Reflexivity Refers to the examination of one's own beliefs, judgments and practices during the research process and how these may have influenced the research.

Rehabilitation The process of returning to a healthy or good way of life, or the process of helping someone to do this after they have been very ill in prison.

Reliability The reliability of a psychological measuring device (such as a test or a scale) is the extent to which it gives consistent measurements. The greater the consistency of measurement, the greater the tool's reliability.

Repertory grid technique A system for eliciting personal constructs and showing how individuals use them to interpret their experience.

Replicability In an experiment, the ability to recreate the experiment in order to support, build upon, or refute the findings by following the procedures set out in the method.

Research gap A topic or area for which missing or insufficient information limits the ability to reach a conclusion to a question.

Research question The main question to be answered by the research, usually stated in general terms and operationalised with one or more hypotheses.

Researcher generated data Data that a researcher produces themselves in the course of a research study, for example, field notes written about behavioural observations, or maps of behavioural occurrence in certain environments.

Resilience Is the ability to withstand and manage advertised.

Respondent generated data Data that research study participants generate throughout a study, for example, diary entries, taking photographs of meaningful places, or producing drawings or charts that capture some element of the phenomenon they have been asked to consider by the researcher.

Response bias Occurs when answers to a question are written in such a way that they encourage a participant to give a particular response (rather than the one that the participant may have typically given).

Response bias effect Is where participants in responding to a survey item may respond inaccurately or falsely to a question.

Response format The way participants answer the questions in your survey.

Reverse coding Where the scores for questions that are negatively worded are flipped so that high scores become low scores and vice versa (e.g., 1 becomes 5, 2 becomes 4, 3 stays as 3, 4 becomes 2, and 5 becomes 1). This then means that all of the questions within a survey are coded in the same direction such that high scores mean the same for all of the items.

Safety and wellbeing Ensuring that participants and the researcher remain physically and emotionally, safe and well, throughout the project.

Satisficing Where participants adopt a strategy of answering items in a questionnaire with the minimum effort (Murphy & Davidshofer, 2005).

Scan sampling This is when the observer scans a group of animals and records the occurrences of behaviours.

Scientific racism The use of bogus scientific arguments to enhance the power of one group of people over another.

Secondary outcome The measure (or outcome) judged to be most important in a trial, and the measure against which the effectiveness of the trial is measured. It must be declared at the design stage.

Selection bias This occurs when participants are allocated to groups in a systematic or non-random fashion. This can occur consciously, or subconsciously.

Self-constructions The ways in which a person believes their thoughts and feelings represent themselves and their identity.

Self-harm An intentional act of self-poisoning or self-injury, irrespective of the apparent purpose of the act.

Self-report A number of popular research methods are based on self-report: for example, questionnaires, interviews, attitude scales and diary methods. These are methods which rely on research subjects' accounts of their own experiences and behaviour.

Semantic differential scale A type of scale where opposite adjectives are used in a response format.

Sequential analysis The structure of social interaction (e.g., openings and closings of talk).

Sexism Using the pervasive power imbalance between men and women to oppress women by devaluing their experience, behaviour and aspirations.

Social constructionism The theoretical perspective that posits that the world is constructed through talk and conversation, and thus conversation and interaction can reveal group level assumptions and norms about phenomena.

Social desirability bias Where participants respond in a way that is perceived to be acceptable or desired by society.

Social Learning Theory A theory of learning process and social behaviour which proposes that new behaviours can be acquired by observing and imitating others.

Sociology The study of society – how it works, why it works, and how it could change. Alleged to be as interesting as Psychology, but by whom we ask?

Spillover This occurs when the treatment effect can be detected in control participants who share the same environment as treated participants, i.e., the treatment effect has 'spilled over' to control participants.

Split-half reliability A system for judging how reliable a psychometric test is.

Standardisation Which involves splitting the test into two, and administering each half.

Standardised procedure/standardisation The test to the same people, then comparing the results.

Stereotaxic surgery The use of a stereotax in brain surgery to enable a specific position in the brain to be reached, for example, for placement of a probe. A stereotax is a piece of equipment that measures in three dimensions (height, breadth, depth) to allow for coordinates to pinpoint a position in space.

Strange situation task Devised by Mary Ainsworth, the task conducted observations on the behaviour of infants with their mother to explore attachment.

Structured observation A method of recording behaviour where the behaviours are pre-categorised into a limited framework.

Subjective Based on or influenced by personal feelings, tastes or opinions.

Synapse Junction between cells across which information is transmitted in electrical or chemical form. Comprises a pre-synaptic and a post-synaptic membrane that are separated by the synaptic cleft.

Synchronous online communication Online communication with individuals responding and interacting with one another in real-time.

Synthesised This is when different components (e.g., of a qualitative and quantitative perspective) are combined and considered together.

Test-retest reliability A system for judging how reliable a psychometric test or measure is, which involves administering the same test to the same people on two different occasions, and comparing the results.

Thematic analysis A qualitative method that aims to find, analyze and interpret patterns of meaning (i.e., themes) in qualitative data. The technique is a method not a methodology as it has no defined theoretically informed foundations.

Time/Interval sampling this is when at regular time intervals the observer records the behaviour occurring at that specific moment. This is a useful technique when observing wild animals/animals in the field.

Timeline As applied to visual data collection methods, timelines are a form of respondent generated data whereby participants are asked to focus on capturing their life experiences and events in a chronological order.

Traditional research methods These are often thought of as surveys, interviews and focus groups.

Transcranial electrical current stimulation (tECS) This is a method of stimulating neurons using an electrical current by applying electrodes to the scalp.

Transferability The degree to which results of a study can be transferred to other groups, contexts or settings.

Translation by committee This method involves two or more individuals who are familiar with both languages, who translate the instrument from the original version. The researcher then uses the independent translators to arrive at a consensus or can even recruit an additional independent party to choose the version that fits best with the original version.

Triangulation A method of cross-checking data from multiple sources and perspectives to increase the credibility of the findings.

True experiment Also known as randomised experiments, an experiment in which the independent variables are under the direct control of the experimenter.

Trustworthiness This refers to the degree of confidence in the methods used to collect and interpret the data presented.

Type 1 error Also known as a false positive, this is when a significant effect is detected by chance rather than due to a true effect, i.e., we fail to correctly reject the null hypothesis.

Type 2 error Also known as a false negative, this is when a true effect is missed, ie we erroneously accept the null hypothesis.

Validity The question of whether a psychometric test or psychological measure.

Variable Anything that is subject to variation, either naturally or through manipulation.

Verbal behaviour Is communicating with others using language. An observational study may observe the behaviour of others in response to the language they hear.

Verbatim In qualitative research, when an interview is transcribed verbatim this means all of the speech on the audio or video recording is transferred exactly word for word into a typed, written record that can be used for analysis purposes.

Vicarious learning Learning that is derived from indirect sources such as hearing or observation, rather than direct, hands-on, instruction.

WEIRD problem In research, the over-recruitment of participants from White, Educated, Industrialised, Rich, and Democratic backgrounds.

Within-groups A research design in which participants take part in each of the experimental conditions.

REFERENCES

Abell, L., & Brewer, G. (2014). Machiavellianism, self-monitoring, self-promotion and relational aggression on Facebook. *Computers in Human Behavior*, *36*, 258–62.

Abrami, P. C., Lysenko, L., & Borokhovski, E. (2020). The effects of ABRACADABRA on reading outcomes: An updated meta-analysis and landscape review of applied field research. *Journal of Computer Assisted Learning*, *36*(3), 260–79. https://doi.org/10.1111/jcal.12417

Abrami, P. C., Savage, R. S., Deleveaux, G., Wade, A., Meyer, E., & Lebel, C. (2010). The design, development, testing and dissemination of evidence-based educational software. In P. Zemliansky & D. M. Wilcox (Eds.), *Design and implementation of educational games: Theoretical and practical perspectives* (pp. 168–87). IGI Global. https://doi.org/http://dx.doi.org/10.4018/978-1-61520-781-7.ch012

Adriansen, H. K. (2012). Timeline interviews: A tool for conducting life history research. *Qualitative Studies*, *3*(1), 40–55. https://doi.org/10.7146/qs.v3i1.6272

Adshead, G. (2010). Written on the body: Deliberate self-harm as communication. *Psychoanalytic Psychotherapy*, *24*(2), 69–80. https://doi.org/10.1080/02668731003707501. Retrieved from Written on the body: deliberate self-harm as communication database.

Adshead, J., Khoubehi, B., Wood, J., & Rustin, G. (2001). Testicular implants and patient satisfaction: A questionnaire-based study of men after orchidectomy for testicular cancer. *BJU International*, *88*(6), 559–62.

Ainsworth, M. D. S., Blehar, M. C., Waters, E., & Wall, S. N. (1978). *Patterns of attachment: A psychological study of the strange situation*. Psychology Press. https://doi.org/10.4324/9780203758045

Ainsworth, M. D., & Bell, S. M. (1970). Attachment, exploration, and separation: Illustrated by the behavior of one-year-olds in a strange situation. *Child Development*, *41*(1), 49–67. https://doi.org/10.1111/j.1467-8624.1970.tb00975.x

American Psychological Association (2002). Ethical principles 5 of psychologists and code of conduct. *American Psychologist*, *57*, 1060–73.

American Psychological Association Ethics Committee Statement (2009). *No Defense to Torture under the APA Ethics Code*. Retrieved from www.apa.org/news/press/statements/ethics-statement-torture.pdf

Ancona, D. G., Okhuysen, G. A., & Perlow, L. A. (2001). Taking time to integrate temporal research. *The Academy of Management Review*, *26*(4), 512–29. https://doi.org/10.5465/amr.2001.5393887

Anderson, C., & Kirkpatrick, S. (2016). Narrative interviewing. *International Journal of Clinical Pharmacy, 38*, 631–34. https://doi.org/10.1007/s11096-015-0222-0

Andrade, C. (2015). The primary outcome measure and its importance in clinical trials. *Journal of Clinical Psychiatry, 76*(10), e1320–e1323. https://doi.org/10.4088/JCP.15f10377

Andrews, M., & Justice, L. (2019). The replication crisis. In P. Banyard, G. Dillon, C. Norman, & B. Winder (Eds.), *Essential psychology* (3rd ed.) (pp. 77–87). SAGE.

Antoun, C., Katz, J., Argueta, J., & Wang, L. (2018). Design heuristics for effective smartphone questionnaires. *Social Science Computer Review, 36*, 557–74.

Anwar, A., Waqas, A., Zain, H. M., & Kee, D. M. (2020). Impact of music and colour on customers' emotional states: An experimental study of online store. *Asian Journal of Business Research, 10*, 104–25.

Anyan, F. (2013). The influence of power shifts in data collection and analysis stages: A focus on qualitative research interview. *The Qualitative Report, 18*(36), 1–9.

Archer, J., & Coyne, S. M. (2005). An integrated review of indirect, relational, and social aggression. *Personality and Social Psychology Review, 9*(3), 212–30.

Archer, K., Savage, R., Sanghera-Sidhu, S., Wood, E., Gottardo, A., & Chen, V. (2014). Examining the effectiveness of technology use in classrooms: A tertiary meta-analysis. *Computers and Education, 78*, 140–49. https://doi.org/10.1016/j.compedu.2014.06.001

Archer, M., Decoteau, C., Gorski, P., Little, D., Porpora, D., Rutzou, T., Smith, C., Steinmetz, G., & Vandenberghe, V. (2020). *What is critical realism? Theory section*. www.asatheory.org/2/post/2016/12/what-is-critical-realism.html

Arendt, H. (1963). *Eichmann in Jerusalem: A report on the banality of evil*. Penguin.

Asch, S. E. (1951). Effects of group pressure upon the modification and distortion of judgments. In H. S. Guetzkow (Ed.), *Groups, leadership and men* (pp. 177–90). Carnegie Press.

Asher, Y., Stark, A., & Fireman, G. D. (2017). Comparing electronic and traditional bullying in embarrassment and exclusion scenarios. *Computers in Human Behavior, 76*, 26–34.

Bacharach, S. B., Bamberger, P. A., & Doveh, E. (2008). Firefighters, critical incidents, and drinking to cope: The adequacy of unit-level performance resources as a source of vulnerability and protection. *Journal of Applied Psychology, 93*(1), 155.

Back, R., & Dana, R. H. (1977). Examiner sex bias and Wechsler Intelligence Scale for children scores. *Journal of Consulting and Clinical Psychology, 45*, 500.

Bagnoli, A. (2009). Beyond the standard interview: The use of graphic elicitation and arts-based methods. *Qualitative Research, 9*(5), 547–70. https://doi.org/10.1177/1468794109343625

Balmer, C., Griffiths, F., & Dunn, J. (2015). A review of the issues and challenges involved in using participant-produced photographs in nursing research. *Journal of Advanced Nursing, 71*(7), 1726–37. https://doi.org/10.1111/jan.12627

Bandura, A. (1963). *Social learning and personality development*. Holt, Rinehart, and Winston.

Bandura, A. (1965). Influence of models' reinforcement contingencies on the acquisition of imitative responses. *Journal of Personality and Social Psychology, 1*(6), 589–95.

Bandura, A., & Huston, A. C. (1961). Identification as a process of incidental learning. *Journal of Abnormal and Social Psychology, 63*(2), 311–18.

Bandura, A., & Walters, R. H. (1977). *Social learning theory* (Vol. *1*). Prentice-Hall.

Bandura, A., Ross, D., & Ross, S. A. (1961). Transmission of aggression through imitation of aggressive models. *The Journal of Abnormal and Social Psychology*, *63*(3), 575–82.

Bandura, A., Ross, D., & Ross, S. A. (1963). Imitation of film-mediated aggressive models. *The Journal of Abnormal and Social Psychology*, *66*(1), 3–11.

Banks, M. (2008). *Using visual data in qualitative research*. Sage.

Bannister, D., & Fransella, F. (1986). *Inquiring man: The psychology of personal constructs* (3rd ed.). Croom Helm.

Banyard, P. (2015). Where is our non-stick frying pan? *The Psychologist*. Available at https://thepsychologist.bps.org.uk/where-psychologys-non-stick-frying-pan

Banyard, P., & Hulme, J. (2015). Giving psychology away: How George Miller's vision is being realised by psychological literacy. *Psychology Teaching Review*, *21*(2), 93–101.

Barbour, R. (2008). *Doing focus groups*. Sage.

Barends, A. J., & de Veries, R. E. (2019). Noncompliant responding: Comparing exclusion criteria in MTurk personality research to improve data quality. *Personality and Individual Differences*, *143*, 84–9.

Barker, L. L. (1971). *Listening behaviour*. Prentice-Hall.

Baron-Cohen, S., Wheelwright, S., Robinson, J., & Woodbury-Smith, M. (2005). The Adult Asperger Assessment (AAA). A diagnostic method. *Journal of Autism and Development Disorders*, *35*(6), 807–19. https://doi.org/10.1007/s10803-005-0026-5

Bateson, P., & Laland, K. N. (2013). Tinbergen's four questions: An appreciation and an update. *Trends in Ecology & Evolution*, *28*(12), 712–18.

BBC (2021). Black scientists say UK research is institutionally racist. Available at https://www.bbc.co.uk/news/science-environment-58795079

Bell, R. (2005). The Abstracts of the 11th Australasian Conference on Personal Construct Psychology 8–10 July 2004. 'Downtowner on Lygon', Melbourne, Victoria. *Australian Journal of Psychology*, *57*(S1), 1–6.

Beninger, K. (2017). Social media users' views on the ethics of social media research. In L. Sloan, & A. Quan-Haase (Eds.), *The SAGE handbook of social media research methods* (pp. 573–92). Sage.

Bennett, C. M., Baird, A. A., Miller, M. B., & Wolford, G. L. (2010). Neural correlates of interspecies perspective taking in the post-mortem Atlantic salmon: An argument for proper multiple comparisons correction. *Journal of Serendipitous and Unexpected Results*, *1*(1), 1–5.

Bergen, N., & Lebonté, R. (2020). 'Everything is perfect, and we have no problems': Detecting and limiting social desirability bias in qualitative research. *Qualitative Health Research*, *30*(5), 783–92. https://doi.org/10.1177/1049732319889354

Berthelette, G., Raftis Y., & Henderson, G. (2001). The sharing circle. A culturally appropriate format for a focus group? *Aboriginal Nurse*, *16*, 17–18.

Billieux, J. (2012). Problematic use of the mobile phone: A literature review and a pathways model. *Current Psychiatry Reviews*, *8*(4), 299–307.

Black, G., Alun, D., Dalis, I., & Chambers, M. (2018). Reflections on the ethics of participatory visual methods to engage communities in global health research. *Global BioEthics, 29*, 22–38. https://doi.org/10.1080/11287462.2017.1415722

Blagden, N. J. (2011). *Understanding denial in sexual offenders: The implications for policy and practice*. Nottingham Trent University.

Blagden, N., Winder, B., Gregson, M., & Thorne, K. (2012). The practical utility of using repertory grids with sexual offenders maintaining their innocence: A case study. *The British Journal of Forensic Practice, 14*, 269–81.

Blagden, N., Winder, B., Gregson, M., & Thorne, K. (2014). Making sense of denial in sexual offenders: A qualitative phenomenological and repertory grid analysis. *Journal of Interpersonal Violence, 29*(2), 1698–731.

Blank, T. O., Schmidt, S. D., Vangsness, S. A., Monteiro, A. K., & Santagata, P. V. (2010). Differences among breast and prostate cancer online support groups. *Computers in Human Behavior, 26*(6), 1400–404.

Blanke, O., Landis, T., Spinelli, L., & Seeck, M. (2004). Out-of-body experience and autoscopy of neurological origin. *Brain, 127*(2), 243–58. https://doi.org/10.1093/brain/awh040

Blumer, H. (1986). *Symbolic interactionism: Perspective and method*. University of California Press.

Boden, Z., & Eatough, V. (2014). Understanding more fully: A multimodal hermeneutic-phenomenological approach. *Qualitative Research in Psychology, 11*(2), 160–77. https://doi.org/10.1080/14780887.2013.853854

Borell, K., Espwall, M., Pryce, J., & Brenner, S. O. (2003). The repertory grid technique in social work research, practice, and education. *Qualitative Social Work, 2*(4), 477–91.

Bowen, G. A. (2009). Document analysis as a qualitative research method. *Qualitative Research Journal, 9*(2), 27–40. https://doi.org/10.3316/QRJ0902027

Bowlby, J. (1969). *Attachment and loss*. Volume *1*, Attachment (2nd ed., Vol. *1*). Basic Books.

Bramley, N., & Eatough, V. (2005). The experience of living with Parkinson's disease: An interpretative phenomenological analysis case study. *Psychology & Health, 20*(2), 223–35. https://doi.org/10.1080/08870440412331296053

Braun, V., & Clarke, V. (2006). Using thematic analysis in psychology. *Qualitative Research in Psychology, 3*(2), 77–101. https://doi.org/10.1191/1478088706qp063oa

Braun, V., & Clarke, V. (2019). To saturate or not to saturate? Questioning data saturation as a useful concept for thematic analysis and sample-size rationales. *Qualitative Research in Sport, Exercise and Health, 13*(2), 201–16.

Bravington, A., & King, N. (2019). Putting graphic elicitation into practice: Tools and typologies for the use of participant-led diagrams in qualitative research interviews. *Qualitative Research, 19*(5), 506–23. https://doi.org/10.1177/1468794118781718

Brislin, R. W. (1970). Back-translation for cross-cultural research. *Journal of Cross-Cultural Psychology, 1*(3), 185–16.

British Psychological Society (2014). *Code of human research ethics*. Available from: https://www.bps.org.uk/news-and-policy/bps-code-human-research-ethics-2nd-edition-2014

British Psychological Society (2017). *Ethics guidelines for internet-mediated research*. INF206/04.2017. British Psychological Society. Available from: https://www.bps.org.uk/sites/www.bps.org.uk/files/Policy/Policy%20-%20Files/Ethics%20Guidelines%20for%20Internet-mediated%20Research.pdf

British Psychological Society (2018). *BPS code of ethics and conduct*. Retrieved from www.bps.org.uk/news-and-policy/bps-code-ethics-and-conduct

British Psychological Society (2017). *Ethics guidelines for internet-mediated research*. British Psychological Society.

Brunsden, V., Goatcher, J., & Hill, R. (2009). Photographic methods: an under used approach. *Social Psychology Review, 11*(1), 45–50.

Bryman, A. (2008). *Social research methods*. Oxford University Press.

Buglass, S. L., Binder, J. F., Betts, L. R., & Underwood, J. D. (2017). Motivators of online vulnerability: The impact of social network site use and FOMO. *Computers in Human Behavior, 66*, 248–55.

Buhrmester, M., Kwang, T., & Gosling, S. D. (2011). Amazon's mechanical turk: A new source of inexpensive, yet high-quality, data? *Perspectives on Psychological Science, 6*, 3–5. https://doi.org/10.1177/1745691610393980

Bulk, L. Y., Kimel, G., King, N., & Nimmon, L. (2020). Understanding experiences in hospice: Exploring temporal, occupational, and relational dimensions using pictor technique. *Qualitative Health Research*. https://doi.org/1049732320926134

Bulman, G., & Fairlie, R. W. (2016). Technology and education: Computers, software, and the internet. In E. A. Hanushek, S. J. Machin, & L. Woessmann (Eds.), *Handbook of the economics of education* (vol. 5) (pp. 239–80). Science Direct.

Burgess, R. (1984). *In the field: An introduction to field research*. Allen & Unwin.

Burr, V. (2015). *Social constructionism*. Routledge.

Burr, V., King, N., & Heckmann, M. (2020). The qualitative analysis of repertory grid data: Interpretive Clustering. *Qualitative Research in Psychology*, 1–25.

Butler, R. J. (2006) Investigating the content of core constructs. *Personal Construct Theory and Practise, 3*, 27–33.

Butt, T. W., & Burr, V. (2004). *Invitation to personal construct psychology* (2nd ed.). Whurr.

Cabassa, L., Parcesepe, A., Nicasio, A., Baxter, E., Tsemberis, S., & Lewis-Fernandez, R. (2013). PMC3818106; health and wellness photovoice project: Engaging consumers with serious mental illness in health care interventions. *Qualitative Health Research, 23*(5), 618–30. https://doi.org/10.1177/1049732312470872

Canter, D., Sarangi, S., & Youngs, D. (2014). Terrorists' personal constructs and their roles: A comparison of the three Islamic terrorists. *Legal and Criminological Psychology, 19*(1), 160–78.

Capuit, P., Viney, L., Walker, B., & Crittenden, N. (2012). *Personal construct methodology*. Wiley-Blackwell.

Castles, A., Rastle, K., & Nation, K. (2018). Ending the reading wars: Reading acquisition from novice to expert. *Psychological Science in the Public Interest, 19*(1), 5–51. https://doi.org/10.1177/1529100618772271

Césaire, A. (1972). *Discourse on colonialism*. Monthly Review Press.

Charmaz, K. (2006). *Constructing grounded theory: A practical guide through qualitative analysis*. Sage.

Charmaz, K. (2008). Grounded theory as an emergent method. In S. Nagy & P. L. Hesse-Biber (Eds.), *Handbook of emergent methods* (pp. 155–72). Guilford Press.

Charmaz, K. (2014). *Constructing grounded theory*. Sage.

Collier, J. (1957). Photography in anthropology: A report on two experiments. *American Anthropologist*, *59*, 843–59.

Corbin, J., & Morse, J. M. (2003). The unstructured interactive interview: Issues of reciprocity and risks when dealing with sensitive topics. *Qualitative Inquiry*, *9*(3), 335–54. https://doi.org/10.1177/1077800403009003001

Corrigan, P. (1979). *Schooling the Smash Street Kids*. Macmillan.

Cox, S. R., Drew, S., Guillemin, M., Howell, C., Warr, D., & Waycot, J. (2014). Guidelines for ethical visual research methods. *Visual Research Collaboratory*, http://vrc.org.au

Cracco, E., Genschow, O., Radkova, I., & Brass, M. (2018). Automatic imitation of pro- and antisocial gestures: Is implicit social behaviour censored? *Cognition*, *170*, 179–89.

Creamer, E. G. (2017). *An introduction to fully integrated mixed methods research*. Sage.

Creighton, G., Oliffe, J., Ferlatte, O., Bottorff, J., Broom, A., & Emily, J. (2018). Photovoice ethics: Critical reflections from men's mental health research. *Qualitative Health Research*, *28*, 446–55. https://doi.org/10.1177/1049732317729137

Creswell, J. W. (2003). *Research design: Qualitative, quantitative, and mixed methods approaches*. Sage.

Creswell, J. W. (2015). *Research design: Qualitative, quantitative, and mixed methods approaches* (4th ed). Sage.

Crossley, M. (2000). *Introducing narrative psychology: Self, trauma and the construction of meaning*. Open University Press.

Crotty, M. (1998). *The foundations of social research: Meaning and perspective in the research process*. Sage.

Culley, L., Hudson, N., & Lohan, M. (2013). Where are all the men? The marginalization of men in social scientific research on infertility. *Reproductive Biomedicine Online*, *27*(3), 225–35.

Cumberbatch, G. (1991) 'Is television violence harmful?' in R. Cochrane and D. Carroll (Eds.), *Psychology and social issues* (pp. 171–81). Falmer Press.

Cunningham, M. R., Roberts, A. R., Barbee, A. P., Druen, P. B., & Wu, C. H. (1995). 'Their ideas of beauty are, on the whole, the same as ours': Consistency and variability in the cross-cultural perception of female physical attractiveness. *Journal of Personality and Social Psychology*, *68*(2), 261.

Cyr, J. (2019). *Focus groups for the social science researcher*. Cambridge University Press.

Daeg de Mott, D. K. (2001). *Ethics. Gale encyclopedia of psychology*. Retrieved February 2011 from www.findarticles.com/p/articles/mi_g2699/is_0004/ai_2699000957/

Dake, K. (1991). Orienting dispositions in the perception of risk an analysis of contemporary worldviews and cultural biases. *Journal of Cross-Cultural Psychology*, *22*(1), 61–82.

Davies, C. (1999). *Interviewing*. In C. Davies, *Reflexive ethnography: A guide to researching selves and others* (pp. 94–116). Routledge.

Day, C. W., Pope, M., & Denicolo, P. (1990). *Insight into teachers' thinking and practice*. Falmer Press.

De Vaus, D. (2002). *Surveys in social research*. Routledge.

DeCuir-Gunby, J. T., & Schutz, P. A. (2017). Mixed methods designs: Frameworks for organizing your research methods. In J. T. DeCuir-Gunby, & P. A. Schutz, (Eds.), *Developing a mixed methods proposal: A practical guide for beginning researchers* (pp. 83–106). Sage.

Demetriou, C., Ozer, B. U., & Eassu, C. A. (2014). Self-report questionnaires. In R. L. Cautin & S. O. Lilienfeld (Eds.), *The encyclopaedia of clinical psychology*, 1–6. https://doi.org/10.1002/9781118625392.wbecp507

Denicolo, P., & Pope, M. (1990). Adults learning – Teachers thinking. In C. Day, M. Pope and P. Denicolo (Eds.), *Insights into teachers' thinking and practice* (pp. 155–69). The Falmer Press.

Denscombe, M. (2008). Communities of practice: A research paradigm for the mixed methods approach. *Journal of Mixed Methods Research, 2*(3), 270–83.

Department for Education. (2018). National curriculum assessments Key stage 1 Teacher assessment frameworks at the end of key stage 1. 14. https://assets.publishing.service.gov.uk/government/uploads/system/uploads/attachment_data/file/740343/201819_teacher_assessment_frameworks_at_the_end_of_key_stage_1_WEBHO.pdf

Department for Education. (2019). Phonics screening check and key stage 1 assessments in England, 2019. September, 1–18. https://assets.publishing.service.gov.uk/government/uploads/system/uploads/attachment_data/file/851296/Phonics_screening_check_and_key_stage_1_assessments_in_England_2019.pdf

DeVellis, R. F. (2017). *Scale development: Theory and applications* (4th ed). Sage.

DiAngelo, R. J. (2018). *White fragility: Why it's so hard for white people to talk about racism*. Penguin.

Dodd, B., Crosbie, S., McIntosh, B., Teizel, T., & Ozanne, A. (2000). *Preschool and primary inventory of phonological awareness*. The Psychological Corporation.

Dorough, S., Grice, J., & Parker, J. (2007). Implicative dilemmas and general psychological well-being. *Personal Construct Theory & Practice*, *4*, 83–101.

Drew, S., & Guillemin, M. (2014). From photographs to findings: Visual meaning-making and interpretive engagement in the analysis of participant-generated images. *Visual Studies*, *29*, 54–67. https://doi.org/10.1080/1472586X.2014.862994

Drew, S., Duncan, R., & Sawyer, S. (2010). Visual storytelling: A beneficial but challenging method for health research with young people. *Qualitative Health Research*, *21*(12), 1677–88. https://doi.org/10.1177/1049732310377455. Retrieved from Visual Storytelling: A beneficial but challenging method for health research with young people. Database.

Duncan, C. J., & Scott, S. (2005). What caused the Black Death? *Postgraduate Medical Journal*, *81*: 315–20.

Dunn, D. M., & Dunn, L. M. (2009). *The British picture vocabulary scale* (3rd ed.). GL Assessment.

Easterby-Smith, M. (1980). The design, analysis and interpretation of repertory grids. *International Journal of Man-Machine Studies*, *13*(1), 3–24.

Eatough, V., & Smith, J. A. (2006). I feel like a scrambled egg in my head: An idiographic case study of meaning making and anger using interpretative phenomenological analysis. *Psychology and psychotherapy*, *79*(Pt 1), 115–35. https://doi.org/10.1348/147608305X41100

Edmondson, A. J. (2013). Listening with your eyes: Using pictures and words to explore self-harm. (University of Leeds). *Psychiatry and Behavioural Sciences*, PhD Retrieved from Listening with your eyes: Using pictures and words to explore self-harm database.

Edmondson, A. J., & Pini, S. (2019). Visual methods in health research: A literature review of the pros and cons of using photographs. *Nurse Researcher*, *27*(2), 8–13. https://doi.org/10.7748/nr.2019.e1620

Edmondson, A. J., Brennan, C., & House, A. O. (2018). Using photo-elicitation to understand reasons for repeated self-harm: A qualitative study. *BMC Psychiatry*, *18*(98). https://doi.org/10.1186/s12888-018-1681-3

Edwards, P., Arango, M., Balica, L., Cottingham, R., El-Sayed, H., Farrell, B., Fernandes, J., Gogichaisvili, T., Golden, N., Hartzenberg, H., Husain, M., Izurieta, M., Jerbi, Z., Khamis, H., Komolafe, E., Laloë, V., Lomas, G., Ludwig, S., Mazairac, G., & Yadav, Y. R. (2005). Final results of MRC CRASH, a randomised placebo-controlled trial of intravenous corticosteroid in adults with head injury-outcomes at 6 months CRASH Trial Collaborators, *Lancet*, *365*, 1957–59. https://doi.org/10.1016/S0140-6736(05)66552-X

Ehri, L. C., Nunes, S. R., Stahl, S. A., & Willows, D. M. (2001). Systematic phonics instruction helps students learn to read: Evidence from the national reading panel's meta-analysis. *Review of Educational Research*, *71*(3), 393–447. https://doi.org/10.3102/00346543071003393

Fancher, R. E. (1996). *Pioneers of psychology* (3rd ed.). W.W. Norton.

Fauls, L. B., & Smith, W. D. (1956). Sex-role learning of five-year-olds. *The Journal of Genetic Psychology*, *89*(1), 105–17.

Feixas, G., & Saúl, L. Á. (2004). The multi-center dilemma project: An investigation on the role of cognitive conflicts in health. *The Spanish Journal of Psychology*, *7*(01), 69–78. http://dx.doi.org/10.1017/S1138741600004765

Ferguson, C. J. (2007). Evidence for publication bias in video game violence effects literature: A meta-analytic review. *Aggression and Violent Behavior*, *12*(4), 470–82.

Ferguson, C. J. (2010). Blazing angels or resident evil? Can violent video games be a force for good? *Review of General Psychology*, *14*(2), 68–81.

Fetters, M. D. (2019). *The mixed methods research workbook: Activities for designing, implementing, and publishing projects*. Sage.

Forum for Research in Literacy and Language. (2012). *Diagnostic test of word reading processes*. GL Assessment.

Fournier, A. K., Berry, T. D., Letson, E., & Chanen, R. (2016). The human–animal interaction scale: Development and evaluation. *Anthrozoös*, *29*(3), 455–67.

Frankowski, S., Lupo, A. K., Smith, B. A., Dane'El, M., Ramos, C., & Morera, O. F. (2016). Developing and testing a scale to measure need for drama. *Personality and Individual Differences*, *89*, 192–201.

Fransella, F., Bell, R., & Bannister, D. (2004). *A manual for repertory grid technique* (2nd ed.). John Wiley and Sons, Ltd.

Freud, S. (1909a). *Analysis of a phobia of a five-year-old boy. In The Pelican Freud Library* (1977), Vol *8*, Case Histories 1, pages 169–306.

Freud, S. (1909b). Bemerkungen über einen Fall von Zwangsneurose (Der 'Rattenmann'). *Jb. psychoanal. psychopathol. Forsch., I*, pp. 357–421; GW, VII, pp. 379–463; Notes upon a case of obsessional neurosis, SE, *10*: 151–318.

Frith, H., & Harcourt, D. (2007). Using photographs to capture women's experiences of chemotherapy: Reflecting on the method. *Qualitative Health Research, 17*(10), 1340–50. https://doi.org/10.1177/1049732307308949. Retrieved from Using Photographs to Capture Women's Experiences of Chemotherapy: Reflecting on the Method database.

Frith, H., Riley, S., Archer, L., & Gleeson, K. (2005). Editorial. *Qualitative Research in Psychology, 2*(3), 187–98. https://doi.org/10.1191/1478088705qp037ed

Fromm, M. (2004). *Introduction to the repertory grid interview*. Waxmann Verlag.

Furr, M. (2011). *Scale construction and psychometrics for social and personality psychology*. Sage.

Fukuyama, F. (2001) Natural rights and human history. *The National Interest, 64*, 19–30.

Ganzel, B. (2007). *Television*. Retrieved from https://livinghistoryfarm.org/farminginthe50s/life_17.html

García-Mieres, H., Ochoa, S., Salla, M., López-Carrilero, R., & Feixas, G. (2016). Understanding the paranoid psychosis of James: Use of the repertory grid technique for case conceptualization. *World Journal of Psychiatry, 6*(3), 381.

Gardner, F. (2000). Methodological issues in the direct observation of parent–child interaction: Do observational findings reflect the natural behavior of participants? *Clinical Child and Family Psychology Review, 3*(3), 185–98.

Gault, R. H. (1907). A history of the questionnaire method of research in psychology. *The Pedagogical Seminary, 14*(3), 366–83. https://doi.org/10.1080/08919402.1907.10532551

Gehlbach, H. (2015). Seven survey sins. *Journal of Early Adolescence, 35*, 883–97.

Gerber, A. S., & Green, D. P. (2012). *Field experiments: Design, analysis and interpretation*. WW Norton and Company.

Gibbs, A. (1997). Focus groups. *Social Research Update, 19*(8), 1–8.

Gibbs, M., Meese, J., Arnold, M., Nansen, B., & Carter, M. (2015). #Funeral and instagram: Death, social media, and platform vernacular. *Information, Communication & Society, 18*(3), 255–68. https://doi.org/10.1080/1369118X.2014.987152

Gijsbers, K., & Nicholson, K. F. (2005). Experimental pain thresholds influenced by sex of experimenter. *Perceptual and Motor Skills, 101*, 803–807.

Gilbert, P., McEwan, K., Bellew, R., Mills, A., & Gale, C. (2009). The dark side of competition: How competitive behaviour and striving to avoid inferiority are linked to depression, anxiety, stress and selfharm. *Psychology and Psychotherapy: Theory, Research and Practice, 82*(2), 123–36.

Gillespie, H., Kelly, M., Gormley, G., King, N., Gilliland, D., & Dornan, T. (2018). How can tomorrow's doctors be more caring? A phenomenological investigation. *Medical Education, 52*(10), 1052–63. https://doi.org/10.1111/medu.13684

Given, L. M. (2008). *The SAGE encyclopedia of qualitative research methods* (Vols. *1–0*). Sage. https://doi.org/10.4135/9781412963909

Gleeson, K. (2011). Polytextual thematic analysis for visual data. In P. Reavey (Ed.), *Visual methods in psychology: Using and interpreting images in qualitative research* (pp. 314–29). Taylor and Francis.

Glegg, S. M. N. (2019). Facilitating interviews in qualitative research with visual tools: A typology. *Qualitative Health Research, 29*(2), 301–10. DOI: 10.1177/1049732318786485

Gómez-Ordóñez, L., Adams, G., Ratele, K., Suffla, S., Stevens, G., & Reddy, G. (2021). Decolonising psychological science: Encounters and cartographies of resistance. *The Psychologist, 34*, 54–7.

Gould, S. J. (1997). *The mismeasure of man*, Revised and Expanded Edition. Penguin.

Gow, K., Lane, A., & Chant, D. (2003). Personality characteristics, beliefs, and the near-death experience. *Australian Journal of Clinical and Experimental Hypnosis, 31*(2), 128–52.

Greyson, B. (1994). Near-death experiences. In R. Corsini (Ed.), *The encyclopedia of psychology* (pp. 460–62). Wiley.

Greyson, B. (2000). Near-death experiences. In E. Cardeña, S. J. Lynn, & S. C. Krippner (Eds.), *Varieties of anomalous experience: Examining the scientific evidence* (pp. 315–52). American Psychological Association. https://doi.org/10.1037/10371-000

Grice, J. W. (2002). Idiogrid: Software for the management and analysis of repertory grids. *Behavior Research Methods, Instruments, & Computers, 34*, 338–41.

Gridley, N., Bywater, T. J., & Hutchings, J. M. (2018). Comparing live and video observation to assess early parent–child interactions in the home. *Journal of Child and Family Studies, 27*(6), 1818–29. https://doi.org/10.1007/s10826-018-1039-y

Griffin, C. (2007). Being dead and being there: Research interviews, sharing hand cream and the preference for analysing 'naturally occurring data'. *Discourse Studies, 9*(2), 246–69.

Griffiths, M. A. (2010). The role of context in online gaming excess and addiction: Some case study evidence. *International Journal of Mental Health and Addiction, 8*, 119–25.

Grysman, A., & Denney, A. (2017). Gender, experimenter gender and medium of report influence the content of autobiographical memory report. *Memory, 25*, 132–45.

Guba, E. G., & Lincoln, Y. S. (1994). Competing paradigms in qualitative research. In N. K. Denzin & Y. S. Lincoln (Eds.), *Handbook of qualitative research* (pp. 105–17). Sage.

Guenther, K. (2017). Monkeys, mirrors and me: Gordon Gallup and the study of self-recognition. *Journal of the History of the Behavioral Sciences, 53*, 1. https://doi.org/10.1002/jhbs.21832.

Guillemin, M., & Drew, S. (2010). Questions of process in participant-generated visual methodologies. *Visual Studies, 25*(2), 175–88. https://doi.org/10.1080/1472586X.2010.502676

Haggbloom, S. J., Warnick, R., Warnick, J. E., Jones, V. K., Yarbrough, G. L., Russell, T. M., … & Monte, E. (2002). The 100 most eminent psychologists of the 20th century. *Review of General Psychology, 6*(2), 139–52.

Halcomb, E. J. (2019). Mixed methods research: The issues beyond combining methods. *Journal of Advanced Nursing, 75*, 499–501.

Halcomb, E. J., Gholizadeh, L., DiGiacomo, M., Phillips, J., & Davidson, P. M. (2007). Literature review: Considerations in undertaking focus group research with culturally and linguistically diverse groups. *Journal of Clinical Nursing, 16*(6), 1000–11.

Halder, M., Binder, J., Stiller, J., & Gregson, M. (2016). An overview of the challenges faced during Cross-Cultural Research. *Enquire, 8*, 1–18.

Hanauer, D. A., Ramakrishnan, N., & Seyfried, L. S. (2013). Describing the relationship between cat bites and human depression using data from an electronic health record. *PLoS One, 8*(8), e70585.

Harder, B. M., & Adams, C. (2020). *Conducting race-based focus groups on health issues: Confronting challenges in design, implementation, and analysis.* Sage Research Methods Cases. https://doi.org/10.4135/9781529743630

Hardison, H. G., & Neimeyer, R. A. (2012). Assessment of personal constructs: Features and functions of constructivist techniques. https://doi.org/10.1002/9781119953616.ch1

Hardy, B., King, N., & Firth, J. (2012). Applying the Pictor technique to research interviews with people affected by advanced disease. *Nurse Researcher, 20*(1), 6–10. https://doi.org/10.7748/nr2012.09.20.1.6.c9302

Hargreaves, C. P. (1979). Social networks and interpersonal constructs. In P. Stringer & D. Bannister (Eds.), *Constructs of sociality and individuality* (pp. 153–75). Academic Press.

Harkin, L. J., & Kuss, D. (2020). 'My smartphone is an extension of myself': A holistic qualitative exploration of the impact of using a smartphone. *Psychology of Popular Media*. Advance online publication. https://doi.org/10.1037/ppm0000278

Harlow, H. F. (1959). Love in infant monkeys. *Scientific American, 200*, 68–74.

Harper, D. (2002). Talking about pictures: A case for photo elicitation. *Visual Studies, 17*(1), 13–26. https://doi.org/10.1080/14725860220137345. Retrieved from Talking about Pictures: a case for photo elicitation database.

Harrison, B. (2002). Seeing health and illness worlds – using visual methodologies in a sociology of health and illness: A methodological review. *Sociology of Health & Illness, 24*(6), 856–72. https://doi.org/10.1111/1467-9566.00322

Hart, K. E., & Kritsonis, W. A. (2006). Critical analysis of an original writing on social learning theory: Limitation of film-mediated aggressive models by: Albert Bandura, Dorothea Ross and Sheila A. Ross. *National Forum of Applied Educational Research Journal, 19*(3), 1–7.

Hartley, J., & Betts, L. R. (2013). Let's be positive: The effects of the position of positive and negative values and labels on Likert-type scale scores. *Chinese Journal of Psychology, 55*, 291–99.

Hawker, D. M., Durkin, J., & Hawker, D. S. (2011). To debrief or not to debrief our heroes: That is the question. *Clinical Psychology & Psychotherapy, 18*(6), 453–63.

Hawton, K., & Harriss, L. (2008). Deliberate self-harm by under-15-year-olds: Characteristics, trends and outcome. *Journal of Child Psychology and Psychiatry, 49*(4), 441–8. https://doi.org/10.1111/j.1469-7610.2007.01852.x

Hawton, K., Bergen, H., Kapur, N., Cooper, J., Steeg, S., Ness, J., et al. (2012). Repetition of self-harm and suicide following self-harm in children and adolescents: Findings from the multicentre study of self-harm in England. *Journal of Child Psychology and Psychiatry, 53*(12), 1212–19. https://doi.org/10.1111/j.1469-7610.2012.02559.x

Hayes, A. F. (2015). The Process Macros for SPSS and SAS. www.processmacro.org/index.html

Haynes, L., Service, O., Goldacre, B., & Torgerson, D. (2013). Test, Learn, Adapt: Randomised Controlled Trials. www.bi.team/publications/test-learn-adapt-developing-public-policy-with-randomised-controlled-trials/

Health & Care Professions Council (2012). Standard of conduct, performance and ethics. Available at https://www.hcpc-uk.org/standards/standards-of-conduct-performance-and-ethics/

Hedden, T., Ketay, S., Aron, A., Markus, H. R., & Gabrieli, J. D. E. (2008) Cultural Influences on Neural Substrates of Attentional Control. *Psychological Science, 19*, 12–17. https://doi.org/10.1111/j.1467-9280.2008.02038.x

Heisley, D. D., & Levy, S. J. (1991). Autodriving: A photoelicitation technique. *Journal of Consumer Research, 18*(3), 257–72. https://doi.org/10.1086/209258. Retrieved from JSTOR database. Retrieved from www.jstor.org/stable/2489338

Heitmann, J., Jonker, N. C., Ostafin, B. D., & de Jong, P. J. (2020). Attentional bias for alcohol cues in visual search – Increased engagement, difficulty to disengage or both? *PLoS one, 15*, e0228272.

Henderson, H. (2017). Difficult questions of difficult questions: The role of the researcher and transcription styles. *International Journal of Qualitative Studies in Education, 31*(2), 143–57.

Henrich, J., Heine, S. J., & Norenzayan, A. (2010). Most people are not WEIRD. *Nature, 466*(7302), 29.

Hepburn, A., & Bolden, G. B. (2013). The conversation analytic approach to transcription. In J. Sidnell & T. Stivers (Eds.), *The handbook of conversation analysis* (pp. 57–76). John Wiley & Sons.

Hill, R. (2015). *Occupational related consequences for relatives of firefighters*. Nottingham Trent University.

Hill, R., & Brunsden, V. (2003). Surviving disaster: Firefighters as victims – preliminary findings. *Fire Safety, Technology and Management, 8*(3), 21–4.

Hill, R., & Brunsden, V. (2009). 'Heroes' as victims: Role reversal in the fire and rescue service. *Irish Journal of Psychology, 30*(1), 73–84.

Hodges, G. C. (2010). Rivers of reading: Using critical incident collages to learn about adolescent readers and their readership. *English in Education, 44*(3), 181–200. https://doi.org/10.1111/17548845.2010.11912414

Hofstede, G. (1980). *Culture's consequences: International differences in work-relate values*. Sage.

Holden, J. M., Long, J., & MacLurg, J. B. (2009). Characteristics of Western near-death experiencers. In J. M. Holden, B. Greyson, & D. James (Eds.), *The handbook of near-death experiences: Thirty years of investigation* (pp. 109–33). Praeger/ABC-CLIO.

Holtby, A., Klein, K., Cook, K., & Travers, R. (2015). To be seen or not to be seen: Photovoice, queer and trans youth, and the dilemma of representation. *Action Research, 13*, 317–35. https://doi.org/10.1177/1476750314566414

Hookway, N. (2008). 'Entering the blogosphere': Some strategies for using blogs in social research. *Qualitative Research, 8*(1), 91–113.

Hopkins, C. (2002). 'But what about the really ill, poorly people?' An ethnographic study into what it means to nurses on medical admissions units to have people who have harmed themselves as their patients. *Journal of Psychiatric and Mental Health Nursing, 9*(2), 147–54.

Horley, J. (2008). *Sexual offenders: Personal construct theory and deviant sexual behaviour.* Routledge.

Horner, A. J., & Burgess, N. (2014). Pattern completion in multielement event engrams. *Current Biology, 24*(9), 988–92.

Horner, A. J., Bisby, J. A., Bush, D., Lin, W. J., & Burgess, N. (2015). Evidence for holistic episodic recollection via hippocampal pattern completion. *Nature Communications, 6*(1), 1–11.

Hosey, G. (2008). A preliminary model of human–animal relationships in the zoo. *Applied Animal Behavioural Science, 109*, 105–27.

Houston, J. (1998). *Making sense with offenders.* John Wiley.

Howe, K. R. (1992). Getting over the quantitative-qualitative debate. *American Journal of Education, 100*(2), 236–56. https://doi.org/10.1086/444015

Hulland, J., Baumgartner, H., & Smith, K. M. (2018). Marketing survey research best practices: Evidence and recommendations from a review of JAMS articles. *Journal of the Academy of Market Science, 46*, 92–108. https://doi.org/10.1007/s11747-017-0532-y

Hulme, C., Bowyer-Crane, C., Carroll, J. M., Duff, F. J., & Snowling, M. J. (2012). The causal role of phoneme awareness and letter-sound knowledge in learning to read: Combining intervention studies with mediation analyses. https://doi.org/10.1177/0956797611435921

Hunter, C., Chantler, K., Kapur, N., & Cooper, J. (2012). Service user perspectives on psychosocial assessment following self-harm and its impact on further help-seeking: A qualitative study. *Journal of Affective Disorders, 145*(3), 315–23. https://doi.org/10.1016/j.jad.2012.08.009

Hustvedt, S. (2005). *Mysteries of the rectangle: Essays on painting.* Princeton Architectural Press.

Iantaffi, A. (2011). Travelling along 'rivers of experience': Personal construct psychology and visual metaphors in research. In P. Reavey (Ed.), *Visual methods in psychology: Using and interpreting images in qualitative research* (pp. 271–83). Taylor and Francis.

Im, E. O., Chee, W., Lim, H. J., Liu, Y., Guevara, E., & Kim, K. S. (2007, May). Patients' attitudes toward Internet cancer support groups. *Oncology Nursing Forum, 34*(3), 705–12.

Jankowicz, D. (2004). *The easy guide to repertory grids*. John Wiley & Sons Ltd.

Jaspal, R. (2018). *Enhancing sexual health, self-identity and wellbeing among men who have sex with men: A guide for practitioners*. Jessica Kingsley Publishers.

Jaspal, R. (2020a). Content analysis, thematic analysis and discourse analysis. In G.M. Breakwell, D.B. Wright & J. Barnett (Eds.), *Research methods in psychology* (5th ed.) (pp. 285–312). Sage.

Jaspal, R. (2020b). *Trans women and HIV: Social psychological perspectives*. Palgrave. https://doi.org/10.1007/978-3-030-57545-8

Jaspal, R., & Bayley, J. (2020). *HIV and gay men: Clinical, social and psychological aspects*. Palgrave. https://doi.org/10.1007/978-981-15-7226-5

Jaspal, R., & Bayley, J. (2019). A minority within a minority? Identity and sexual health among Black & Minority Ethnic men who have sex with men. *Journal of the Association of Nurses in AIDS Care, 30*(6), 607–9. https://doi.org/10.1097/JNC.0000000000000101

Jaspal, R., Lopes, B., Wignall, L., & Bloxsom, C. (2021). Predicting sexual risk behaviour in British and European Union university students in the United Kingdom. *American Journal of Sexuality Education, 16*(1), 140–59. https://doi.org/10.1080/15546128.2020.1869129

Jefferson, G. (2004). Glossary of transcript symbols with an introduction. In G. H. Lerner (Ed.), *Conversation analysis: Studies from the first generation* (pp. 13–31). John Benjamins Publishing Company.

Jefferson, G. (1985). An exercise in the transcription and analysis of laughter. In T. Van Dijk (Ed.), *Handbook of discourse analysis: Discourse and dialogue*, vol. *3*: (pp. 25–34). Academic Press.

Johnson, H., McNally, S., Rolfe, H., Ruiz-Valenzuela, J., Savage, R., Vousden, J., & Wood, C. (2019). Teaching assistants, computers and classroom management. *Labour Economics, 58*(February), 21–36. https://doi.org/10.1016/j.labeco.2019.02.006

Johnson, L. (2015). *A straight talking introduction to psychiatric diagnosis*. PCCS Books.

Johnson, R. B., & Onwuegbuzie, A. J. (2004). Mixed methods research: A research paradigm whose time has come. *Educational Researcher, 33*(7), 14–26.

Kalekin-Fishman, D. (2009). Blood–territory–rights–duties: Constructing and construing citizenship as a form of life. In J. C. Thomas & L. M. Leitner (Eds.), *Personal constructivism: Theory and applications* (pp. 89–113). Pace University Press.

Kamberelis, G., & Dimitriadis, G. (2011). Focus groups: Contingent articulations of pedagogy, politics, and inquiry. In N. K. Denzin & Y. S. Lincoln (Eds.), *The SAGE handbook of qualitative research* (pp. 545–61). Sage.

Kamin, L. (1977). *The science and politics of IQ*. Penguin.

Katz, J. (1972). *Experimentation with human beings*. Russell Sage Foundation.

Kean, S. (2014). Phineas Gage, neuroscience's most famous patient. Retrieved from www.slate.com/articles/health_and_science/science/2014/05/phineas_gage_neuroscience_case_true_story_of_famous_frontal_lobe_patient.html (accessed July 21, 2015).

Keeves, J. P. (1997). *Educational research methodology and measurement.* Cambridge University Press.

Kelly, G. (1991). *The psychology of personal constructs.* Norton.

Kelly, G. A. (1955a/1991). *The psychology of personal constructs.* W.W. Norton.

Kelly, G. A. (1955b). *The psychology of personal constructs.* Norton.

Kelly, G. A. (1964). The language of hypothesis: Man's psychological instrument. *Journal of Individual Psychology, 20*(2), 137–52.

King, N., & Horrocks, C. (2010). *Interviews in qualitative research.* Sage.

King, N., Bravington, A., Brooks, J., Hardy, B., Melvin, J., & Wilde, D. (2013). The Pictor Technique: A method for exploring the experience of collaborative working. *Qualitative Health Research, 23*(8), 1138–52. https://doi.org/10.1177/1049732313495326

King, N., Bravington, A., Brooks, J., Hardy, B., Melvin, J., & Wilde, D. (2017a). The Pictor technique: Exploring experiences of collaborative working from the perspectives of generalist and specialist nurses. In J. Brooks & N. King (Eds.), *Applied qualitative research in psychology* (pp. 221–34). Macmillan Education/Palgrave.

King, N., Bravington, A., Brooks, J., Melvin, J., & Wilde, D. (2017b). 'Go make your face known': Collaborative working through the lens of personal relationships. *International Journal of Integrated Care, 17*(4), *3*, 1–11. https://doi.org/10.5334/ijic.2574

King, N., Horrocks, C., & Brooks, J. (2018). *Interviews in qualitative research* (2nd ed.). Sage.

Kitson-Boyce, R., Blagden, N., Winder, B., & Dillon, G. (2018). 'This time it's different' preparing for release through CoSA (The prison model): A phenomenological and repertory grid analysis. *Sexual Abuse: A Journal of Research and Treatment, 31*(2).

Kitson-Boyce, R., Wheatley, R., & Blagden, N. (2020). The application of the repertory grid in forensic practice. *Journal of Constructivist Psychology*, 1–22.

Kitzinger, J. (1994). The methodology of focus groups: The importance of interaction between research participants. *Sociology of Health & Illness, 16*(1), 103–21.

Kitzinger, J. (1995). Qualitative research: Introducing focus groups. *BMJ, 311*, 299–302.

Kiyimba, N., Lester, J. N., & O'Reilly, M. (2018). *Using naturally occurring data in qualitative health research: A practical guide.* Springer.

Kline, P. (2000). *The handbook of psychological testing* (2nd ed.). Routledge.

Kühnen, U., & Oyserman, D. (2002). Thinking about the self-influences thinking in general: Cognitive consequences of salient self-concept. *Journal of Experimental Social Psychology, 38*(5), 492–99.

Kutchins, H., & Kirk, S. (2001). *Making us crazy: DSM- the psychiatric bible and the creation of mental disorders.* Constable.

Kvale, S., & Brinkmann, S. (2009). *Interviews: Learning the craft of qualitative research interviewing* (2nd ed.). Sage.

Kvale, S. (1996). *Interviews: An introduction to qualitative research interviewing.* Sage.

Lachal, J., Speranza, M., Taïeb, O., Falissard, B., Moro, M., & Revah-Levy, A. (2012). Qualitative research using photo-elicitation to explore the role of food in family relationships among obese adolescents. *Appetite, 58*(3), 1099–105. https://doi.org/10.1016/j.appet.2012.02.045

Retrieved from Qualitative research using photo-elicitation to explore the role of food in family relationships among obese adolescents database.

Laconi, S., Kaliszewska-Czeremska, K., Gnisci, A., Sergi, I., Barke, A., Jeromin, F., … & Király, O. (2018). Cross-cultural study of problematic internet use in nine European countries. *Computers in Human Behavior, 84*, 430–40.

Laestadius, L. (2017). Instagram. In L. Sloan, & A. Quan-Haase (Eds.), *The SAGE handbook of social media research methods* (pp. 573–92). Sage.

Laestadius, L. I., Wahl, M. M., & Cho, Y. I. (2016). #Vapelife: An exploratory study of electronic cigarette use and promotion on instagram. *Substance Use & Misuse, 51*(12), 1669–73. https://doi.org/10.1080/10826084.2016.1188958

Langmann, S., & David, P. (2014). Dignity and ethics in research photography. *International Journal of Social Research Methodology, 17*, 709–21. https://doi.org/10.1080/13645579.2013.825473

Larsen, L., Kohnen, S., Nickels, L., & McArthur, G. (2015). The Letter-Sound Test (LeST): A reliable and valid comprehensive measure of grapheme–phoneme knowledge. *Australian Journal of Learning Difficulties, 20*(2), 1–14. https://doi.org/10.1080/19404158.2015.1037323

Latané, B., & Darley, J. M. (1970). *The unresponsive bystander: Why doesn't he help?* Prentice Hall.

Leach, C., Freshwater, K., Aldridge, J., & Sunderland, J. (2001). Analysis of repertory grids in clinical practice. *British Journal of Clinical Psychology, 40*, 225–48.

Leedy, P. D., & Ormrod, J. E. (2001). *Practical research: Planning and design* (7th ed.). Merrill Prentice Hall.

Levenson, J. S., Willis, G. M., & Prescott, D. S. (2016). Adverse childhood experiences in the lives of male sex offenders: Implications for trauma-informed care. *Sexual Abuse, 28*(4), 340–59.

Lewis, D. J., & Duncan, C. P. (1958). Vicarious experience and partial reinforcement. *Journal of Abnormal Psychology, 57*(3), 321–26.

Lieberman, M. A. (2008). Gender and online cancer support groups: Issues facing male cancer patients. *Journal of Cancer Education, 23*(3), 167–71.

Lievesley, R., Winder, B., Norman, C., & Banyard, P. (2018). A life sentence in instalments: A qualitative analysis of repeat offending among short-sentenced offenders. *Victims & Offenders, 13*(3), 409–26. https://doi.org/10.1080/15564886.2017.1354112

Likert, R. (1932). A technique for the measurement of attitudes. *Archives of Psychology, 22*(140), 55.

Lincoln, Y. S., & Guba, E. G. (1985). *Naturalistic inquiry*. Sage.

Littlewood, R., & Lipsedge, M. (1998). *Aliens and alienists* (2nd ed.). Unwin Hyman.

Lukes, S. (2005). *Power: A radical view* (2nd ed.). Macmillan.

Lytton, H. (1971). Observation studies of parent – child interaction: A methodological review. *Child Development, 42*(3), 651–84. https://doi.org/10.1017/CBO9781107415324.004

Magnusson, E., & Marecek, J. (2015). *Doing interview-based qualitative research: A learner's guide*. Cambridge University Press.

Malik, S. H., & Coulson, N., (2008). The male experience of infertility: A thematic analysis of an online infertility support group bulletin board. *Journal of Reproductive and Infant Psychology, 26*(1), 132–48.

Mancuso, J. C. (2003). Children's development of personal constructs. In F. Fransella (ed.), *International handbook of personal construct psychology* (pp. 275–82). Wiley.

Marin, G., & Marin, B. V. (1991). *Research with hispanic populations*. Sage.

Martin, P., Bateson, P. P. G., & Bateson, P. (2007). *Measuring behaviour: an introductory guide* (3rd ed.). Cambridge University Press.

Mason, J. (2003). The use of the repertory grid as an aid to assessment and formulation in a sex offender with a learning disability. *The British Journal of Forensic Practice, 5*(3), 37–44.

Mason, J. (2008). Measuring psychological change in offenders with intellectual disabilities and alcohol misuse using repertory grids: Two case examples. *British Journal of Forensic Practice, 10*, 37–44.

Maxwell, J. A. (2012). *A realist approach for qualitative research*. Sage.

Mays, N., & Pope, C. (2000). Assessing quality in qualitative research. *British Medical Journal, 320*(7226), 50–52.

McCarty, C., & Ruttle, K. (2010). *Progress in reading assessment*. Hodder Education.

McCrudden, M. T., Marchand, G., & Schutz, P. A. (2021). Joint displays for mixed methods research in psychology. *Methods in Psychology*, 100067.

McGorry, S. Y. (2000). Measurement in cross-cultural environment: Survey translation issues. *Qualitative Market Research: An International Journal, 3*(2), 74–81.

McNally, S. (2014). *Online reading support*. London School of Economics. https://educationendowmentfoundation.org.uk/public/files/Projects/Evaluation_Protocols/EEF_Project_Protocol_OnlineReadingSupport.pdf

McNally, S., Ruiz-valenzuela, J., & Rolfe, H. (2016). *ABRA: Online reading support*. Addendum added March 2018 Independent evaluators: October 2016.

McNeill, F. (2006). A desistance paradigm for offender management. *Criminology & Criminal Justice, 6*(1), 39–62.

Mendes, K.; Ringrose, J., & Keller, J. (2019). *Digital feminist activism: Girls and women fight back against rape culture*. Oxford University Press.

Merriam, S. B., & Tisdell, E. J. (2015). *Qualitative research: A guide to design and implementation* (4th ed.). Josey Bass: Wiley.

Merton, R. K., & Kendall, P. L. (1946). The focused interview. *American Journal of Sociology, 51*(6), 541–57.

Miles, M. B., Huberman, A. M., & Saldana, J. (2014). *Qualitative data analysis: A methods sourcebook*. Sage.

Miller A. H., Jones J. F., Drake D. F., Tian H., Unger E. R., & Pagnoni G. (2014). Decreased basal ganglia activation in subjects with chronic fatigue syndrome: Association with symptoms of fatigue. *PLoS ONE, 9*(5): e98156. https://doi.org/10.1371/journal.pone.0098156

Miller, G. (1969) Psychology as a means of promoting human welfare. *American Psychologist, 24*, 1063–75.

Mo, P. K., Malik, S. H., & Coulson, N. S. (2009). Gender differences in computer-mediated communication: a systematic literature review of online health-related support groups. *Patient Education and Counseling*, *75*(1), 16–24.

Moors, A. C. (2020). Research methods in psychology: A feminist exercise to facilitate students' understanding of operational definitions, observation, and inter-rater reliability. *Psychology of Women Quarterly*, *44*(2), 266–70. https://doi.org/10.1177/0361684319900349

Morgan, D. L. (1996). Focus groups. *Annual Review of Sociology*, *22*(1), 129–52.

Morse, J. M., Barrett, M., Mayan, M., Olson, K., & Spiers, J. (2002). Verification strategies for establishing reliability and validity in qualitative research. *International Journal of Qualitative Methods*, *1*(2), 13–22.

Moseholm, E., & Fetters, M. D. (2017). Conceptual models to guide integration during analysis in convergent mixed methods studies. *Methodological Innovations*, *10*(2). https://doi.org/10.1177%2F2059799117703118.

Murphy, K. R., & Davidshofer, C. O. (2005). *Psychology testing: Principles and applications* (6th ed.). Pearson.

Naffi, N., & Davidson, A. L. (2017). Engaging host society youth in exploring how they construe the influence of social media on the resettlement of Syrian refugees. *Personal Construct Theory and Practice*, *14*, 116–28.

Nagel, T. (1974). What is it like to be a bat? *The Philosophical Review*, *83*(4): 435–50.

National Institute of Child Health and Human Development. (2000). Report of the National Reading Panel. Teaching children to read: an evidence-based assessment of the scientific research literature on reading and its implications for reading instruction: Reports of the subgroups (NIH Publication No. 00–4754). US Government Printing Office.

Neale, A. V. (1991). Work stress in emergency medical technicians. *Journal of Occupational Medicine*, 991–7.

Needs, A. P. C. (1988). *The subjective context of social difficulty*, (Doctoral dissertation, University of York).

Neimeyer, G., Bowman, J., & Saferstein, J. (2005). The effects of elicitation techniques on repertory grid outcomes: Difference, opposite, and contrast methods. *Journal of Constructivist Psychology*, *18*, 237–52.

Neimeyer, R. A. (2004). Repertory grid methods. Available at www.pcp-net.org/encyclopaedia/repgrid-methods.html

Neuman, W. L. (2007). *Basics of social research: Qualitative and quantitative approaches* (2nd ed.). Pearson.

Newman, I., & Benz, C. R. (1998). *Qualitative-quantitative research methodology: Exploring the interactive continuum*. Southern Illinois University Press.

Nijdam-Jones, A., Rosenfeld, B., Gerbrandij, J., Quick, E., & Galietta, M. (2018). Psychopathology of stalking offenders: Examining the clinical, demographic, and stalking characteristics of a community-based sample. *Criminal Justice and Behavior*, *45*(5), 712–31.

Norris, H., & Makhlouf-Norris, F. (1976). *The measurement of self-identity* (Vol. *1*, pp. 79–82). Wiley.

O'Reilly, M., Kiyimba, N., Lester, J. N., & Edwards, D. (2020). Establishing quality in discursive psychology: Three domains to consider. *Qualitative Research in Psychology, 18*(3), 1–20.

O'Reilly, M., Ronzoni, P., & Dorga, N. (2013). *Research with children: Theory and practice.* Sage.

Open Science Collaboration (2015). Estimating the reproducibility of psychological science. *Science, 349*, 6251. https://doi.org/10.1126/science.aac4716

Oppenheim, A. N. (1992). *Questionnaire design, interviewing and attitude measurement.* Continuum.

Orland, L. (2000). What's in a line? Exploration of a research and reflection tool. *Teachers and Teaching: Theory and Practice, 6*(2), 197–213. https://doi.org/10.1080/713698715

Orne, M. T. (1962). On the social psychology of the psychological experiment: With particular reference to demand characteristics and their implications. *American Psychologist. 17*(11), 776–83.

Oyserman, D., & Lee, S. W. (2008). Does culture influence what and how we think? Effects of priming individualism and collectivism. *Psychological Bulletin, 134*(2), 311–42. http://dx.doi.org/10.1037/0033-2909.134.2.311

Packard, J. (2008). 'I'm gonna show you what it's really like out here': The power and limitation of participatory visual methods. *Visual Studies, 23*(1), 63–77. https://doi.org/10.1080/14725860801908544

Pain, H. (2012). A literature review to evaluate the choice and use of visual methods. *International Journal of Qualitative Methods, 11*(4), 303–19. https://doi.org/10.1177/160940691201100401

Patton, M. Q. (1999). Enhancing the quality and credibility of qualitative analysis. *Health Services Research, 34*(5 Pt 2), 1189.

Patton, M. Q. (2002). *Qualitative research and evaluation methods.* Sage.

Pavlov, I. (1927). *Conditioned reflexes.* Oxford University Press.

Pedersen, P. B. (1991). Multiculturalism as a generic approach to counselling. *Journal of Counseling & Development, 70*(1), 6–12. http://dx.doi.org/10.1002/j.15566676.1991.tb01555.x

Pembroke, L. (Ed.). (1994). *Self-harm: Perspectives from personal experience.* http://studymore.org.uk/shpfpe.pdf

Pietrantoni, L., & Prati, G. (2009). Resilience among first responders. *Resilience among First Responders*, 1000–19.

Pink, S. (2006). *Doing visual ethnography: Images, media and representation in research* (2nd ed.). Sage.

Pink, S. (2013). *Doing visual ethnography* (3rd ed.). Sage.

Plumwood, V. (1992). Feminism and ecofeminism: Beyond the dualistic assumptions of women, men and nature. *The Ecologist, 22*(1), 8–13.

Poland, B. D. (1995). Transcription quality as an aspect of rigor in qualitative research. *Qualitative Inquiry, 1*(3), 290–310.

Polit, D. F., & Beck, C. T. (2010). Generalization in quantitative and qualitative research: Myths and strategies. *International Journal of Nursing Studies, 47*(11), 1451–58.

Ponterotto, J. G., & Casas, J. (1993). *Handbook of ethnic/racial minority counselling research*. Charles C. Thomas.

Pope, K., & Gutheil, T. (2009). The interrogation of detainees: How doctors' and psychologists' ethical policies differ. *British Medical Journal, 338*, 1178–80.

Potter, J. (2002). Two kinds of natural. *Discourse Studies, 4*(4), 539–42.

Potter, J., & Hepburn, A. (2005). Qualitative interviews in psychology: Problems and possibilities. *Qualitative Research in Psychology, 2*(4), 281–307.

Preacher, K. J., & Hayes, A. F. (2008). Asymptotic and resampling strategies for assessing and comparing indirect effects in multiple mediator models. *Behavior Research Methods, 40*(3), 879–91.

Prikrylova, E. (2019). Attending to gender identities and new add-on treatments: A discursive investigation of heterosexual couples' infertility treatment. PhD, Nottingham Trent University IREP. Available only by special request with stated reason for request from irep.ntu.ac.uk

Procter, H. G. (1985). Repertory grid techniques in family therapy and research. In N. Beail (Ed.), *Repertory grid technique and personal constructs: Application in clinical and educational settings* (pp. 218–39). Groom Helm.

Prosser, J. (2006). Researching with visual images: Some guidance notes and a glossary for beginners. Real Life Methods Working Papers: Researching with visual images.

Przybylski, A. K., Murayama, K., DeHaan, C. R., & Gladwell, V. (2013). Motivational, emotional, and behavioral correlates of fear of missing out. *Computers in Human Behavior, 29*(4), 1841–8.

Pyle, A. (2013). Engaging young children in research through photo elicitation. *Early Child Development and Care*, (-), 1–15. Retrieved from Engaging young children in research through photo elicitation database.

Reavey, P. (2016). *Visual methods in psychology: Using and interpreting images in qualitative research* (pp. 271–83). Taylor and Francis.

Regehr, C. (2009). Social support as a mediator of psychological distress in firefighters. *The Irish Journal of Psychology, 30*(1–2), 87–98.

Reicher, S., Haslam, S., & Smith, J. (2012). Working toward the experimenter: Reconceptualizing obedience within the Milgram Paradigm as identification-based followership. *Perspectives on Psychological Science, 7*(4), 315–24.

Rhodes, T., & Fitzgerald, J. (2006). Visual data in addictions research: Seeing comes before words? [Editorial]. *Addiction Research & Theory, 14*(4), 349–63. https://doi.org/10.1080/16066350600826180

Ritchie, J., & Lewis, J. (2003). *Qualitative research practice: A guide for social science students and researchers*. Sage.

Robson, C. (2002). *Real world research: A resource for social scientists and practitioner researchers* (2nd ed.). Blackwell Publishing.

Robson, C. (2011). *Real world research* (3rd ed.). Hoboken.

Ronay, R. & von Hippel, W. (2010). The presence of an attractive woman elevates testosterone and physical risk taking in young men. *Social Psychological and Personality Science, 1*, 57–64.

Rose, D. (2000). Analysis of moving images. In M. W. Bauer & G. Gaskell (Eds.), *Qualitative researching with text, image and sound* (pp. 246–62). Sage.

Rose, J. (2006). Independent review of the teaching of early reading final report. *Independent Review*. www.standards.dcsf.gov.uk/phonics/report.pdf

Rose, S., Kamin, L. J., & Lewontin, R. C. (1984). *Not in our genes*. Penguin.

Rosenthal, R., & Fode, K. L. (1963). The effect of experimenter bias on the performance of the albino rat. *Behavioural Science, 8*(3), 183–89.

Rust, J., & Golombok, S. (1999). *Modern psychometrics: The science of psychological assessment*. Routledge.

Ryle, A., & Breen, D. (1972). Some differences in the personal constructs of neurotic and normal subjects. *The British Journal of Psychiatry, 120*, 483–89.

Saini, M., & Polak, S. (2014). The ecological validity of parent – child observations: A review of empirical evidence related to custody evaluations. *Journal of Child Custody, 11*(3), 181–201. https://doi.org/10.1080/15379418.2014.953661

Saldaña, J. (2015). *The coding manual for qualitative researchers*. Sage.

Salkind, N. J. (2010). *Encyclopedia of research design* (Vols. *1–0*). Sage. https://doi.org/10.4135/9781412961288

Salmons, J. (2017). Using social media in data collection: Designing studies with the qualitative e-research framework. In L. Sloan and A. Quan-Haase (Eds.), *The SAGE handbook of social media research methods* (pp. 177–97). Sage.

Sanderson, L. (2017). *Posttraumatic growth in firefighters*. Nottingham Trent University.

Saúl, L. A., Lopez-Gonzalez, M. A., Moreno-Pulido, A., Corbella, S., Compan, V., & Feixas, G. (2012). Bibliometric review of the repertory grid technique: 1998–2007. *Journal of Constructivist Psychology, 25*(2), 112–31.

Savage, R. S., Abrami, P., Hipps, G., & Deault, L. (2009). A randomized controlled trial study of the ABRACADABRA reading intervention program in Grade 1. *Journal of Educational Psychology, 101*(3), 590–604. https://doi.org/10.1037/a0014700

Scheib, J. W. (2003). Role stress in the professional life of the school music teacher: A collective case study. *Journal of Research in Music Education, 51*(2), 124–36. https://doi.org/10.2307/3345846

Scherer, L. (2016). Children's engagement with visual methods through qualitative research in primary school as 'art that didn't work'. *Sociological Research Online, 21*(1), 1–16. https://doi.org/10.5153/sro.3805

Schoch, K. W. (2016). Case study research. In G. J. Burkholder, K. A. Cox, & L. M. Crawford (Eds.), *The scholar-practitioner's guide to research design* (pp. 227–41). Sage.

Schön, D. A. (1983). *The reflective practitioner: How professionals think in action*. Basic Books, Inc.

Schulz, K. F., Chalmers, I., Hayes, R. J., & Altman, D. G. (1995). Empirical evidence of bias with estimates of treatment effects in controlled trials. *Journal of the American Medical Association, 273*(5), 408–12. https://doi.org/10.1001/jama.273.5.408

Schulz, W. F. (2000). The humanist basis for human rights. *American Humanist Association, 60*(5).

Schumm, W. R., Bell, D. B., & Resnick, G. (2001). Recent research on family factors and readiness: Implications for military leaders. *Psychological Reports*, *89*(1), 153–65.

Scott, D. (2005). Critical realism and empirical research methods in education. *Journal of Philosophy of Education*, *39*(4), 633–46. https://doi.org/10.1111/j.1467-9752.2005.00460.x

Sekaran, U. (1983). Methodological and theoretical issues and advancements in cross-cultural research. *Journal of International Business Studies*, *14*(2), 61–73.

Serin, R. C., & Lloyd, C. D. (2009). Examining the process of offender change: The transition to crime desistance. *Psychology, Crime & Law*, *15*(4), 347–64.

Seymour-Smith, S. (2015). Applying discursive approaches to health psychology. *Health Psychology*, *34*(4), 371.

Seymour-Smith, S., Wetherell, M., & Phoenix, A. (2002). 'My wife ordered me to come!': A discursive analysis of doctors' and nurses' accounts of men's use of general practitioners. *Journal of Health Psychology*, *7*(3), 253–67.

Sheldon, P., & Bryant, K. (2016). Instagram: Motives for its use and relationship to narcissism and contextual age. *Computers in Human Behavior*, *58*, 89–97. http://dx.doi.org/10.1016/j.chb.2015.12.059

Sheridan, J., Chamberlain K., & Dupuis, A. (2011). Timelining: Visualizing experience. *Qualitative Research*, *11*(5), 552–69. https://doi.org/10.1177/1468794111413235

Shotter, J. (2007). Re-visiting George Kelly: Social constructionism, social ecology, and social justice-all unfinished projects. *Personal Construct Theory & Practice*, *4*, 68–82.

Silverman, D. (2011). *Interpreting qualitative data: A guide to the principles of qualitative research* (4th ed.). Sage.

Silverman, D. (2013). *Doing qualitative research: A practical handbook*. Sage.

Siraj A. (2011). Isolated, invisible, and in the closet: The life story of a Scottish Muslim lesbian. *Journal of Lesbian Studies*, *15*(1), 99–121. https://doi.org/10.1080/10894160.2010.490503

Skinner, B. F. (1953). *Science and human behavior*. Macmillan.

Slavin, R. E., Lake, C., Davis, S., & Madden, N. A. (2011). Effective programs for struggling readers: A best-evidence synthesis. *Educational Research Review*, *6*(1), 1–26. https://doi.org/10.1016/j.edurev.2010.07.002

Sloan, L., & Quan-Haase, A. (2017). *The SAGE handbook of social media research methods*. Sage.

Smith, B. (2018). Generalizability in qualitative research: Misunderstandings, opportunities and recommendations for the sport and exercise sciences. *Qualitative Research in Sport, Exercise and Health*, *10*(1), 137–49.

Smith, J. A. (2003). *Qualitative psychology: A practical guide to research methods*. Sage.

Smith, J. A. (2017). Interpretative phenomenological analysis: Getting at lived experience. *Journal of Positive Psychology*, *12*(3), 303–4. https://doi.org/10.1080/17439760.2016.1262622

Smith, J. A., & Osborn, M. (2007). Interpretative Phenomenological Analysis. In J. A. Smith (Ed.), *Qualitative Psychology. A Practical Guide to Research Methods* (2nd ed.) (pp. 51–80). Sage.

Smith, J. A., Flowers, P., & Osborn, M. (2009). *Interpretative phenomenological analysis: Theory, method and research*. Sage.

Smith, J. A., Harré, R., & Van Langenhove, L. (Eds.). (1995). *Rethinking methods in psychology*. Sage.

Smith, L. R., & Sanderson, J. (2015). I'm going to instagram it! An analysis of athlete self-presentation on instagram. *Journal of Broadcasting & Electronic Media, 59*(2), 342–58. https://doi.org/10.1080/08838151.2015.1029125

Smithson, J. (2000). Using and analysing focus groups: Limitations and possibilities. *International Journal of Social Research Methodology, 3*(2), 103–19. https://doi.org/10.1080/136455700405172

Spandler, H. (2001). *Who's hurting who?: Young people, self-harm and suicide*. Handsell.

Speer, S. A. (2002). 'Natural' and 'contrived' data: A sustainable distinction?. *Discourse Studies, 4*(4), 511–25.

Spybrook, J., Bloom, H., Congdon, R., Hill, C., Martinez, A., & Raudenbush, S. (2011). Optimal Design Plus Empirical Evidence: Documentation for the 'Optimal Design' Software.

Stake, R. E. (2003). Case studies. In N. K. Denzin & Y. S. Lincoln (Eds.), *Strategies of qualitative inquiry* (pp. 134–64). Sage.

StataCorp (2019). Stata Statistical Software Release 16. StataCorp LLC.

Stewart, K., & Williams, M. (2005). Researching online populations: The use of online focus groups for social research. *Qualitative Research, 5*(4), 395–416.

Stokoe, E. (2012). Moving forward with membership categorization analysis: Methods for systematic analysis. *Discourse studies, 14*(3), 277–303.

Stokoe, E. (2013). The (in)authenticity of simulated talk: Comparing role-played and actual interaction and the implications for communication training. *Research on Language & Social Interaction, 46*(2), 165–85.

Streptomycin in the treatment of pulmonary tuberculosis. (1948). *British Medical Journal, 2*(4582), 769–82. https://doi.org/10.1016/S0366-0869(50)80004-7

Stroop, J. R. (1935). Studies of interference in serial verbal reactions. *Journal of Experimental Psychology, 18*(6), 643–62.

Sullivan, C. F. (2003). Gendered cybersupport: A thematic analysis of two online cancer support groups. *Journal of Health Psychology, 8*(1), 83–104.

Sullivan, C., Gibson, S., & Riley, S. C. (Eds.). (2012). *Doing your qualitative psychology project*. Sage.

Sutcliffe, J. (2018). 'Nature is Part of Me and I'm Part of Nature': Exploring How People Understand Their Relationships with Nature and How These Relationships Develop (Doctoral dissertation, University of Huddersfield). University of Huddersfield Repository.

Takahashi, A. R. W., & Araujo, L. (2019). Case study research: Opening up research opportunities. *RAUSP Management Journal, 55*(1), 100–11. https://doi.org/10.1108/RAUSP-05-2019-0109

Tan, F. B., & Hunter, G. M. (2002). The repertory grid technique: A method for the study of cognition in information systems. *MIS Quarterly, 26*, 39–57.

Taylor, S. (2001). Locating and conducting discourse analytic research. In M. Wetherell, S. Taylor & S. Yates (Eds.), *Discourse as data* (pp. 5–48). Sage.

Terry, R. (2019). Capturing learning: Using visual elicitation to investigate the workplace learning of 'newly qualified' in-service teachers in further education. *Research in Post-Compulsory Education*, *24*(2–3), 268–89. https://doi.org/10.1080/13596748.2019.1596430

Teti, M. (2019). The murky ethics of visual qualitative methods: Picturing a clear path forward. *International Journal of Qualitative Methods*, *18*, 1–4. https://doi.org/10.1177/1609406919884810

Tewksbury, R., & Copes, H. (2013). Incarcerated sex offenders' expectations for reentry. *The Prison Journal*, *93*(1), 102–22.

Tewksbury, R., & Lees, M. (2006). Perceptions of sex offender registration: Collateral consequences and community experiences. *Sociological Spectrum*, *26*(3), 309–34.

Throuvala, M. A., Christidi, S., Papastefanou, Y., Hourmouzoglou, M., Ferentinou, M., Destounis, G., Poulakida, A., Griffiths, M. D., Rennoldson, M. A., & Kuss, D. J. (2018). Treatment of problematic internet use and patient characteristics: The case of Problematic Internet Use Unit 18 Ano in Greece. *Journal of Behavioral Addictions*, *7*(S1), 1–177. https://doi.org/10.1556/JBA.7.2018.Suppl.1

Tiggemann, M., & Zaccardo, M. (2015). 'Exercise to be fit, not skinny': The effect of fitspiration imagery on women's body image. *Body Image*, *15*, 61–7. https://doi.org/10.1016/j.bodyim.2015.06.003

Tiggemann, M., Hayden, S., Brown, Z., & Veldhuis, J. (2018). The effect of Instagram 'likes' on women's social comparison and body dissatisfaction. *Body Image*, *26*, 90–97. https://doi.org/10.1016/J.BODYIM.2018.07.002

Torres-Rodríguez, A., Griffiths, M. D., Carbonell, X., Farriols-Hernando, N., & Torres-Jimenez, E. (2019). Internet gaming disorder treatment: A case study evaluation of four different types of adolescent problematic gamers. *International Journal of Mental Health and Addiction*, *17*(1), 1–12. https://doi.org/10.1007/s11469-017-9845-9

Townsend, L., & Wallace, C. (2016) *Social media research: A guide to ethics*. University of Aberdeen. Available at www.gla.ac.uk/media/Media_487729_smxx.pdf

Tsiachristas, A., McDaid, D., Casey, D., Brand, F., Leal, J., Park, A., et al. (2017). General hospital costs in England of medical and psychiatric care for patients who self-harm: A retrospective analysis. *The Lancet Psychiatry*, *4*(10), 759–67. https://doi.org/10.1016/S2215-0366(17)30367-X

UN General Assembly, Universal Declaration of Human Rights, 10 December 1948, 217 A (III), available at: www.refworld.org/docid/3ae6b3712c.html (accessed 14 September 2021).

Van IJzendoorn, M. H., & Kroonenberg, P. M. (1988). Cross-cultural patterns of attachment: A meta-analysis of the strange situation. *Child Development*, 147–56.

Van Lommel, P., Van Wees, R., Meyers, V., & Elfferich, I. (2001). Near-death experience in survivors of cardiac arrest: A prospective study in the Netherlands. *The Lancet*, *358*(9298), 2039–45. https://doi.org/10.1016/S0140-6736(01)07100-8

Walker, B. M., & Winter, D. A. (2007). The elaboration of personal construct psychology. *Annual Review of Psychology, 58*, 453–77.

Wang, C., & Burris, M. A. (1997). Photovoice: Concept, methodology, and use for participatory needs assessment. *Health Education & Behavior, 24*(3), 369–387. https://doi.org/10.1177/109019819702400309. Retrieved from NLM; Photovoice: concept, methodology, and use for participatory needs assessment database.

Wang, J. (2006). Questions and the exercise of power. *Discourse and Society, 17*, 529–48. https://doi.org/10.1177/0957926506063127

Weaver, B., & McNeill, F. (2015). Lifelines: Desistance, social relations, and reciprocity. *Criminal Justice and Behavior, 42*(1), 95–107.

Whitehurst, T. (2006). Liberating silent voices – Perspectives of children with a profound and complex learning needs on inclusion. *British Journal of Learning Disabilities, 35*, 55–61. https://doi.org/10.1111/j.1468-3156.2006.00405.x. Retrieved from Liberating silent voices – perspectives of children with a profound and complex learning needs on inclusion database.

Wiggins, B. E. (2019). *The discursive power of memes in digital culture: Ideology, semiotics, and intertextuality*. Routledge.

Wiggins, S., (2017). *Discursive psychology: Theory, method and applications*. Sage.

Wiggins, S., & Potter, J. (2013). Discursive psychology. In C. Willig & W. S. Rogers (Eds.), *The SAGE handbook of qualitative research in psychology* (2nd ed.) (pp. 93–109). Sage.

Wilde, D. J. (2012). Finding meaning in out-of-body experiences: An interpretative phenomenological analysis. [Doctoral thesis, The University of Manchester] The University of Manchester Repository: www.research.manchester.ac.uk/portal/en/theses/finding-meaning-in-outofbody-experiences-an-interpretative-phenomenological-analysis(f7eb8e48-093c-4e55-a917-8103fdd781fd).html

Wilde, D. J., & Murray, C. D. (2009). The evolving self: Finding meaning in near-death experiences using Interpretative Phenomenological Analysis. *Mental Health, Religion and Culture, 12*(3), 223–39. https://doi.org/10.1080/13674670802334910

Wilkinson, S. (2004). *Focus groups. Doing social psychology research* (pp. 344–76). Wiley.

Williams, S., Clausen, M. G., Robertson, A., Peacock, S., & McPherson, K. (2012). Methodological reflections on the use of asynchronous online focus groups in health research. *International Journal of Qualitative Methods, 11*(4), 368–83.

Williams, S. (2009). Understanding anorexia nervosa: An online phenomenological approach. (Unpublished doctoral dissertation). Queen Margaret University, Edinburgh, United Kingdom. Retrieved from http://etheses.qmu.ac.uk/135/

Willig, C., (2013), From recipes to adventures. In C. Willig, *Introducing qualitative research in psychology: Adventures in theory and method* (pp. 1–13). Open University Press.

Willis, G. M., Levenson, J. S., & Ward, T. (2010). Desistance and attitudes towards sex offenders: Facilitation or hindrance? *Journal of Family Violence, 25*(6), 545–56.

Winter, D. A. (1992). *Personal construct psychology in clinical practice: Theory, research and applications*. Routledge.

Winter, D. A. (2003). Repertory grid technique as a psychotherapy research measure. *Psychotherapy Research*, *13*(1), 25–42.

Wooffitt, R. (2005). *Conversation analysis and discourse analysis: A comparative and critical introduction*. Sage.

Yardley, L. (2000). Dilemmas in qualitative health research. *Psychology & Health*, *15*(2), 215–28. https://doi.org/10.1080/08870440008400302

Yorke, L., & Dallos, R. (2015). An interpretative phenomenological analysis and repertory grid exploration of anger in young offenders. *Journal of Constructivist Psychology*, *28*(2), 126–38.

Zakowski, S. G., Harris, C., Krueger, N., Laubmeier, K. K., Garrett, S., Flanigan, R., & Johnson, P. (2003). Social barriers to emotional expression and their relations to distress in male and female cancer patients. *British Journal of Health Psychology*, *8*(3), 271–86.

INDEX

Page numbers in *italics* refer to figures; page numbers in **bold** refer to tables.

Kolibri 360 GmbH
Ferdinand-Jühlke-Straße 7
99095 Erfurt, Deutschland
produktsicherheit@kolibri360.de